Lecture Notes in Computer Science 11048

Commenced Publication in 1973
Founding and Former Series Editors:
Gerhard Goos, Juris Hartmanis, and Jan van Leeuwen

More information about this series at http://www.springer.com/series/7408

Carlos E. Cuesta · David Garlan
Jennifer Pérez (Eds.)

Software Architecture

12th European Conference on Software Architecture, ECSA 2018
Madrid, Spain, September 24–28, 2018
Proceedings

 Springer

Editors
Carlos E. Cuesta 🆔
King Juan Carlos University
Móstoles, Madrid
Spain

Jennifer Pérez 🆔
Technical University of Madrid
Madrid
Spain

David Garlan 🆔
School of Computer Sciences
Carnegie Mellon University
Pittsburgh, PA
USA

ISSN 0302-9743   ISSN 1611-3349   (electronic)
Lecture Notes in Computer Science
ISBN 978-3-030-00760-7   ISBN 978-3-030-00761-4   (eBook)
https://doi.org/10.1007/978-3-030-00761-4

Library of Congress Control Number: 2018954495

LNCS Sublibrary: SL2 – Programming and Software Engineering

This Springer imprint is published by the registered company Springer Nature Switzerland AG
The registered company address is: Gewerbestrasse 11, 6330 Cham, Switzerland

Preface

This volume contains the proceedings of the 12th European Conference on Software Architecture (ECSA 2018), held in Madrid, Spain, during September 24–28, 2018. Specifically, these are the proceedings of the main program, i.e., the conference itself.

This edition had the special meaning of an anniversary. ECSA 2018 was not only the 12th edition of the full-fledged ECSA conference, it was also the 15th installment in the series if we include the three previous meetings held in the original European workshop (EWSA 2004 to 2006, held in St. Andrews, Pisa, and Nantes).

It was also the second time that the conference was held in Spain, and also the second time in Madrid. This was also a commemoration to some extent, as Madrid was also the location of the first ECSA in 2007. Even the current Program Co-chairs shared a close relationship with that edition. Back then, Prof. Cuesta was the Organizing Chair, while Prof. Garlan was one of the keynote speakers — indeed, the first one in the history of ECSA. Since then, the conference has been celebrated in Paphos, Cambridge, Copenhagen, Essen, Helsinki, Montpellier, Vienna, Dubrovnik, Copenhagen again, and Canterbury. This rich tradition will continue next year, when the conference returns to France, for the first time in the historic city of Lille.

ECSA is now the center of a complex ecosystem gathering a number of additional meetings around the main conference. These included three specific tracks, namely the industrial track, the posters, tools and demo track, and the Women in Software Architecture (WSA) track, focusing on diversity. It also included the PhD symposium, along with a full set of eight co-celebrated workshops and the innovator bootcamp — three of these were organized for the first time. The contributions of all these meetings are included in the Companion Proceedings, published in the ACM Digital Library.

This volume, gathering just the papers of the main conference, is published again by Springer, following a tradition which dates back to its origins in 2004. Every edition of the ECSA conference, except for the two joint venues, has been published in the *Lecture Notes in Computer Science* series, creating a timeline which has already become a series itself: LNCS 3047, 3527, and 4344; 4758, 5292, 6258, and 6903; 7957, 8627, 9278, 9839, and 10475; and now this volume, LNCS 11048.

For this reason, and honoring this tradition, Springer provided a 1,000 Euro funding for the 2018 meeting. This was used to bestow the ECSA 2018 Best Paper Award, which was announced during the Gala Dinner. Also for this reason, Springer itself was recognized as a Bronze Sponsor for the ECSA 2018 edition.

The 2018 edition was one of the most successful meetings in ECSA's recent history. Apart from the interest generated by the many co-located events, the main program alone attracted more than a hundred abstracts, which finally solidified in 96 submissions; this was downsized to the final number of 86 submissions after several of them were desk-rejected. Then, each of these was reviewed by our Program Committee (PC); every paper was reviewed by at least three PC members, and several of the papers had additional reviews when necessary.

After a thorough and careful process, the PC selected 17 submissions as full papers and 7 additional ones as short papers. This resulted in a 19,77% acceptance ratio for full papers and an additional 8,14% acceptance ratio for short papers, taking into account just the papers which were considered for review. The global figures added up to a 27,91% ratio, not distinguishing between full and short papers. These calculations reached a 25,00% ratio when all submissions are considered.

ECSA accepted three kinds of submissions: research, industrial, and educational papers, both full and short. After the reviewing process, the majority of accepted papers were still research-oriented: 10 full papers and 3 short ones, encompassing 54,17% of the accepted submissions. The second biggest subset was that of industry-oriented papers: 6 full ones and 2 short ones, comprising one third (33,33%) of the published papers. The remaining 12,50% included 1 full paper and another 2 short ones.

One of the emphases of the ECSA 2018 organization was to stimulate industry participation: the above figures reflect that. Moreover, one third of the accepted papers, belonging to the main program, equaled the submissions sent to the co-located industry track, and were included in the Companion proceedings. These contributions were presented separately but together, during the conference's industry day.

Research, industrial, and educational papers are combined in this volume, as they had exactly the same reviewing process, and the contributions are thematically grouped. So there is not any indication of their nature either in the table of contents or in the papers themselves. As already noted, most of the papers are research-oriented. For information only, the industrial contributions are those beginning with the pages 49, 103, 115, 131, 159, 203, 303, and 336. Again, their aggregation in thematical groups shows how close research is to the actual practice in our field.

The conference also had three outstanding keynote speakers, which honored our community with their presence. These were:

- Rick Kazman from Carnegie Mellon University and the University of Hawaii. His keynote addressed the difficulty of measuring the effects of software architecture, in the context of estimating (and reducing) the architectural debt.
- Michael Keeling from IBM. His keynote outlined the extreme complexity of any real-world architecture problem, and how the definition and use of cognitive landmarks can help to deal with it.
- Siobhán Clarke from the Trinity College at Dublin. Her keynote described how the changing landscape requires the definition of adaptive systems, and how these adaptations are to be affected by the corresponding architectural styles.

The abstracts for their keynote addresses are included later in this volume, specifically after this preface.

In spite of being "European" both in name, location, and inspiration, ECSA has always had an international vocation. Many of the submissions were from Europe, but papers were received from all continents. After the reviewing process, 83,33% of the contributions were European in origin, while 12,50% were from America, and the remaining 4,17% were from Oceania. Contributions were accepted from Germany, Italy, Sweden, France, Austria, Belgium, Brazil, Denmark, Estonia, Ireland, the Netherlands, New Zealand, the United States, and Colombia, in descending order.

The Program Committee itself had an international composition. Again, and as probably expected, it had a majority of Europeans, which composed 69,49% of the members; but also 23,73% of the members were American, and 6,78% were from Oceania. However, the distribution of countries was very different, particularly within Europe; so that countries with an important presence in the PC did not have a significant representation in the final program, and vice versa. This just serves as a testimony of the rigour and independence of the excellent work done by this committee.

This year's program showed the thematical richness which has always been a defining feature of ECSA. To a great extent, the conference dealt with the challenges posed by brand-new technology and the consequence of its presence, as in the case of, e.g., cyber-physical systems or the Internet of Things. It also studied the effects of applying new architectural styles, such as the recent surge on microservices, while still developing the consequences of well-known patterns, such as service-orientation. It elaborated on hard, long-term goals, such as self-adaptation, while also building up on everyday domain-specific issues, as in the case of security and data architectures. And while the classic strategies to deal with knowledge, i.e. design decisions, in the field are still being refined, it is ultimately defined by its actual practice.

Due to the extent and quality of the research presented in this volume, a virtual special issue on the *Journal of Systems and Software* issued an open call for papers, which specifically targeted extended and refined versions of the better qualified papers in the ECSA program. The topic of this *JSS* special issue was defined as "The Next Generation of Software Architecture," and had this edition's Program Co-chairs and General Chair as its guest editors.

ECSA is currently the only meeting on software architecture which is included in the CORE 2018 conference ranking, having achieved an A-rank. Now it is also the eldest research venue in this area, with the current name and acronym; though this is circumstantial, just while the others are undergoing a change of name and orientation. In any case, for more than a decade now, it has been recognized as one of the premier conferences in this branch of software engineering.

Though it has always been present, both in theory and in practice, in the last few years software architecture has recovered a central position in the field, together with a renewed popularity and a considerable interest from the industry. The discipline is now recovering the importance it already had in the first decade of the century – to the extent that even industrial conferences are already happening.

The research and expertise that our conference has been developing for the last 15 years are now more relevant than ever. Our findings and results, both the classic and the more recent ones, are now applied in day-to-day operation and practice. Let's continue building — and defining — the future of this discipline.

July 2018

Carlos E. Cuesta
David Garlan
Jennifer Pérez

Organization

General Chair

Jennifer Pérez   Universidad Politécnica de Madrid, Spain

Program Co-chairs

Carlos E. Cuesta   Rey Juan Carlos University, Spain
David Garlan   Cargenie Mellon University, USA

Program Committee

Jesper Andersson	Linnaeus University, Sweden
Paris Avgeriou	University of Groningen, The Netherlands
Muhammad Ali Babar	University of Adelaide, Australia
Rami Bahsoon	University of Birmingham, UK
Thais Batista	Federal University of Rio Grande do Norte, Brazil
Steffen Becker	University of Stuttgart, Germany
Stefan Biffl	Technical University Wien, Austria
Jan Bosch	Chalmers University of Technology, Sweden
Tomas Bures	Charles University, Czech Republic
Javier Cámara	Carnegie Mellon University, USA
Carlos Canal	University of Málaga, Spain
Rafael Capilla	Universidad Rey Juan Carlos, Spain
Khalil Drira	LAAS-CNRS, France
Laurence Duchien	University of Lille, France
Matthias Galster	University of Canterbury, New Zealand
Juan Garbajosa	Universidad Politécnica de Madrid, Spain
Carlo Ghezzi	Politecnico di Milano, Italy
Ian Gorton	Northeastern University, USA
Volker Gruhn	Universität Duisburg-Essen, Germany
Paola Inverardi	Universitá degli Studi dell'Aquila, Italy
Pooyan Jamshidi	Carnegie Mellon University, USA
Anton Jansen	Philips Innovation Services, The Netherlands
Rick Kazman	Carnegie Mellon University, USA
Michael Keeling	IBM, USA
Patricia Lago	Vrije Universiteit Amsterdam, The Netherlands
Nuno Laranjeiro	University of Coimbra, Portugal
Rogerio De Lemos	University of Kent, UK
Grace Lewis	Carnegie Mellon University, USA
Anna Liu	University of New South Wales and Amazon, Australia
Antónia Lopes	Universidade de Lisboa, Portugal

Sam Malek	University of California, Irvine, USA
Tommi Mikkonen	University of Helsinki, Finland
Mehdi Mirakhorli	Rochester Institute of Technology, USA
Raffaela Mirandola	Politecnico di Milano, Italy
Henry Muccini	Universitá degli Studi dell'Aquila, Italy
Juan Manuel Murillo	University of Extremadura, Spain
Elisa Yumi Nakagawa	University of São Paulo, Brazil
Elena Navarro	University of Castilla-La Mancha, Spain
Elisabetta Di Nitto	Politecnico di Milano, Italy
Flavio Oquendo	IRISA (UMR, CNRS) and Université Bretagne Sud, France
Ipek Ozkaya	Carnegie Mellon University, USA
Claus Pahl	Free University of Bozen-Bolzano, Italy
Cesare Pautasso	University of Lugano, Switzerland
Claudia Raibulet	University of Milano-Bicocca, Italy
Ralf Reussner	Karlsruhe Institute of Technology, Germany
Riccardo Scandariato	Chalmers University of Technology, Sweden
Clemens Szyperski	Microsoft, USA
Bedir Tekinerdogan	Wageningen University, The Netherlands
Chouki Tibermacine	University of Montpellier, France
Rainer Weinreich	Johannes Kepler University Linz, Austria
Danny Weyns	Katholieke Universiteit Leuven, Belgium
Uwe Zdun	University of Vienna, Austria
Liming Zhu	University of New South Wales, Australia
Olaf Zimmermann	Hochschule für Technik Rapperswill FHO, Switzerland

Steering Committee

Paris Avgeriou	University of Groningen, The Netherlands
Muhammad Ali Babar	University of Adelaide, Australia
Ivica Crnkovic	Chalmers University of Technology, Sweden
Carlos E. Cuesta	Rey Juan Carlos University, Spain
David Garlan	Carnegie Mellon University, USA
Patricia Lago	Vrije Universiteit Amsterdam, The Netherlands
Antónia Lopes	University of Lisbon, Portugal
Rogério de Lemos	University of Kent, UK
Raffaela Mirandola	Politecnico di Milano, Italy
Flavio Oquendo	IRISA and Université de Bretagne Sud, France
Jennifer Pérez	Universidad Politécnica de Madrid, Spain
Bedir Tekinerdogan	Wageningen University, The Netherlands
Danny Weyns	Katholieke Universiteit Leuven, Belgium
Uwe Zdun	University of Vienna, Austria

Organizing Committee

Industrial Co-chairs

Grace Lewis	Carnegie Mellon University, USA
Manuel Gómez Langley	GMV, Spain

Workshop Co-chairs

Raffaela Mirandola	Politecnico di Milano, Italy
Hong-Mei Chen	University of Hawaii at Manoa, USA

Doctoral Symposium Co-chairs

Paris Avgeriou	University of Groningen, The Netherlands
Juan Garbajosa	Universidad Politécnica de Madrid, Spain

Poster, Tools and Demo Chair

Elisa Yumi Nakagawa	University of São Paulo, Brazil

Publicity Chair

Elena Navarro	University of Castilla-La Mancha, Spain

WSA Track Co-chairs

Laurence Duchien	University of Lille, France
Thais Batista	Federal University of Rio Grande do Norte, Brazil

Local Co-chairs

Agustín Yagüe	Universidad Politécnica de Madrid, Spain
Jessica Díaz	Universidad Politécnica de Madrid, Spain

Local Organization

Héctor Humanes	Universidad Politécnica de Madrid, Spain
Norberto Cañas	Universidad Politécnica de Madrid, Spain
Javier García	Universidad Politécnica de Madrid, Spain
Almudena Sánchez	GMV, Spain
Germania Rodríguez	Universidad Técnica Particular de Loja, Ecuador
Daniel Guamán	Universidad Técnica Particular de Loja, Ecuador

Additional Reviewers

Ana Paula Allian	Daniel Feitosa
Javier Berrocal	Vincenzo Ferme
Georg Buchgeher	Paolo Di Francesco
Everton Cavalcante	Markus Frank
Mariam Chaabane	Lina Garcés

Joshua Garcia
José García-Alonso
Amal Gassara
Negar Ghorbani
Iris Groher
Mahmoud Hammad
Sara Hasan
Marianne Huchard
Nesrine Khabou
Houda Khlif
Floriment Klinaku
Lucas Klostermann
Imene Lahyani
Cristiane Aparecida Lana
Jair Leite
Jun-Wei Lin

Ivano Malavolta
Christian Manteuffel
Jürgen Musil
Brauner Oliveira
Ben Ramsey
Anja Reuter
Daniel Romero
Darius Sas
Bruno Sena Da Silva
Aly Syed
Theo Theunissen
Nguyen Tran
Faheem Ullah
Sylvain Vauttier
Roberto Verdecchia
Huaxi Yulin Zhang

Keynote Talks

Measuring and Managing Architecture Debt: Tales from the Trenches

Rick Kazman (iD)

Carnegie Mellon and University of Hawaii, USA

Abstract. In this talk I will present my experiences in transitioning and validating an automated software architecture measurement system in two large multinational corporations. I will describe the measures that we employed and the tool chains that we constructed to automatically calculate these measures. I will also describe how we got the development teams to accept and apply these measures through pilot studies, surveys, and constantly adjusting the measures based on feedback and correlations with productivity measures. This experience shows that it is critical to guide the development teams to focus on the underlying problems behind each measure, rather than on the scores themselves. It is also critical to both quantify architecture debt and prove to development teams and management alike that these measures matter, and that we can calculate the return on investment of paying down the debt.

Finding Our Way in the Software Wilderness

Michael Keeling

IBM, USA
http://neverletdown.net

Abstract. Over time, even modestly large or complex software systems can become an untamed wilderness. Anyone who dares venture into one of these wild systems can quickly become entangled in the serpentine vines of past design decisions, sliced by the razor-sharp barbs of hidden assumptions, and lost in a labyrinth of code and documentation. Software architects can help their teams navigate this harsh landscape by creating cognitive landmarks that can be used as reference points and by building trails other designers can follow. In this talk we'll explore techniques for creating architectural landmarks in the code, in documentation, and even in the physical workspace, that your fellow developers can use to navigate the wilds of your software system.

Exploring Different Architecture Styles for Adaptive Systems

Siobhán Clarke ⓘ

Trinity College Dublin, Ireland

Abstract. Modern software encompasses a dizzying range of application types operating in changing environments. This inherent complexity requires adaptive execution models operating within a range of architectural styles. Over the last decade, my team has explored the requirements for, and execution of, adaptation in a range of application types. We found that we naturally veered towards different software architecture styles in different circumstances – e.g., decentralised multi-agent systems when autonomous entities were required, or service-oriented computing when large-scale adaptive composition of behaviours was required. In this talk, I share our experiences with different classes of systems, and discuss open challenges for the research community.

Contents

Microservices Architectures

Service-Oriented Architectures

Architectural Design Decisions

Software Architecture in Practice

Security and Data Architectures

Self-adaptive Architectures

A DSL for MAPE Patterns Representation in Self-adapting Systems

Paolo Arcaini[1]([✉]) [ID], Raffaela Mirandola[2] [ID], Elvinia Riccobene[3] [ID], and Patrizia Scandurra[4] [ID]

[1] National Institute of Informatics, Tokyo, Japan
`arcaini@nii.ac.jp`
[2] Politecnico di Milano, Milan, Italy
`raffaela.mirandola@polimi.it`
[3] Dipartimento di Informatica, Università degli Studi di Milano, Milan, Italy
`elvinia.riccobene@unimi.it`
[4] DIGIP, Università degli Studi di Bergamo, Bergamo, Italy
`patrizia.scandurra@unibg.it`

Abstract. In architecture-based self-adaptation, the adaptation logic is usually structured in terms of MAPE-K (Monitor-Analyze-Plan-Execute over a shared Knowledge) control loops dealing with the adaptation concerns of the managed system. In case of large, complex and decentralized systems, multiple interacting MAPE loops are introduced. Some common design patterns of interactive MAPE components have been proposed in the literature; however, a well-defined way to document them and to express the semantics of their interactions is still missing.

This paper presents a domain-specific language, *MAPE Specification Language* (MSL), as modeling front-end to define and instantiate common patterns of interacting MAPE components when architecting the adaptation logic of a self-adaptive system. We also provide a *semantic mapping* (implemented by a model generator) to transform MSL descriptions of MAPE pattern instances into formal executable models based on the formalism of *self-adaptive Abstract State Machines* (ASMs). Such a mapping provides a link to the modeling back-end of ASMs for formally specifying and analyzing the behavior of instances of MAPE patterns.

1 Introduction

Modern software systems typically operate in dynamic environments and deal with highly changing operational conditions; *self-adaptation* is nowadays considered [8,10,14] as an effective approach to deal with the increasing complexity, uncertainty and dynamicity of these systems. Feedback control loops that monitor and adapt managed parts of a software system are widely accepted as the main architectural solution [6] to realize self-adaptation in software systems.

P. Arcaini—This author is supported by ERATO HASUO Metamathematics for Systems Design Project (No. JPMJER1603), JST.

According to the original definition of Kephart and Chess [14], we refer to these control schemas as MAPE-K (Monitor, Analyze, Plan, and Execute over a shared Knowledge) – or simply MAPE – feedback loops.

In case of complex and distributed systems, multiple interacting MAPE loops with a decentralized control may be introduced to deal with system adaptation. Some common design patterns of interactive MAPE loops have been proposed in the literature [20], together with a graphical notation for representing them; however, a well-defined way to document them and to express the semantics of their (components) interactions is still missing.

To overcome these limitations, we here propose a domain-specific language, called *MAPE Specification Language* (MSL), for architecting self-adaptive systems by explicitly modeling the interaction pattern among MAPE components. The aim is to have, at the early design stage, a lightweight formalism for representing MAPE patterns and their instances as first-class citizens. MSL is to be intended as a modeling front-end framework for structuring the adaptation logic, on top of richer and more specific modeling and/or analysis back-end frameworks (such as: UML-like modeling notations, other ADLs, or formal methods). Starting from a concise and simple definition of an MSL model of a structure of interactive MAPE loops, the corresponding representation in a target back-end framework can be obtained using model transformations and then tailored/refined according to the target scope.

MSL adopts the same modeling concepts of the MAPE graphical notation presented in [20] to express the structure of MAPE components interactions, and in addition it provides constructs to fix some semantic variations in component interactions. MSL has been developed using the grammarware approach of Xtext, which is combined with the modelware approach of the Eclipse Modeling Framework (EMF); this allows the automatic generation of a model editor, a parser, and a basic validator, and it facilitates the development of compilers/-generators toward other (back-end) frameworks by using principles and tools of *model-driven engineering*. The language allows the definition and instantiation of MAPE patterns in an expressive and concise manner using a textual notation. The rationale in this decision is that textual notations should scale better than visual ones with increasing system design size [16].

As a first example of a back-end framework, we here propose that for formal analysis of (instances of) MAPE patterns. To this aim, we adopt a formal executable description of MAPE loops in terms of *self-adaptive Abstract State Machines* (self-adaptive ASMs) [3]. To bring this approach to fruition, we developed a model generator, called MSL2ASM, that transforms an MSL model into a self-adaptive ASM model automatically. The aim of this mapping is twofold: (i) specifying the MSL semantics through a *semantic mapping* [11] approach, and (ii) providing a connection with a back-end framework [3] that uses multi-agent ASMs as the underlying formal model for early simulation and formal analysis of distributed self-adaptive systems. Indeed, the ASM-based MSL semantics is executable, i.e., the ASM models obtained from MSL models express and guarantee by construction the interaction semantics a user wants to give and can be

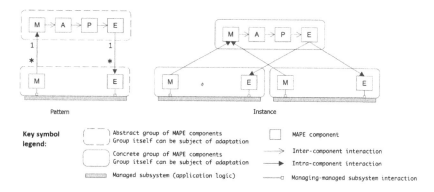

Fig. 1. Aggregate MAPE pattern (left) and an instance of it (right) from [20]

simulated, refined, and verified to provide early feedback about the correct loops interactions (e.g., absence of interferences) as devised in [3].

Paper Organization. Some background on MAPE patterns for self-adaptation is given in Sect. 2. The MSL language is presented in Sect. 3, while the semantic mapping from the MSL to the back-end framework of self-adaptive ASMs is presented in Sect. 4. Section 5 provides a description of some related work. Section 6 concludes the paper and outlines some future directions of our work.

2 Background on MAPE-Patterns for Self-adaptation

In architecture-based adaptation, the self-adaptive layer (the managing subsystem) is typically conceived as a set of interacting MAPE loops, one per each adaptation concern. In [20], some recurring structures of interacting MAPE components, *MAPE patterns*, have been defined for designing decentralized adaptation solutions, where controllers make independent decisions but have some kind of interaction. Figure 1 shows an example of such a pattern (the *Aggregate* MAPE pattern), an instance of this pattern in a configuration, and the key symbols of the graphical notation adopted in [20].

A MAPE pattern defines the structure of a composite MAPE loop as a set of *abstract groups* of MAPE components representing the roles of the feedback processes and the *type of interactions* between MAPE components. A *pattern instance* describes the structure of the pattern for one particular configuration. The annotated multiplicity of the interactions between the groups of MAPE components determines the allowed occurrences of the different groups in the pattern. Notationally, there are different types of interactions.

- *Managing-managed subsystem interactions* are those between M components and the managed subsystem for monitoring purposes, and between E components and the managed subsystem for performing adaptations.
- *Inter-component interactions* are those between different types of MAPE components. Typically, M interacts with A, A with P, and P with E.
- *Intra-component interactions* between MAPE components of the same type, e.g., interactions between M components.

Although it is undoubted the importance of MAPE patterns to represent known design solutions and support their reuse, the semantics of their graphical representation is often ambiguous and may intentionally leave *semantic variation points* (as in UML). Given the MAPE pattern in Fig. 1, elements of ambiguous interpretation are, for example, the AND/OR semantics of signals when an M computation of the higher MAPE group is triggered by the M computations of the lower groups. In MSL, we allow the specification of such semantic variations and support the designer in fixing the semantics at configuration level.

3   MSL: A DSL for MAPE Patterns Specification

In designing the MSL language, we tried to adhere to the following three proven principles in software architecture design [17]:

- *Separation of concerns*: Introduce language abstractions that allow dividing the adaptation logic into distinct adaptation concerns by structuring it into different MAPE loops with as little overlap in functionality as possible.
- *Principle of Least Knowledge*: A MAPE loop/component should not know about internal details of other MAPE loops/components.
- *Minimize upfront design*: Introduce language constructs allowing designing what is necessary, thus to avoid making a large design effort prematurely.

We adopted the same concepts of the graphical notation introduced in Sect. 2 as core concepts of MSL for defining MAPE patterns and their instances. Additionally, further language constructs were added for modeling semantic variation points about MAPE component interactions explicitly.

The MSL language has been developed using the grammarware approach of Xtext combined with the modelware approach of EMF. The Xtext grammar of the MSL textual notation, together with the running example used in this paper and introduced below, is available online at [18]. The MSL model editor can be installed as eclipse plugin[1]. We introduce the MSL modeling constructs in Sect. 3.1, while MSL parsing and validation are discussed in Sect. 3.2. The language operational semantics is given in Sect. 4 in terms of ASMs.

Running Example. An adaptation scenario considering a smart home, inspired by the case study in [19], is used to illustrate the MSL language. Specifically, we focus on the heating system that can work on different settings according to the user needs expressed through adaptation concerns. Hereafter, we consider the adaptation concern *Comfortable Heating* (CH): the application monitors the comfort level of its residents and activates the heating when the temperature is too low, or switches off the heating when the temperature is too warm.

3.1   MSL Modeling Notation

Pattern Definition. In MSL, a MAPE pattern is defined by introducing a named element *abstract pattern* (by the keyword abstract pattern) that

---

[1] The update site is http://fmse.di.unimi.it/sw/msl/updatesite/.

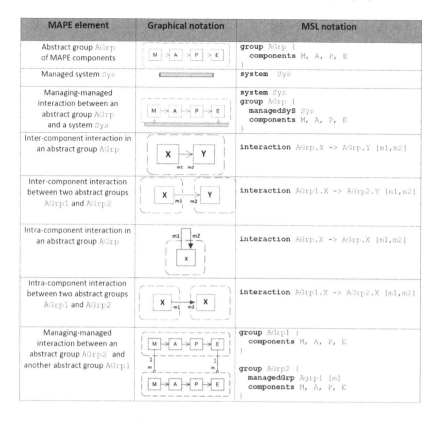

Fig. 2. MAPE pattern definition

declares the managed subsystems' type, the abstract groups of MAPE components, and the type of interactions between MAPE components. Figure 2 reports
the core modeling elements to define a MAPE pattern in terms of abstract groups
of MAPE components, managed subsystems, and their interactions with multiplicities. For each element, the corresponding graphical notation adopted in [20]
and the textual notation in MSL are shown. The MSL syntax is intuitive and
self-explanatory[2]. As an example, Code 1 reports the MSL representation of the
Aggregate MAPE pattern shown in Fig. 1.

All patterns proposed in [20] can be expressed in MSL (see the pattern library
available online at [18]). As another (more complex) example, Code 2 shows the
hierarchical control pattern from [20] (on the left) and its corresponding MSL definition (on the right). This pattern captures a hierarchical distribution control,
where higher-level MAPE components manage subordinate MAPE components
(i.e., the managed subsystems can be managing subsystems themselves).

---

[2] Note that we do not provide keywords to distinguish between intra- and inter- interactions, since they are already characterized by the kind of MAPE components
connected by the interaction.

| abstract pattern AggregateMAPE {
  system Sys
  group Main {
    components M, A, P, E
  }
  group Interface {
    managedSyS Sys
    components M, E
  } | interaction Interface.M −> Main.M [*−ALL,1]
interaction Main.E −> Interface.E [1,*−ALL]
interaction Main.M −> Main.A [1,1]
interaction Main.A −> Main.P [1,1]
interaction Main.P −> Main.E [1,1]
} |

Code 1. Aggregate MAPE pattern definition in MSL

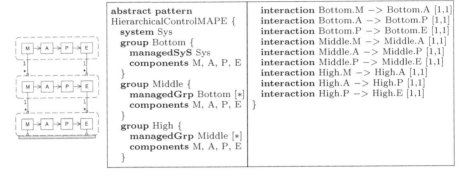

| abstract pattern
HierarchicalControlMAPE {
  system Sys
  group Bottom {
    managedSyS Sys
    components M, A, P, E
  }
  group Middle {
    managedGrp Bottom [*]
    components M, A, P, E
  }
  group High {
    managedGrp Middle [*]
    components M, A, P, E
  } | interaction Bottom.M −> Bottom.A [1,1]
interaction Bottom.A −> Bottom.P [1,1]
interaction Bottom.P −> Bottom.E [1,1]
interaction Middle.M −> Middle.A [1,1]
interaction Middle.A −> Middle.P [1,1]
interaction Middle.P −> Middle.E [1,1]
interaction High.M −> High.A [1,1]
interaction High.A −> High.P [1,1]
interaction High.P −> High.E [1,1]
} |

Code 2. Hierarchical Control pattern

Semantic Variation Points at Interaction Level. One of the ambiguities of the MAPE loop representation proposed in [20] is related to the interpretation of the interactions [1, *], [*, 1], and [*, *] among multiple components of different MAPE groups. Indeed, it is not clear whether, in order to trigger the interaction, the communication must be established among all the involved components or only some of them. Therefore, in MSL, in addition to the standard multiplicity 1, we allow to specify exactly the intended semantics of * by means of multiplicities *-ALL, *-SOME, and *-ONE (see interactions in Code 1). When used as starting multiplicity of the interaction, these multiplicities respectively mean that the target group must receive the communication from *all* the interacting groups, from *at least one* of them, or from *exactly one* of them. In a similar way, when used as target multiplicity of the interaction, they mean that the starting group must communicate with *all* the interacting target groups, a *non-empty subset* of them, or *exactly one* of them.

Pattern Instantiation and Configuration. Once defined, in MSL an abstract MAPE pattern can be instantiated by first defining a *concrete pattern* (a named element preceded by the keyword `concrete pattern`) to rename the roles (the abstract MAPE groups and managed subsystems) of the abstract pattern for a certain adaptation concern. Roles renaming is realized by *name binding*, i.e., through identifiers. Then, to effectively instantiate the concrete pattern for a specific scenario, a *configuration* (a named element introduced by the keyword `configuration`) must be defined. Such a configuration instantiates the concrete groups of MAPE components and managed subsystems that effectively play the renamed roles of the concrete pattern and their (concrete) interactions.

```
import AggregateMAPE                          h0 : ComfortableHeatingMAPE.IntTemp {
concrete pattern ComfortableHeatingMAPE         managedSyS hs0
          concretizationOf AggregateMAPE {      components m_h0:M, e_h0:E
  system Heater : AggregateMAPE.Sys           }
  group MainCH: AggregateMAPE.Main            h1 : ComfortableHeatingMAPE.IntTemp {
  group IntTemp: AggregateMAPE.Interface        managedSyS hs1
}                                               components m_h1:M, e_h1:E
                                              }
configuration ComfortableHeating              ch.m_ch −> ch.a_ch
          instanceOf ComfortableHeatingMAPE { ch.a_ch −> ch.p_ch
  hs0: ComfortableHeatingMAPE.Heater          ch.p_ch −> ch.e_ch
  hs1: ComfortableHeatingMAPE.Heater          h0.m_h0 −> ch.m_ch
                                              h1.m_h1 −> ch.m_ch
  ch : ComfortableHeatingMAPE.MainCH {        ch.e_ch −> h0.e_h0
    components m_ch:M, a_ch:A, p_ch:P, e_ch:E ch.e_ch −> h1.e_h1
  }                                         }
```

Code 3. A MAPE pattern instance in MSL

Running Example. The MSL Code 3[3] shows a concretization, called
ComfortableHeatingMAPE, of the pattern AggregateMAPE for the adaptation
concern CH. Essentially, there is a concrete MAPE group, IntTemp, that is
responsible for monitoring rooms temperature via sensors and manage the heating system accordingly. So it plays the role of Interface w.r.t. the heating system by providing both a component M and a component E. The group MainCH
has a main sequential MAPE loop. It is responsible for realizing the adaptation concern; therefore, its component M aggregates temperature data from all
temperature sensors through the components M of IntTemp, and then its component A decides to increase/decrease the heating or to turn it off. To this last
purpose, components P and E plan adaptation actions and drive the components
E of IntTemp, respectively. To complete the pattern instantiation, a configuration of the concrete pattern is also given in the second part of the MSL Code 3
as introduced by the keyword configuration. In this configuration, there are
two managed systems for the heating (hs0 and hs1), and their interface MAPE
groups (h0 and h1) interacting with one main MAPE group (ch).

3.2   MSL Parsing and Validation

The MSL parser generated automatically by Xtext is complemented by a validator to perform static analysis of MSL models and give informative feedback
to the users. In particular, in addition to standard Xtext validation, we specified some constraints for pattern matching, i.e., to check whether a given pattern
instance conforms to its pattern. We formalized such constraints in terms of OCL
(Object Constraint Language) formulas (see an example below) over the MSL
metamodel (automatically generated by Xtext), and then implemented them
into the Xtext validator.

– *Checking concrete groups in a concrete pattern w.r.t. the abstract pattern*:
  each concrete pattern must declare one concrete group per abstract group.

---

[3] We allow the definition and instantiation of a MAPE pattern in the same MSL file
with extension .msl, and also the definition of patterns in separate files without
instantiation and their import in order to create a library of patterns.

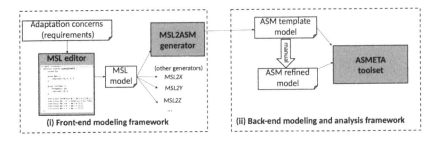

Fig. 3. Pattern-driven tooling for modeling and analyzing self-adaptive systems

```
context Pattern
def: ap: AbstractPattern = self.absPattern
inv: ap.abstractGroups?->forAll(ag:AbstractGroup |
self.groups-->select(g:ConcreteGroup | g.name = ag.name)-->size() = 1)
```

4   A Back-End Framework for Formal Analysis of MAPE Patterns

We here propose a mapping from an MSL model of a MAPE pattern (and its instance) to a self-adaptive ASM [3]. To this aim, we use the *semantic mapping* technique of the ASM-based semantic framework [11], which allows the specification of the dynamic semantics of metamodel-based languages.

The aim of the proposed mapping is twofold: (i) specifying the language semantics, and (ii) providing a connection with the ASM-based back-end framework ASMETA[4] (ASM mETAmodeling) [2] for formal analysis. The ASMETA toolset is just an example of all possible target back-end frameworks. Figure 3 shows our high-level view of possible tooling for modeling the adaption layer of a self-adaptive system using MAPE patterns: the ASMETA back-end allows basic validation in terms of simulation (either guided or automatized), and verification in terms of static analysis and model checking. Specifically, the resulting (possibly further refined) ASM models can be used, as devised in [3], for early prototyping of MAPE loop controllers and for verifying properties of distributed MAPE loops such as non-conflict, minimality, as well as correct interactions.

The model generator MSL2ASM, that automatically translates MSL models into self-adaptive ASMs, has been developed in Java using a Model-to-Text (M2T) approach. According to the mapping rules synthesized in Table 1, the generator visits the MSL ecore metamodel instance – i.e., the abstract syntax tree (AST) of an MSL model[5] – to produce the corresponding ASM model. The generator can be installed as eclipse plugin together with the MSL editor.

---

[4] http://asmeta.sourceforge.net/.

[5] This AST is the EMF ecore model of MSL used as the in-memory objects representation of any parsed MSL text file.

In Sect. 4.1, we briefly recall the formalism of self-adaptive ASMs for MAPE loops modeling, and in Sect. 4.2 we describe the mapping and exemplify it with the running application example. In Sect. 4.3, we show some possible uses of the ASMETA framework for formal analysis of MAPE loops.

4.1 Theoretical Background on Self-adaptive ASMs

ASMs [5] are an extension of FSMs where unstructured control states are replaced by states comprising arbitrary complex data (i.e., domains of objects with functions defined on them), and transitions are expressed by transition rules describing how data (state function values saved into *locations*) change from one state to the next. ASM models can be easily read as "pseudocode over abstract data" which comes with a well defined semantics: at each run step, all transition rules are executed in parallel by leading to simultaneous (consistent) updates of a number of locations.

By exploiting the notion of *multi-agent ASM* – where each agent executes its own ASM in parallel with other agents' ASMs and the agent's *program* is the set of all transition rules of its own ASM –, in [3] we provide the definition of *self-adaptive ASMs* as a multi-agent ASM where the set *Agents* is the disjoint union of the set *MgA* of *managing agents* and the set *MdA* of *managed agents*. Managing agents encapsulate the logic of self-adaptation, while managed agents encapsulate the system's functional logic. Still in [3], a MAPE loop (or interactive MAPE loops) for an adaptation concern *adj* is defined as:

$$MAPE(adj) = \left\langle R_{adj}, \xrightarrow{adj}, K(adj) \right\rangle \tag{1}$$

R_{adj} is the set of transition rules, executed by managing agents, modeling the MAPE computations involved in the control loop; $\xrightarrow{adj}$ is a relation on R_{adj} and is used to express MAPE computations interaction (e.g., M infers an A, which infers a P, which infers an E); $K(adj)$ is the knowledge (part of the locations of the self-adaptive ASM) used to keep the information necessary to enact and coordinate MAPE computations.

By the interaction relation definition, we can express a *decentralized* and *centralized* execution schema (also a mixed schema is possible) among MAPE computations. In the decentralized schema, rules in R_{adj} are executed by different agents, which interact with each other *indirectly* by sharing locations of the knowledge $K(adj)$ – and, therefore, rules are executed in different run steps. In the centralized schema, rules in R_{adj} are executed by the same managing agent either *indirectly*, or *directly* where each rule invokes the rule it is in interaction relation with – and, therefore, all rules are executed in one step (*waterfall* style).

4.2 Mapping MSL Models into Self-adaptive ASMs

We here describe a transformation process from an MSL model to a self-adaptive ASM. An informal description of the mapping rules is reported in Table 1.

Table 1. Mapping from MSL models into self-adaptive ASMs

MAPE element	ASM construct
Managed system Sys	Agent type SysMda with program r_Sys modeling its behavior
Managing group Grp	Agent type GrpMga with program r_Grp modeling its behavior
Component X ($X \in \{M, A, P, E\}$) of group Grp	Macro rule r_GrpX (called from program r_Grp) that models the behavior of component X. The rule contains a *placeholder* <<TODO>> for indicating that the designer must supply an implementation.
Decentralized interaction $Grp1.X \rightarrow Grp2.Y[m_1, m_2]$	Functions modeling the interaction among agents of Grp1Mga and Grp2Mga: - fromGrp1toGrp2 associating agents of Grp1Mga to agents of Grp2Mga. The signature is fromGrp1toGrp2: Grp1Mga -> Grp2Mga if m_2=1, and fromGrp1toGrp2: Grp1Mga -> Powerset(Grp2Mga) if $m_2 \in \{$*-ALL,*-SOME,*-ONE$\}$. - fromGrp2toGrp1 associating agents of Grp2Mga to agents of Grp1Mga. The signature is fromGrp2toGrp1: Grp2Mga -> Grp1Mga if $m_1 = 1$, and fromGrp2toGrp1: Grp2Mga -> Powerset(Grp1Mga) if $m_1 \in \{$*-ALL,*-SOME,*-ONE$\}$. - sgnGrp1Grp2: Prod(Grp1Mga,Grp2Mga) -> Boolean modeling the *signals* exchanged among agents in order to trigger the interaction.
Centralized interaction $Grp.X \rightarrow Grp.Y[1, 1]$	Components rules X, Y of the same group Grp are called in a waterfall style by the agent of type GrpMga
Variation point semantics of multiplicity $m_1 \in \{$*-ALL,*-SOME,*-ONE$\}$ in interaction $Grp1.X \rightarrow Grp2.Y[m_1, m_2]$	A derived function startGrp2Y: Grp1Mga -> Boolean (read in rule r_Grp2Y) is used to combine the different values of the signals going from Grp1Mga agents to a single Grp2Mga agent \$b; function implementation depends on the variation point semantics: *-ALL: (**forall** \$a **in** fromGrp2toGrp1(\$b) **with** sgnGrp1Grp2(\$a, \$b)) *-SOME: (**exist** \$a **in** fromGrp2toGrp1(\$b) **with** sgnGrp1Grp2(\$a, \$b)) *-ONE: (**exist unique** \$a **in** fromGrp2toGrp1(\$b) **with** sgnGrp1Grp2(\$a, \$b))
Variation point semantics of multiplicity $m_2 \in \{$*-ALL,*-SOME,*-ONE$\}$ in interaction $Grp1.X \rightarrow Grp2.Y[m_1, m_2]$	Rule r_Grp1X of agent Grp1Mga sends signals to Grp2Mga agents. The selected Grp2Mga agents depend on the variation point semantics: *-ALL: to all associated agents *-SOME: to a randomly selected subset of agents: chooseone({\$a **in** Powerset(Grp2Mga)| not(isEmpty(\$a)): \$a}) *-ONE: to a randomly selected agent: chooseone({\$a **in** Grp2Mga:\$a})
Concrete interactions in the **configuration** section	Declaration of agents, instances of agents types SysMda and GrpMga, and initialization of interaction functions fromGrp1toGrp2 and fromGrp2toGrp1

The agents set of the self-adaptive ASM is obtained by creating an agent in *MdA* for each managed system and an agent in *MgA* for each managing group of a concrete pattern.

The set of rules R_{adj} involved in the *MAPE* loop is built by creating a rule r_GrpX for each component X of each group Grp.

A decentralized interaction $Grp1.X \rightarrow Grp2.Y$ determines a relation between rules r_Grp1X and r_Grp2Y in $\xrightarrow{adj}$; the correct interaction between the two rules is obtained by creating, in the knowledge $K(adj)$, two functions, fromGrp1toGrp2 and fromGrp2toGrp1, specifying the interacting agents, and a function sgnGrp1Grp2 modeling the *signals* the agents use for establishing the communication. A centralized interaction between components X and Y of the same group Grp is obtained by directly invoking rule r_GrpY from r_GrpX.

The mapping also captures the desired semantics of * multiplicity; a starting multiplicity of * kind is modeled by means of a formula (used as guard of a component rule) that requires that *all/some/exactly one* signal(s) must be received by the target agent in order to trigger the interaction. A target multiplicity of * kind, instead, is modeled by forcing the starting agent to write the signal to *all/some/exactly one* target agent(s).

The generated ASM model is already executable as coordination schema of MAPE components, but with empty implementation (marked by placeholders `<<TODO>>`) for component rules in R_{adj} (only standard writing and reading of signals is added to the model). Therefore, in order to reflect the specific adaptation scenario, the model has to be refined by the designer. The starting point of this refinement consists in replacing the placeholders with effective ASM rules specifying the M, A, P, E computations; the effort for this refinement is domain-specific. Moreover, the designer can also refine the standard implementation of * multiplicity by selecting the set of agents from/to which the signals must be received/sent. Backward compatibility between MSL and ASM models is not currently supported; it is addressed as future work.

Running Example. As mapping example, Code 4 reports the ASM model (in the AsmetaL notation) generated automatically from the MSL model shown in Code 3. According to the framework of self-adaptive ASMs presented in Sect. 4.1 (see Eq. 1) and the resulting ASM in Code 4, the MAPE loop for the adaptation concern CH is defined as $MAPE(CH) = \left\langle R_{CH}, \xrightarrow{CH}, K(CH) \right\rangle$, where

$R_{CH} = \{$r_IntTempM,r_IntTempE,r_MainCHM,r_MainCHA, r_MainCHP, r_MainCHE$\}$
$\xrightarrow{CH} = \{$(r_IntTempM,r_MainCHM),(r_MainCHM,r_MainCHA), (r_MainCHA,r_MainCHP),
        (r_MainCHP,r_MainCHE), (r_MainCHE,r_IntTempE)$\}$
$K(CH) = \{$fromIntTempMtoMainCHM, fromMainCHMtoIntTempM,
        sgnIntTempMMainCHM, fromMainCHEtoIntTempE,
        fromIntTempEtoMainCHE, sgnMainCHEIntTempE$\}$

As an example of refinement, a complete version of the ASM model for the smart heating application is available online [18]. Code 5 reports an excerpt of the elements added in the refined model. For example, a monitored function `roomTemp` has been added to model the rooms temperature; indeed, in ASMs monitored functions represent the inputs coming from the environment. Moreover, the refined model also contains a function `desiredHeating` that models the adaptation logic (i.e., how the heating should be set). Finally, placeholders of component rules have been refined. For example, in `r_IntTempE`, the `IntTempMgA` agents trigger the actuators of the manged heaters (`HeaterMdA` agents) by setting the function `setHeatingStatus` according to the desired heating.

4.3   Formal Analysis of the ASM Model

As we already said, the resulting ASM models guarantee by construction the correct loop interaction. However, the designer could have wrongly designed

```
asm ComfortableHeating
import StandardLibrary

signature:
  //ComfortableHeatingMAPE
  domain HeaterMdA subsetof Agent
  domain MainCHMgA subsetof Agent
  domain IntTempMgA subsetof Agent
  derived startMainCHM: MainCHMgA −> Boolean
  derived startMainCHA: MainCHMgA −> Boolean
  derived startMainCHP: MainCHMgA −> Boolean
  derived startMainCHE: MainCHMgA −> Boolean
  controlled heaterManagedByIntTemp: IntTempMgA −> HeaterMdA
  derived startIntTempM: IntTempMgA −> Boolean
  derived startIntTempE: IntTempMgA −> Boolean
  //l: IntTemp.M −> MainCH.M [∗−ALL,1]
  controlled sgnIntTempMMainCHM: Prod(IntTempMgA, MainCHMgA) −> Boolean
  controlled fromIntTempMtoMainCHM: IntTempMgA −> MainCHMgA
  controlled fromMainCHMtoIntTempM: MainCHMgA −> Powerset(IntTempMgA)
  //l: MainCH.E −> IntTemp.E [1,∗−ALL]
  controlled sgnMainCHEIntTempE: Prod(MainCHMgA, IntTempMgA) −> Boolean
  controlled fromMainCHEtoIntTempE: MainCHMgA −> Powerset(IntTempMgA)
  controlled fromIntTempEtoMainCHE: IntTempMgA −> MainCHMgA
  //ComfortableHeating
  static hs0: HeaterMdA
  static hs1: HeaterMdA
  static ch: MainCHMgA
  static h0: IntTempMgA
  static h1: IntTempMgA

definitions:
  function startMainCHM($b in MainCHMgA) =
    (forall $a in fromMainCHMtoIntTempM($b) with sgnIntTempMMainCHM($a, $b))
  function startMainCHA($b in MainCHMgA) = true
  function startMainCHP($b in MainCHMgA) = true
  function startMainCHE($b in MainCHMgA) = true
  function startIntTempM($b in IntTempMgA) = true
  function startIntTempE($b in IntTempMgA) =
    sgnMainCHEIntTempE(fromIntTempEtoMainCHE($b), $b)

  rule r_Heater = skip //<<TODO>>
  rule r_CleanUp_MainCHE = skip //<<TODO>>
  rule r_CleanUp_MainCHM =
    forall $a in fromMainCHMtoIntTempM(self) do
      sgnIntTempMMainCHM($a, self) := false

  rule r_CleanUp_IntTempE =
    sgnMainCHEIntTempE(
      fromIntTempEtoMainCHE(self), self) := false
    ...

  rule r_MainCHE =
    if startMainCHE(self) then
      par
        skip //<<TODO>>
        forall $a in fromMainCHEtoIntTempE(self) do
          sgnMainCHEIntTempE(self, $a) := true
        r_CleanUp_MainCHE[]
      endpar
    endif

  rule r_MainCHP =
    if startMainCHP(self) then
      par
        skip //<<TODO>>
        r_MainCHE[]
        r_CleanUp_MainCHP[]
      endpar
    endif
```

```
rule r_MainCHA =
  if startMainCHA(self) then
    par
      skip //<<TODO>>
      r_MainCHP[]
      r_CleanUp_MainCHA[]
    endpar
  endif

rule r_MainCHM =
  if startMainCHM(self) then
    par
      skip //<<TODO>>
      r_MainCHA[]
      r_CleanUp_MainCHM[]
    endpar
  endif

rule r_MainCH = r_MainCHM[]

rule r_IntTempM =
  if startIntTempM(self) then
    par
      skip //<<TODO>>
      if not sgnIntTempMMainCHM(self
        fromIntTempMtoMainCHM(self)) then
        sgnIntTempMMainCHM(self,
          fromIntTempMtoMainCHM(self)) := true
      endif
      r_CleanUp_IntTempM[]
    endpar
  endif

rule r_IntTempE =
  if startIntTempE(self) then
    par
      skip //<<TODO>>
      r_CleanUp_IntTempE[]
    endpar
  endif

rule r_IntTemp =
  par
    r_IntTempM[]
    r_IntTempE[]
  endpar

main rule r_mainRule =
  forall $a in Agent with true do
    program($a)

default init s0:
function sgnIntTempMMainCHM($a in IntTempMgA,
  $b in MainCHMgA) = false

function fromIntTempMtoMainCHM($a in IntTempMgA) =
  switch($a)
    case h0: ch   case h1: ch
  endswitch

function fromMainCHMtoIntTempM($a in MainCHMgA) =
  switch($a)
    case ch: {h0, h1}
  endswitch
  ...

agent MainCHMgA: r_MainCH[]
agent IntTempMgA: r_IntTemp[]
agent HeaterMdA: r_Heater[]
```

Code 4. ASM model of the Comfortable Heating MAPE loop

the system and/or refined the ASM model; therefore, on the refined ASM model, the designer can perform some validation and verification activities in order to check that the designed system behaves as expected for the considered adaptation scenario. For example, (s)he can simulate the model by means of the ASMETA simulator in order to observe a MAPE loop execution, as shown in Fig. 4 for the **running case study**. In the initial state State 0, the user interacts with the simulator for specifying rooms temperatures, by setting the values of the locations of the monitored function roomTemp. Starting from State 1, the ASM evolves autonomously executing all the computations of the MAPE pattern:

asm ComfortableHeating_ref
import StandardLibrary
 	
signature:
...
   //signature added in refinement
   enum domain HeatingStatus = {FAIRLY_HOT | VERY_HOT | OFF}
   domain Temperature subsetof Integer
   monitored roomTemp: IntTempMgA — > Temperature
   controlled desiredHeating: MainCHMgA — > HeatingStatus
   controlled setHeatingStatus: HeaterMdA — > HeatingStatus
   ...
	definitions:
	...
	   rule r_TriggerActuators_Heater($s in HeaterMdA, $b in IntTempMgA) =
	      setHeatingStatus($s) := desiredHeating(fromIntTempEtoMainCHE($b))
	
	   rule r_IntTempE =
	      if startIntTempE(self) then
	         par
	            r_TriggerActuators_Heater[heaterManagedByIntTemp(self), self]
	            r_CleanUp_IntTempE[]
	         endpar
	      endif

Code 5. Excerpt of the refined ASM model of the Comfortable Heating MAPE loop

- the interaction between the M components of the `IntTempMgA` agents `h0` and `h1` and the `MainCHMgA` agent `ch` is triggered by the dispatching and reception of signals in `sgnIntTempMMainCHM` (written by `IntTempMgA` agents in State 1 and read by the `MainCHMgA` agent in State 2);
- in State 2, the `MainCHMgA` agent `ch` performs all its MAPE computations (all the rules corresponding to the four MAPE components are called in a waterfall manner);
- the interactions between the E components of the `MainCHMgA` agent and of the `IntTempMgA` agents is triggered by the dispatching and reception of signals in `sgnMainCHEIntTempE` (written by the `MainCHMgA` agent in State 2 and read by the `IntTempMgA` agents in State 3);
- in State 3, the `IntTempMgA` agents inform the managed system that the heaters of the rooms must be turned on by setting to `FAIRLY_HOT` the actuators `setHeatingStatus`.

Monitoring phase of the Interface group

```
Insert a constant in Temperature
of type Integer for roomTemp(h0):
15
...
<State 0 (monitored)>
roomTemp(h0)=15
roomTemp(h1)=16
sensorsActivatedHeater(hs0)=true
sensorsActivatedHeater(hs1)=true
</State 0 (monitored)>
```

Interaction between the Interface group and the Main group

```
<State 1 (controlled)>
...
setHeatingStatus(hs0)=undef
setHeatingStatus(hs1)=undef
sgnIntTempMMainCHM(h0,ch)=true
sgnIntTempMMainCHM(h1,ch)=true
...
</State 1 (controlled)>
```

Analysis, Planning and Execute phases of the Main group

```
<State 2 (controlled)>
...
setHeatingStatus(hs0)=undef
setHeatingStatus(hs1)=undef
sgnIntTempMMainCHM(h0,ch)=false
sgnIntTempMMainCHM(h1,ch)=false
sgnMainCHEIntTempE(ch,h0)=true
sgnMainCHEIntTempE(ch,h1)=true
</State 2 (controlled)>
```

Interaction between Main and Interface groups

```
<State 3 (controlled)>
...
setHeatingStatus(hs0)=FAIRLY_HOT
setHeatingStatus(hs1)=FAIRLY_HOT
sgnIntTempMMainCHM(h0,ch)=false
sgnIntTempMMainCHM(h1,ch)=false
sgnMainCHEIntTempE(ch,h0)=false
sgnMainCHEIntTempE(ch,h1)=false
</State 3 (controlled)>
```

Fig. 4. Simulation trace (bold titles are not part of the simulation)

Validation is very useful as it can provide a quick feedback about the system behavior; however, if we want to gain a higher confidence on the correctness of the designed system, formal verification should be used. For example, for the **running example**, we used the AsmetaSMV model checker of the ASMETA framework [2] to verify some properties regarding adaptation correctness:

- *whenever necessary, the adaptation is performed*: if the average temperature is below 18, the heaters will be turned on. This is captured by the following Linear Time Logic (LTL) formula[6]:

$\mathbf{G}($avgTemp(ch) < 18 implies
$\qquad\mathbf{F}($setHeatingStatus(hs0) $!=$ OFF and setHeatingStatus(hs1) $!=$ OFF$))$

- *the adaptation is only performed when necessary*: if the heaters have been turned on, an average temperature below 18 has been observed in the past. This is captured by the following Past LTL formulas:

$\mathbf{G}($setHeatingStatus(hs0) $!=$ OFF implies $\mathbf{O}($avgTemp(ch) $< 18))$
$\mathbf{G}($setHeatingStatus(hs1) $!=$ OFF implies $\mathbf{O}($avgTemp(ch) $< 18))$

- *all possible kinds of adaptation can be executed*: the heaters can be turned both to `FAIRLY_HOT` and `VERY_HOT`. This can be proved by falsifying these four LTL properties[7]:

not $\mathbf{F}($setHeatingStatus(hs0) $=$ FAIRLY_HOT$)$//*this is expected to be false*
not $\mathbf{F}($setHeatingStatus(hs0) $=$ VERY_HOT$)$//*this is expected to be false*
not $\mathbf{F}($setHeatingStatus(hs1) $=$ FAIRLY_HOT$)$//*this is expected to be false*
not $\mathbf{F}($setHeatingStatus(hs1) $=$ VERY_HOT$)$//*this is expected to be false*

5   Related Work

We give an overview of selected works that are related to notations for modeling MAPE loops (and patterns) of self-adaptation explicitly and that we identified as the most relevant to the context of this work.

Contributions in [7,13] exploit the use of a network of Timed Automata to specify the behavior of MAPE components, and the Uppaal model checker for property verification. A development methodology, called ENTRUST, supports the systematic engineering and assurance of self-adaptive systems. In ENTRUST, a template-based approach to the design and verification of a "specific family" of self-adaptive systems is used, namely a target domain of distributed applications in which self-adaptation is used for managing resources for robustness and openness requirements via adding/removing resources from the system. In MSL, instead, we clearly elevate MAPE loops to first-class entities for structuring the adaptation logic of any self-adaptive system in the early design phases and for fostering (in a broad sense) *pattern-oriented modeling*.

---

[6] For the semantics of the used temporal logics, we remind the reader to [4].
[7] Note that, in order to verify the desired property, we need to find counterexamples for the properties stating that the heater cannot be turned to `FAIRLY_HOT` and `VERY_HOT`.

In [12], a UML profile is proposed to model control loops as first-class entities when architecting software with UML. The UML profile supports modeling of interactions between coarse-grained controllers, while the MSL language aims at modeling finer-grained interactions between the MAPE components. Moreover, the UML profile does not support pattern modeling for MAPE loops explicitly.

SOTA (State Of The Affairs) [1], tool-supported by the Eclipse plug-in Sim-SOTA, is a goal-oriented modeling and simulation framework for self-adaptive systems. SOTA adopts UML activity diagrams as primary notation to model the behavior of feedback control loops. The framework ACTRESS [15] is grounded on an actor-oriented component meta-model and provides support for structural modeling of feedback loops, model well-formedness checking (through structural OCL or Xbase invariants), and generation of Java-like code for the actor- and JVM- based runtime platform Akka. Both SOTA and ACTRESS do not support pattern modeling and do not adopt a formal notation, as self-adaptive ASMs, for the behavior specification and verification of MAPE components.

CYPHEF (CYber-PHysical dEvelopment Framework) [9] provides a graphical notation for modeling the control architecture of a cyber-physical system by MAPE loop patterns. Differently from our approach, CYPHEF does not provide support for formal verification.

Despite similarities and differences with our approach, all the works mentioned above can be used as back-end frameworks to complement and complete for different purposes the adaptation logic design started in MSL.

6   Conclusion and Future Work

We proposed the textual language MSL for defining and instantiating MAPE patterns in structuring the adaptation logic of self-adaptive systems. MSL can be used to model complex composite MAPE loops structures, as all those devised in [20]. The language provides a textual counterpart of the graphical notation originally presented in [20] for specifying MAPE patterns, but never developed and exposing a number of ambiguities. A semantic mapping (and a model generator) from MSL to self-adaptive ASMs has been also presented. It provides a connection to the modeling back-end of ASMs for specifying and analysing the behavior of instances of MAPE patterns formally.

As future work, we want to extend the MSL pattern library (available online at [18]) with other common patterns of interacting MAPE loops, and the language itself to allow composition strategies of patterns instances in the same design. Moreover, we plan to evaluate the usability and usefulness of the framework on a certain number of case studies. We also plan to extend our framework in order to support backward compatibility between an MSL model and its ASM counterpart.

References

1. Abeywickrama, D.B., Hoch, N., Zambonelli, F.: SimSOTA: engineering and simulating feedback loops for self-adaptive systems. In: International C* Conference on Computer Science & Software Engineering, C3S2E13, Porto, Portugal, 10–12 July 2013, pp. 67–76 (2013)
2. Arcaini, P., Gargantini, A., Riccobene, E., Scandurra, P.: A model-driven process for engineering a toolset for a formal method. Softw. Pract. Exp. **41**(2), 155–166 (2011)
3. Arcaini, P., Riccobene, E., Scandurra, P.: Formal design and verification of self-adaptive systems with decentralized control. ACM Trans. Auton. Adapt. Syst. **11**(4), 25:1–25:35 (2017)
4. Baier, C., Katoen, J.-P.: Principles of Model Checking. Representation and Mind Series. The MIT Press, Cambridge (2008)
5. Börger, E., Raschke, A.: Modeling Companion for Software Practitioners. Springer, Heidelberg (2018). https://doi.org/10.1007/978-3-662-56641-1
6. Brun, Y., et al.: Engineering self-adaptive systems through feedback loops. In: Cheng, B.H.C., de Lemos, R., Giese, H., Inverardi, P., Magee, J. (eds.) Software Engineering for Self-Adaptive Systems. LNCS, vol. 5525, pp. 48–70. Springer, Heidelberg (2009). https://doi.org/10.1007/978-3-642-02161-9_3
7. Calinescu, R., Gerasimou, S., Habli, I., Iftikhar, M.U., Kelly, T., Weyns, D.: Engineering trustworthy self-adaptive software with dynamic assurance cases. CoRR abs/1703.06350 (2017)
8. Cheng, B.H.C., et al.: Software engineering for self-adaptive systems: a research roadmap. In: Cheng, B.H.C., de Lemos, R., Giese, H., Inverardi, P., Magee, J. (eds.) Software Engineering for Self-Adaptive Systems. LNCS, vol. 5525, pp. 1–26. Springer, Heidelberg (2009). https://doi.org/10.1007/978-3-642-02161-9_1
9. D'Angelo, M., Caporuscio, M., Napolitano, A.: Model-driven engineering of decentralized control in cyber-physical systems. In: 2017 IEEE 2nd International Workshops on Foundations and Applications of Self* Systems, FAS*W, pp. 7–12, September 2017
10. de Lemos, R., et al.: Software engineering for self-adaptive systems: a second research roadmap. In: de Lemos, R., Giese, H., Müller, H.A., Shaw, M. (eds.) Software Engineering for Self-Adaptive Systems II. LNCS, vol. 7475, pp. 1–32. Springer, Heidelberg (2013). https://doi.org/10.1007/978-3-642-35813-5_1
11. Gargantini, A., Riccobene, E., Scandurra, P.: A semantic framework for metamodel-based languages. Autom. Softw. Eng. **16**(3–4), 415–454 (2009)
12. Hebig, R., Giese, H., Becker, B.: Making control loops explicit when architecting self-adaptive systems. In: Proceedings of the 2nd International Workshop on Self-Organizing Architectures, SOAR 2010, pp. 21–28. ACM, New York (2010)
13. Iglesia, D.G.D.L., Weyns, D.: MAPE-K formal templates to rigorously design behaviors for self-adaptive systems. ACM Trans. Auton. Adapt. Syst. **10**(3), 15:1–15:31 (2015)
14. Kephart, J.O., Chess, D.M.: The vision of autonomic computing. IEEE Comput. **36**(1), 41–50 (2003)
15. Křikava, F., Collet, P., France, R.B.: ACTRESS: domain-specific Modeling of Self-adaptive Software Architectures. In: Proceedings of the 29th Annual ACM Symposium on Applied Computing, SAC 2014, pp. 391–398. ACM, New York (2014)
16. Meliá, S., Cachero, C., Hermida, J.M., Aparicio, E.: Comparison of a textual versus a graphical notation for the maintainability of MDE domain models: an empirical pilot study. Softw. Qual. J. **24**(3), 709–735 (2016)

17. Microsoft: Microsoft Application Architecture Guide, 2nd edn. Microsoft Press, Redmond (2009)
18. The MSL language (2018). https://github.com/fmselab/msl
19. Song, H., Barrett, S., Clarke, A., Clarke, S.: Self-adaptation with end-user preferences: using run-time models and constraint solving. In: Moreira, A., Schätz, B., Gray, J., Vallecillo, A., Clarke, P. (eds.) MODELS 2013. LNCS, vol. 8107, pp. 555–571. Springer, Heidelberg (2013). https://doi.org/10.1007/978-3-642-41533-3_34
20. Weyns, D., et al.: On patterns for decentralized control in self-adaptive systems. In: de Lemos, R., Giese, H., Müller, H.A., Shaw, M. (eds.) Software Engineering for Self-Adaptive Systems II. LNCS, vol. 7475, pp. 76–107. Springer, Heidelberg (2013). https://doi.org/10.1007/978-3-642-35813-5_4

Formally Describing Self-organizing Architectures for Systems-of-Systems on the Internet-of-Things

Flavio Oquendo[(⊠)]

IRISA – UMR CNRS/Univ. Bretagne Sud, Vannes, France
flavio.oquendo@irisa.fr

Abstract. Nowadays, the Internet-of-Things (IoT) enables the engineering of Software-intensive Systems-of-Systems (SoS), which are opportunistically created for achieving specified missions in specific operational environments.

A challenging issue in the architectural design of SoS on IoT is to conceive concepts and mechanisms for describing how an SoS architecture is able to create, on the fly, emergent behaviors from elementary IoT systems/devices.

To address this challenge, this paper investigates the theory of self-organization, which makes possible that, in an SoS, its constituent systems spontaneously create and maintain a valid SoS architecture enabling the evolutionary development of the required emergent behavior to fulfill the specified SoS mission. In particular, it describes how SosADL, a formal SoS Architecture Description Language (ADL), based on the novel π-Calculus for SoS, was enhanced to support the architectural description of self-organizing SoSs on the IoT, upwardly causing SoS emergent behaviors at run-time.

Keywords: Software architecture description
Software-intensive System-of-Systems · Self-organization · Emergence
Internet-of-Things · SosADL

1 Introduction

Software-intensive systems are often independently developed, operated, managed, and evolved. Progressively, communication networks enabled these independent systems to interact, yielding a new kind of complex system, i.e. a system that is itself composed of systems, the so-called System-of-Systems (SoS).

SoSs are evolutionary developed from independent systems to achieve missions not possible to be accomplished by a single system alone [15]. They are architected to produce emergent behavior, i.e. a behavior that stems from the interactions among constituents, but that cannot be predicted from behaviors of the constituents themselves [14].

The SoS defining characteristics [15] are: operational independence, managerial independence, and geographical distribution of the constituent systems; and evolutionary development and emergent behavior of the SoS as a whole.

Recently, the Internet-of-Things (IoT), by providing a ubiquitous communication network, has made possible to opportunistically create software-intensive SoSs, on-the-fly, for achieving a specific mission in a given operational environment by opportunistically creating appropriate emergent behaviors [33].

Oppositely to usual SoSs, the architect of an SoS on IoT generally does not know at design-time which are the concrete systems that will become constituents of the SoSs at run-time. Additionally, the SoS architecture depends not only on the constituents of the SoS but also on the operational environment where the SoS will operate on the IoT.

Architecturally speaking, two recursive levels of scale can be observed in an SoS: (i) the SoS as a whole, called the macro-scale; and (ii) the SoS constituents and their connections organized in an architecture, called the micro-scale.

Knowing that an emergent behavior is a macro-scale property which, in the case of supervenience [17], the type of emergence suitable for SoS [25], is deducible from the micro-scale architecture, the research question posed is: how to formally describe (in terms of concepts and mechanisms) the SoS architecture at micro-scale in order to spontaneously create the required emergent behavior at macro-scale for fulling the specified SoS mission on the IoT?

This paper addresses this challenging question, by investigating the theory of self-organization [30], and conceiving a novel approach based on self-organization as a mechanism for spontaneously creating concrete software-intensive SoS architectures on the IoT. The outcome is thereby that some independent IoT systems/devices themselves will create the required connectivity enabling the production of the required emergent behaviors for fulling SoS missions. In addition, when compared with man-made organized SoSs, self-organizing SoSs are more robust and more resilient [29].

In particular, this paper brings contributions beyond the state-of-the-art on the formalization of self-organizing SoS architectures. It describes how SosADL [20, 24], a formal SoS Architecture Description Language (ADL), based on the novel π-Calculus for SoS [21], was enhanced to support the formal description of self-organizing SoS architectures and presents its application on the IoT.

This paper extends previous published work on SosADL at the IEEE System-of-Systems Engineering Conference (SoSE) 2016, where the architectural language was presented in [20] and SoSE 2017, where the features to describe SoS emergent behaviors were described in [26].

The novelty of this paper regarding these previous publications is the presentation of a novel architectural formalism for self-organization based on concurrent constraints and the enhancements of SosADL for describing self-organizing SoS architectures based on an exogenous architectural approach.

The remainder of this paper is organized as follows. Section 2 presents the principles of self-organization and how they can be applied to software architecture. Section 3 overviews the concepts and constructs of SosADL for supporting self-organization, enabling emergent behavior. Section 4 presents how SosADL can be applied to describe self-organizing SoS architectures, demonstrated through an excerpt of a real application for architecting a Reconnaissance SoS, focusing on the flocking behavior of a fleet of Unmanned Aerial Vehicles (UAVs). In Sect. 5, we outline the implemented toolset as well as the validation of SosADL for supporting self-organizing SoS architectures. In Sect. 6, we position our proposal for describing self-organizing architectures of SoSs with related work. To conclude we summarize, in Sect. 7, the main contributions of this paper and outline future work.

2   Self-organization Principles for Software Architecture

2.1   Phenomenon of Self-organization

Self-organization can be basically defined as the spontaneous creation and preservation of an emergent arrangement out of local connections between initially independent constituents [1, 25, 30]. It is spontaneous in the sense that it is not triggered by external events (it is internally produced). It is in particular resilient, being able to be restructured when subject to perturbations, attaining new valid self-organizations.

Motivated by the spontaneity and resilience of self-organization, during the last decade, the engineering of self-organizing systems has attracted increasing attention [29].

The phenomenon of self-organization is largely present in nature, e.g. in an atom, a molecule, a cell, an organism, and a society [1]. Indeed, we live in a world that exhibits self-organization at different scales. A snowflake, a flock of birds, a herd of land animals, a swarm of insects, and a school of fishes are examples of natural systems that exhibit self-organization. A flock of UAVs, a swarm of robots, and the Web are examples of artificial systems that similarly exhibit self-organization. Indeed, self-organization is a general principle that is exhibited in natural and artificial systems.

In particular, Ilya Prigogine showed the universality of the phenomenon of self-organization on both natural and artificial systems [30]. He developed the fundamental research that led to the general theory of self-organization, for which he was awarded the Nobel Prize in 1977, studying open systems that are far from equilibrium, called dissipative structures. He showed that self-organization is naturally present in far from equilibrium systems in Physics, in Chemistry, in Biology, in Sociology and in Computing when conditions are present.

Based on the work of Ilya Prigogine, we have proposed the theory of self-organization for SoS and the principles to adopt it to architect SoSs [25].

2.2   Architectural Perspective of Self-organization

From an architectural perspective, self-organization is the ability of a whole to spontaneously arrange its parts in a purposeful (non-random) manner, under appropriate constraints and without the assistance of an external intervention. It can be defined as the mechanism that enables an SoS to create, preserve, and evolve its architecture without external intervention, and in particular, without explicit command and control.

For instance, coming back to natural systems, as Ilya Prigogine demonstrated, convection within the atmosphere is the result of the self-organization of water molecules when they reach a critical point obtained by varying imposed constraints (thereby increasing or decreasing its order).

Similarly, SoSs are complex systems far from equilibrium when compared to single systems that are essentially systems near equilibrium [25, 30]. Therefore, self-organization is reachable in critical points located in the transition space between disorder and order, far from equilibrium, in the so-called edge of chaos [9, 25]. It is at an attractor that a valid organization is reached through self-organization [8].

Fundamentally, Ilya Prigogine demonstrated that to make self-organization possible in a complex system, on the one hand the system must be in a state far from equilibrium and on the other hand we need to be able to vary the order/disorder of the system by adding or removing constraints, thereby increasing or decreasing order (oppositely, disorder) in the edge of chaos.

To reach a valid self-organization, it is thereby necessary to reach an attractor and to reach an attractor it is needed to tie or relax constraints, until the attractor is achieved.

Thereby, for initiating and maintaining self-organization in an SoS that is far from equilibrium, all what is needed is to apply the appropriate balance of constraints. Consequently, the ADL for describing self-organizing SoS architectures must be able to express and manipulate architectural constraints.

3   Self-organization Principles in SosADL

SosADL was conceived to overcome limitations of existing ADLs by providing the expressive power to describe the architectural concerns of SoSs, and in particular to enable the description of emergent behaviors in evolutionary architectures [23] according to different approaches, including self-organization [25].

For architecturally describing a single system architecture, the core concepts are those of component, connector and configuration. In SosADL, an SoS architecture is described in terms of abstract specifications of possible constituent systems, mediators, and their coalitions [20]. The core concepts are hence the one of *system* to represent the constituents, the one of *mediator* to represent the enforced interactions among constituents, and the one of *coalition* to represent their formation as an SoS.

In SosADL, SoS architectures are represented in abstract terms (as concrete systems which will become constituents of the SoS are not necessarily known at design-time, as e.g. on the IoT) [20]. The defined abstract architecture will then be evolutionarily concretized at run-time, by identifying and incorporating concrete constituent systems (see [6] for details on the automated synthesis of concrete SoS architectures from abstract architectures in SosADL).

Based on the theory of self-organization for SoS, our approach for architecting self-organizing SoSs on the IoT with SosADL is first to specify a coalition and then to apply constraints to the behavior of its constituent systems in order to eventually attain an attractor. Semantically, it follows the constraint interpretation of emergence through self-organization [2].

Indeed, behaviors of the parts (the micro-scale) constrained by their interactions (in the micro-scale) as well as by coalition policies (also in the micro-scale) cause (upward causation) the emergent behavior of the whole (at macro-scale) through self-organization. In fact, it is by constraining the behaviors of the parts that self-organization is enabled and the emergent behavior is produced.

Achieving self-organization in SoS is based on the application of constraints to systems that will participate to the SoS. That is, before the existence of an SoS, the different candidate systems that will participate in the SoS work independently from one to another on the IoT. Thereby, no emergent behavior appears. Once constraints are applied to the identified IoT systems/devices, imposing constrained interactions among them, the necessary condition to create self-organization possibly holds. It is by applying suitable constraints that the self-organizing behavior will definitely emerge at an attractor.

More precisely, SosADL was enhanced to support self-organization in a principled way by two novel features: (i) *the mechanism of concurrent constraints* and (ii) *the architectural concept of mediator*. Therefore, to reach an attractor in a self-organizing SoS on the IoT, we must add or remove constraints to make the order of the SoS vary. To manage the degree of freedom of constituent systems in an SoS, SosADL apply mediators to constrain or relax their behaviors through concurrent constraints. Note that mediators are explicitly specified through constraints among constituent systems at micro-scale, where each micro-scale behavior expresses what are the actions to execute for enforcing constraints.

It is indeed, based on the general theory of self-organization from Ilya Prigogine, who demonstrated that very simple micro-scale rules can describe highly complex dissipative macro-scale structures, that we developed this novel architectural approach for self-organizing SoSs on the IoT supported by SosADL.

Therefore, in our approach following the theory of self-organization for SoS [25], it is by constraining the behavior of the constituent systems through the creation and application of mediators regulating their behaviors that we enable the phenomenon of self-organization which will always appear whenever the appropriate conditions to reach attractors are met.

To achieve this goal, we designed a novel formal calculus, the π-Calculus for SoS [21], which generalizes the π-Calculus [18] with the notion of computing based on concurrent constraints and in particular on the principles of constraint-based calculi [19].

In particular, the π-Calculus for SoS supports the specification of the coalition of mediated concurrent systems by means of constraints. In an SoS, the constituents can tell new constraints (i.e. adding constraints to the environment) as well as can ask about constraints (i.e. determining whether a given constraint can be inferred from the told constraints to the environment), or by untelling constraints (i.e. removing constraints from the environment).

Based on the π-Calculus for SoS, in SosADL, a behavior is described by the actions that it can carry out as well as the constraints that it enforces or copes with. It provides: (i) a `tell` construct for adding a constraint to the local environment; (ii) an `ask` construct for querying if a constraint can be inferred from the local environment; (iii) a `compose` construct to express concurrent composition of behaviors and constraints; (iv) a `connection` construct to restrict the interface that a behavior can use to interact with others; (v) an `untell` construct for removing a constraint from the local environment.

4   Describing Self-organizing Architectures in SosADL

For describing self-organizing SoS architectures in SosADL, we declare the micro-scale behaviors which will determine the emergence of self-organization and imply the desired macro-scale behavior as well as the related constraints in SosADL, through supervenience (see [26] for details on how SosADL supports supervenience for describing emergence).

To present how SosADL can be applied to architecturally describe self-organization, we will show hereafter an extract of a real SoS that we have designed in cooperation with its stakeholders, in the framework of the IoT.

Flood Monitoring and Emergency Response addresses the problem of flash floods. To address this critical problem, we have architected, with SosADL, a Flood Monitoring and Emergency Response SoS. In order to fulfill its mission [34], the Flood Monitoring and Emergency Response SoS must be able to create and maintain several self-organizing emergent behaviors in different coalitions, such as in the WSN-based Urban River Monitoring SoS and the UAV-based Reconnaissance SoS [16].

The UAV-based Reconnaissance SoS is formed by Unmanned Aerial Vehicles (UAVs) deployed from different city councils. Identified UAVs are microcopters with eight propellers, a camera and a wireless network access point. A fleet of UAVs can be activated by the gateway of the WSN-based Urban River Monitoring SoS for accomplishing a reconnaissance mission and can fly autonomously using built-in GPS.

Let us now focus on one of the emergent behaviors of the UAV-based Reconnaissance SoS: the flocking behavior of the fleet of deployed UAVs.

The intended macro-scale behavior, i.e. flocking, aims to create and maintain a flock of UAVs through self-organization. A flock is defined as a clustered group of individuals (called flockmates), moving with a common velocity. In nature, there are numerous examples of this sort of self-organization, for instance flocks of birds and schools of fishes. In engineering, it is a common collective behavior applied to engineered systems, including UAVs.

The flocking behavior was originally presented in [32], from which several works have proposed adaptations for designing flocks of engineered systems [16].

4.1   Describing Behaviors for Enabling Self-organizing SoSs

The macro-scale emergent behavior of flocking is the resultant of three micro-scale behaviors for flockmates [16, 32] shown in Fig. 1: separation, alignment, and cohesion.

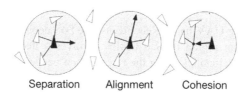

Separation   Alignment   Cohesion

Fig. 1. Separation, alignment, and cohesion micro-scale behaviors

These three micro-scale behaviors enforce the three constraints that are required for enabling self-organization, thus making the flocking behavior emerge in attractors:

- *Separation behavior* (collision avoidance): every flockmate must avoid collisions with nearby flockmates;
- *Alignment behavior* (velocity matching): every flockmate must attempt to match velocity (heading and speed) with nearby flockmates;
- *Cohesion behavior* (flock centering): every flockmate must attempt to stay close to nearby flockmates.

The separation micro-scale behavior for collision avoidance, shown in Fig. 1 (left), moves a flockmate away from other flockmates when their distance becomes shorter than a predefined threshold (first constraint), independently from the speed.

The alignment micro-scale behavior for velocity matching, shown in Fig. 1 (middle), matches the flockmate speed and heading with the speed and heading of its neighboring flockmates (second constraint).

The cohesion micro-scale behavior for flock centering, shown in Fig. 1 (right), drives a flockmate towards neighboring flockmates (third constraint). Note that, as a flockmate sees only its neighbors, the cohesion behavior drives a flockmate towards their center and not toward the center of the whole flock.

These three micro-scale behaviors (alignment, cohesion, and separation) combined together determine the acceleration vector that drives a UAV. From the UAV viewpoint, every micro-scale behavior generates an independent request for a steering maneuver to be executed by the UAV.

It is worth highlighting that these micro-scale behaviors governing alignment, cohesion, and separation (enforcing the respective constraints in flocking), also constrained by the relative positions of nearby flockmates, has been demonstrated sufficient to guarantee a suitable self-organization for enabling flocking [32], in line with the general theory of self-organization from Ilya Prigogine in terms of dissipative structures [30].

By the application of these three micro-scale behaviors, every UAV in the fleet, will behave to align and get closer to neighboring UAVs, while avoiding collision. For an external observer, at the macro-scale level, the UAVs will evolve to form a flock through self-organization. It is also worth to note that even if there are disturbances in the flock, the UAVs will smoothly form again a flock through self-organization.

In the architecture description of the UAV-based Reconnaissance SoS with SosADL, UAVs are declared as constituent systems of the flock and mediators are deduced according to the position of a UAV and its neighboring UAVs. The coalition is formed by the participating UAVs interacting under the constraints enforced by mediators.

In our case study, the UAV-based Reconnaissance SoS deployed in the Monjolinho river in the metropolitan region of Sao Carlos involves a fleet of identified UAVs located at different municipalities along the river. When needed, they are commanded to takeoff and reach an area with high risk of flooding for a reconnaissance mission (triggered by the monitoring of the urban river). Along the way and at destination, they get together for flying in flock, through self-organization, to carry out the reconnaissance of the zone of flood. They fly autonomously and form flocks spontaneously.

4.2 Describing Abstract SoS Architectures with SosADL

For achieving the emergent behavior of flocking through self-organization, the architecture of the UAV-based Reconnaissance SoS needs to be rigorously designed.

In our exogenous SoS architecture description for flocking, first, we will describe the constituent systems of the SoS, i.e. the UAVs, and next the mediators enforcing the micro-scale behaviors and inferred constraints required for creating and maintaining flocks. Then, we will describe the architecture of the SoS as a whole in terms of a coalition for achieving the macro-scale flocking behavior.

In SosADL, UAVs are declared as constituent systems of the flock. As shown in Listing 1, UAV is described as a system abstraction: we declare the interface and capabilities that must have all UAVs participating in the flock, without addressing how these interfaces and capabilities are implemented.

```
with FlightInformation //user-defined library for flight information
//abstract system declaration of UAV constituent systems
system UAV() is {
 //gate to output the position of the UAV
 gate position is {
  //connection to output UAV's latitude, longitude, altitude
  connection uav_coordinate is out{Coordinate}
  //connection to output UAV's direction with heading angle
  connection uav_heading is out{Direction}
  //connection to output UAV's direction with pitch angle
  connection uav_pitch is out{Direction}
 }
 //gate to input the command for steering the UAV
 gate command is {
  //connection to input command to the UAV
  connection fly_control is in{[heading:Direction,pitch:Direction]}
 }
 //behavior for steering the UAV through gates
 behavior autopilot() is {…}
}
```

Listing 1. UAV system declaration in SosADL

As declared in Listing 1, every UAV holds a gate, named position, having connections to outputting its coordinate in terms of latitude, longitude, and altitude, and its direction in terms of heading and pitch angles. Next, gate command enables to steer the UAV. Finally, the UAV behavior, named autopilot, is declared (not shown for sake of brevity), perceived as a black box behavior.

Note that connection uav_coordinate of gate position transmits values of datatype Coordinate for determining the location of a UAV in terms of latitude, longitude and altitude, and that connections uav_heading and uav_pitch of the same gate transmit values of datatype Direction for determining the flying direction of a UAV in terms of heading and pitch. Datatype Direction is equipped with operations to compute new headings or pitches from current ones, passed in parameter.

Let us now declare, in SosADL, the mediator `Flocking` which will make possible the emergence of the flocking macro-scale behavior of the SoS.

As shown in Listing 2, `Flocking` is described as a mediator abstraction: we declare the duties of the mediated UAV in terms of `uav_position` and `uav_command` and the behavior among UAVs participating in the flock as `mediating`. By creating concretions, a mediator will be synthesized for each UAV that participates in the flock.

Before presenting the mediating behavior, let us now describe the three micro-scale behaviors used during mediation for flocking by declaring behavior abstractions, respectively named `separation`, `alignment`, and `cohesion`.

In the exogenous approach, for achieving the flocking emergent behavior, these three required micro-scale behaviors are declared in the behavior part of the mediators, as shown in Listings 3, 4 and 5 (oppositely to the endogenous approach presented in [26], where these micro-scale behaviors are declared as embedded in the UAVs).

```
//use user-defined library for flight information
with FlightInformation
//abstract mediator declaration of flocking mediators
mediator Flocking(range:Distance,min:Distance) is {
 //duty to determine the position of the mediated UAV
 duty uav_position is {
  //connection to input UAV's latitude, longitude, altitude
  connection uav_coordinate is in{Coordinate}
  //connection to input UAV's direction with heading angle
  connection uav_heading is in{Direction}
  //connection to input UAV's direction with pitch angle
  connection uav_pitch is in{Direction}
 }
 //duty to steer the mediated UAV
 duty uav_command is {
  //connection to output command to the mediated UAV
  connection fly_control is out{[heading:Direction,pitch:Direction]}
 }
 //micro-scale behaviors for flock: separation, alignment, cohesion
 abstraction separation(…) is {…}
 abstraction alignment(…) is {…}
 abstraction cohesion(…) is {…}
 //behavior for mediating the UAV through duties
 behavior mediating(…) is {…}
}
```

Listing 2. Mediator declaration in SosADL

They handle data structures for representing on the one hand the position of the mediated UAV as well as the positions of the other UAVs in its neighborhood. Based on relative positions, the mediator decide which maneuvers to apply to the UAV.

```
abstraction separation(uav:Position,mate:Position) is {
  value new_away_heading is uav::heading::turn_away(mate::heading)
  value new_away_pitch is uav::pitch::pitch_away(mate::pitch)
  via uav_command::fly_control send [heading=new_away_heading,
  pitch=new_away_pitch]
}
```

Listing 3. Separation micro-scale behavior in SosADL

The separation micro-scale behavior, shown in Listing 3, gives the capability to compute, using trigonometry, the minimum angular difference between two UAVs (the mediated UAV heading and the heading of its nearest flockmate), and turns away from it following that calculated direction (given by calculated angles) to avoid coalition.

```
abstraction alignment(uav:Position,hood:set{Position}) is {
  value avg_heading is hood::heading->avg_heading()
  value avg_pitch is hood::pitch->avg_pitch()
  value new_aligned_heading is uav::heading::turn_towards(
  avg_heading)
  value new_aligned_pitch is uav::pitch::pitch_towards(avg_pitch)
  via uav_command::fly_control send [heading=new_aligned_heading,
  pitch=new_aligned_pitch]
}
```

Listing 4. Alignment micro-scale behavior in SosADL

The alignment micro-scale behavior, shown in Listing 4, gives the capability to a UAV to turn for moving in the same direction that nearby UAVs are moving. Using trigonometry, it can compute a new heading and a new pitch for the mediated UAV based on the headings and pitches of the neighbors and then command the UAV to follow that new direction.

```
abstraction cohesion(uav:Position,hood:set{Position}) is {
  value avg_towards_heading is hood::heading->avg_towards_heading()
  value avg_towards_pitch is hood::pitch->avg_towards_pitch()
  value new_towards_heading is uav::heading::turn_towards(
  avg_towards_heading)
  value new_towards_pitch is uav::pitch::pitch_towards(
  avg_towards_pitch)
  via uav_command::fly_control send [heading=new_towards_heading,
  pitch=new_towards_pitch]
}
```

Listing 5. Cohesion micro-scale behavior in SosADL

The cohesion micro-scale behavior, shown in Listing 5, gives the capability to compute, using trigonometry, a new heading and a new pitch for the mediated UAV (the direction to fly) based on the neighboring bearings (the direction to getting close to the neighbors). It will thereby move to get closer to neighboring UAVs.

```
behavior mediating() is {
 repeat {
  //get the coordinate of the mediated UAV
  via uav_position::uav_coordinate receive uav_coordinate
  //get the heading of the mediated UAV
  via uav_position::uav_heading receive uav_heading
  //get the pitch of the mediated UAV
  via uav_position::uav_pitch receive uav_pitch
  //tell the position to other mediators
  tell uav is [coordinate=uav_coordinate, heading=uav_heading,
   pitch=uav_pitch]
  //ask if any other UAV is in the neighborhood
  value hood is ask which uav[coordinate,heading,pitch]
   suchthat { //uav is in vision range (the vision range of the UAV)
    uav_coordinate::distance(coordinate)<range }
    //if there are UAVs in the vision range, i.e. it is not empty
  if not(hood::empty()) then { //then, get the nearest flockmate
   value nearest_mate is uav_coordinate::nearest(hood)
   //if it is too close, i.e. < min separation
   if (uav_coordinate::distance(nearest_mate::coordinate)<min)
   //then command mediated UAV to execute separation micro-behavior
   then separation(uav,nearest_mate)
   //else command mediated UAV to execute alignment micro-behavior
   else {alignment(uav,hood)
   //and command mediated UAV to execute cohesion micro-behavior
       cohesion(uav,hood)}
  }
 }
}
```

Listing 6. Flock mediating behavior in SosADL

By the application of these three micro-scale behaviors, commanding the mediated UAV, every UAV in the fleet, will stepwise behave to align and get closer to neighboring UAVs, while avoiding collision.

Let us now declare the mediating behavior in Listing 6. Once the `mediating` behavior receives the position of the mediated UAV (first getting its coordinate, second getting its heading, and third getting its pitch), the **tell** construct asserts the received position into its local environment, enabling sharing with other mediated UAVs. Next, the **ask** construct is used to ask for the positions of all flockmates that are in the vision range of the mediated UAV. With the result assigned to hood, the mediator first checks if there is any. If not, i.e. if no other UAV is in the neighborhood of the mediated UAV, the mediated UAV continues to fly in the same direction, moving forward. If there are UAVs in the neighborhood of the mediated UAV, the flocking mediator looks for the nearest flockmate and check whether it is too close to the mediated UAV. If their distance is less than a minimum separation value, the `mediating` behavior applies the `separation` micro-scale behavior. If not, the `mediating` behavior commands the mediated UAV applying the `alignment` micro-scale behavior and then the `cohesion` micro-scale behavior based on the positions of the neighboring flockmates.

It is worth to note that if there are disturbances in the flock, the UAVs will smoothly form again a flock based on the flocking mediators.

Let us now describe the SoS architecture making possible the flocking macro-scale emergent behavior.

The SoS architecture is described by declaring the constituent systems that can participate in the SoS, the mediators that can be created and managed for coordinating the constituent systems and the possible coalitions that can be formed to achieve the SoS emergent behaviors.

The SoS architecture description, shown in Listing 7, comprises the declaration of a sequence of constituent systems complying with the system abstraction of UAV (as declared in Listing 1) and a sequence of mediators conforming with the mediator abstraction of Flocking (as declared in Listing 2).

Based on these systems and mediator abstractions, the coalition for creating emergent behavior is declared, as shown in Listing 7. In particular, the coalition of UAVs is described as a collection of UAVs where each UAV has an associated steering mediator created in the coalition (with the specified vision range and minimum separation distance as parameters). The emergent behavior of the coalition is giving by the macro-scale behavior created by supervenience from the mediating behaviors, which apply the micro-scale behaviors.

```
with UAV,Flocking //use system and mediator abstractions
//abstract architecture declaration for the flocking SoS
architecture FlockingSoS(range:Distance,min:Distance) is {
  //coalition defined by a fleet of UAVs and flocking mediators
  behavior coalition is compose{
    fleet is sequence{UAV()}
    flocking is sequence{Flocking(range,min)}
  } binding {//forall UAV in coalition there is a flocking mediator
      forall {uav in fleet suchthat exists{one steer in flocking
        suchthat unify one{steer::uav_position} to one{uav::position}
              unify one{steer::uav_command} to one{uav::command}}
      }
    }
}
```

Listing 7. SoS architecture description for flocking in SosADL

It is by the application of the mediating behaviors, commanding the UAVs by applying the defined micro-scale behaviors, that every UAV in the fleet, will stepwise behave to align and get closer to neighboring UAVs, while avoiding collision. For an external observer at the macro-scale level, the fleet of UAVs will evolve to form a flock.

From this abstract SoS architecture, different concrete SoS architectures may be created based on the identified UAVs for each particular operational environment. For instance, as mentioned, in the case of flood monitoring of the Monjolinho river, the fleet of identified UAVs are microcopters located at different cities of the metropolitan region of Sao Carlos along the river. They are then commanded to takeoff and reach an area with high risk of flooding for a reconnaissance mission (triggered by the monitoring of the urban river). At the destination, they eventually get together for flying in flock to carry out the reconnaissance of the targeted zone of flood.

5   Validating Self-organizing Architectures with SosADL

A major impetus behind developing formal foundations for SoS architecture description is that formality renders them suitable to be manipulated by software tools. The usefulness of providing the π-Calculus for SoS underlying SosADL is thereby directly related to the tools it provides to support architecture modeling of self-organization, but also analysis and evolution of self-organizing architectures.

We have developed an SoS Architecture Development Environment, named SosADL Studio [27, 28], for supporting architecture-centric formal development of self-organizing SoSs using SosADL.

This toolset is constructed as plugins in Eclipse (http://eclipse.org/). It provides a model-driven architecture development environment where the SosADL meta-model is defined in EMF/Ecore (http://eclipse.org/modeling/emf/), with the textual concrete syntax expressed in Xtext (http://eclipse.org/Xtext/), the graphical concrete syntax developed in Sirius (http://eclipse.org/sirius/), and the type checker implemented in Xtend (http://www.eclipse.org/xtend/), after having being proved using the Coq proof assistant (http://coq.inria.fr/) [28].

Applying model-to-model transformations, SoS architecture descriptions are transformed to input languages of analysis tools, including UPPAAL (http://www.uppaal.org/) for model checking, DEVS (http://www.ms4systems.com/) for simulation, and PLASMA (http://project.inria.fr/plasma-lab/) for statistical model checking.

The constraint solving mechanism implemented to support the **tell**, **ask**, and **untell** constraint handling constructs are based on the Kodkod SAT-solver (http://alloy.mit.edu/kodkod/).

Of particular interest for validating self-organizing behavior is the automated generation of concrete SoS architectures, transformation from SosADL to DEVS, and the subsequent simulation in DEVS enabling to observe and tune the described self-organizing emergent behavior of an SoS [27].

For supporting verification of self-organizing SoS architectures, we have conceived a novel logic, named DynBLTL [31], for expressing correctness properties of evolving architectures and verifying these properties with statistical model checking [5].

For validating SosADL as well as its accompanying SosADL Studio, we have carried out a field study of a real SoS for Flood Monitoring and Emergency Response and studied its concretization in the Monjolinho river, which crosses the city of Sao Carlos, SP, Brazil. The aim of this field study (of which an extract is presented in this paper) was to assess the fitness for purpose and the usefulness of, on the one hand, SosADL as a formal SoS architectural language, and on the other hand, the SosADL Studio as a software environment to support the architectural description and analysis of real self-organizing SoSs.

The result of this field study (see [22] for details) shows that SosADL meet the requirements for modeling SoS architectures and its emergent behaviors, in particular for self-organizing SoS architectures. As expected, using a formal ADL compels the SoS architects to study different architectural alternatives and take key architectural decisions to make possible the emergence of self-organizing behaviors in SoS architectures.

In particular, the result of this field study showed that the different tools integrated in the SosADL Studio provides the appropriate features for describing and analyzing

SoS architectures and their emergent behaviors, in particular regarding description, validation, and verification of self-organizing SoS architectures.

In fact, a key identified benefit of using SosADL Studio was the ability to validate and verify the studied self-organizing SoS architectures very early in the SoS lifecycle with respect to its correctness properties, as well as for studying the extreme conditions in which self-organizing behaviors were not able to satisfy the SoS mission.

6 Related Work

Self-organization, as a mechanism for modeling complex systems, has been extensively discussed in the literature [29, 38]. In the Computing discipline, different workshops haven been dedicated to the topic, e.g. [3], and since 2007 a dedicated conference series has been organized, i.e. the IEEE International Conferences on Self-Adaptive and Self-Organizing Systems (SASO) [10] targeting foundations and applications of principled approaches to engineering systems, networks and services based on self-adaptation or self-organization.

Regarding software architecture, while self-adaptive architectures have been extensively discussed in the community, self-organizing architectures have been much less addressed, and even when tackled they were often as an adjunct consideration [3, 29].

More recently, the importance of explicitly describing the architecture in the development of self-organizing systems has been increasingly highlighted in publications [35]. Predictably, most of the works on the software architecture of self-organizing systems has been developed in the area of SoS engineering [13]. Self-organization is indeed of major interest for SoS, as emergent behavior is a foundational characteristic and self-organization a well-founded mechanism for producing emergent behavior. Since 2006, more than 30 papers addressing emergence and self-organization for SoS engineering have been published in the IEEE SoS Engineering (SoSE) proceedings [11], however none proposed an ADL for describing self-organizing SoS architectures [13, 23, 35]. In ECSA proceedings, several papers addressed self-adaptive architectures, but none addressed self-organizing architectures.

Regarding self-organizing SoSs, Häner et al. [7] address the importance of self-organization for developing large SoSs. It does not provide a formalization of self-organization for SoS architectures, limiting to apply the self-organization principle in practice in the domain of natural crisis management. In their work, self-organization is established on the basis of autonomous and concurrent tasks that are enacted by choreographies specifying the expected behavior of the set of SoS constituent systems. It is complementary to our work in the sense that their designed self-organizing SoS architecture can be formally described with SosADL, in particular supporting the description and formalization of self-reconfiguration in the choreographies.

Regarding self-organizing flocking architectures, Jaimes et al. [12] present a realistic situation where an autonomous fixed-wing UAV and semi-autonomous swarm of quad-rotor UAVs work together to carry out the surveillance on a given area. This work demonstrates the practical interest of using a flock of UAVs for surveillance. This kind of SoS architecture can be straightforwardly described with SosADL, enabling to analyze its deployment in different environments as well as in different UAV platforms.

Another thread of related work on SoSs is the one of implementation platforms, in particular, for the case of the so-called "ensembles" (an SoS that is only composed of homogeneous systems), e.g. DEECo (Dependable Ensembles of Emerging Components) [4] and SCEL (Service Component Ensemble Language) [36]. In this case, SoS homogeneous architectures described and analyzed with SosADL can be transformed to implementation models in SCEL or DEECo. SosADL also supports transformation to service-oriented architectural styles [37] applied to SoS implementation.

In summary, based on the study of the state-of-the-art [23], SosADL enhanced with concurrent constraints is positioned as a pioneering ADL having the expressive power to formally describe self-organizing SoS architectures, no existing ADL being able to express these evolutionary architectures.

7   Conclusion and Future Work

This paper presented the notion of self-organization, briefly introduced the general theory of self-organization of Nobel laureate Ilya Prigogine on dissipative structures, applied this theory for SoS, and explained the enhancements of SosADL that support the rigorous description of self-organizing architectures.

We established that software-intensive SoSs on the IoT are dissipative structures, far from equilibrium [25] and that, consequently, self-organization provides a spontaneous mechanism to find new instable equilibriums again far from equilibrium.

Thereby, as an SoS is a complex system that is far from equilibrium, to support self-organization, we enhanced SosADL with concurrent constraints, where we substituted the constructs for manipulating and exchanging values by constructs that manipulates and exchanges concurrent constraints, i.e. **tell**, **ask**, and **untell** as well as extended the semantics of **compose** and **connection** to support the concurrent composition among systems and the intentional binding between connections of these systems.

In particular, this paper presented the enhancements of SosADL which bring main contributions beyond the state-of-the-art on self-organizing SoS architectures on the IoT, grounded on concurrent constraint satisfaction.

In addition, this paper demonstrated how architectural mediators expressed with SosADL supports exogenous architecture descriptions through an excerpt of a real application for architecting a UAV-based Reconnaissance SoS, focusing on the flocking behavior. It provides the first exogenous architectural description of flocking, all others being based on the endogenous approach, which is not adequate to the IoT.

SosADL has been applied in several case studies and pilots where the suitability of the language itself and the supporting toolchain has been validated for both self-organizing architectures and traditional, non-self-organizing ones [22].

On-going and future work is mainly related with the application of SosADL in industrial-scale projects. Regarding the IoT, they include joint work with IBM for applying SosADL to architect smart-farms in cooperative settings, and with SEGULA for applying SosADL to architect SoSs in the naval engineering domain. Description of real-scale self-organizing SoS architectures, and their validation and verification using the SosADL toolchain, are main threads of these pilot projects.

References

1. Ashby, W.R.: Principles of the self-organizing system. In: Von Foerster, H., Zopf Jr., G.W. (eds.) Principles of Self-Organization, Pergamon, UK (1962)
2. Blachowicz, J.: The constraint interpretation of physical emergence. J. Gen. Philos. Sci. **44**, 21–40 (2013)
3. Brueckner, S.A., Di Marzo Serugendo, G., Karageorgos, A., Nagpal, R. (eds.): Engineering Self-Organising Systems: Methodologies and Applications. Springer, Heidelberg (2005). https://doi.org/10.1007/b136984
4. Bures, T., Gerostathopoulos, I., Hnetynka, P., Keznikl, J., Kit, M., Plasil, F.: Gossiping components for cyber-physical systems. In: Avgeriou, P., Zdun, U. (eds.) ECSA 2014. LNCS, vol. 8627, pp. 250–266. Springer, Cham (2014). https://doi.org/10.1007/978-3-319-09970-5_23
5. Cavalcante, E., Quilbeuf, J., Traonouez, L.-M., Oquendo, F., Batista, T., Legay, A.: Statistical model checking of dynamic software architectures. In: Tekinerdogan, B., Zdun, U., Babar, A. (eds.) ECSA 2016. LNCS, vol. 9839, pp. 185–200. Springer, Cham (2016). https://doi.org/10.1007/978-3-319-48992-6_14
6. Guessi, M., Oquendo, F., Nakagawa, E.Y.: Checking the architectural feasibility of systems-of-systems using formal descriptions. In: 11th IEEE System-of-Systems Engineering Conference, SoSE, Kongsberg, Norway, June 2016
7. Häner, R., et al.: TRIDEC system-of-systems. In: 11th IEEE International Symposium on Autonomous Decentralized Systems, Mexico City, Mexico (2013)
8. Heylighen, F.: Science of self-organization and adaptivity. In: Knowledge Management, Organizational Intelligence, Complexity. The Encyclopedia of Life Support Systems (1999)
9. Holland, J.H.: Emergence from Chaos to Order. Oxford University Press, Oxford (1998)
10. IEEE Conferences on Self-Adaptive and Self-Organizing Systems (SASO), March 2018. http://www.saso-conference.org/
11. IEEE System-of-Systems Engineering Conferences (SoSE). http://sosengineering.org/
12. Jaimes, A., Kota, S., Gomez, J.: An approach to surveillance of an area using swarm of fixed wing and quad-rotor unmanned aerial vehicles UAV(s). In: 3rd IEEE System-of-Systems Engineering Conference, SoSE, Singapore, June 2008
13. Klein, J., van Vliet, H.: A systematic review of system-of-systems architecture research. In: 9th ACM Conference on the Quality of Software Architecture, QoSA, June 2013
14. Kopetz, H., Höftberger, O., Frömel, B., Brancati, F., Bondavalli, A.: Towards an understanding of emergence in systems-of-systems. In: 10th IEEE System-of-Systems Engineering Conference, SoSE, San Antonio, Texas, USA, May 2015
15. Maier, M.W.: Architecting principles for systems-of-systems. Syst. Eng. J. **1**(4), 267–284 (1998)
16. Maza, I., Ollero, A., Casado, E., Scarlatti, D.: Classification of multi-UAV architectures. In: Valavanis, K.P., Vachtsevanos, G.J. (eds.) Handbook of Unmanned Aerial Vehicles, pp. 953–975. Springer, Dordrecht (2015). https://doi.org/10.1007/978-90-481-9707-1_119
17. McLaughlin, B., Bennett, K.: Supervenience. In: Stanford Encyclopedia of Philosophy (2014)
18. Milner, R.: Communicating and Mobile Systems: The π-Calculus. Cambridge Press, Cambridge (1999)
19. Olarte, C., Rueda, C., Valencia, F.D.: Models and emerging trends of concurrent constraint programming. Int. J. Constr. **18**(4), 535–578 (2013)
20. Oquendo, F.: Formally describing the software architecture of systems-of-systems with SosADL. In: 11th IEEE System-of-Systems Engineering Conference, SoSE, June 2016

21. Oquendo, F.: The π-calculus for SoS: novel π-calculus for the formal modeling of software-intensive systems-of-systems. In: 38th International Conference on Communicating Process Architectures, CPA, Copenhagen, Denmark, August 2016

22. Oquendo, F.: Case study on formally describing the architecture of a software-intensive system-of-systems with SosADL. In: 15th IEEE International Conference on Systems, Man, and Cybernetics, SMC, Budapest, Hungary, October 2016

23. Oquendo, F.: Software architecture challenges and emerging research in software-intensive systems-of-systems. In: Tekinerdogan, B., Zdun, U., Babar, A. (eds.) ECSA 2016. LNCS, vol. 9839, pp. 3–21. Springer, Cham (2016). https://doi.org/10.1007/978-3-319-48992-6_1

24. Oquendo, F.: Formally describing the architectural behavior of software-intensive systems-of-systems with SosADL. In: 21st IEEE International Conference on Engineering of Complex Computer Systems, ICECCS, Dubai, UAE, November 2016

25. Oquendo, F.: Software architecture of self-organizing systems-of-systems. In: 12th IEEE System-of-Systems Engineering Conference, SoSE, Waikoloa, Hawaii, USA, June 2017

26. Oquendo, F.: Architecturally describing the emergent behavior of software-intensive system-of-systems with SosADL. In: 12th IEEE SoSE, Waikoloa, Hawaii, USA, June 2017

27. Oquendo, F., Buisson, J., Leroux, E., Moguérou, G., Quilbeuf, J.: The SosADL studio: an architecture development environment for software-intensive systems-of-systems. In: ECSA Colloquium on Software-Intensive SoS. ACM, Copenhagen, November 2016

28. Oquendo, F., Buisson, J., Leroux, E., Moguérou, G.: A formal approach for architecting software-intensive systems-of-systems with guarantees. In: 13th IEEE SoSE, Paris (2018)

29. Parunak, H., Brueckner, S.A.: Software engineering for self-organizing systems. Knowl. Eng. Rev. **30**(4), 419–434 (2015)

30. Prigogine, I.: Nobel Lecture: Time, Structure and Fluctuations (1977). Nobelprize.org

31. Quilbeuf, J., Cavalcante, E., Traonouez, L.-M., Oquendo, F., Batista, T., Legay, A.: A logic for the statistical model checking of dynamic software architectures. In: Margaria, T., Steffen, B. (eds.) ISoLA 2016. LNCS, vol. 9952, pp. 806–820. Springer, Cham (2016). https://doi.org/10.1007/978-3-319-47166-2_56

32. Reynolds, C.W.: Flocks, herds, and schools: a distributed behavioral model, in computer graphics. In: 14th ACM SIGGRAPH Conference, Anaheim, USA (1987)

33. Roca, D., Nemirovsky, D., Nemirovsky, M., Milito, R., Valero, M.: Emergent behaviors in the Internet-of-Things: the ultimate ultra-large-scale system. IEEE Micro **36**, 36–44 (2016)

34. Silva, E., Batista, T.V., Oquendo, F.: A mission-oriented approach for designing system-of-systems. In: 10th IEEE System-of-Systems Engineering Conference, SoSE, May 2015

35. Weyns, D., Malek, S., de Lemos, R., Andersson, J. (eds.): Self-Organizing Architectures. Springer, Heidelberg (2010). https://doi.org/10.1007/978-3-642-14412-7

36. Wirsing, M., Hölzl, M., Koch, N., Mayer, P. (eds.): Software Engineering for Collective Autonomic Systems. Springer, Cham (2015). https://doi.org/10.1007/978-3-319-16310-9

37. Wirsing, M. (ed.): Software Engineering for Service-Oriented Systems. Springer, Heidelberg (2015)

38. Ye, D., Zhang, M., Vasilakos, A.V.: A survey of self-organization mechanisms in multiagent systems. IEEE Trans. Syst. Man Cybern.: Syst. **47**, 441–461 (2017)

Guidance of Architectural Changes in Technical Systems with Varying Operational Modes

Lukas Märtin[1(✉)], Nils-André Forjahn[1], Anne Koziolek[2], and Ralf Reussner[2]

[1] TU Braunschweig,Braunschweig, Germany
{l.maertin,n.forjahn}@tu-braunschweig.de
[2] Karlsruhe Institute of Technology,Karlsruhe, Germany
{koziolek,reussner}@kit.edu

Abstract. Technical systems often rely on redundant platforms. One way to increase dependability is to define various QoS modes, applied to different hardware resources. Switching between modes is limited by resource availability and causes costs for structural changes. Hence, selecting appropriate system architectures for specific resource sets and defining cost-efficient mode sequences is challenging. This short paper proposes an approach to support reconfiguration decisions for varying modes. We extend our decision graphs for traversing architectures towards multi-purpose applicability. We optimise reconfigurations within individual modes while reducing costs of mode changes simultaneously. Graph-based differentiations lead to most efficient mode sequences, transition configurations and visualisations. To respect high reconfigurability, we particularly inspect impacts of resource faults. For evaluation, we apply a subsystem of a micro satellite with multiple operational modes.

1 Introduction

Developing *technical systems* often incorporates grouping of redundant resources. Each feasible *system configuration* is evaluated by quality demands wrt. an *operational mode*. A *multi-purpose system* executes tasks in varying modes and redundancy groups. Due to modes changes and resources faults this is challenging. Thus, for cost-efficient maintenance, it is essential to identify relations between modes and optimal transitions. Here, we propose to prioritise configurations according architectural quality at design time to reduce maintenance costs. Thus, a prioritised reconfiguration space is tailored to modes and continuously synchronised to resource availability for reducing efforts of manual exploration.

 In previous work, we introduced an architecture-oriented approach to support reconfiguration decisions, the *Deterministic Architecture Relation Graph* (*DARG*) [10]. Our existing approach is integrated [9] with the concept of *Degrees of Freedom* [6] for architecture optimisation to generate quality-accessed configurations from large decision spaces.

© Springer Nature Switzerland AG 2018
C. E. Cuesta et al. (Eds.): ECSA 2018, LNCS 11048, pp. 37–45, 2018.
https://doi.org/10.1007/978-3-030-00761-4_3

In this short paper, we refine our work towards multi-purpose application. Thus, an *DARG* instance is exchanged for each mode change and appropriate transition configurations are explored. To define a cost-efficient *ordering of modes* and *efficient transitions*, we inspect commonalities and efficient reconfigurations in intersections of *DARG* pairs. For evaluation, we apply our approach to a satellite subsystem with varying resource constellations and multiple modes. For dependability, the result stability is checked to assure a fault-aware solution.

The remainder of this paper is organised as follows. Section 2 summarises related work. Our approach is described in Sect. 3 and evaluated in Sect. 4. We conclude and promote future work in Sect. 5.

2 Related Work

We make use of knowledge from configuration generator to relate alternate solutions with slight differences in resource demands and qualities. Similar to that, Barnes et al. [1] define relations between architectures on candidate evolution paths. These paths specify a search-based reconfiguration process from a source to a user-defined target architecture via a sequence of transient architectures. We intend to explore such targets automatically. Jung et al. [5] determine policies to adapt running systems in the cloud. A decision-tree learner that is trained with feasible system configurations, generated by queuing models, derives these policies at design time. Close to that, Frey et al. [4] inspect reconfigurations as deployment options derived by genetic algorithms. The authors define rules at design time to systematically change the deployment of a system at run time. Both approaches neither explicitly represent the reconfiguration space nor the qualitative trade-offs between design options. Our approach preserves knowledge from the configuration generation to prioritise near-optimal candidates. Malek et al. [8] proposes a more hardware-oriented approach in context of self-adaptive systems. The authors provide a trade-off model to identify a suitable deployment architecture. Even though that approach is applicable to distinguish between configurations, the authors did not integrate a prioritisation of all feasible design alternatives for decision support at run time.

3 Reconfiguration Support for Varying Operation Modes

We extend our work by multi-purpose capabilities to reduce maintenance efforts.

3.1 Baseline Models

Due to space constraints all models [9, 10] are summarised here. A resource platform *RP* defines properties and constraints of resources. Redundancies are represented by groups. Properties provide value assignments for quality attributes from the configuration generation. We model configurations as sets of software components with bindings *bind* to resources in *RP*. A configuration has a unique

id and holds aggregated values *val* for attributes. An *ARG* defines an unsorted reconfiguration space. Its nodes are parametrised by generated configurations and their bindings to *RP*. Edges relate configurations via transient nodes or directly. Changes in resource bindings and reconfiguration costs are annotated as edge labels. Initially an *ARG* is ambiguous as labels might be non-deterministic. To fix that, we adapt *Quality Attribute Directed Acyclic Graphs* [3] (*QADAG*) to describe operational modes as weighted sums with constraints for attributes. Values for attributes are extracted from *ARG* nodes. For aggregation, each value is normalised. The user customises a *QADAG* wrt. an operational mode by setting weightings and *minimal acceptance values*. A value drops to 0 if its minimal acceptance is violated. *DARG* instances are derived as mode-specific refinements of the *ARG* for each *QADAG* instance by evaluating a *utility* for all configuration results. Hence, edges are qualitatively definable now. A *DARG* instance is an architecture-based model of the *reconfiguration space* for a specific mode.

3.2   Aligning Changes of Operational Modes and DARG Instances

The interrelationships of multiple *QADAG* and *DARG* instances are considered by deriving optimal orders. Built on existing analysis methods a *QADAG* is customised to derive a corresponding *DARG* instance. The *multi-mode analysis* inspects the importance of a configuration within its origin instance and extracts an optimal order between all instances. Faults are injected to check robustness.

Prioritise Configurations for Mode Transitions. Each configuration in a *DARG* instance is rated by its fitness for mode transitions. In addition to existing indicators, we apply *centralities* to specify the intra-graph importance of each node. According to graph size, the inexpensive *degree centrality*, the path-oriented *closeness centrality* or the expensive graph-spanning *betweenness centrality* might be applied.

Three *transition criteria* result to rate reconfiguration abilities. The (1) normalised *utility* defines the fitness to the mode, the (2) amount of resource bindings *bind* characterises the degree of redundancies and the (3) centrality *cen* of the corresponding node quantises the reconfiguration options wrt. related configurations. The resource amounts and centrality is normalised over all occurrences. By setting constant weighting the criteria are prioritised. Each configuration c_i is rated by a *transition value* in its reconfiguration space D_i, defined by $tv_{c_i,D_i} := w_1 * utility_{c_i} + w_2 * cen_{c_i} + w_3 * |bind_{c_i}|$.

Extracting Optimal Mode Sequences. For extracting optimal mode sequences, we inspect all transition values of configurations in pairs of *DARG* instances. Because of the common *ARG*, the configurations of *DARG* instances intersect, matched by id. Let D_s and D_t be reconfiguration spaces in $\mathcal{D}$, then $D_s \cap_{id} D_t \iff \forall c_i \in D_s, c_j \in D_t : c_{i_{id}} == c_{j_{id}}$ is the configuration intersection of the pair. Although it is unlikely that an intersection is empty, then an ordering of this pair is infeasible and is done randomly instead. To inspect the transition values between reconfiguration spaces, we aggregate the values to sums. Due to asymmetries in the values wrt. the source spaces, we inspect two values per pair. For the pair of reconfiguration spaces D_s and D_t the *transition value sum* is defined by $tvs_{D_s \cap_{id} D_t} := \left(\sum_{i=1}^{|D_s \cap_{id} D_t|} tv_{c_i, D_s} + tv_{c_i, D_t} \right) \mid c_i \in D_s \cap_{id} D_t$.

To explore all pairs, we permute over D by $S \subset \mathcal{P}(\mathcal{D})$ with $S_i \in S$ is an *ordered sequence* and $|S_i| == |\mathcal{D}|$ the permutation size equals the amount of all $DARG$ instances. All transition value sums in S are inspected for the overall maximum by $tvs_{max} := \max \sum_{i=1}^{|S|} (tvs_{D_s \cap_{id} D_t} \forall D_s, D_t \in S_i) \mid S_i \in S$.

The highest sum characterises the *optimal sequence* of all $DARG$ instances with the set of *transition configurations*. By backtracking $DARG$ to $QADAG$ instances, the order of reconfiguration spaces lead to the *optimal mode sequence*.

Consideration of Resource Faults. Each resource fault reduces the amount of configurations. If all options in a redundancy group are affected, a configuration is invalid. This causes changes in commonalities between reconfiguration spaces as well as centralities within the graphs. Thus, faults have significant impacts on the selection of transition configurations and optimal mode sequences. Hence, expected resource faults are injected in $DARG$ instances. The transition configurations and the optimal sequence are checked for stability in an iterative process. If a pair of $DARG$ instances is affected by a fault in the resource platform, it is marked for re-ordering and all transition values are recalculated. The ordering might be updated due to the new maximum transition value sums.

4   Validation

We validate our approach along a subsystem of the TET-1 satellite.

4.1   Application Scenario

TET-1 is designed for verifying experimental hardware. We apply our approach to the *attitude control system* (ACS) [7]. The ACS architecture is threefold. Sensor resources *estimate* the position and orientation then necessary attitude changes are *predicted* and at least required actions are *controlled* on actuation resources. Such resource dependencies are represented by components on the lowest level. To enhance reconfiguration abilities for heterogeneous redundancies, we relaxed constraints and added sensing variations to the original design. For actuation two groups with reaction wheels (RWS) and magnetic coils (MCS) exist. Sensing is performed by five groups consisting of star compasses (ASC), sun sensors (CSS), magnetic field sensors (MFS), inertial measurement units (IMU) and on-board navigation systems (ONS). We model the ACS as variant-rich *Palladio Component Model* [2] instance with several degrees of freedom with PALLADIO DSE. Our tool AREVA[1] generates an ARG model and a default $QADAG$. We

---

[1] AREVA tool and **validation data**, https://www.github.com/lmaertin/areva.

apply three experiments [7] with varying modes: A Li-Polymer battery ($N1$), a pico propulsion system ($N7$) and an infra-red camera ($N15$). Based on six quality attributes and data sheets, three $QADAG$ with corresponding $DARG$ instances are derived for validation. For sake of space, we leave out details.

4.2 Design of Experiment

The exploration is challenging if operational modes vary and faults occur. Thus, we (1) define optimal mode sequences and (2) approve its fault robustness.

The importance of a configuration in a $DARG$ is vital to define appropriate transition configurations for sequencing modes. Maximum classification values for configurations are identified to differentiate pairs of reconfiguration spaces efficiently. For that, we aggregate transition values within each $DARG$ instance to rate orders of mode sequences. The maximum sums over all transition values in intersections of all pairs of reconfiguration spaces are calculated. By ordering of the sums, an optimal mode sequence is determined.

High reconfigurability is only assured if the mode sequence is robust against faults. Thus, if a fault affects a valid configuration the corresponding mode sequence must hold. The impact of faults on the validity of mode ordering is examined on level of relative changes of transition values. The ordering needs to be proven as stable. Here, we adapt the previous fault-less measurements to estimate impacts of faults. For that, we inspect the distance of changes in the sums of transition values. The order of these relative values is checked for compliance to the recent order of modes. If the maximum changes, the mode sequence is no longer stable and a re-ordering is initiated.

4.3 Measurements and Explanation

Our measurement are done on basis of our ACS model and the sequence of expected faults from Table 1. For each experiment, we choose an initial configuration with a high amount of resources to enhance reconfigurability.

(1) Identifying Optimal Mode Sequences. We perform a multi-mode analysis on basis of $DARG$ instances for each experiment. At first, we explore transition configurations and optimal mode sequences in a faultless setting. Afterwards, we inject a fault sequence and observe impacts on the initial results. For both settings, the calculation of the transition values is parametrised to 0.33 for w_1, w_2 and w_3. We applied all three kinds of centralities. Even though all measurements perform well, we show the results for betweenness due to lack of space. The analysis calculates individual transition values and explores maximum sums in *six possible orders* of intersecting $DARG$ instances. For each order, the transition value sum consists of sums from two transitions. The order $N15 \rightarrow N1 \rightarrow N7$ has the highest sum and is the optimal mode sequence when no faults occur. It is followed by $N1 \rightarrow N15 \rightarrow N7$ and $N7 \rightarrow N1 \rightarrow N15$.

For explanation, we take a deeper look into the amount of transition configurations between a pair of modes and their transition value distribution. A transition between $N1$ and $N7$, and vice versa, has the most transition configurations with 86. $N17 \leftrightarrow N15$ has a sum of 85 and $N77 \rightarrow N15$ at least 77. Therefore, mode orders containing transitions between $N1$ and $N7$ are more likely to have higher transition value sums than other transitions if the transition value distributions are similar. This means that reconfigurations due to mode transitions between $N1$ and $N7$ are more effective because the reconfiguration spaces are more structurally similar than all other combinations. Figure 1 shows the transition value distribution of the configurations for each mode transition. While the medians and value ranges for each transition are different, they are still within similar value ranges. For instance, the transition $N15 \rightarrow N1$ provides higher rated transition configurations in average. Therefore, this transition probably leads to highly rated configurations to perform the experiment $N1$ well. The high amount of transition configurations in both transitions of $N15 \rightarrow N1 \rightarrow N7$ leads to reduced reconfiguration costs. Additionally, high average transition values promote appropriate configurations.

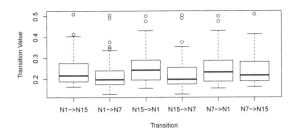

Fig. 1. Transition value distribution per transition direction

(2) Inspecting Fault Robustness. We derived a sequence of faults that effectively harms the ACS wrt. fault analysis methods in Table 1. To examine the robustness of our results, the changes of transition value sums for each possible order is shown after fault injection. The initial optimal mode order of $N15 \rightarrow N1 \rightarrow N7$ that was calculated under a faultless state is stable for most of the injected faults. However, when RW1 fails the transition value sum of $N1 \rightarrow N15 \rightarrow N7$ beats the original optimal order. After injecting the fault of RW2, no transition configurations are left and the reconfiguration process stops. Overall, the complete failure of the ONS, CSS and the majority of actuation resources have the biggest impacts on available transition configurations. At the beginning in particular, the redundancy groups are thinned out. If a group becomes disadvantageous or invalid, similar resources from other groups are used. However, other resources in the affected resource groups already failed before, like the first GPS Antenna1+LNA1 or the second CSS RearHead2. That is why the fault of the second GPS LNA2+Antenna2, the CSS RearHead1 and the MC1x led to the complete failure of their corresponding group.

Table 1. Fault sequence and impacts on transition value sums

Fault	1→7→15	7→1→15	7→15→1	1→15→7	15→1→7	15→7→1
GPS LNA1+Antenna1	37.33	39.93	37.36	40.03	**41.30**	37.48
GPS Receiver1	37.24	38.65	36.98	40.26	**42.33**	37.03
GPS LNA2+Antenna2	10.09	12.31	11.55	12.86	**13.02**	10.08
MFS Fluxgate1	10.11	12.20	11.61	12.83	**13.07**	10.12
CSS RearHead2	9.90	12.19	11.61	12.78	**12.90**	10.12
ASC DPU1 High Res	10.15	12.41	11.63	13.01	**13.11**	10.13
ASC DPU2 Low Res	10.07	12.21	11.53	12.77	**13.04**	10.03
CSS Chipset1 High Res	9.88	12.07	11.49	12.65	**12.78**	10.06
CSS RearHead1	2.15	3.28	2.92	3.11	**3.36**	2.10
CSS FrontHead2	2.14	3.27	2.93	3.10	**3.35**	2.10
CSS Chipset2 Low Res	2.13	3.27	2.92	3.11	**3.34**	2.10
RW1	1.84	2.68	2.60	**2.78**	2.74	1.81
MC1x	0.58	0.74	0.73	**0.76**	0.76	0.57
RW2, MC2y, MC2x	-, -, -	-, -, -	-, -, -	-, -, -	-, -, -	-, -, -

Following, we inspect the reasons for the change of the optimal order after RW1. While the amount of transition configurations has already been heavily reduced by faults before, transitions of $N1 \leftrightarrow N7$ and $N1 \leftrightarrow N15$ are still more beneficial from a structural standpoint with 8 and 13 transition configurations respectively. After the failure of RW1 the transitions of $N1 \leftrightarrow N15$ and $N7 \leftrightarrow N15$ are both equally disadvantageous in terms of structural similarity compared to $N1 \leftrightarrow N15$ with only 6 transition configurations left. Even though, $N15 \rightarrow N1 \rightarrow N7$ overall had more transition configurations than $N1 \rightarrow N15 \rightarrow N7$, now both have the same amount. Therefore, the choice of optimal mode order is completely reliant on the transition value distribution and the highest average. Figure 2 shows the distribution of transition values per mode transition direction. The plot shows that the two partial transitions of $N15 \rightarrow N1 \rightarrow N7$ as well as $N1 \rightarrow N15 \rightarrow N7$ both are very similar. The first transitions $N15 \rightarrow N1$ and $N1 \rightarrow N15$ have almost the same high median. The second transitions $N15 \rightarrow N7$ and $N1 \rightarrow N7$ both have a similar low median. So both orders are also very similar in terms of average transition value. The biggest impact on the final result of ranking $N1 \rightarrow N15 \rightarrow N7$ higher than $N15 \rightarrow N1 \rightarrow N7$ is the first transition value sum, which is sufficient at this point to induce a higher overall sum.

Overall $N15 \rightarrow N1 \rightarrow N7$ should remain as optimal mode sequence because it is stable until the 13th fault. Additionally, it provides the best trade-off between the amounts of similarities between all modes, and thus keeping the reconfiguration cost low, and the average transition values for each configuration, improving the experiments by providing alternate configurations with high utilities.

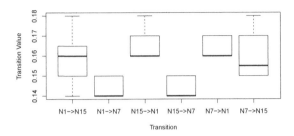

Fig. 2. Transition value distribution per transition direction

5 Conclusions

We presented an approach to support maintenance of fault-tolerant technical systems in multi-purpose setting. By performing pre-calculations at design time, we generate knowledge for efficient reconfigurations at run time for varying operational modes. The extended decision model $DARG$ supports mode transitions and guides architectural changes by mode sequences. We evaluated our tool-supported approach on a satellite subsystem and proven fault robustness of results. Because of extensive efforts in processing the reconfiguration space, we settled our approach at design time and build upon static data for quality predictions. Consequently, the results might have a lack of precision.

In on-going research, we are doing an empirical study with experts from space industry to explore possible integrations of the approach in the development process. Further improvements are possible by integrating runtime data to continuously update the $DARG$. Here, the computational efforts and delays for reconfiguration at runtime need to be respected to justify our analyses against traditional explorations.

Acknowledgments. This work was partially supported by the DFG under Priority Programme SPP1593: Design For Future Managed Software Evolution.

References

1. Barnes, J.M., Pandey, A., Garlan, D.: Automated planning for software architecture evolution. In: 28th International Conference on Automated Software Engineering, pp. 213–223 (2013)
2. Becker, S., Koziolek, H., Reussner, R.: The palladio component model for model-driven performance prediction. Syst. Softw. **82**(1), 3–22 (2009)
3. Florentz, B., Huhn, M.: Embedded systems architecture: evaluation and analysis. In: Hofmeister, C., Crnkovic, I., Reussner, R. (eds.) QoSA 2006. LNCS, vol. 4214, pp. 145–162. Springer, Heidelberg (2006). https://doi.org/10.1007/11921998_14
4. Frey, S., Fittkau, F., Hasselbring, W.: Search-based genetic optimization for deployment and reconfiguration of software in the cloud. In: 35th International Conference on Software Engineering, pp. 512–521 (2013)

5. Jung, G., Joshi, K., Hiltunen, M., Schlichting, R., Pu, C.: Generating adaptation policies for multi-tier applications in consolidated server environments. In: 5th International Conference on Autonomic Computing, pp. 23–32 (2008)
6. Koziolek, A., Reussner, R.: Towards a generic quality optimisation framework for component-based system models. In: 14th International ACM Sigsoft Symposium on Component Based Software Engineering, pp. 103–108 (2011)
7. Löw, S., Herman, J., Schulze, D., Raschke, C.: Modes and more - finding the right attitude for TET-1. In: 12th International Conference on Space Operations (2012)
8. Malek, S., Medvidovic, N., Mikic-Rakic, M.: An extensible framework for improving a distributed software system's deployment architecture. IEEE Trans. Softw. Eng. **38**(1), 73–100 (2012)
9. Märtin, L., Koziolek, A., Reussner, R.H.: Quality-oriented decision support for maintaining architectures of fault-tolerant space systems. In: 2015 European Conference on Software Architecture Workshops, pp. 49:1–49:5 (2015)
10. Märtin, L., Nicolai, A.: Towards self-reconfiguration of space systems on architectural level based on qualitative ratings. In: 35th International Aerospace Conference (2014)

IoT Architectures

Applying Architecture-Based Adaptation to Automate the Management of Internet-of-Things

Danny Weyns[1,2]([⊠]), M. Usman Iftikhar[2], Danny Hughes[1,3], and Nelson Matthys[3]

[1] imec-DistriNet, Department of Computer Science,
Katholieke Universiteit Leuven, 3001 Heverlee, Belgium
`danny.weyns@kuleuven.be`
[2] Linnaeus University, 351 95 Vaxjo, Sweden
[3] VersaSense, 3001 Heverlee, Belgium
`info@versasense.com`
`https://www.versasense.com/`

Abstract. Architecture-based adaptation equips a software-intensive system with a feedback loop that enables the system to adapt itself at runtime to changes to maintain its required quality goals. To guarantee the required goals, existing adaptation approaches apply exhaustive verification techniques at runtime. However these approaches are restricted to small-scale settings, which often limits their applicability in practice. To tackle this problem, we introduce an innovative architecture-based adaptation approach to solve a concrete practical problem of VersaSense: automating the management of Internet-of-Things (IoT). The approach, called MARTAS, equips a software system with a feedback loop that employs Models At Run Time and Statistical techniques to reason about the system and adapt it to ensure the required goals. We apply MARTAS to a building security case system, which is a representative IoT system deployed by VersaSense. The application comprises a set of IoT devices that communicate sensor data over a time synchronized smart mess network to a central monitoring facility. We demonstrate how MARTAS outperforms a conservative approach that is typically applied in practice and a state-of-the-art adaptation approach for different quality goals, and we report lessons learned from this industrial case.

Keywords: Architecture-based adaptation · Self-adaptation
Feedback loop · Internet-of-Things · Automated management

1 Introduction

Handling change is an increasingly important challenge for software engineers. Change can manifest itself in different forms, ranging from market-driven evolution of products to uncertainties a system faces during operation (e.g., sudden

C. E. Cuesta et al. (Eds.): ECSA 2018, LNCS 11048, pp. 49–67, 2018.
https://doi.org/10.1007/978-3-030-00761-4_4

changes in the environment or dynamics in the availability of resources). Our particular focus in this paper is on the ability of software systems to handle changes at runtime autonomously. A prominent approach to deal with runtime change is so called architecture-based adaptation [11,14,16,21,29]. Architecture-based adaptation equips a software system with an external feedback loop that collects data of the system and its environment that was difficult or impossible to determine before deployment. The feedback loop uses the collected data to reason about itself and to adapt itself to changes in order to provide the required quality goals, or gracefully degrade if needed. A typical example is a self-managing Web-based client-server system that continuously tracks and analyzes changes in load and available bandwidth and dynamically adapts the server configuration to provide the required quality of service to its users, while minimizing costs [11].

Over the past two decades, researchers and engineers have put extensive efforts in understanding how to engineer self-adaptive systems [6,8,18,19,23]. In recent years, the particular focus of research has been on how to provide assurances for the quality goals of self-adaptive systems that operate under uncertainty [4,19]. According to [27], after a relatively slow start, research in the field of self-adaptation has taken up significantly from 2006 onwards. The field is now – according to the Redwine and Riddle model [22] – following the regular path of maturation and is currently in the phases of internal and external enhancement and exploration. Self-adaptation techniques have found their way to industrial applications, a prominent example is cloud elasticity [9,10]. However, there is a broad agreement – at least in the research community – that self-adaptation can contribute to solving many practical problems that originate from the continuous change that systems are exposed to during operation.

Architecture-based adaptation is one prominent approach to realise self-adaptation. In this approach, the external feedback loop is realised by different interacting components that share runtime models. These models include an architectural model of the managed system that allows the feedback loop to reason about different system configurations and adapt the system to realise the adaptation goals. Other prominent complementary approaches to realise self-adaptation are self-aware computing [15], self-organisation [7], and control-based software adaptation [24]. The focus of state-of-the art approaches for architecture-based adaptation that aim at providing assurances for the quality goals are primarily based on applying formal techniques [4,19,30]. Some approaches employ formal methods to provide guarantees by construction. More recently, the use of probabilistic models to handle uncertainties at runtime has particular gained interest. These models are used during operation to verify properties using model checking techniques to support decision-making for adapting the system. However, these approaches use exhaustive verification, which is very demanding in the resources and time required to make adaptation decisions. Hence, these approaches are restricted to small-scale settings, which often limits their applicability in practice. This is particularly the case for resource constrained systems and large-scale IoT setups.

To tackle the limitations of current formal approaches for architecture-based adaptation, we propose MARTAS, a novel approach that combines Models At RunTime And Statistical techniques to realise adaptation. We validate MARTAS for a building security monitoring system, which is a representative case of IoT applications developed by VersaSense, a provider of industrial IoT solutions. The test results show that MARTAS outperforms a conservative approach that is typically used in practice as well as a state-of-the-art adaptation approach that uses exhaustive verification.

The remainder of this paper is structured as follows. In Sect. 2, we explain the basic principles of architecture-based adaptation. Section 3 introduces the IoT application that we use for the evaluation of this research. In Sect. 4, we present MARTAS, the novel approach for architecture-based adaptation that combines formal models with statistical techniques at runtime to make adaptation decisions. In Sect. 5, we evaluate MARTAS for a real-world IoT system deployment. Section 6 discusses related work. In Sect. 7, we highlight lessons learned, and we draw conclusions in Sect. 8.

2   Architecture-Based Adaptation in a Nutshell

Self-adaptation and architecture-based adaptation in particular can be considered from two angles: (1) the ability of a system to adapt in response to changes in the environment and the system itself [6]; the "self" prefix indicates that the system adapts with minimal or no human involvement [2], and (2) the feedback loop mechanisms that are used to realize self-adaptation that explicitly separate the part of a system that deals with the domain concerns (goals for which the system is built) from the part that deals the adaptation concerns (the way the system realizes its goals under changing conditions).

In architecture-based adaptation, the feedback loop system maintains an architectural model of the managed system, possibly extended with relevant aspects of the environment in which the system operates. This model is kept up to date at runtime and used to make adaptation decisions, in order to achieve the goals of the system. Using a model at an architectural level provides the required level of abstraction and generality to deal with the self-adaptation problem [16,28].

An architecture-based adaptive system comprises two key building blocks: a *managed system* and a *managing system*. The managed system comprises the application code that realizes the system's domain functionality. The managing system manages the managed system; that is, the managing system comprises the adaptation logic that deals with one or more adaptation goals. The adaptation goals represent concerns about how the managed system realises the domain functionality; they usually relate to software qualities of the managed system. Adaptation goals can be subject of change themselves.

A typical approach to structure the software of the managing system is by means of a so-called Monitor-Analyzer-Planner-Executer + Knowledge feedback loop (MAPE-K in short). The Knowledge that is shared among the MAPE components contains various types of runtime models, including models of representative parts of the managed system and the environment, models of the qualities that are subject to adaptation, and other working models that are shared among the MAPE components. The *Monitor* collects runtime data from the managed system and the environment and uses this to update the content of the Knowledge, resolving uncertainties (e.g., the interference of the links in an IoT network is tracked to update the relevant runtime models). Based on the current knowledge, the *Analyzer* determines whether there is a need for adaptation of the managed system using the adaptation goals. If adaptation is required, the *Planner* puts together a plan that consists of a set of adaptation actions that are then enacted by the *Executor* that adapts the managed system as needed.

An example state-of-the-art approach that provides guarantees at runtime for the adaptation goals is QoSMOS (Quality of Service Management and Optimisation of Service-based systems) [3]). QoSMOS models a service-based application as a Discrete Time Markov Chain. The feedback loop employs this formal model to identify the service configurations that satisfy the Quality of Service (QoS) goals using a *model checker*. The result of the analysis is a ranking of the configurations based on the required QoS requirements. The best option is used to reconfigure the service-based system to guarantee the adaptation goals. QoSMOS is a representative state-of-the-art approach that uses exhaustive verification to make adaptation decisions. Due to the state explosion problem (the number of states of the models grows exponentially with the model size, hence also the resources and time required for verification), such approaches are restricted to small-scale settings, which often limits their applicability in practice. MARTAS aims at contributing to tackle this challenging problem.

3   IoT Application

In this section, we describe a building security monitoring application that we use throughout the remainder of the paper for illustration and to evaluate MARTAS. We start with introducing the problem context. Then, we give an overview of the application setting. The section concludes with explaining the challenge VersaSense faces with the management of this kind of IoT applications.

3.1   Problem Context

VersaSense is a provider of wireless IoT products for industrial sensing and control systems. The company employs an in-house developed IoT technology known as Micro Plug and Play (MicroPnP) [20], which includes a suite of ultra-low power wireless IoT devices (*motes*), a wide range of sensors and actuators, and management either as a cloud integration service or as a dedicated appliance. The company uses an 802.15.4e wireless mesh network (SmartMesh IP[TM]) for short range factory scenarios and a Long Range low power star network (LoRa[1])

---

[1] https://www.lora-alliance.org/; https://www.semtech.com/technology/lora.

for applications that require multi kilometer range. VersaSense provides IoT solutions directly to industry in the areas of surveillance, facility management, manufacturing, consumer goods, and precision agriculture.

The solutions developed by VersaSense support substantial automation, including automatic identification of sensing and actuation peripherals, installation of their drivers, and static network configuration. However, the management of deployed IoT applications, and in particular handling interference in network connections and sudden changes in traffic load remains a challenge. This is a major impediment to ensuring high quality of service (e.g., multi-year battery lifetimes and high levels of reliability).

The typical approach to tackle this challenge is either by over-provisioning (e.g., power settings are set to maximum and duplicate packets are sent to parents) and/or by hand-tuning the network settings. While this conservative approach may achieve good reliability (low packet loss), it is suboptimal in energy consumption. Furthermore, this approach requires manual interventions for network maintenance that are costly and error prone. In a joint R & D effort between VersaSense and imec-DistriNet we studied and developed an innovative self-adaptation solution to tackle this challenging problem.

3.2 IoT Application

To build a solution that automates the management of IoT applications in an efficient way, VersaSense deployed an IoT application at the Computer Science Campus of KU Leuven using their state-of-the-art technology. This application is a representative case for a medium-scale IoT facility/factory developed by VersaSense. Figure 1 shows a schematic overview of the application that is set up as a smart mesh network with 15 motes that are equipped with different types of sensors. The network uses time synchronized communication with communication slots fairly divided among the motes.

Motes are strategically placed to provide access control to labs (RFID sensors), to monitor the movements and occupancy status passive infrared sensors) and to sense the temperature (heat sensors). The sensor data is relayed from the motes to the IoT gateway that is deployed at a central monitoring facility. Communication in the network is organized in cycles, each cycle comprising a fixed number of communication slots. Each slot defines a sender and receiver mote that can communicate.

The domain concern for the IoT network is to relay sensor data to the gateway. The adaptation concerns are to ensure reliable and energy-efficient communication. The VersaSense stakeholders defined the adaptation goals as follows: (1) the average packet loss over a given time period should not exceed a required threshold, (2) the average latency of packets should be below a given fraction of the cycle time, (3) the energy consumed by the motes should be minimized to optimize the lifetime of the network.

Achieving these goals is challenging due to two primary types of uncertainty: (1) network interference and noise due to factors such as weather conditions and the presence of other WiFi signals in the neighborhood; interference affects the

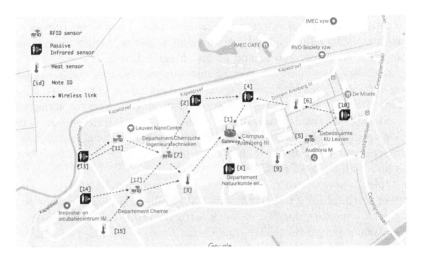

Fig. 1. IoT system deployed by VersaSense at the computer science campus in Leuven

quality of communication which may lead to packet loss; (2) fluctuating traffic load that may be difficult to predict; e.g., packets produced by a passive infrared sensor are based on the detection of motion of humans, which may be difficult to anticipate.

Two factors determine the critical qualities: the power settings of the motes used for communication (from 0 for min power to 15 for max power) and the distribution of the packets sent by each mote over the links to its parents (e.g., for two parents: 0% to one parent and 100% to the other, 20/80, ... 100/0). Operators can set the power settings and the distribution of packets of the motes in the network via an interface.

The user interface also offers access to sensor data based on user defined properties. These include the traffic load generated by motes, the energy consumed by the motes, the Signal-to-Noise (SNR) ratio of the communication links (SNR represents the ratio between the level of the signal used for communication and the level of the noise from the environment. Lower SNR implies higher interference, resulting in higher packet loss.), and statistical data about the QoS of the overall network for a given period.

3.3   Challenge

The general challenge we aim to tackle in this joint R & D effort is the following:

How to automate the maintenance of smart mess IoT networks to ensure the required quality goals in the face of uncertain operating conditions?

For the evaluation of MARTAS, we defined the following concrete quality requirements that need to be realised regardless of possible network interference and fluctuating load of packets generated in the network:

R1: The average packet loss over 24 h should not exceed 10%;

R2: The average packet latency over 24 h should not exceed 5% of the cycle time;

R3: The energy consumed by the motes should be minimized.

When architecture-based adaptation is applied, these quality requirements become the adaptation goals.

4   MARTAS: Novel Approach to Architecture-Based Adaptation

We now present MARTAS, the novel approach to architecture-based adaptation that combines formal models with statistical techniques at runtime to make adaptation decisions. We start with a general overview of MARTAS. Then we show how we instantiated the approach to realise the adaptive IoT application.

4.1   Decision Making with Formal Models and Statistical Techniques

The key driving requirements for MARTAS are the following: (i) the approach should provide guarantees for the adaptation goals with sufficient confidence (sufficient is defined by the stakeholders), and (ii) the approach should make adaptation decisions efficiently, paving the way to apply it to system settings at an increasing scale.

The central idea of MARTAS is to equip a MAPE loop with a separate runtime quality model for each adaptation goal. Each quality model takes care of one adaptation concern of the system (e.g. a stochastic automaton that models the packet loss of a network). Quality models can capture different uncertainties that are represented as model parameters (e.g. interference of network links or the traffic generated by motes). These parameters are monitored at runtime to update the runtime models. The adaptation goals are modeled as a set of rules that are used to select configurations that comply with the required adaptation goals (e.g., packet loss < 10%, minimize energy consumption). To make an adaptation decision, the MAPE loop estimates the qualities for the different configurations that are considered for adaptation (i.e., the adaptation options).

To that end, the MAPE loop uses runtime statistical model checking (RSMC). RSMC combines runtime simulation with statistical techniques to estimate the qualities of each adaptation option with a required level of confidence. By combining the estimated qualities per adaptation option with the adaptation goals of the system, the MAPE loop can then select the best configuration to realize the adaptation goals. RSMC offers an efficient verification approach compared to exhaustive approaches; it also allows balancing the confidence of the verified quality properties with the time and resources that are needed to compute them. MARTAS' modularity (separate definition of quality models and adaptation goals) also provides flexibility, paving the way for on-the-fly updating/changing models and goals.

Figure 2 shows a blueprint architecture of MARTAS.

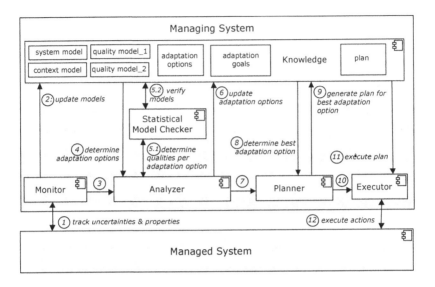

Fig. 2. Blueprint architecture of MARTAS

The approach works as follows:

1. The monitor tracks uncertainties and relevant properties of the managed system and the environment in which the system is deployment;
2. The collected data is used to update the corresponding runtime models;
3. The monitor triggers the analyser;
4. The analyser reads the adaptation options from the knowledge repository. The set of adaptation options is determined by the different configurations that can be selected to adapt the current configuration. An adaptation option has a placeholder for each quality property that is subject to adaptation;
5. For each adaptation option, the analyser estimates the expected qualities that are subject to adaptation. To that end, the analyser employs the statistical model checker that simulates the corresponding quality model with the settings of the adaptation option using a verification query in order to determine the expected quality with sufficient confidence (details are presented below).
6. The analyser updates the adaptation options with the verification results, i.e., it adds the estimated qualities to the placeholders for each adaptation option; it then determines whether the current configuration is able to achieve the adaptation goals;
7. If the current configuration is not able to achieve the adaptation goals the analyser triggers the planner;

8. The planner ranks the adaptation options by applying the adaptation goals to the different adaptation options and determines the best configuration;
9. The planner generates a plan for the best adaptation option;
10. The planner triggers the executor;
11. The executor executes the plan;
12. That is, the executor executes the adaptation actions to adapt the managed system.

In step 5, MARTAS employs RSMC. The central idea of RSMC is to check the probability $p \in [0,1]$ that a model M satisfies a property φ, i.e., to check $P_M(\varphi) \geq p$ by performing a series of simulations. RSMC applies statistical techniques on the simulation results to decide whether the system satisfies the property with some degree of confidence. To verify a quality property it has to be formulated as a verification query. We use two types of queries: probability estimation $(p = Pr[bound](\varphi))$ and simulation $(simulate \ N[\leq bound]\{E1, ..., Ek\})$. For a probability estimation query the statistical model checker applies statistical techniques to compute the number of runs needed to produce a probability estimation p for expression φ of the quality model with an approximation interval $[p - \epsilon, p + \epsilon]$ and confidence $(1 - \alpha)$ for a given time $bound$. The values of ϵ and α that determine the accuracy of the results can be set for each query. For a simulation query, the value of N determines the number of simulations the model checker will apply in time $bound$ to return values for state expressions $E1, ..., Ek$ of the quality model. For this type of query, the designer has to determine how many runs are needed to obtain a required accuracy. In our current research, we use the relative standard error of the mean (RSEM) as a measure to determine the accuracy of the simulation queries. The standard error of the mean (SEM) quantifies how precisely a simulation result represents the true mean of the population (and is thus expressed in units of the data). RSEM is the SEM divided by the sample mean and is expressed as a percentage. E.g., an RSEM of 5% represents an accuracy with a SEM of plus/minus 0.5 for a mean value of 10. In our current research, we rely on offline experiments only to compute the number of simulations required for a particular accuracy.

Note that the different adaptation goals applied in step 8 may not be completely independent, e.g., optimizing one of the goals may affect some other goals. In such cases, the order in which the goals are applied to the adaptation options may provide a means to determine the priority of goals.

4.2 Applying MARTAS to the IoT Application

We now show how we instantiated MARTAS to realise the adaptive IoT application. We start with an overview of the concrete architecture. Then we illustrate the runtime quality models that we used to estimate energy consumption together with the verification query. The evaluation and lessons learned are presented in the next sections.

To solve the problem of optimising and reconfiguring the IoT network, VersaSense and imec-DistriNet applied the innovative architecture-adaptive solution to the case. Figure 3 gives an overview of the layered architecture of the approach.

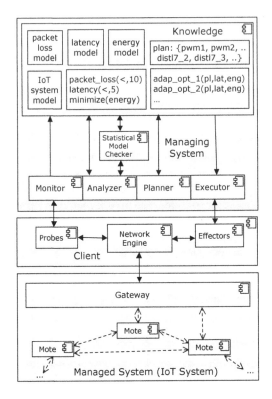

Fig. 3. MARTAS solution for the IoT application

The bottom layer consists of the managed system with the network of motes and the gateway. The middle layer comprises a client that runs on a dedicated machine. This client offers an interface to the IoT network via a probe and an effector. The probe can be used to monitor the IoT network (status of motes and links, data about the packet loss, the energy consumption, latency of the network, etc.) and the effector adapts the mote settings (power settings of the motes, distribution of packets sent to parents, etc.). The network engine collects data of the network in a repository and performs analyses on the data. In manual mode, an operator can access the IoT network via the client to track its status and perform reconfigurations manually. Reconfigurations include changing the power settings per communication link and changing the routing of packets by adapting the distribution of packets sent to parents. In the architecture-based adaptive solution, the top layer is added to the system that automatically adapts the configuration such that the adaptation goals of the IoT network are guaranteed.

The monitor uses the probe to track the traffic load and network interferences as well as the quality properties of interest. This data is used to update a set of models in the knowledge repository, including a model of the IoT system with the relevant aspects of the environment, and a set of quality models, one for each adaptation goal. As an example, Fig. 4 shows the energy model that is specified as a set of timed automata.

The energy model is used by the statistical model checker to estimate the expected energy consumption per adaptation option (recall that the set of adaptation options is determined by the range of power settings of the motes for each outgoing link and the distribution of packets sent to parents). To that end it uses the following query:

$$simulate\ 1[<=30]\ Gateway\,.\,avgEnergyConsumption$$

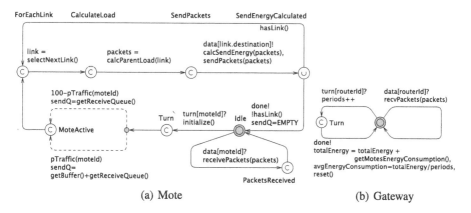

(a) Mote   (b) Gateway

Fig. 4. Quality model used in the IoT application to predict energy consumption

This query performs 30 simulations to compute the expected average energy consumed for the next cycle. This number of simulations provides an RSEM of 0.5%, which was determined using offline experiments.

When the query is invoked, the model parameters for the adaptation option that is verified are set using the data collected by the monitor; e.g., the probability that each mote will generate traffic is set using the $pTraffic(moteID)$ parameter, for motes with multiple parents, the distributions of packets sent to parents are set, etc. The model is then simulated to determine its expected energy consumption. The automaton on the left represents a mote. The automaton is evaluated for each mote in the network in the order they communicate packets (time synchronised). When a mote gets its turn ($turn[moteID]$), the probability that it will send packets is determined based on its recently observed traffic load ($pTraffic(moteID)$). The mote then sends the packets in its queue to its parents one by one ($sendPackets(packets)$), i.e., the packets it received from children and the locally generated packets. As soon as the queue is empty ($sendQ=EMPTY$) the mote returns to the idle state. An idle mote can receive packets at any time ($receivePackets(packets)$). The automaton on the right shows the model for the gateway. When the gateway gets its turn, it computes the average energy consumption that was required to communicate packets in the cycle ($avgEnergyConsumption$).

When the different quality estimates are determined for all the adaptation options, the analyser updates the adaptation options, i.e., it adds the values for packet loss (*pl*), latency (*lat*), and energy consumption (*eng*) to the placeholders of the adaptation options (*adap_opt_i(pl,lat,eng)*, see Fig. 4. The planner is then triggered to plan an adaptation if required. The planner starts by selecting the best adaptation option based on the quality properties determined during analysis. The planner then checks whether this option is: (i) in use, implying that no adaptation is required, (ii) no valid configuration is found, in this case a failsafe strategy is applied (i.e., the network is reconfigured to a default setting), (iii) a better option is found that can achieve the adaptation goals. If adaptation is required, the planner creates a plan consisting of steps, where each step either adapts the power setting of a mote for a link (e.g., *pwm1* sets the power setting of mote 1) or it adapts the distribution of packets sent over a link to a parent of a mote (e.g., *distl7_2*, sets the percentage of packets send by mote 7 over the link to mote 2). As soon as the plan is ready, the executer enacts the adaptation steps via the effectors.

Central to the novelty of MARTAS are two concepts that work in tandem: (i) a distinct runtime quality model for each adaptation goal, and (ii) the use of statistical model checking at runtime that performs a series of simulations and uses statistical techniques to estimate the qualities of the different adaptation options using the quality models. Compared to exhaustive model checking, statistical model checking is very efficient in terms of verification time and required resources. The tradeoff is that the results are not exact, but subject to a level of accuracy and confidence. The engineer can set this level, but higher confidence requires more time and resources.

5   Evaluation

We now evaluate MARTAS using the IoT application. We compare the novel approach with a conservative approach that is typically used in practice. Then we compare MARTAS with a state-of-the-art adaptation approach that uses exhaustive verification.

5.1   Comparison with Conservative Approach

We used the IoT application with 15 motes that is described in Sect. 3.2 (see also Fig. 1) to compare MARTAS with a conservative approach that uses over-provisioning to deal with uncertainties (maximum power setting and all packets are sent to all parents). Each mote consists of: (1) a Raspberry Pi that is responsible for sensing, local processing, and network management operations, and (2) a LoRa module[2] that deals with the radio communication. The gateway runs on a regular server machine.

As explained in Sect. 3.2, to adapt the IoT system, the power settings of the motes can be set from 0 to 15 (min to max power), and the distribution of

---

[2] http://ww1.microchip.com/downloads/en/DeviceDoc/50002346C.pdf.

packets sent over the links to multiple parents can be set in steps of 20%. This resulted in an adaptation space of in total 256 possible configurations.

We evaluated the packet loss, latency, and energy consumption of the IoT network for both approaches over a period of 24 h. The IoT system was configured with a cycle time of 570 s, i.e., 9.5 min, hence a period of 24 h consists of 153 cycles. Each cycle comprises 285 slots of 2 s. For each link, 40 slots are allocated for communication between the motes. During the first 8 min of the cycle the motes can communicate packets upstream to the gateway. The next half second is slack time and during the remaining 1 min the gateway can communicate adaptation packets downstream to the motes. Each mote can generate up to 10 packets per cycle, depending on the type of sensor deployed and the conditions in the environment. The size of the queue is set to 60. Packets from children that arrive when the queue is full are discarded. The values for SNR are based on the actual conditions of the wireless communication. For the evaluation of MARTAS we used verification queries with an approximation interval of 1% and confidence of 90%, and simulations queries with a relative standard error of the mean of 0.5%. Figure 5 shows the test results.

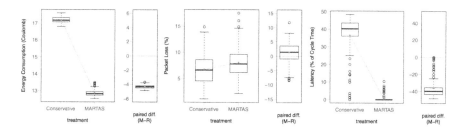

Fig. 5. Test results for conservative approach versus MARTAS

The boxplots show that the average energy consumption of MARTAS is significantly better compared to the conservative approach (p value < 0.000), and the same applies for latency (p < 0.000). For the packet loss, both approaches have similar results and realize the adaptation goal (mean of paired differences is 1.4%). Finally, the mean time required to realise adaptation is $45.7s$ [44.5...48.5], which is only a fraction of the available adaptation time (8 min) for this setting. In conclusion, the test results demonstrate a substantial added value of applying self-adaptation, compared to the conservative approach that is typically used in practice.

5.2   Comparison with a State-of-the-Art Adaptation Approach

To compare MARTAS with runtime quantitative verification – RQV [3], a state-of-the-art adaptation approach that uses exhaustive verification, we used a simulation of the same IoT application setup used in the previous experiment[3]. We

---

[3] The simulator: https://people.cs.kuleuven.be/~danny.weyns/software/DeltaIoT/.

compare the packet loss and energy consumption of the IoT network, and the adaptation time for both approaches over a period of 12 h, corresponding to 76 cycles. For the interference of links and the packets generated by the motes of the simulated system, we used profiles based on data that we collected from the physical deployment over a period of one week. For RQV, we translated the automata model for packet loss to a Discrete Time Markov Chain, and the model for energy consumption to a Markov Decision Process model. For runtime verification we used the PRISM model checker [17] with the default settings. Figure 6 shows the test results.

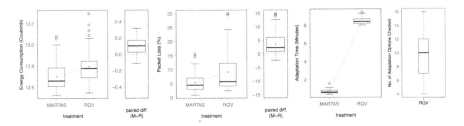

Fig. 6. Test results for MARTAS versus RQV

The boxplots show that the average energy consumption of MARTAS is sightly better compared to RQV (mean of 12.70 for MARTAS versus 12.79 for RQV, i.e., an energy saving of 4%). MARTAS achieves substantially better results for packet loss (mean of 5.45% versus 9.11%). The results for the adaptation time (that is primarily used for verification of adaptation options) show that MARTAS only uses a fraction of the available 8 min to select an adaptation option ($43s$ [$30\ldots46$]). RQV on the other hand consumes all the available time to select an adaptation option ($508s$ ($8m\ 28s$) [$787s\ldots529s$][4]). Moreover, the boxplot most right of Fig. 6 reveals that within the available time of 8 min RQV was able to verify only a fraction of the available adaptation options (9 [$6\ldots12$]). Testing the scalability of MARTAS in simulation (by increasing the number of motes and their connectivity) showed that the approach scales up to similar types of networks with 25 motes. In conclusion, MARTAS achieves better results compared to a state-of-the-art adaptation approach for all quality requirements, while it requires only a fraction of the available adaptation time. On the other hand, the results confirm the limitations of a state-of-the-art adaptation approach based on exhaustive verification in terms of the time it requires to make adaptation decisions.

6 Related Work

Various leading ICT companies have invested significantly in the study and application of self-adaptation techniques [14], including initiatives such as IBM's

---

[4] RQV could complete the ongoing verifications that were started within 8 min.

Autonomic Computing, Sun's N1, HP's Adaptive Enterprise, and Microsoft's Dynamic Systems. These efforts have resulted in industrial applications, such as automated server management, cloud elasticity and automated data center management. These efforts are often based on control-based adaptation solutions. For architecture-based adaptation on the other hand, there is still little understanding about the validity and tradeoffs of incorporating it into real-world software-intensive systems [5].

A number of recent R & D efforts have explored the application of architecture-based adaptation in practical applications. Georgas and Taylor [12] present a domain-independent approach for building adaptive robotic systems and discuss two case studies. Asadollahi et al. [1] apply the StarMX framework to self-manage an internet commerce environment that simulates the activities of a business oriented transactional web server. Happe et al. [13] argue for hierarchically structured models to manage self-healing and self-adaptation and discuss different viewpoints on this in the context of a robotic case. Cámara et al. [5] apply architecture-based adaptation to an industrial middleware to monitor and manage highly populated networks of devices. Van Der Donckt et al. [26] investigated a novel cost-benefit adaptation schema for different QoS requirements and evaluated this approach on a real world IoT deployment. Recently, da Silva et al. [25] apply architecture-based techniques to role-based access control for business processes. While these related efforts apply architecture-based adaptation to practical applications, the only related effort that targets guarantees for the compliance of the systems with the adaptation goals is [25]. Overall, this paper contributes to existing efforts by applying a novel architecture-based adaptation approach in a different but important emerging domain: automation of the management of IoT networks.

7 Experiences and Lessons Learned

To conclude we report the results of a semi-structured interview we performed with two members of the technical staff of VersaSense. The aim was to get further insights in the experiences of the company with the self-adaptive solution. The interview was structured around six key questions. We summarise the main outcome of the interview.

Q1: What do you consider the most important benefits of the self-adaptive solution? Business and economical benefits, in particular: (i) removing manual interventions reduces costs to manage IoT deployments; (ii) being able to handle changes whenever they occur faster, (iii) achieving more optimal configurations in which the self-adaptive system is in the driver seat, avoiding conservative and sub-optimal configurations with as a result longer system lifetime (energy) and better customer experience; (iv) being able to offer 24/7 service to customers, without interruption.

Q2: What are potential risks of the self-adaptive solution and how could these risks be mitigated? Replacing experienced human interventions by self-adaptation requires trust and faith in the outcome the automated decision making. For IoT applications that are subject to very frequent changes, the overhead cost of self-adaptation may be an issue. E.g., when a system is optimized for a particular range of situations, and the operational context frequently changes, the system has to continuously adapt itself to accommodate new changes. A traditionally over-provisioned manually configured system might be able to accommodate more situations without the overhead of having to adapt itself at every change. A mitigation strategy could be finding a good balance between (1) a super-optimized self-adaptation policy for a particular situation, and (2) a less optimized policy that can accomodate more situations. Furthermore, good system monitoring, in combination with predicting patterns/trends of potential changes beforehand, might allow to determine a more optimal self-adaptation.

Q3: What are the most significant experiences gained from deploying and trialing the self-adaptive approach? The benefits of adaptation were already visible for small IoT deployments. The risks for the company are limited as the approach can be added as an add-on module so it can be tested in a controlled proof-of-concept setup. It will be particularly interesting to investigate now how the adaptive approach will scale towards bigger deployments with different application features and quality requirements.

Q4: Why do you think the adaptation approach presented in the paper is innovative or valuable for others. MARTAS is one of the first solutions that applies self-adaptation in the context of the new domain of IoT. It is one of the first solutions that actually applies automated management in the context of an existing IoT deployment.

Q5: Do you see a broader applicability of the proposed solution for your business? As IoT deployments and applications continue to grow in scale (i.e. number of assets being monitored and controlled by IoT devices), heterogeneity (types of devices and technologies involved), and complexity (i.e. application features and quality requirements), manual maintenance will require more and more efforts and become increasingly error-prone. We will investigate how the proposed solution can translate to other types of existing IoT applications, and how it can be integrated to the rest of the elements inside the infrastructure spanning from IoT devices towards cloud. Applying the proposed approach to automatically ensure optimal quality levels while keeping the entire system operating flawlessly, will certainly be a game-changer in this field.

Q6: What are your main lessons learned from this R & D effort? This interesting experiment showed how cutting-edge R & D efforts can be integrated with existing products and solutions. This may lead to improved products and additional competitive services that can be offered to customers. Solving the problem of automating the management of IoT deployments required the combined expertise from researchers and engineers from different areas: software architectures, adaptation, IoT system engineering.

8   Conclusions

Architecture-based adaptation is a well-studied approach to mitigate uncertainties of software-intensive systems that are difficult to anticipate before deployment. The interference of the network links in an IoT system or the traffic generated by the motes are concrete examples of uncertainties that VersaSense faces that drove the research presented in this paper. However, existing adaptation approaches to handle uncertainties and provide guarantees for the required adaptation goals apply exhaustive verification techniques at runtime, which often limits their applicability in practice. To tackle this problem, we presented MARTAS, an innovative architecture-based adaptation approach to solve VersaSence problem: automating the management of Internet-of-Things (IoT). This novel approach equips an IoT application with a feedback loop that employs runtime models and statistical techniques to reason about the system and to adapt it to ensure the required goals. We applied MARTAS to a building security monitoring system, which is a representative case for a class of IoT applications deployed by VersaSense, and we demonstrated how MARTAS outperforms the current manual approach and a state-of-the-art approach for different quality goals. The main benefits of automating the management of IoT deployments are reduced costs, handle changes whenever they occur faster, achieve more optimal configurations, longer system lifetimes and better customer experience. The main risks are the need for trust in the automated decision making and potentially substantial overhead costs in settings that are subject to very frequent changes. These risks could be mitigated by balancing the quality optimality adaptation can achieve with the range of situation the approach can accommodate. This $R \& D$ effort demonstrated that solving a self-adaptation problem in practice required the combined expertise from researchers and engineers.

References

1. Asadollahi, R., et al.: StarMX: a framework for developing self-managing java-based systems. In: Software Engineering for Adaptive and Self-Managing Systems. IEEE (2009)
2. Brun, Y., et al.: Engineering self-adaptive systems through feedback loops. In: Cheng, B.H.C. (ed.) Software Engineering for Self-Adaptive Systems. LNCS, vol. 5525, pp. 48–70. Springer, Heidelberg (2009). https://doi.org/10.1007/978-3-642-02161-9_3
3. Calinescu, R.: Dynamic QoS management and optimization in service-based systems. IEEE Trans. Softw. Eng. **37**(3), 387–409 (2011)
4. Cámara, J.: Assurances for Self-Adaptive Systems. LNCS, vol. 7740. Springer, Heidelberg (2013). https://doi.org/10.1007/978-3-642-36249-1
5. Cámara, J., et al.: Evolving an adaptive industrial software system to use architecture-based self-adaptation. In: International Symposium on Software Engineering for Adaptive and Self-Managing Systems. IEEE Press (2013)
6. Cheng, B.H.C., et al.: Software engineering for self-adaptive systems: a research roadmap. In: Cheng, B.H.C. (ed.) Software Engineering for Self-Adaptive Systems. LNCS, vol. 5525, pp. 1–26. Springer, Heidelberg (2009). https://doi.org/10.1007/978-3-642-02161-9_1

7. Di Marzo Serugendo, G., Gleizes, M.P., Karageorgos, A.: Self-organization in multi-agent systems. Knowl. Eng. Rev. **20**(2), 165–189 (2005)

8. Dobson, S.: A survey of autonomic communications. ACM Trans. Auton. Adapt. Syst. **1**, 223–259 (2006)

9. Dustdar, S.: Principles of elastic processes. IEEE Internet Comput. **15**(5), 66–71 (2011)

10. Galante, G., de Bona, L.: A survey on cloud computing elasticity. In: International Conference on Utility and Cloud Computing. IEEE Computer Society (2012)

11. Garlan, D.: Rainbow: architecture-based self-adaptation with reusable infrastructure. Computer **37**(10), 46–54 (2004)

12. Georgas, J.C., Taylor, R.N.: Policy-based architectural adaptation management: robotics domain case studies. In: Cheng, B.H.C., et al. (eds.) Software Engineering for Self-Adaptive Systems. LNCS, vol. 5525, pp. 89–108. Springer, Heidelberg (2009). https://doi.org/10.1007/978-3-642-02161-9_5

13. Happe, J., Koziolek, H., Bellur, U., et al.: The role of models in self-adaptive and self-healing systems. In: Self-Healing and Self-Adaptive Systems, Dagstuhl Report (2009)

14. Kephart, J.O., Chess, D.M.: The vision of autonomic computing. Computer **36**(1), 41–50 (2003)

15. Kounev, S.: Self-Aware Computing Systems. Springer, Heidelberg (2017). https://doi.org/10.1007/978-3-319-47474-8

16. Kramer, J., Magee, J.: Self-managed systems: an architectural challenge. In: Future of Software Engineering. IEEE Computer Society (2007)

17. Kwiatkowska, M., Norman, G., Parker, D.: PRISM 4.0: verification of probabilistic real-time systems. In: Gopalakrishnan, G., Qadeer, S. (eds.) CAV 2011. LNCS, vol. 6806, pp. 585–591. Springer, Heidelberg (2011). https://doi.org/10.1007/978-3-642-22110-1_47

18. de Lemos, R., et al.: Software engineering for self-adaptive systems: a second research roadmap. In: de Lemos, R., Giese, H., Müller, H.A., Shaw, M. (eds.) Software Engineering for Self-Adaptive Systems II. LNCS, vol. 7475, pp. 1–32. Springer, Heidelberg (2013). https://doi.org/10.1007/978-3-642-35813-5_1

19. de Lemos, R., et al.: Software engineering for self-adaptive systems: research challenges in the provision of assurances. In: de Lemos, R., Garlan, D., Ghezzi, C., Giese, H. (eds.) Software Engineering for Self-Adaptive Systems III. Assurances. LNCS, vol. 9640, pp. 3–30. Springer, Cham (2017). https://doi.org/10.1007/978-3-319-74183-3_1

20. Matthys, N., et al.: μpnp-mesh: the plug-and-play mesh network for the internet of things. In: IEEE 2nd World Forum on Internet of Things (2015)

21. Oreizy, P., Medvidovic, N., Taylor, R.N.: Architecture-based runtime software evolution. In: International Conference on Software Engineering. IEEE Computer Society (1998)

22. Redwine, S., Riddle, W.: Software technology maturation. In: International Conference on Software Engineering. IEEE Computer Society Press (1985)

23. Salehie, M., Tahvildari, L.: Self-adaptive software: landscape and research challenges. Trans. Auton. Adapt. Syst. **4**, 14:1–14:42 (2009)

24. Shevtsov, S.: Control-theoretical software adaptation: a systematic literature review. IEEE Trans. Softw. Eng. **44**, 784–810 (2017)

25. da Silva, C.E., et al.: Self-adaptive role-based access control for business processes. In: Software Engineering for Adaptive and Self-Managing Systems. IEEE Press (2017)

26. Van Der Donckt, J., et al.: Cost-benefit analysis at runtime for self-adaptive systems applied to an IoT application. In: Evaluation of Novel Approaches to Software Engineering (2018)
27. Weyns, D.: Software Engineering of Self-Adaptive Systems: An Organised Tour and Future Challenges. In: Handbook of Software Engineering. Springer, Heidelberg (2018). https://people.cs.kuleuven.be/danny.weyns/papers/2017HSE.pdf. (forthcoming)
28. Weyns, D., Iftikhar, U., Söderlund, J.: Do external feedback loops improve the design of self-adaptive systems? A controlled experiment. In: International Symposium on Software Engineering of Self-Managing and Adaptive Systems. SEAMS 2013 (2013)
29. Weyns, D., Malek, S., Andersson, J.: FORMS: unifying reference model for formal specification of distributed self-adaptive systems. ACM TAAS **7**(1), 8:1–8:61 (2012)
30. Weyns, D., et al.: Perpetual assurances for self-adaptive systems. In: de Lemos, R., Garlan, D., Ghezzi, C., Giese, H. (eds.) Software Engineering for Self-Adaptive Systems III. Assurances. LNCS, vol. 9640, pp. 31–63. Springer, Cham (2017). https://doi.org/10.1007/978-3-319-74183-3_2

IoT Architectural Styles

A Systematic Mapping Study

Henry Muccini and Mahyar Tourchi Moghaddam[(✉)]

University of L'Aquila, 67100 L'Aquila, Italy
{henry.muccini,mahtou}@univaq.it

Abstract. IoT components are becoming more and more ubiquitous. Thus, the necessity of architecting IoT applications is bringing a substantial attention towards software engineering community. On this occasion, different styles and patterns can facilitate shaping the IoT architectural characteristics. This study aims at defining, identifying, classifying, and re-designing a class of IoT styles and patterns at the architectural level. Conforming a systematic mapping study (SMS) selection procedure, we picked out 63 papers among over 2,300 candidate studies. To this end, we applied a rigorous classification and extraction framework to select and analyze the most influential domain-related information. Our analysis revealed the following main findings: *(i)* facing by various architectural styles that attempted to address various aspects of IoT systems, cloud and fog are discerned as their most important components. *(ii)* distributed patterns are not widely discussed for IoT architecture, however, there is foreseen a grow specially for their industrial applications. *(iii)* starting from the last few years on, there is still a growing scientific interest on IoT architectural styles. This study gives a solid foundation for classifying existing and future approaches for IoT styles beneficial for academic and industrial researchers. It provides a set of abstract IoT reference architectures to be applicable on various architectural styles.

Keywords: IoT · Software architecture · Styles · Patterns
Systematic mapping study

1 Introduction

It is foreseen that 26 billion devices by 2020 and 500 billion devices by 2030 will be connected to the Internet [1, 2] and business to business spending on IoT technologies, apps and solutions will reach 267 billion dollars by 2020 [3]. Another estimation says that the IoT has a potential economic impact of $11 trillion per year by 2025, which would be equivalent to about 11% of the world economy [4]. Such predictions are a matter of encouragement for companies to invest on IoT based applications and to build their pillars on IoT in order to achieve their desired value creation and sustained competitive advantage. Along with a suitable degree of maturity regarding technologies and solutions applied on the identification, connectivity, and computation of IoT components, a slope up over architectural concerns is further apparent. Hence, a role of the academic community might be providing a set of standard architectures to assure the efficiency and quality of IoT hardware and software components in practice.

© Springer Nature Switzerland AG 2018
C. E. Cuesta et al. (Eds.): ECSA 2018, LNCS 11048, pp. 68–85, 2018.
https://doi.org/10.1007/978-3-030-00761-4_5

Our attention goes to one specific pillar of software architecture, that is, architectural styles and patterns for engineering IoT applications. Such a focus is driven by a concrete need: since our team is involved in the design and implementation of IoT-based urban security systems, we have been looking for architectural styles and patterns driving the way IoT components shall be combined together. Since we found a dispersed body of knowledge on the subject, we decided to run this study.

The goal of this research is not only to classify and identify the domain state of the art, but also to redesign a class of IoT architectural patterns according to the philosophy and granularity of software architectures. In order to tackle this goal, a well-established systematic mapping study has been performed. The primary studies have been chosen based on an accurate inclusion and exclusion criteria and a deep analysis.

The main contributions of this study are: *(i)* Addressing to an up to date state of the art class for IoT architectural styles and patterns, which can be used as a future research reference. *(ii)* Providing a sustainable map to be used as a framework to learn and evaluate architectural styles, patterns, and descriptions. *(iii)* Identifying current characteristics, challenges and publication trends with respect to IoT architectures approach. *(iv)* Classifying IoT architectures according to their specific computation and communication attributes.

The audience of this study are both research and industry communities interested to improve their knowledge and select a suitable architectural style for their IoT system.

This paper is structured as follows. Section 2 motivates the need for this study. Section 3 reveals the design of this systematic study. Section 4 presents a taxonomy on IoT architectures and provides background. Sections 5, 6, 7 and 8 elaborate on the obtained results whilst Sect. 9 runs a number of horizontal analysis over the results and discusses the obtained results. Section 10 analyses threats to validity and Sect. 11 closes the paper and discusses future works.

2   Motivation

This section discusses the motivation that this research arose from and argues the potential scientific value of it. Thus, an extensive search has been performed in Subsect. 2.1 to discover the related existed systematic reviews. Subsection 2.2 gives a concise reasoning upon the necessity for a systematic mapping study on IoT Architectural styles.

2.1   Existing Mapping Studies Related to IoT Architectures

Toward learning the already conducted systematic studies (literature review (SLR) and SMS) related to this research topic, we performed a manual search using the following search string:

("systematic mapping study" OR SMS OR "systematic literature review" OR SLR OR "Literature Review" OR LR) AND (IoT OR "Internet of Things" OR "Internet-of-things" OR "Internet of Everything" OR "Internet-of-everything") AND ("software architecture" OR "system architecture" OR architecture).

Subsequently, in order to best organize the search, following inclusion and exclusion criteria are determined.

Inclusion Criteria: (i) Studies performed a systematic literature review or mapping study on architectural solutions, methods, styles, patterns or languages specific for IoT and IoE; *(ii)* Studies written in English language and available in full-text; *(iii)* Studies subject to peer review.

Exclusion Criteria: (i) Studies that are focusing only on architecture or only on IoT (and IOE); *(ii)* Studies that are NOT secondary (systematic literature reviews and mapping studies); *(iii)* Studies in the form of tutorial papers, editorials, etc.

Further, a multi-stage search and selection process has been performed based on three authentic databases: the *ACM Digital Library, ISI Web of Science,* and *Wiley Inter Science.* We initially found a total number of 317 papers and after impurity removal, merge and duplication removal, the selection process applied on 214 remaining studies. After all, we did not find any systematic study on the topic. However, a slightly related study with different objective and scope has been chosen to be compared with our research. The search and selection procedure can be find at the following link: https://www.dropbox.com/s/bxri9gv91sv5ttu/DE.ECSA-IoT.Style.xlsx?dl=0.

The research [5] conducted a systematic survey that purposed on categorizing the challenges arise from cloud-based software systems architecture. *Strengths:* The paper is well-structured and follow a clear methodology and research questions, concluded by a framework for future researches. *Why it is different from our work:* the paper [5] tries to discover the related literature on software architecture of cloud-based systems; it is merely a review and they do not conclude it with proposing any architecture pattern; it is not specifically related to IoT. Our objective is instead to propose different styles and patterns for IoT architecture, applicable on all IoT domain solutions, whether based on cloud or not.

2.2   The Need for a SMS on IoT Architectural Styles

This research complements the existing studies regarding the IoT architectures with introducing a literature-based classification of its styles and patterns. So far, a large body of knowledge has been proposed in both IoT systems and software architecture styles, however, a lack of harmonizing and integrating them together is undeniable.

Although the IoT has been introduced more than one decade ago, the research and industry communities are still trying to define its different aspects effectively. Trying to discover the impact of existing literature on proposing a new set of IoT architectures, we identify, describe, and classify different styles to help the community to choose the best architecture for their IoT models.

3   Research Method

The goal of this research is formulated based on the Goal-Question-Metric perspectives [6] as follow:

Purpose—to propose a class of IoT architectures
Issue—with identifying, describing, and classifying different styles and patterns

Object—based on existing IoT architecture approaches
Viewpoint—from the research and industry viewpoints.

3.1   Search Strategy

To achieve the aforementioned goal, we arranged for a set of questions along with their rationale:

- **RQ1.** *What sort of architectural styles can be used in order to model an IoT system?* This research question aims at categorizing different types of IoT architecture styles in detail.
- **RQ2.** *How IoT architectures can be categorized based on their distribution level?* This research question aims at classifying the IoT architectures based on their intelligent edge and element collaboration.
- **RQ3.** *How scientific publications on IoT architectural styles evolved over time? What strategy they used to structure their research?* This research question aims at identifying and classifying the interest of researchers in IoT architectural styles and their various characteristics over time.
- **RQ4.** *What type of evidence (evaluation or assurance) is provided by existing literature on IoT architectural styles?* This question reviews whether the primary studies guaranteed their functionality through a kind of validation or not.

Furthermore, an optimum search strategy is expected to provide effective solutions to the following questions: which, where, what, and when [7].

Which Approaches? The search strategy consists of two phases: *(i)* an automatic search on academic database; and *(ii)* a snowballing. The first step has been performed using a search string (Listing 1) followed by the selection criteria applied on the set of results. Then a snowballing procedure on the included results of the automatic search has been applied in order to structure the final set of primary studies. In the course of snowballing, if a paper considered to be included, snowballing has been applied iteratively and the procedure ended when no new papers have been found. The snowballing has been performed starting from the 30 primary studies resulting from the automatic search, leading to the final set of 63 primary studies.

Where to Search? The electronic databases that we used for the automatic search (ACM, IEEE, ELSEVIER, SPRINGER, ISI Web of Science, and WILEY Inter Science) are known as the main source of literature for potentially relevant studies on software engineering [8].

What to Search? Following some test executions and refinements, the search string has been finalized as shown in Listing 1. We tried to codify the string in a way to be best adapted to specific syntax and criteria of each selected electronic data source.

Listing 1. Composed Search String

```
(IoT OR "Internet of Things" OR "Internet-of-things" OR IoE OR "Internet of Everything" OR "Internet-of-everything") AND (Architecture OR "Software Architecture") AND (patterns OR styles)
```

Further, we combined all studies into a single dataset, after removal of impurities and duplicates.

When and What Time Span to Search? We did not consider publication year as a criterion for the search and selection steps. Thus, all studies coming from the selection steps, until February 2018, were included regardless of their publication time.

3.2   Selection Strategy

A multi-stage selection process (Fig. 1) has been designed to give a full control on the number and characteristics of the studies coming from different stages.

As it is shown in Fig. 1, we are not mentioning Science Direct since we did not achieve any result on that. Furthermore, we used "Software Engineering" as a refinement criterion for Springer engine as it led to over 183,000 results that were potentially outside of our intended research area. We did not use Google Scholar since it may generate many irrelevant results and have considerable overlap with ACM and IEEE; nevertheless, we used Google Scholar in the forward snowballing procedure. Hence, we considered all the selected studies and filtered them according to a set of well-defined inclusion and exclusion criteria (Table 1).

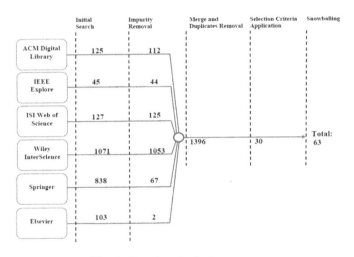

Fig. 1. Search and selection process

Data Extraction. This step is aimed at identifying, collecting, and classifying data from the selected primary studies (the list is available on online data extraction file) to answer the research questions. To this end, a detailed classification framework has been designed to structure the extracted data. Indeed, designing an effective classification framework needs a comprehensive analysis of the primary studies' content. Furthermore, the IoT standards and formal software architecture classifications supported us through categorizing the data extraction. The systematic process that we followed for this phase consists of collecting and clustering the keywords of primary studies.

Table 1. Inclusion and exclusion criteria

Inclusion criteria	Exclusion criteria
Studies proposing, leveraging, or analysing architectural solutions, methods, techniques, or styles and patterns, specific for IoT and IoE	Studies that, while focusing on IoT, do not explicitly deal with their architecture (e.g., studies focussing only on technological aspects, inner details of IoT)
studies subject to peer review (e.g., journal papers, papers published as part of conference proceedings, workshop papers, and book chapters)	Secondary or tertiary studies (e.g., systematic literature reviews, surveys, etc.)
Studies written in English language and available in full-text	Studies in the form of tutorial papers, editorials, etc. because they do not provide enough information

Data Synthesis. The data synthesis activity involves collating and summarizing the data extracted from the primary studies [9] with the main goal of understanding, analysing, and classifying current research on IoT architectures. The data synthesis has been structured of following two phases. *Vertical analysis: (i)* analysis of extracted data individually to track the trends and collect information of each study with respect to the research questions; *(ii)* analysis the discrete extracted data as a whole to reason about potential patterns and trends. *Horizontal analysis: (i)* analysis of extracted data to explore possible relations across different dimensions and facets of the research. *(ii)* using contingency tables analysis to cross-tabulate and group the data and made comparisons between two or more concepts of the classification framework.

Study Replicability. A replication package is provided to tackle the page limits of a conference paper: (https://www.dropbox.com/s/bxri9gv91sv5ttu/DE.ECSA-IoT.Style. xlsx?dl=0). The package is available as an excel file with different sheets that include all necessary information such as primary studies, data extraction, keywording and clustering, snowballing, primary studies distribution, validity examination and etc.

4 Background and Taxonomy

4.1 Reference Definition of IoT

This section provides some various definitions of IoT mostly derived from our primary studies, then suggest a reference definition for the purpose of this work.

According to P5 [10], the Internet of Things comprises large numbers of smart devices at the network edge that may have to collaborate and interact with each other in real time. P54 [11] defines IoT as an environment in which objects (devices) are given unique identifiers and the ability to transfer data over a network without having human-to-human or human-to-computer interaction. From another view (P32) [12], IoT could be specified as a worldwide network of interconnected entities. As stated in P21 [13] IoT is an ecosystem that interconnects physical objects with telecommunication networks, joining the real world with the cyberspace and enabling the development of new kinds of services and applications.

All aforementioned definitions have their focus on the networking aspect of IoT, whilst the following two definitions emphasize on its computational environment too. IoT is a construction paradigm of computational systems where the objects around us will be in the network in order to extend the capabilities of the environment (P16) [14]. The Internet of Things is a technological revolution that represents the future of computing and communications (P34) [15].

IoT can be considered as the future evaluation of the Internet that realizes machine-to-machine (M2M) learning. Thus, IoT provides connectivity for everyone and everything (P48) [16]. P9 [17] focuses on IoT objectives that are: Convergence, Communication, Connectivity, Content, Computing, and Collections. In the Cluster of European Research Projects report, IoT is defined as an integrated part of the future Internet, which ensures that 'things' with identities can communicate with each other [18].

From our point of view, IoT is: *the internal/external communication of intelligent components via internet in order to improve the environment through proving smarter services.*

4.2   Taxonomy

By analyzing the primary studies under such a dimension, a set of representative concepts have been identified as shown in Fig. 2. The taxonomy shows various architectural concerns on IoT systems. The focus of this study goes to the *architectural styles* and *distribution patterns* in the following sections, hence, the remaining features are briefly addressed here.

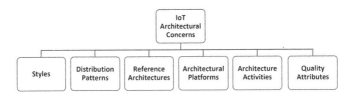

Fig. 2. IoT architectures taxonomy

Reference Architectures. An IoT reference architecture shall provide a uniform basis to understand, compare and evaluate different IoT solutions. Among our primary studies, (15/63) papers try to develop a kind of IoT reference architecture. For instance, P61 [19] introduces an abstract IoT reference architecture with an abstract view on the components of IoT and their possible connections, in order to ensure a broad applicability. However, a number of more extendable, scalable and flexible IoT reference architectures are presented as architectural platforms.

Architectural Platforms. Most of IoT platforms are cloud- based and open-source. *Amazon web service IoT platform* (AWS) dominates the consumer cloud market. AWS provides multiple data processing services (Amazon S3, Amazon DynamoDB, AWS

Lambda, Amazon Kinesis, Amazon SNS, Amazon SQS). However, the core logic of the platform is located within the Message Broker, Thing Registry, Thing Shadows, Rules Engine, and the Security & Identity component, and hence, they are encompassed by the IoT Integration Middleware [19]. *Microsoft Azure IoT Hub* is another example. Its reference architecture is composed of core platform services and application-level components to facilitate the processing needs across three major areas of a typical IoT solution: *(i)* device connectivity, *(ii)* data processing, analytics, and management *(iii)* presentation and business connectivity [20]. There are other platforms such as OpenMTC, FIWARE, and SiteWhere, that can be find over selected primary studies.

Architecture Activities. The architecture activities variables have been extracted from Li et al. [21] paper. Most discussed activities in architectural level are *analysis* (32/63) and *understanding* (30/63) a kind of IoT architecture. This denotes that each study tries to define its own IoT architecture to address a specific problem. However, (19/63) studies *reused* a special style of architecture that was mostly layered architecture. *Evaluation* (22/63), *description* (18/63), *synthesis* (14/63) are among the superlative used activities but *impact analysis* (11/63), *implementation* (10/63), *recovery* (9/63), and *maintenance* (8/63) are rarely discoursed.

Quality Attributes. The standard used to categorize quality attributes comes from ISO 25010 tied with some specific IoT attributes derived from the primary studies keywording. The architectural style of an IoT system can have effect on quality attributes but does not guarantee all of them. The most recognized quality attributes that are supposed to be satisfied with a proper IoT architecture are *scalability* (45/63), *security* (43/63), *interoperability* (38/63), and *performance* (37/63). Scalability is an essential attribute as IoT should be capable to perform at an acceptable level with this scale of devices. Furthermore, security gains a high concern in an IoT system, in which different components and entities are connected to each other through a network. Interoperability helps heterogenous components of IoT to work together efficiently. *Privacy* (32/63), *availability* (28/63), *mobility* (26/63), *reliability* (24/63), *resiliency* (12/63), and *evolvability* (9/63) are positioned in the lower degree of concern. *Resiliency*, that is effective handling the failures and is a critical aspect, is not addressed vastly through primary studies but has a huge capacity to be studied in future researches.

5   Architectural Styles (RQ1)

The primary studies used one or more overlaid style(s) to design their software architecture. However, among the various IoT architectural styles, layered architecture (34/63) was the clear winner as reported in Table 2. In the Layered View the system is viewed as a complex heterogeneous entity that can be decomposed into interacting parts [22].

The primary studies designed their layered architecture in different ways, ranged from 3 to 6 layers. As shown in Fig. 3, a three-layer IoT architecture is composed of the perception layer, processing and storage layer, and application layer.

Table 2. Architectural styles

Architecture style	#studies	Studies
Layered	34	P1, P3, P4, P7, P12, P17, P18, P20, P21, P25, P26, P27, P33, P34, P35, P39, P41, P42, P43, P44, P45, P48, P49, P50, P52, P53, P54, P55, P57, P58, P59, P61, P62, P63
Cloud based	32	P1, P2, P5, P6, P8, P9, P10, P11, P15, P16, P20, P21, P24, P26, P28, P29, P32, P33, P40, P44, P45, P48, P51, P52, P55, P56, P57, P58, P60, P61, P62, P63
Service oriented	15	P3, P9, P13, P14, P16, P19, P22, P23, P26, P28, P37, P38, P51, P55, P63
Microservices	6	P6, P13, P16, P19, P46, P47
Restful	5	P22, P29, P30, P37, P43
Publish/subscribe	3	P10, P27, P31
Information Centric Networking	2	P14, P18

The *perception* layer consists of the physical objects and sensor devices (P48) [16] in order to identify and collect environmental information and bring them to the virtual space. The *Processing and storage* layer is in charge of analysing and storing the data gathered by sensors. Various techniques such as cloud computing, ubiquitous computing, database software and intelligent processing are being used to best handle the collected information. The *application* layer provides the service requested by customers (P63) [23] ranging from agriculture to smart healthcare.

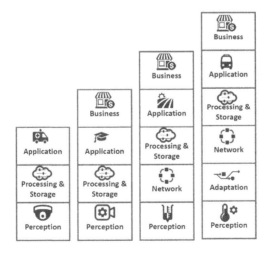

Fig. 3. Layered IoT architecture

Four-layer IoT architecture has one more substrate on the top, that is called **business** layer. This layer is responsible for the handling of entire IoT system. By creating the business models according to dynamic value propositions, this layer designs the roadmap of IoT system. To build a five-layer IoT architecture, a **network** layer can be added to transfer information from perception to processing layer. The transmission medium can be wired or wireless and technology can be 3G, UMTS, Wi-Fi, Bluetooth, infrared, ZigBee, etc. depending upon the sensor devices (P48) [16]. A number of studies brought an **adaptation** layer into the IoT architecture to make it six-layer. This layer is positioned between perception and network layers. This layer is an adapter that facilitate interoperability of IoT heterogenous devices.

Cloud-based architecture (32/63) that has a cloud as the core of their computational part has the second position. Capability of processing and storing big amount of data and providing contextual information, is making cloud computing as an inseparable part of IoT. Fog Computing is a significant extension to cloud environment. Few studies (7/63) addressed fog, as it is a new cloud computing paradigm. Fog brings virtualized cloud services to the edge of the network to control the devices in the IoT (P5) [10].

Cloud architecture is characterized by its various services towards providing an IoT system. As mentioned in P1 [24], Infrastructure as a Service (*IaaS*), provides virtualized computing resources. The physical machines and virtual machines are stored in the IaaS, and the task of the engines in the IaaS is to mine the data. Data Storage as a Service (*DSaaS*) provides data storage and information retrieval by a database manager. Platform as a Service (*PaaS*) provides the tools to work with the machines in the cloud. Software as a Service (SaaS) provides resources to the users for interpretation and visualization of data in the cloud. *Fog* is positioned between cloud and IoT devices and facilitates the devices to communicate with cloud and provides them processing, storage, and networking services.

Service oriented architectures (SoA) (15/63) put the service at the centre of their IoT service design. In fact, the core application component makes the service available for other IoT components over a network. SOA consists of following three elements. A service provider that is the primary engine underlying the services. A service broker that describes the location of the service and ensures its availability. A service consumer or client that asks the service broker to locate a service and determine how to communicate with that service [25].

Microservices (6/63) and the SOA approach in the IoT have the same goal, that is building one or multiple applications from a set of different services (P19) [26]. A microservice is a small application which can be deployed independently, scaled independently, tested independently and which has a single responsibility [27]. Literally, the microservice architecture approach utilizes the SoA together with knowledge of software virtualization to overtake the architecture quality limitations like scalability. In this style, an application is built by the composition of several microservices.

Restful (5/63) is underlying architecture organization style of the Web and provides a decoupled architecture, and light weight communication between service producer and service consumers, that is suitable for cloud-based APIs. Restful has its essence on creating loosely coupled services on the Web so that it can be easily reused. It further has advantages for a decentralized and massive-scale service system align well the field of pervasive computing [28].

In Publish/subscribe architectural style (3/63) publisher sends a message on a specific topic, regardless of receiver, and a subscriber can subscribe and receive the same topic asynchronously. The system is generally mediated by a number of brokers which receive published messages from publishers and send them to subscribers.

Information Centric Networking (ICN) (2/63) instead, makes the information as a base of the device communication. ICN matches the application pattern of IoT systems and provides an efficient and intelligent communication paradigm for IoT [29].

6   Distribution Patterns (RQ2)

On the other hand, IoT distribution patterns classify the architectures according to *edge intelligence* and *elements collaboration* (P32) [12]. The IoT architecture patterns are classified as: centralized, collaborative, connected intranets, and distributed based on a layered architectural style (Fig. 4).

Centralized. In this pattern, the perception layer provides data for the central processing and storage component to be provided as services in the next layer. Connecting to this central component is mandatory to use the IoT service. The central component can be a server, cloud, or a fog network connected to cloud.

Collaborative. Here a network of central intelligent components can communicate in order to form and empower their services.

Connected Intranets. In this pattern, sensors provide data within a local intranet to be used locally, remotely, and centrally. The advantage is that if the central component fails, local service is still in access. The disadvantage is that there is no fully distributed framework to facilitate the communication among components.

Distributed. Here all components are fully interconnected and capable to retrieve, process, combine, and provide information and services to other components towards the common goals.

Table 3 shows the distribution patterns that are used by the primary studies. Most of studies used centralized pattern (51/63) followed by collaborative (10/63), fully distributed (4/63) and connected intranets (2/63) patterns. Distributed patterns are not widely discussed for IoT architecture, however, there is foreseen a grow specially for industrial applications.

Towards our objectives, we present a three and four layered architecture that are composed of the following layers (Fig. 4). *Perception*: represents the physical sensors and actuators of the IoT that aim to collect information. *Processing and Storage*: is the central IoT component that stores and analyses the data gathered by perception components to be in access of other entities for their application purposes. *Application*: determines the class of services provided by IoT. *Business*: manages the IoT system for its specific goal, by creating business models derived from the information of application layer. The styles are described as follow:

Table 3. IoT distribution patterns

Distribution patterns	#studies	Studies
Centralized	51	P1, P2, P5, P6, P7, P9, P10, P11, P12, P13, P14, P16, P17, P18, P19, P20, P21, P22, P23, P24, P27, P28, P29, P31, P32, P33, P34, P35, P37, P38, P40, P41, P42, P43, P44, P46, P47, P48, P49, P50, P51, P53, P54, P55, P56, P57, P59, P60, P61, P62, P63
Collaborative	10	P3, P8, P15, P25, P26, P32, P36, P45, P51, P58
Connected intranets	4	P4, P32, P39, P58
Distributed	2	P32, P52

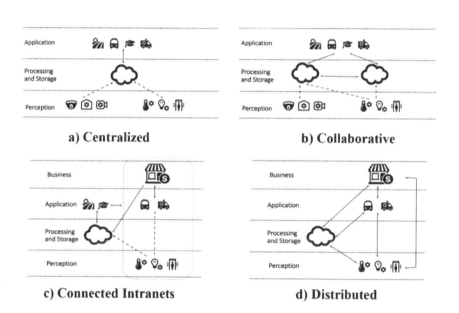

a) Centralized   b) Collaborative

c) Connected Intranets   d) Distributed

Fig. 4. IoT architectural patterns

7 Publication Trend (RQ3)

In this section the publication evolution on IoT architectural styles are presented. To this end, publication year, venue, type and strategy are extracted and discussed below.

Publication Year. Figure 5 shows the distribution of IoT architectural styles literature. It noticeably indicates that the number of papers grows by time and there are few papers published before 2014. This result confirms the scientific interest and research necessity on IoT architecture issues in the last few years.

Publication Type. The most common publication type is conference paper (35/63), followed by journal (21/63), book chapter (4/63) and workshop paper (3/63). Such a high number of conference and journal papers may point out that architecting IoT is maturing as a research topic despite its still relatively young.

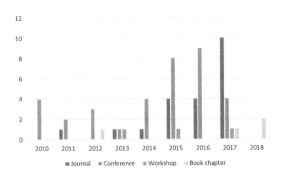

Fig. 5. Distribution of primary studies by type of publication

Publication Venues. From the extracted data we can notice that research on IoT architecture is spread across many venues, spanning different research areas such as telecommunications, software engineering, cloud computing, security, etc. This can be figured out as an indication, which IoT architectural styles area is perceived today as orthogonal with respect to many other research areas, rather than a specific research topic.

Research Strategies. To learn the dispersion of research strategy across primary studies, we take advantage of well-known research approaches proposed by Wieringa et al. in [30]. *Solution proposal* (39/63) is the most common strategy, followed by *philosophical papers* (17/63). Considering the IoT as a novel concept, it is justifiable that most of studies try to provide their own solution for architecting it. *Evaluation research* (16/63) is the third most common strategy highlighting the efforts through industrializing the conducted studies. *Validation* (10/63) comes afterward, to show the degree of evidence provided by researches. *Experience* (2/63) and *opinion* (1/63) research strategies are also used but rarely.

8   Provided Evidence (RQ4)

Empirical Method. Lots of primary studies did not provide any type of evaluation to validate their work (26/63). However, the other empirical methods are used as follows: *Experiments* (13/63), *illustrative examples* for evaluation (13/63), *case studies* (12/63), and *prototype* (10/63).

Assurance. Concerning assurances, (15/63) studies provide some level of evidence for claims using *experimental* results and (10/63) of the studies use *simulation*. Few studies used *emulation* (3/63), *formal method* (3/63) and *consistency checking* (2/63) to assure their study functionality. However, in most of studies (41/63), no assurance is provided at all.

These results confirm that the evidence provided by studies is often obtained from experiments, and application of the researches results to toy examples.

9   Horizontal Analysis and Discussion

This section reports the results orthogonal to the vertical analysis presented in the previous sections. For the purpose of this section, we cross-tabulated and grouped the data, we made comparisons between pairs of concepts of our classification framework and identified perspectives of interest.

9.1   Architectural Styles VS IoT Distribution Patterns

Here the question is, *"Which architectural style is more often used for different IoT distribution patterns?"* As shown in Table 4, (26/63) studies used the centralized layered architecture and again (26/63) based the centralized architecture on a cloud component. 4 over 11 studies that used collaborative pattern, presented their architecture in a layered style, whilst (7/11) made it based on cloud. The attention on cloud confirms the close relation between IoT and DevOps culture, and the necessity of developing a software computational core for such a system.

Table 4. Styles vs distribution patterns

IoT distr. patterns	IoT styles						
	Layered	Cloud based	SOA	Micro service	Restful	Pub/sub	ICN
Centralized (#: 58)	26	26	12	6	4	3	2
Collaborative (#: 11)	4	7	3	-	-	-	-
Connected intranets (#: 4)	3	2	-	-	-	-	-
Distributed (#: 2)	1	2	-	-	-	-	-

However, there is a clear research shortcoming on IoT distributed patterns development. The level of distribution has a direct impact on quality attributes satisfaction.

9.2   IoT Elements vs Quality Attributes

"What quality attributes need to be best satisfied for each main element of IoT?" Previous paragraph investigated on deciphering the best software architectural style for IoT. A software architectural style over another, exposes a set of specific quality attributes for the IoT system. Moreover, the wisdom of various IoT elements over the architecture is crucial to design a quality-oriented system. Six main elements of

IoT [23] along with their relevant primary studies count are: communication (55/63), sensing (55/63), computing (39/63), service (30/63), identification (27/63), and semantics (22/63). However, we made this horizontal analysis to learn what quality attributes should be focused on for each IoT element. Scalability is the most respected feature for identification element. To improve the scalability of this element, a certain design choice of identification devices can be made. Security is also in the center of attention for IoT elements, despite, interoperability is strongly tied with security and privacy in IoT.

9.3   Distribution Patterns vs Quality Attributes

Which IoT quality attributes should particularly be assured to design an appropriate IoT pattern? To answer, the horizontal analysis shows that other than security, scalability, and interoperability that are most respected; IoT distribution patterns are strongly addressing the IoT system's performance. Regarding the rapid development and extension of devices in the edge of the network, performance of IoT should be maintained in an appropriate level. Performance highly depends on the data storage and application logic distribution among edge and central servers. Fog computing is introduced to improve performance level tied with the response time.

10   Threats to Validity

According to Petersen et al. [31], the quality rating for this systematic mapping study assessed and scored as 73%. This value is the ratio of the number of actions taken in comparison to the total number of actions reported in the quality checklist. The quality score of our study is far beyond the scores obtained by existing systematic mapping studies in the literature, which have a distribution with a median of 33% and 48% as absolute maximum value. However, the threats to validity is unavoidable. Below we shortly define the main threats to validity of our study and the way we mitigated them.

External Validity: In our study, the most severe threat related to external validity may consist of having a set of primary studies that is not representative of the whole research on IoT architectural styles. We mitigated this potential threat by *(i)* following a search strategy including both automatic search and backward-forward snowballing of selected studies; *(ii)* defining a set of inclusion and exclusion criteria. Along the same lines, gray and non-English literature are not included in our research as we want to focus exclusively on the state of the art presented in high-quality scientific studies in English.

Internal Validity: It refers to the level of influence that extraneous variables may have on the design of the study. We mitigated this potential threat to validity by *(i)* rigorously defining and validating the structure of our study, *(ii)* defining our classification framework by carefully following the keywording process, *(iii)* and conducting both the vertical and horizontal analysis.

Construct Validity: It concerns the validity of extracted data with respect to the research questions. We mitigated this potential source of threats in different ways. *(i)* performing automatic search on multiple electronic databases to avoid potential biases; *(ii)* having a strong and tested search string; *(iii)* Complementing the automatic by the snowballing activity; *(iv)* rigorously screen the studies according to inclusion and exclusion criteria.

Conclusion Validity: It concerns the relationship between the extracted data and the obtained results. We mitigated potential threats to conclusion validity by applying well accepted systematic methods and processes throughout our study and documenting all of them in the excel package.

11   Conclusion

In this paper we present a systematic mapping study with the goal of classifying and identifying the domain state-of-the-art and redesign a class of IoT architectural styles respecting the philosophy and granularity of architectural patterns. Starting from over 2,300 potentially relevant studies, we applied a rigorous selection procedure resulting in 63 primary studies. The results of this study are both research and industry oriented and are intended to make a framework for future research in IoT architectural styles field. As a future work, we will assess the potential integration of existing research to an industrial level of IoT.

Acknowledgment. This research was financially supported by the Area of Advance ICT at Chalmers University of Technology. We acknowledge the support provided by the Internet of Things and People (IOTAP) Research Center at Malmö University.

References

1. https://www.ericsson.com/res/docs/2015/mobility-report/ericsson-mobility-report-nov-2015.pdf
2. http://www.cisco.com/c/r/en/us/internet-of-everything-ioe/internet-of-things-iot/index.html
3. Forbes: Internet of Things Market to Reach $267B by 2020. https://www.forbes.com/sites/louiscolumbus/2017/01/29/internet-of-things-market-to-reach-267b-by-2020/#65580872609b
4. Institute MG: Unlocking the potential of the Internet of Things. http://www.mckinsey.com/business-functions/business-technology/our-insights/the-internet-of-things-the-value-of-digitizing-the-physical-world
5. Chauhan, M.A., Muhammad, A.B., Benatallah, B.: Architecting cloud-enabled systems: a systematic survey of challenges and solutions. Softw. Pract. Exp. **47**(4), 599–644 (2017)
6. Basili, V.R., Caldiera, G., Rombach, H.D.: The goal question metric approach. In: Encyclopedia of Software Engineering. Wiley (1994)
7. Zhang, H., Babar, M.A., Tell, P.: Identifying relevant studies in software engineering. Inf. Softw. Technol. **53**(6), 625–637 (2011). https://doi.org/10.1016/j.infsof.2010.12.010

8. Chen, L., Babar, M.A., Zhang, H.: Towards an evidence-based understanding of electronic data sources. In: Proceedings of the 14th International Conference on Evaluation and Assessment in Software Engineering. EASE 2010, Swinton, UK (2010)
9. Kitchenham, B.A., Charters, S.: Guidelines for performing systematic literature reviews in software engineering (2007)
10. Syed, M.H., Fernandez, E.B., Ilyas, M.: A pattern for fog computing. In: Proceedings of the 10th Travelling Conference on Pattern Languages of Programs. ACM (2016)
11. Tyagi, N.: A reference architecture for IoT. Int. J. Comput. Eng. Appl. **10**, 19–24 (2016)
12. Roman, R., Zhou, J., Lopez, J.: On the features and challenges of security and privacy in distributed internet of things. Comput. Netw. **57**(10), 2266–2279 (2013)
13. Nunes, L.H., Estrella, J.C., Perera, C., Reiff-Marganiec, S., Botazzo Delbem, A.C.: Multi-criteria IoT resource discovery: a comparative analysis. Softw. Pract. Exp. **47**(10), 1325–1341 (2017)
14. Martins, L., Júnior, R.T., Giozza, W.F., da Costa, J.P.C.: Increasing the dependability of IoT middleware with cloud computing and microservices. In: Companion Proceedings of the10th International Conf on Utility and Cloud Computing, pp. 203–208. ACM (2017)
15. Wu, M., Lu, T.J., Ling, F.Y., Sun, J., Du, H.Y.: Research on the architecture of Internet of Things. In: 2010 3rd International Conference on Advanced Computer Theory and Engineering (ICACTE), vol. 5, pp. V5–484. IEEE (2010)
16. Khan, R., Khan, S.U., Zaheer, R., Khan, S.: Future internet: the internet of things architecture, possible applications and key challenges. In: 2012 10th International Conference on Frontiers of Information Technology (FIT), pp. 257–260. IEEE (2012)
17. Gómez Romero, C.D., Díaz Barriga, J.K., Rodríguez Molano, J.I.: Big Data Meaning in the Architecture of IoT for Smart Cities. In: Tan, Y., Shi, Y. (eds.) International Conf on Data Mining and Big Data, pp. 457–465. Springer, Cham (2016). https://doi.org/10.1007/978-3-319-40973-3_46
18. http://www.rfid-in-action.eu/cerp
19. Guth, J., Breitenbücher, U., Falkenthal, M., Leymann, F., Reinfurt. L.: Comparison of IoT platform architectures: a field study based on a reference architecture. In: Cloudification of the Internet of Things (CIoT), pp. 1–6. IEEE (2016)
20. https://azure.microsoft.com/en-us/updates/microsoft-azure-iot-reference-architecture-available/
21. Li, Z., Liang, P., Avgeriou, P.: Application of knowledge-based approaches in software architecture: a systematic mapping study. Inf. Softw. Technol. **55**(5), 777–794 (2013)
22. Paris, A., Zdun, U.: Architectural patterns revisited-a pattern language, pp. 1–39 (2005)
23. Al-Fuqaha, A., Guizani, M., Mohammadi, M., Aledhari, M., Ayyash, M.: Internet of things: a survey on enabling technologies, protocols, and applications. IEEE Commun. Surv. Tutor. **17**(4), 2347–2376 (2015)
24. Pena, P.A., Sarkar, D., Maheshwari, P.: A big-data centric framework for smart systems in the world of internet of everything. In: 2015 International Conference on Computational Science and Computational Intelligence (CSCI), pp. 306–311. IEEE (2015)
25. http://docs.huihoo.com/oracle/e-business-suite/12/doc.121/e12064/T291171T509748.htm
26. Butzin, B., Golatowski, F., Timmermann, D.: Microservices approach for the internet of things. In: 2016 IEEE 21st International Conference on Emerging Technologies and Factory Automation (ETFA), pp. 1–6. IEEE (2016)
27. Thones, J.: Microservices. IEEE Softw. **32**(1), 116 (2015)
28. Guinard, D., Trifa, V., Wilde, E.: A resource oriented architecture for the web of things. In: Internet of Things (IOT) 2010. IEEE (2010)
29. Hail, M.A., Fischer, S.: IoT for AAL: an architecture via information-centric networking. In: Globecom Workshops (GC Wkshps) IEEE, pp. 1–6. IEEE (2015)

30. Wieringa, R., Maiden, N., Mead, N., Rolland, C.: Requirements engineering paper classification and evaluation criteria: a proposal and a discussion. Requir. Eng. **11**(1), 102–107 (2006)
31. Petersen, K., Vakkalanka, S., Kuzniarz, L.: Guidelines for conducting systematic mapping studies in software engineering: an update. Inf. Softw. Technol. **64**, 1–18 (2015)
32. The set of Primary Studies can be find at the following link. https://www.dropbox.com/s/bxri9gv91sv5ttu/DE.ECSA-IoT.Style.xlsx?dl=0

ECo-IoT: An Architectural Approach for Realizing Emergent Configurations in the Internet of Things

Fahed Alkhabbas[1,2]([⊠]), Romina Spalazzese[1,2], and Paul Davidsson[1,2]

[1] Department of Computer Science and Media Technology, Malmö University,
Malmö, Sweden
{fahed.alkhabbas,romina.spalazzese,paul.davidsson}@mau.se
[2] Internet of Things and People Research Center, Malmö University,
Malmö, Sweden

Abstract. The rapid proliferation of the Internet of Things (IoT) is changing the way we live our everyday life and the society in general. New devices get connected to the Internet every day and, similarly, new IoT services and applications exploiting them are developed across a wide range of domains. The IoT environment typically is very dynamic, devices might suddenly become unavailable and new ones might appear. Similarly, users enter and/or leave the IoT environment while being interested in fulfilling their individual needs. These key aspects must be considered while designing and realizing IoT systems.

In this paper we propose ECo-IoT, an architectural approach to enable the automated formation and adaptation of Emergent Configurations (ECs) in the IoT. An EC is formed by a set of things, with their services, functionalities, and applications, to realize a user goal. ECs are adapted in response to (un)foreseen context changes e.g., changes in available things or due to changing or evolving user goals. In the paper, we describe: (i) an architecture and a process for realizing ECs; and (ii) a prototype we implemented for (iii) the validation of ECo-IoT through an IoT scenario that we use throughout the paper.

Keywords: Internet of Things · Emergent configurations
Self-adaptive systems · Software architecture

1 Introduction

The rapid proliferation of the Internet of Things (IoT) is changing the way we live and work. New things, (smart) connected objects and devices with their services, functionalities, and applications become available everyday. Leveraging such things, new IoT systems are continuously developed providing new types of services and applications in various fields such as home automation, transportation and health-care to mention a few [7,12].

© Springer Nature Switzerland AG 2018
C. E. Cuesta et al. (Eds.): ECSA 2018, LNCS 11048, pp. 86–102, 2018.
https://doi.org/10.1007/978-3-030-00761-4_6

The context of IoT systems continuously changes as things, which are possibly resource-constrained and mobile, can join at anytime or become suddenly unavailable. The high dynamicity of the context makes it hard, if not impossible, to fully specify at design time which things constitute IoT systems, which things contribute to perform what tasks, and in which order. Therefore, to enable the IoT, it should be possible to automatically form IoT systems based on dynamically discovered things and adapt the systems in response to emergent user needs and unforeseen context changes. To meet the aforementioned requirements, we exploit the concept of Emergent Configurations (ECs) to engineer IoT systems. The term EC refers to a set of things that connect and cooperate temporarily to achieve a user goal. A thing is any (smart) connected object or device, with its functionalities and services or applications [2,5].

A concrete use case that we use throughout the paper is the smart meeting room scenario presented in [2]. Imagine a person who enters an unknown smart meeting room and intends to deliver a presentation. The smart room is equipped with several things including light and temperature sensors, curtains and light actuators, a smart screen, and a smart projector. The user expresses her/his goal to deliver a presentation e.g., via an application installed on her/his smartphone. The goal is interpreted and a set of suitable things are automatically chosen to form an EC which satisfies it. For instance, the EC constituents could be the smartphone, the smart projector, the light sensor and the curtains actuator. The smartphone connects and streams the presentation to the projector which illustrates it while curtains are closed automatically due to the high light levels detected by the light sensor. Suppose that, during the presentation, the projector turns off suddenly. The failure is automatically detected and the user is proposed to continue the presentation using the available smart screen.

ECo-IoT consists of: (1) a process which enables the automated formation and adaptation of ECs in response to dynamic context changes; (2) an architecture which enables the realization of ECs and refines the abstract architecture presented in [2]. We also present a first prototype implementing both the architecture and the process and validate the feasibility of ECo-IoT through the smart meeting room scenario. In this paper, we *assume* that: (i) the user goal specification and interpretation process is already performed and correctly terminated, i.e., we take as input a decomposed goal (we plan to investigate this as future work); (ii) ECs are formed, enacted and adapted within well-defined spatial boundaries: ECs goals are achieved within locations e.g., room, building. Consequently, the number of things involved in forming and adapting an EC is not expected to be massive. This notably mitigates the well-known IoT scalability problem [12]. (iii) ECs are realized to achieve goals within non-critical time constraints: we envision that ECs are realized within the timescale of seconds; (iv) ECs are formed and enacted at runtime: ECs are realized to achieve user goals expressed at runtime; (v) ECs constituents share a context ontology.

The remainder of this paper is organized as follows. Section 2 discusses related works. Section 3 presents an overview about ECs. Section 4 introduces the ECo-IoT approach. Section 5 presents the prototype implementation. Section 6 presents an experiment which validates the feasibility of the approach. Finally, Sect. 7 concludes the paper and outlines future work directions.

2   Related Work

In the context of architectures, a number of works have been proposed. The IoT-A project presented a service-based reference model architecture for the IoT [8]. The architecture we propose in this paper is compliant with the IoT reference architecture and refines the process management and the service organization layers presented in the reference architecture functional view. Kramer et al. [11] proposed an architectural reference model to support automatic (re)configuration of self-managed systems. The model relies on a set of predefined plans to achieve system goals. When new goals are introduced, new plans are generated in a timely consuming process. Aura is an architectural framework designed to enable users to continue their tasks in mobile contexts where they can move between different environments and to adapt progressing computations apropos the dynamic availability of services [22]. User tasks are precompiled at design time and appropriate services are (re-)assigned at runtime. Another architecture which adopts a similar approach is SIA, a service oriented architecture designed to enable the integration of the IoT in enterprise services [18]. In SIA, business processes are modelled at design time using an extended version of BPEL which allows dynamic assignment of services during the processes execution. Although services can be (re)assigned at runtime, specifying execution flows at design time limits systems flexibility as updating execution flows automatically, in response to unforeseen context changes or emergent user needs, is not supported in both Aura and SIA. Dar et al. [10] proposed a high level service oriented architecture designed to enable adaptive service composition for the IoT. The reconfiguration of the composed services is performed at design time through user interfaces. Thus, automated adaptations in response unforeseen context changes are not supported.

Hussein et al. [14] proposed a model-driven approach to enable IoT systems to adapt at runtime. A set of system states and adaptation triggers are modelled at design time based on anticipated context changes. When an adaptation is triggered, the system is switched from one state to another based on the designed models. Ciortea et al. [1] proposed an agent-based approach for composing goal-driven IoT mashups. IoT things are modelled offline as agents or artefacts according to their capabilities. Agents rely on predefined plans which specify how their goals are achieved. In cases where goals cannot be achieved individually, agents interact and cooperate, in a network like system called STN, to compose IoT mashups which achieve the goals. Marrella et al. [15] presented SmartPM, a framework for enabling automated adaptation of processes using situation calculus and AI planning. Processes are defined by designers using a graphical editor. Events and exceptions which disrupt the processes enactment are automatically detected and recovery procedures are automatically generated to adapt faulty processes. Seigcr et al. [21] proposed another framework for enabling workflow-based Cyber-physical Systems to self adapt. The framework utilizes the MAPE-K loop notion to automatically adapt workflows in response to detected failures. Relying on predefined plans in [1], process (or workflows) in [15,21] or models of possible system states and adaptation triggers in [14] limit systems flexibility as it is hard to foresee at design time IoT systems constituents in dynamic and mobile contexts.

The MobIoT is a service-oriented middleware designed to address the heterogeneity, interoperability and scalability in mobile IoT contexts [19]. User requests are achieved by applying an ontological-based composition approach which exploits the notation of probabilistic registration and lookup mechanisms. The approach addresses specific types of requests related to real world measurement in the physics and chemistry domains. Mayer et al. [20] proposed an approach to achieve user goals by dynamically composing service-based IoT mashups. IoT things are described by means of semantic services. User goals are described in a machine understandable way and can be expressed via a user interface. Given the semantic description of the user goal and a list of services, a plan which comprises a set of services is generated to achieve the goal. The proposed approach supports adaptation apropos the dynamic availability of services. Compared to our approach, we consider additional intrinsic contextual properties of IoT things including connectivity status, operational status (i.e., on/off) and if they rely on batteries. In addition, exploiting the notion of events, our approach possesses more effective reasoning capabilities about performed adaptations.

3   Emergent Configurations Background

In [2], we presented an abstract architecture for ECs describing how they are automatically formed and adapted. In this section, we first overview the proposed architecture, then refine it by presenting the ECo-IoT. The abstract architecture, illustrated in Fig. 1, comprises a set of components. The *User Agent* (UA) is an application running on one of the existing smart devices (e.g., smartphone) and

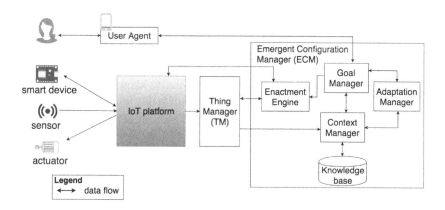

Fig. 1. A high level architecture for realizing ECs

used to enable users to interact with the system. The *Emergent Configuration Manager* (ECM) is responsible for automatically forming ECs to achieve user goals (if possible) and for adapting ECs in response to runtime context changes. The *Thing Manager* (TM) is responsible for discovering and registering available IoT things, monitoring their statuses and reporting any changes to the ECM. Finally, a *set of (IoT) things* which, following indications of the ECM, communicate and collaborate to realize ECs. The ECM comprises the following subcomponent:

(i) *Goal Manager*: is responsible for interpreting user goals and forming ECs which achieve them;

(ii) *Adaptation Manager*: is responsible for adapting ECs in response to context changes. ECs are adapted by executing the Monitor-Analyze-Plan-Execute plus Knowledge (MAPE-K) loop -better described in Sect. 4.1;

(iii) *Context Manager*: is responsible for maintaining ECs context;

(iv) *Enactment Engine*: is responsible for enacting ECs by commanding or requesting ECs constituents to perform functionalities in specific orders;

(v) *System Knowledge Base*: is the container of the context of ECs.

In this paper, we mainly focus on the realization of the ECM component while the realization of the TM and UA are planned for future works.

4   The ECo-IoT Approach

In this section, we present the `ECo-IoT` approach for realizing ECs. More specifically, we present a process and a refined architecture developed to enable the automatic formation and adaptation of ECs.

4.1   The ECo-IoT Process

Figure 2 shows the `ECo-IoT` process[1] for enabling the automated formation and adaptation of ECs. The *EC formation process* starts with a user interacting with the goal manager (via the user agent) to express her/his goal by sharing a goal description. The goal manager expects that the shared description comprises (at least) a goal type (e.g., deliver presentation) and spatial boundaries (e.g., a specific room). After analyzing the goal description, the goal manager requests the context manager to provide the semantic knowledge about the goal type and the context of the specified spatial boundaries including, for instance, available things and their capabilities. In cases where the goal type or the spatial boundaries are not known to the context manager, the goal interpreter engages in a complex process which involves interactions with the user to better analyze her/his goal description. It also interacts with the user to identify e.g., her/his

---

[1] For presentation purposes, in Fig. 2, we omit some details. The process is modelled using the standard Business Process Model and Notation (BPMN) http://www. bpmn.org.

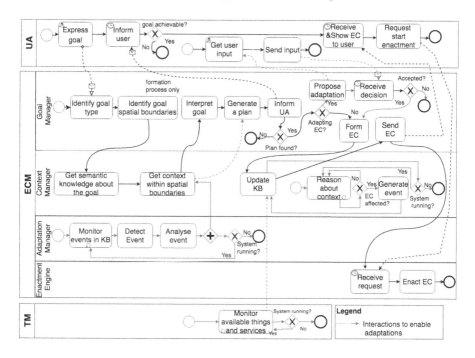

Fig. 2. ECs formation and adaptation process

preferences (when applicable). Based on the goal interpretation and the retrieved context, the goal manager tries to generate a plan which achieves the user goal when enacted. The user is informed whether or not the requested goal is achievable. If a plan is found, the goal manager forms an EC and forwards it to the context manager which updates knowledge base. Afterwards, the goal manager sends the EC to the user agent which illustrates needed info to the user (e.g., EC constituents). Then, the user agent requests the enactment engine to enact the EC. The user goal interpretation and ECs enactment processes are out of the scope if this paper and planned for future works.

To enable the automated adaptation of ECs, the *EC adaptation process* exploits the notion of Monitor-Analyze-Plan-Execute plus Knowledge (MAPE-K) loop adopted from the field of Self-adaptive Systems. In general, ECs are adapted due to: (i) changes in available things and their status; (ii) evolving user goals. Several components *monitor* various parts of the context. The thing manager continuously *monitors* available things and their status. It mainly *monitors* things connectivity status, operational status (i.e., on/off), locations and battery levels (when applicable). The thing manager periodically reports detected changes to the context manager which updates the knowledge base. The context manager continuously *monitors* the context and *analyzes* if context changes affect any running EC. If an EC is affected, the context manager generates events about the detected changes and updates the knowledge base. In this paper, we consider the following types of events: (1) an IoT thing is disconnected; (2) an IoT thing is no longer situated within the spatial boundaries of an EC which comprises it; (3) an IoT thing is running out of battery. As can be noted, these events model only the loss of IoT things. We plan to consider events which model the availability of new things and evolving user goals in our future work.

The adaptation manager continuously *monitors* events in the knowledge base. When an event is detected, the adaptation manager *analyzes* it and decides a proper adaptation procedure. Based on the detected event type, adaptation procedures can be *reactive* or *proactive*. Reactive adaptations procedures are applied in response to events of type (1) and (2), while proactive adaptations are applied in response to events of type (3). An example of a reactive adaptation is to propose the user to continue the presentation using an available smart screen after the sudden loss of the used smart projector. An example of a proactive adaptation is to propose the user to switch to an available laptop to stream the presentation as the battery level of the used smartphone is less than a specific threshold and expected to turn off soon. The number of proactive events that can be generated about a thing battery level is configurable in order not to overwhelm the user with many messages. The goal manager then tries to find a new plan that maintains the achievement of the user goal. If a plan is found, the goal manager proposes the adaptation to the user and asks for her/his approval. If the user accepts the proposal, the goal manager forms a new version of the EC, changes the status of the former version and links both ECs via the event which triggered the adaptation process. The status of an EC is *ready for execution* when it is newly formed, *in execution* when it is being enacted, *adapted* in case it is adapted, *enacted successfully* in case it achieves the goal and *failed* in case it cannot be adapted to maintain the goal achievement. The EC versioning subprocess enables the reasoning about all performed adaptations. The process then continues as described in EC formation process.

4.2   A Refined Architecture for Realizing ECs

Figure 3 illustrates a refined architecture based on the abstract architecture and the ECs realization requirements formulated in [2]. The architecture also complies with the well known architectural design principles such as separation of

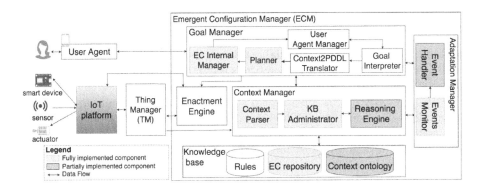

Fig. 3. A refined architecture for realizing ECs

concerns and modularity. In the following, we describe in more details the ECM subcomponents which we mainly focused on for the realization of ECs in this paper.

4.3 Managers Components

Goal Manager. This component comprises five subcomponents responsible for forming ECs which achieve user goals when enacted. The *User Agent Manager* is responsible for interacting with the User Agent. The *Goal Interpreter* is responsible for analyzing goals descriptions in the context of their spatial boundaries. The *Planner* is responsible for generating (if possible) plans which achieve the goals when enacted. It supports the system to cope with dynamic (unforeseen) context changes and to utilize heterogeneous IoT things. Generated plans comprise a set of actions (i.e., tasks) which might have different complexity levels based on the autonomy of available things. The *Context2PDDL Translator* is responsible for generating files needed for the planning process by translating goals interpretations and the context of identified spatial boundaries to the Planning Domain Definition Language (PDDL) [6].

The *EC Internal Manager* is responsible for updating the user agent manager about ECs formation and adaptation processes, instantiating ECs when plans are found by the planner, maintaining their statuses and versioning them when they are adapted.

Context Manager. This component comprises three subcomponents responsible for maintaining and reasoning about ECs context. The *Context Parser* is responsible for receiving and parsing information about available things and their statuses. This information is forwarded to the *Knowledge Base Administrator* which is responsible for manipulating the knowledge base. The *Reasoning Engine* comprises two subcomponents, the *Semantic Reasoner* and the *Rule-based Engine*. The semantic reasoner is responsible for querying the context ontology and inferring semantic knowledge. The rule-based engine is responsible for monitoring the KB and generating events when the conditions of the rules defined in the rules repository are met.

Adaptation Manager. This is an event-based component which comprises two subcomponents responsible for adapting ECs in response to context changes. The *Event Monitor* is responsible for detecting events created by the reasoning engine. The *Event Handler* is responsible for analyzing how detected events affect running ECs and for triggering proper adaptation processes when needed.

4.4 Knowledge Base Component

Context Ontology. This component contains the semantic representation of ECs context. The context of IoT systems can be represented by various means such as graphical based modelling, markup scheme based modelling, key-value based modelling and ontology based modelling to mention a few [3]. Ontologies are composed of a set of concepts represented by classes, relations represented by properties and concept instances represented by individuals. They are considered among the most suitable techniques to maintain systems contexts [3,23]. Reasons for this include: their expressiveness, representation of shared understanding of knowledge among involved parties and the availability of several tools and reasoning engines which support their usage [3,17,24]. Figure 4 illustrates the main classes of the ECs context ontology.

Fig. 4. Main classes of the ECs context ontology

The *owl:Thing* class is the superclass for all classes in the ontology. The *IoT-Thing* class models the types of IoT things supported by the system. It has three subclasses, *Sensor*, *Actuator* and *SmartDevice*. The *Service* class models external services which can be consumed by the system. For instance, a service which can be used to convert a presentation to a format supported by a smartphone. The *User* class models system users. The *Goal* class models the types of goals which are supported by the system. The exploration of this class is out of the scope of this paper and is planned for future works. The *Capability* class models the types of functionalities provided by things types. Functionalities types are modelled as subclasses e.g., senseLightLevel. The *Event* class models specific types of events in the context of ECs. It has three subclasses *GoalBasedEvents*, *AvailabilityEvents* and *UnavailabilityEvents*. The UnavailabilityEvents class has three subclasses which model the events described in Sect. 4.1. The GoalBasedEvents and AvailabilityEvents classes model respectively events related to evolving user goals and the availability of new things. The exploration of these classes is planned for future works. The *GeographicalSpace* class models available locations. The structure of this class is adopted from the SOUPA space ontology [4].

The ontology also comprises object properties which model the following relations: (1) users have goals and locations; (2) IoT things have capabilities and locations; (3) services have capabilities; (4) IoT things are connectable; (5) IoT things are connected; (6) Geographical spaces have sub spaces. The ontology also comprises a set of data properties which model: (1) things operational status; (2) things connectivity status; (3) if a thing relies on batteries or not; (4) a thing battery level when applicable; (5) capabilities preconditions and effects written in the PDDL language; (6) timestamps of triggered events.

Our approach requires that a developer models offline the mentioned context ontology. However, note that several parts of the knowledge (e.g., things individuals, locations, battery levels, connectivity statuses, etc.) can be *automatically* populated from the data sent by the thing manager with the support of an IoT platform. For instance, the Amazon AWS-IoT platform[2] supports the management and runtime monitoring of registered things. Geographical spaces (i.e., locations) can be populated automatically by consuming services in a smart building. Still, developers need to extend the ontology when introducing new types of things and defining things capabilities.

EC Repository. This component is a container of active and archived ECs. An EC comprises a user goal and its' spatial boundaries, a set of things and capabilities, the plan generated to achieve the goal, the EC version and status.

Rules repository. This component comprises business rules which are application specific and generic rules which are required to realize ECs. An example of a business rule is to lower light levels in a room if a presentation is ongoing via a projector. An example of a generic rule is that two things are connectable if they have Wifi capabilities.

5   Prototype Implementation

In this section, we present some implementation[3] details about the prototype we developed to validate the feasibility of ECo-IoT. The prototype is implemented in Java (version 1.8) and integrates the OWLAPI (version 5.1.3)[4] with the JavaFF planner (version 2.1.5)[5]. The context ontology is represented by OWL [16] and the EC repository is realized by a relational PostgreSQL database.

5.1   The Knowledge Base

The Context Ontology. Let us consider that "room19" is a smart meeting room which contains a set of IoT things. Tables 1 and 2 illustrate (partially) how the available things are modelled in the context ontology. As capabilities preconditions and effects are modelled in PDDL, they are explored in Sect. 5.4. We created an individual of the user class and set the user location to "room19".

Table 1. Representation of some object properties in the context ontology

Individual	Individual class	hasCapability	Capability class	hasLocation
smart_projector_a	SmartProjector	illustrate_presentation_a	IllustratePresentation	room19
smart_screen_b	SmartScreen	illustrate_presentation_b	IllustratePresentation	room19
smart_phone_c	SmartPhone	stream_presentation_c	StreamPresentation	room19
laptop_d	Laptop	stream_presentation_d, illustrate_presentation_d	StreamPresentation, IllustratePresentation	room19

---

[2] https://aws.amazon.com/iot/.

[3] The prototype code is available at https://github.com/iotap-center/eco-iot.

[4] http://owlapi.sourceforge.net.

[5] http://personal.strath.ac.uk/david.pattison/#software.

Table 2. Representation of some data properties in the context ontology

Individual	Individual class	isConnected	hasStatus	reliesOnBattery	hasBatteryLevel
smart_projector_a	SmartProjector	True	False	False	N/A
smart_screen_b	SmartScreen	True	False	False	N/A
smart_phone_c	SmartPhone	True	True	True	20%
laptop_d	Laptop	True	False	True	60%

5.2 The Context Manager

To enable the ECM to receive status updates about available things from the thing manager, we implemented the *context parser* component based on the Publish/Subscribe model and subscribed it to topics defined at the simulated thing manager. The KB administrator utilizes the OWLAPI to maintain the knowledge represented in the context ontology.

To dynamically generate events, we implemented a thread which periodically checks the EC context ontology for new changes in the status of available things (see Sect. 4.1). We plan to integrate a rule-based engine to enable the dynamic manipulations of rules at runtime. This will enable developers and end users to define business rules at runtime to better configure their smart environments.

5.3 The Adaptation Manager

In this first prototype implementation, the *event monitor* is implemented as a thread which continuously checks if new events are created in the KB. The *event handler* implements the part of adaptation process which handles the events detected by the event monitor.

5.4 The Goal Manager

In the implemented prototype, we integrated the JavaFF planner which is an open source planner based on [9]. The JavaFF planner requires two PDDL files to generate a plan, namely, the domain file and the problem file. For the prototype, we have manually defined both files. We plan to implement the Context2PDDL component to automatically generate these files. The domain file comprises three basic parts, namely, types, predicates and actions. Types represent the hierarchy of information structure in the planning domain. More specifically, they are the translation of the classes hierarchy in the context ontology. For instance, as illustrated below, smart devices, sensors and actuators are sub-types of the type IoT-Thing.

```
(:types ... smartDevice sensor actuator - IoT-Thing ...
```

Predicates are the result of translating data and object properties. For instance, as illustrated below, the ontology data property *hasStatus* is translated to the hasStatus predicate in the domain file. The symbol ? is used to declare a variable (e.g., ?t) of the type which directly follows it (e.g., IoT-Thing).

```
(:predicates ... (hasStatus ?t - IoT-Thing ?st - status) ...
```

Finally, actions represent the translation of things capabilities modelled in the ontology. We recall that capabilities data properties are already specified in strings that are described in PDDL. As illustrated in below, actions are described by parameters, preconditions and effects. Parameters of a capability are represented by variables. Preconditions specify the conditions needed to perform actions. For example, it is only possible to turn on a thing if it is already turned off. Effects represent changes in the state of the world if actions are executed successfully. For instance, executing successfully the action defined below results in turning on a specific IoT thing.

```
(:action turnThingOn
    :parameters (?thing - IoTThing)
    :precondition (hastatus ?thing off)
    :effect (hastatus ?thing on))
)
```

The planning problem file comprises three basic parts, namely, objects, initial states and desired states. As illustrated below, objects represent instances of the types defined in the domain file. The set of instantiated objects in the problem file is the same set of individuals in the context ontology.

```
(:objects ... smart_projector_a - smartProjector...
```

The initial state of the world is a set of predicates representing a particular situation. As illustrated below, the status of the smart_projector_a object is *false* meaning that the smart projector is turned off.

```
(:init ...(hasStatus smart_projector_a false)...
```

Desired states are described by means of predicates which specify desired changes in the state of the world. Desired states represent the translation of goals interpretations. The desired state in the smart meeting room scenario is illustrated below. The *EC internal manager* is implemented to perform its responsibility described in Sect. 4.1.

```
(:goal (illustrate smartProjector1  presentation1))
```

6   Experimenting ECo-IoT

In this section we validate the feasibility of our approach by putting in action the prototype we implemented. We recall that we already realized a number of the ECo-IoT components in this first prototype, as shown in Fig. 3. The additional effort is planned for future work. This means that here we validate the feasibility of ECo-IoT while gaining initial insights about the performances of a subset of it.

6.1   Forming ECs

We assume that the user has expressed her/his goal to be "deliver a presentation in room19" and that the goal is received by the goal manager which derived the goal type (i.e., deliver a presentation) and the spatial boundaries (i.e., room19). In the current implementation, the goal interpretation process is prespecified and is dedicated to run the smart meeting room scenario. The goal manager queried context manager about the (capabilities of) things which are situated in room19. The context manager responded with the set of individuals presented in the Tables 1 and 2. We envision that the output of the goal interpretation correlates decomposed goals with available capabilities. More specifically, to specify which of the existing devices can store a presentation file, can stream it and which of them can illustrate it.

To specify where the presentation file is stored, the goal interpreter interacted with the user through the user agent manager and the user agent. In addition, it asked the user about the preferred device to stream and illustrate the presentation by highlighting possible options. In the current implementation, the user interacted with the goal interpreter through the console. The user selected her/his smartphone as the source of the presentation and the available smart projector as the preferred illustration device. Based on that, the plan illustrated below was generated to achieve the user goal. First, the thing manager turns the projector on and connects it to the user smartphone. Then, the smartphone streams the presentation to the smart projector which illustrates it. The formation process then continued as described in Sect. 4.1.

```
(turn_on_thing smart_projector_a)
(connect_things smart_phone_c smart_projector_a)
(stream_presentation presentation1 smart_phone_c smart_projector_a)
(illustrate_presentation smart_projector_a presentation1)
```

6.2   Adapting ECs

To simulate the enactment of the EC formed in Sect. 6.1, we updated manually the system knowledge base simulating the supposed execution of the generated plan. For instance, we changed the status of smart_projector_a to be true meaning that the smart projector is turned on. As already mentioned, this process will be automated when the thing manager and the enactment engine are realized. Then, we published two messages to the context manager to trigger *reactive* and *proactive* adaptation processes. We illustrate one scenario per each category. The first message stated that smart_projector_a is disconnected. The message was received by the context manager which generated an event that was detected by the adaptation manager. In response, the adaptation manager triggered the adaptation process which generated a plan that substitutes smart_projector_a with smart_screen_b. The adaptation was proposed to the user (via a printed message on the console) and the EC was versioned properly after the user accepted the proposal.

The second message stated that the battery level of smart_phone_c is 12% which was less than the configured threshold to trigger the proactive adaptation process. The context manager automatically created an event which was detected by the adaptation manager. The adaptation manager triggered the proactive adaptation process as described in Sect. 4.1. The user was proposed to switch to laptop_d to continue the presentation. The user accepted the proposed adaptation by communicating via the console and the EC was versioned properly.

6.3   Discussion

The dynamicity of IoT contexts and the involvement of the human in the loop require ECs to be responsive. Designing ECs to be goal-oriented, supports meeting this requirement. Indeed, specifying the goal spatial boundaries notably mitigates the well-known scalability issue in the IoT [12]. The implemented prototype presents an evidence about the feasibility of the ECo-IoT approach. Although some components are not implemented yet, they do not seem to require intensive resources for performing their responsibilities. The semantic model of the context ontology, having the goal ontology defined, is expected to reduce the complexity of the goal interpretation process. Although it is required that the context ontology be modelled by developers, several parts of the operational (dynamic) knowledge can be populated automatically as described briefly in Sect. 4.4. From a user perspective, we envision that the user needs only to express her/his goal without being concerned about how available things can achieve it. In addition, the goal interpretation process should not overwhelm the user with many requests. We plan to investigate these aspects in our future work.

In Sect. 5.4, we explained the mapping between the PDDL files structures and the context parameters. The process of translating context to PDDL is not expected to be computationally complex as we do not expect to deal with a huge number of things due to goals spatial boundaries and to the responsiveness of the context retrieval process (see below). The process of creating events is not complex either, as it creates events when rules preconditions are met. Likewise, the process of detecting events is not complex as it is not more than continuously querying the KB for new events. The process of enacting ECs may impose some complexity in cases where ECs aim to achieve contradicting goals, when ECs compete on available resources or when ECs are formed, enacted or adapted in uncertain contexts.

The fast retrieval of the context contributes to the responsiveness of the system. Therefore, we conducted an experiment to evaluate the knowledge retrieval process when the number of individuals in the context ontology increases. Figure 5a illustrates the response time of a query which retrieves an increasing number of fully specified things situated within specific spatial boundaries. Things were automatically instantiated, specified and persisted. As can be noted, it is evident that the KB administrator scales well when the number of individuals in the ontology increases.

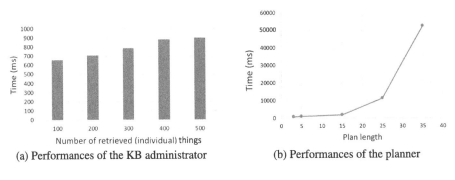

(a) Performances of the KB administrator   (b) Performances of the planner

Fig. 5. Performances of the KB administrator and the planner

The planner is another key component which is involved whenever an EC is formed or adapted. AI planning is well known for being a resource intensive process [13]. Therefore, we conducted an experiment to evaluate how the planner performs in a smart room that has 200 IoT things which possess 800 capabilities on average. Note that these numbers do not represent an upper bound or a limitation of the approach. To setup the experiment, the planning domain file was automatically generated. To simulate realistic conditions, several initial states were declared, many generated actions were complex with respect to their preconditions and effects and goals were achievable by multiple possible plans. Figure 5b illustrates that the planer responds in the order of a few seconds when generated plans comprise up to 24 actions. All experiments were conducted on a dual-core CPU running at 2.7 GHz, with 16 Gb memory.

In the future, we expect to have some additional computational complexity from the components to be developed. In order to mitigate the complexity, we plan to work on proposing intelligent and efficient goal interpretation techniques that reduce, as much as possible, domain and problem spaces of AI planning processes.

7   Conclusion and Future Work

New things get continuously connected and embedded everywhere. This gives to the Internet of Things (IoT) an increasingly important role in all aspects of our society. Devising concrete architectures and approaches is then a needed enabler to support the effective use of IoT systems. In this paper, we presented the ECo-IoT approach to enable the automated formation and adaptation of Emergent Configurations while dealing with realistic IoT scenarios including runtime changes. We also described our first prototype for the validation of ECo-IoT in terms of its feasibility and performances of some key components.

Some future directions we plan to investigate include: devising a suitable goal language; exploring (intelligent) processes and techniques for effective and efficient goal interpretation; investigating automated mechanisms supporting rule-based reasoning; handling situations where concurrent ECs compete on available resources or aim to achieve contradicting goals; proposing mechanisms to enable the automated adaptation of ECs in response to evolving user goals and the availability of new things; devising mechanisms to enable the formation, enactment and adaptation of ECs in uncertain contexts. Additionally, we aim at: extending the prototype by implementing e.g., a thing manager exploiting an IoT platform, rule engine, a Context2PDDL translator, a goal interpreter, and an enactment engine; conducting trade off analysis among existing IoT deployment models to support decision making about the ECo-IoT deployment; and performing a more extensive evaluation.

Acknowledgment. This work is partially financed by the Knowledge Foundation through the Internet of Things and People research profile (Malmö University, Sweden).

References

1. Ciortea, A., Boissier, O., Zimmermann, A., Florea, A. M.: Responsive decentralized composition of service mashups for the internet of things. In: 6th ACM International Conference on the Internet of Things, pp. 53–61. ACM (2016)
2. Alkhabbas, F., Spalazzese, R., Davidsson, P.: Architecting emergent configurations in the internet of things. In: IEEE International Conference on Software Architecture (ICSA), pp. 221–224. IEEE (2017)
3. Perera, C., Zaslavsky, A., Christen, P., Georgakopoulos, D.: Context aware computing for the internet of things: a survey. IEEE Commun. Surv. Tutor. **16**, 414–454 (2014)
4. Chen, H., Perich, F., Finin, T., Joshi, A.: SOUPA: standard ontology for ubiquitous and pervasive applications. In: 1st Annual International Conference on Mobile and Ubiquitous Systems: Networking and Services, pp. 258–267. IEEE (2004)
5. Ciccozzi, F., Spalazzese, R.: MDE4IoT: supporting the internet of things with model-driven engineering. In: Badica, C., et al. (eds.) Intelligent Distributed Computing X. SCI, vol. 678, pp. 67–76. Springer, Cham (2017). https://doi.org/10.1007/978-3-319-48829-5_7
6. McDermott, D., et al.: PDDL - the planning domain definition language (1998)
7. Miorandi, D., Sicari, S., De Pellegrini, F., Chlamtac, I.: Internet of things: vision, applications and research challenges. Ad Hoc Netw. **10**, 1497–1516 (2012)
8. Bauer, M.: IoT reference architecture. In: Bassi, A., et al. (eds.) Enabling Things to Talk, pp. 163–211. Springer, Heidelberg (2013). https://doi.org/10.1007/978-3-642-40403-0_8
9. Hoffmann, J., Nebel, B.: The FF planning system: fast plan generation through heuristic search. J. Artif. Intell. Res. **14**, 253–302 (2001)
10. Dar, K., Taherkordi, A., Rouvoy, R., Eliassen, F.: Adaptable service composition for very-large-scale internet of things systems. In: 8th Middleware Doctoral Symposium, p. 2. ACM (2011)
11. Kramer, J., Magee, J.: Self-managed systems: an architectural challenge. In: Future of Software Engineering, pp. 259–268. IEEE Computer Society (2007)
12. Atzori, L., Iera, A., Morabito, G.: The internet of things: a survey. Comput. Netw. **54**, 2787–2805 (2010)
13. Ghallab, M., Nau, D., Traverso, P.: Automated Planning: Theory and Practice. Elsevier, New York (2004)

14. Hussein, M., Li, S., Radermacher, A.: Model-driven development of adaptive IoT systems. In: 4th International Workshop on Interplay of Model-Driven and Component-Based Software Engineering, pp. 20–27 (2017)
15. Marrella, A., Mecella, M., Sardina, S.: Intelligent Process Adaptation in the SmartPM System. ACM Trans. Intell. Syst. Technol. (TIST) **8**, 25 (2017)
16. McGuinness, D.L., Van Harmelen, F. et al.: OWL web ontology language overview. W3C recommendation (2004)
17. Noy, N.F., McGuinness, D.L. et al.: Ontology development 101: a guide to creating your first ontology. Stanford Knowledge Systems (2001)
18. Spiess, P., et al.: SOA-based integration of the internet of things in enterprise services. In: IEEE International Conference on Web Services, pp. 968–975. IEEE (2009)
19. Hachem, S., Pathak, A., Issarny, V.: Service-oriented middleware for the mobile internet of things: a scalable solution. In: IEEE GLOBECOM: Global Communications Conference. IEEE (2014)
20. Mayer, S., Verborgh, R., Kovatsch, M., Mattern, F.: Smart configuration of smart environments. IEEE Trans. Autom. Sci. Eng. **13**, 1247–1255 (2016)
21. Seiger, R., Huber, S., Heisig, P., Aßmann, U.: Toward a framework for self-adaptive workflows in cyber-physical systems. Softw. Syst. Model. **17**, 1–18 (2017)
22. Sousa, J.P., Garlan, D.: Aura: an architectural framework for user mobility in ubiquitous computing environments. In: Bosch, J., Gentleman, M., Hofmeister, C., Kuusela, J. (eds.) Software Architecture. ITIFIP, vol. 97, pp. 29–43. Springer, Boston, MA (2002). https://doi.org/10.1007/978-0-387-35607-5_2
23. Strang, T., Linnhoff-Popien, C.: A Context modeling survey. In: 1st International Workshop on Advanced Context Modelling, Reasoning and Management, Ubi-Comp (2004)
24. Wang, X.H., Zhang, D.Q., Gu, T., Pung, H.K.: Ontology based context modeling and reasoning using OWL. In: 2nd IEEE Annual Conference on Pervasive Computing and Communications Workshops, pp. 18–22. IEEE (2004)

A Catalogue of Architectural Decisions for Designing IIoT Systems

Somayeh Malakuti[1(✉)], Thomas Goldschmidt[2], and Heiko Koziolek[1]

[1] ABB Corporate Research Center, Ladenburg, Germany
{somayeh.malakuti,heiko.koziolek}@de.abb.com
[2] ABB Digital, Ladenburg, Germany
thomas.goldschmidt@de.abb.com

Abstract. Designing Industrial IoT (IIoT) systems enforces new sets of architectural decisions on software/system architects. Although a rich set of materials for architecting enterprise software systems exist, there is a lack of reference documents on architectural decisions and alternatives that architects face to design IIoT systems. Based on our experience in designing IIoT systems in various domains such as process automation, discrete manufacturing and building automation, we provide a catalogue of architectural decisions, their impacts on the quality attributes of systems, and technology options to realize each design alternative.

Keywords: IIoT systems · Architecture design · Cloud platform

1 Introduction

In designing software systems, including Industrial IoT (IIoT) systems, architects face various design alternatives, which have different impacts on the desired quality attributes of the target system. Unlike enterprise software systems [1], there is a lack of reference documents on architectural decisions and alternatives that architects face when designing IIoT systems. There have been however several attempts to define reference architectures [2–4] and design patterns for IoT systems [5]. Although in these reference architectures and patterns, certain architectural decisions are already made, architects still face several alternatives and decisions to derive concrete architectures from them and to realize the patterns. This paper presents a set of architectural decisions, which we collected based on our experience in five IIoT projects in the domains of process automation, building automation and IIoT platforms.

As depicted in Fig. 1, in this paper we consider three layers in IIoT systems: *Asset*, *Platform* and *Application*. Assets are constituents of an IIoT system, which must interact with each other and with the rest of the system towards fulfilling the system's goals. These are physical devices such as motors and controllers, as well as software entities such as an application running on a robot.

S. Malakuti was partially supported by German Federal Ministry of Education and Research in the scope of the BaSys 4.0 project (01—S16022).

C. E. Cuesta et al. (Eds.): ECSA 2018, LNCS 11048, pp. 103–111, 2018.
https://doi.org/10.1007/978-3-030-00761-4_7

A core part of an IIoT system is the platform on which it is built. The IIoT platform can be extracted as common services/components that are independent of a specific application. This may include communication paradigms, APIs, security concepts, data models, cloud environments and even hardware components such as communication gateways.

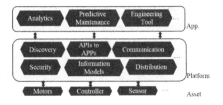

Fig. 1. Three layers in IIoT systems

Various applications such as data analytics and predictive maintenance applications can be developed on top. A special class of applications in industrial systems is the engineering tools, which will be considered in this paper. These tools offer features to, for example, define the structure of a plant, define location of devices, configure devices, etc.

Category	Decision	Alternatives	Quality Attributes	Example Technology Options
Asset	Information model content	Standardized	+Interoperability, -Functional Suitability	FDI, AutomationML, PLCOpen
		Proprietary	-Interoperability, +Functional Suitability	Company-specific
		Raw	-Interoperability	OPC UA DI
		Semantically augmented	+Interoperability	ecl@ss, CDD, OWL
	Information acquisition	Manual	-Efficiency, -Maintainability	Industrial engineering tools
		(semi-) Automatic	+Efficiency, +Maintainability	mDNS, UPnP, DHCP
	Information model deployment	Embedded in Asset	+Interoperability,+/-Performance, -Security	Embedded OPC UA Server, Plain objects, Docker
		On Edge	+Interoperability,+Security,-Performance	Aggregating OPC UA server
		On Cloud	+Interoperability,+Security,-Performance	GraphDb, DocumentDB, SQL, WebAPI
Platform	Discovery of assets on-premise	Manual asset configuration	-Maintainability, -Efficiency	Connectivity engineering tool
		Auto-discovery of assets	+Maintainability, +Efficiency	UPnP, mDNS
	Discovery of cloud endpoints	Manual configuration of cloud endpoints	-Maintainability, -Efficiency, -Availability	Connectivity engineering tool
		Auto-discovery of cloud endpoints	+Maintainability, +Availability, +Efficiency	Azure DPS, AWS Registry & Device Gateway
	Communication towards edge	Generic protocol support	+Maintainability, +Compatibility, +Interoperability, -Performance	OPC UA, oneM2M
		Domain-specific protocol	-Maintainability, +Compatibility, -Interoperability, -Performance	Adapter hosted in Docker
	Communication towards cloud	Message-oriented	+Scalability,+Performance	MQTT, AMQP
		Transaction-oriented	-Scalability,-Performance	AWS CloudFront, Azure Service Fabric
	Interface-level interoperability	Standardized	+Interoperability,-Functional Suitability	MIMOSA
		Custom	-Interoperability,+Functional Suitability	REST/Swagger, OPC UA
	Information model interoperability	Common model	+Interoperability,-Functional Suitability	OPC UA
		Peer mapping	-Interoperability,+Functional Suitability	Custom service implementation
Engineering Tools	User experience and mobility	Desktop-based engineering client	+Useability, +Functional Suitability, -Installability	Microsoft WPF, QT, GTK
		Web-based engineering client	-Useability, -Functional Suitability, +Installability	AngularJS, BackboneJS, React
		Native mobile engineering client	-Useability, -Functional Suitability, +Installability	ReactNative, Xamarin
	Open data models	Standardized	+Interoperability	AutomationML, PLCOpen, Collada, IEC61499, eCl@ss
		Proprietary	-Interoperability	Company-specific
	Configuration capability	Manual	-Efficiency, -Maintainability, +Functional Suitability	Industrial engineering tools
		(semi-) Automatic	+Efficiency, +Maintainability, -Functional Suitability	mDNS, UPnP, DHCP

Note: *Functional suitability is concerned with whether a system meets stated and implied users' needs*

Fig. 2. The catalogue of architectural decisions

Figure 2 depicts parts our catalogue of architectural decisions, which will be explained throughout the paper. This table depicts design alternatives, their positive and negative impacts on various quality attributes and possible implementation options. Figure 3 shows the dependencis among the decisions.

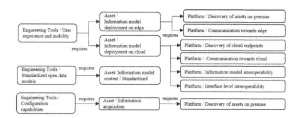

Fig. 3. Dependencies among design alternatives

2   Architectural Decisions for the Asset Layer

2.1   Representation of Assets in Information Models

The assets in IIoT systems must be connected to the cyber world to be accessed and manipulated by applications running in the cyber world. This indicates the need for an information model for the assets, which maintains various information about them, and is used as an interface to access and communicate with the assets. Various terms such as digital twins and administration shell are being used to refer to such information models [6]. While designing the information model of an asset, an architect must make the following decisions.

Information Model Content. The following decisions exist:

Standardized vs. Proprietary Information: The content of information models is in general domain- and application-specific; nevertheless, there are various proposals to standardize the content, which can be adopted by architects as means to increase the interoperability of the information models. AutomationML [7] is an example. If the adopted standards are not expressive enough to define desired information, their functional suitability for a system reduces. To overcome this problem, companion standards may be proposed to extend the existing standards.

Raw vs. Semantically Augmented Information: Even if information is represented based on some standards, due to the multiplicity of industrial standards, it is necessary to ensure that the semantics/meaning of the information is known in a machine-readable form. This would help to increase the interoperability of IIoT systems. The information can be augmented with semantic tags, and/or ontologies can be adopted to define the semantics of the information. The information provided by eCl@ss [8] or semantic ontologies in format of OWL can be used as the source for semantic tags. For example, by tagging an information item with the eCl@ss classification number 0173-1#02-BAA036#009, we indicate that the information item represents the maximum operating temperature of a temperature transmitter.

Information Acquisition. Two alternatives are considered for populating the content of information models:

Manual vs. (Semi-) Automatic: The content might be provided manually, for example, during the engineering process. This would require suitable engineering tools for IIoT systems (see Sect. 4). Alternatively, it might be possible to (semi) automatically infer the content of information models. For this, discovery and network scanning mechanisms must be adopted to discover assets on the IIoT network and scan their information. Various technologies such as UPnP [9] can be adopted for this matter.

Depending on the desired functionality of an IIoT system, both manual and (semi) automatic information acquisition might be needed, otherwise the functional suitability of the system will be influenced. For example, design and simulation models of a sensor are added manually, and its live parameters might be acquired after its installation by scanning network.

Information Deployment. An architect must decide which part of information must be deployed on which target. The key prerequisite to have flexible deployment is to support modularity in information models, so that information pieces can be deployed separately. The three following alternatives are distinguished for deployment targets, which are not mutually exclusive.

Embedded in Assets: If assets are physical devices, depending on their computation power and the complexity of their information models, the information models might be embedded alongside their other business objects; e.g. via a container-based architecture such as using Docker containers. Delivering assets with embedded information models, which comply with industry standards, help to increase the interoperability of the assets. However, if it is the only supported way of deploying the information models, it may reduce the functional suitability of the systems in scenarios where complex information models are required. Besides, depending on the adopted network architecture, it may also reduce the security of systems because the assets must be directly accessible; i.e. the security boundaries are at the level of the assets.

On Edge: IIoT systems may also contain many legacy assets, whose internal architecture does not support embedded information models. Here, the alternative for making such assets interoperable with other IIoT assets is to deploy the information models on-premise on a server/gateway (e.g. OPC UA server [10]). Such a server acts as the standardized communication gateway, using which the assets are connected to IIoT systems; hence, interoperability requirements are fulfilled. Even if IIoT systems only consist of IIoT-compatible assets with embedded information models, on-premise gateways are still a promising solution to increase the security of the systems by bringing the security boundaries at the edge level.

On Cloud: Information models might also be deployed on external clouds. This is normally the way to expose information outside a premise. As for the on-premise alternative, cloud-based deployment might be needed to fulfill desired functionality of IIoT systems, e.g. remote monitoring, and helps to improve the security of the systems. This alternative might have negative impact on the performance of the systems because of network communications.

3   Architectural Decisions for the Platform Layer

3.1   Discovery Mechanisms

A core responsibility of an IIoT platform is to ensure that assets as well as their information models can be found efficiently. Therefore, a discovery mechanism is an important component in such a platform.

Manual vs. Automatic Asset Discovery On-premise: Assets can be made known in IIoT systems by manually configuring their connections. This may help to improve the interoperability of the assets because one may easily add additional hacks to make the assets discoverable. Manual discovery reduces the maintainability and efficiency of the systems because the (re-)configuration activity must be done manually. These problems can be overcome by adopting an auto-discovery mechanism as it is facilitated by some protocols such as UPnP [9].

Manual vs. Automatic Cloud Endpoint Discovery: When a regional cloud gateway is not available due to network issues, a discovery mechanism needs to provide an alternative for the edge gateway to send its data to. In cloud-based scenarios, manual configuration and discovery of cloud endpoints reduces the maintainability and efficiency of the systems, because of large number of assets that have to be configured. Besides, the availability of the systems reduces, because the necessary fallback mechanisms to cope with the cases that an endpoint is down are not by default in place.

3.2   Communication Aspects

Communications Towards Edge. The following alternatives exist:

Generic vs. Domain-specific Protocols: On the edge level, modern protocols such as OPC UA [10] support multiple communication paradigms, i.e. client/server and publish/subscribe. This enables architects to choose the best suiting combination for the specific environment where communication takes place. Additionally, domain-specific communication protocols (e.g., Modbus) may need to be taken into account to support the installed bases. When adopting generic protocols, we may run into compatibility issues if assets do not support the adopted protocols. On the other hand, due to their generality, the maintainability and interoperability of the target system will improve. In contrary, domain-specific protocols are tailored and optimized for a specific domain; hence they deliver better performance, while compromising maintainability and inter-operability because one has to deal with many protocols in an IIoT system.

Communications Toward the Cloud. The following alternatives exist:

Message-oriented vs. Transaction-oriented: It mostly makes sense to choose a firewall-friendly message-based protocol to be able to route the traffic securely and efficiently towards the cloud. For an IIoT system that is mostly about sending messages out towards the cloud, a combination of a secured channel via WebSockets [11] as transport channel with a tunneling of a message based protocol such as MQTT [12] or AMQP [13] seems a good fit. Alternatively, OPC UA using its publish/ subscribe model might also be used for such communication paths.

Although message-oriented protocols offer better scalability and performance, they may fall short in providing the desired functionality of a system. It is because they are mainly focusing on 'sending' message and one has to offer workaround to emulate scenarios where 'receiving' responses are needed. For more interactive communications, traditional HTTP(S) request/response paradigms should be used.

3.3 Cloud-Level Interoperability

Larger IIoT systems might consist of multiple cloud-based IIoT systems that must interact with each other. Cloud-level interoperability is studied from two perspectives: (a) interface-level, and (b) information-level.

Interface-Level Interoperability. Two alternatives are distinguished:

Standardized vs. Specific Interfaces: Easily accessible, yet at the same time controllable interfaces need to be provided to other clouds. This can either be based on standards (e.g. OPC UA) or at least easily discoverable state-of-the-art REST interfaces which allow for a technology-independent implementation of the corresponding connectors. Adhering to specific interface standards improves the interoperability of systems, but may also limit the possibility to implement certain functionality of the systems if the standards are not expressive enough.

Information-Level Interoperability. When exchanging data, it must be possible to identify what the data is about and how various data sources relate to each other. Two alternatives exist to make the information models of cloud-based IIoT systems map-able to each other:

Common Model vs. Peer Mapping: Mapping of the information models can be achieved by either mapping to a common intermediate model definition (e.g. using OPC UA) or by providing custom mappings between peer clouds. The former increases the interoperability, but may negatively affect the functionality of the systems because the common model may not be expressive enough to define desired information models. Custom mappings resolve these issues with the price of reduced interoperability.

4   Architectural Decisions for Engineering Tools

4.1   User Experience and Mobility

Desktop-based vs. Web-based: With respect to usability and functional suitability, desktop-based engineering tools offer advantages over web-based tools because they can offer more complex features such as richer functionality for 3D modelling. Web-based tools on the other hand reduce the load of installation.

Mobile vs. PC-based: An architect may strive for the mobile-based engineering and configuration of IIoT devices. Since IIoT devices usually have a large set of correlated parameters, mobile-based configuration becomes very complex and complicates engineering tasks on more constrained mobile devices. Hence, mobile-based engineering have limited functional suitability and useability, but are easier to install, e.g. through App stores. Architects may define an abstraction over all configuration parameters (e.g., NAMUR NE131 Core Parameters [14]) to enable simple, but important engineering tasks on a mobile device, while leaving the full engineering capabilities to a richer desktop application.

4.2   Open Data Models

In an IIoT system, there may be an increased desire to seamlessly access engineering data from heterogeneous devices, possibly from different vendors. This can for example help 3rd parties to implement services for predictive maintenance and production optimization.

Standardized vs. Proprietary Data Models: If engineering data adhers to industry standards, it will be feasible to exchange the engineering data across heterogeneous devices; hence, improving interoperability while increasing the complexity to map proprietary models to standards. In some cases, device vendors consider engineering data as intellectual property and there is a keen interest to protect the underlying business models by keeping the data in a proprietary format. Architects can plan to support export functions from internal data structures to open data format such as AutomationML [7] and eCl@ss [8].

4.3   Configuration Capabilities

An essential task in commissioning IIoT systems is to configure devices with necessary parameters. Due to the large number of parameters, this task is inherently complicated and is nowadays performed manually to a large extent.

Manual vs. (Semi-)Automatic Configuration: With more and more devices directly accessible over the Internet, it is possible to automate many formerly manual engineering task. For example, an engineer may no longer need to enter network addresses from a paper-based list, but instead simply scan the local network for IIoT devices. (Semi-)automatic configuration capabilities of an engineering tool improves the efficiency and maintainability of the engineering tasks because users must not deal with configuring many parameters. On the other hand, it may reduce the functional suitability if it is not possible to customize parameterizations of devices.

5   Related Work and Conclusion

To the best of our knowledge, there is no similar work on defining a catalogue of architectural decisions for IIoT systems. There are, however, various reference architectures proposed [2–4]. Since they are reference architectures, certain architectural decisions are already made. This is in contrary to our work, which elaborates on design alternatives and their impacts on quality attributes of software. Based on this catalogue, an architect may design a reference or a technical architecture for his system of interest. In [5] various patterns for IoT systems are introduced, where no discussion is provided on architectural decisions and alternatives to realize the patterns. Our design catalogue can be used as complementary to these patterns. Regardless of domain for which an IIoT system is designed, our proposed catalogue helps architects to have a consolidated view on relevant architectural decisions. In future, we would like to extend this catalogue to cover more aspects of IIoT systems, for example, by considering other applications such as predictive maintenance.

References

1. Zimmermann, O., Gschwind, T., Küster, J., Leymann, F., Schuster, N.: Reusable architectural decision models for enterprise application development. In: Proceedings of the QoSA 2007 (2007)
2. Hankel, M.: The Reference Architectural Model Industrie 4.0 (RAMI 4.0). VDE VERLAG; Neuerscheinung edition (2015)
3. Industrial Internet Consortium, The Industrial Internet of Things Volume G1: Reference Architecture, Technical report (2017)
4. Bauer, M., Bui, N., De Loof, J., Magerkurth, C.: Enabling Things to Talk: Designing IoT Solutions with the IoT Architectural Reference Model. Springer, Heidelberg (2013). https://doi.org/10.1007/978-3-642-40403-0
5. Reinfurt, L., Breitenbücher, U., Falkenthal, M., Leymann, F., Riegg, A.: Internet of Things patterns. In: EuroPlop 2016, ACM (2016)
6. Wagner, C., et al.: The role of the industrie 4.0 asset administration shell and the digital twin during the life cycle of a plant. In: 22nd IEEE International Conference on Emerging Technologies and Factory Automation (2017)
7. Schmidt, N., Lder, A.: AutomationML in a Nutshell (2015)
8. eCl@ss Classification and Product Description. https://www.eclass.eu

9. UPnP Forum Technical Committee, UPnP Device Architecture (2014)
10. Mahnke, W., Leitner, S.-H., Damm, M.: OPC Unified Architecture. Springer-Verlag, Heidelberg (2009). https://doi.org/10.1007/978-3-540-68899-0
11. Fette, I., Melnikov, A.: The WebSocket Protocol (2011)
12. ISO/IEC JTC Information Technology, ISO/IEC 20922:2016: Message Queuing Telemetry Transport (2016)
13. Godfrey, R., Ingham, D., Schloming, R.: OASIS Advanced Message Queuing Protocol (2012)
14. Klettner, C.: Namur open architecture. ATP Ed. **59**(01), 20–37 (2017)

Embedded and Cyber-Physical Systems

Enabling Continuous Software Engineering for Embedded Systems Architectures with Virtual Prototypes

Pablo Oliveira Antonino[1], Matthias Jung[1], Andreas Morgenstern[1(✉)], Florian Faßnacht[2], Thomas Bauer[1], Adam Bachorek[1], Thomas Kuhn[1], and Elisa Yumi Nakagawa[3]

[1] Fraunhofer IESE, Fraunhofer-Platz 1, 67663 Kaiserslautern, Germany
{pablo.antonino,matthias.jung,andreas.morgenstern,thomas.bauer,
adam.bachorek,thomas.kuhn}@iese.fraunhofer.de
[2] Ergosign GmbH, Europaallee 12, 66113 Saarbrücken, Germany
florian.fassnacht@ergosign.de
[3] Department of Computer Systems, University of Sao Paulo, Sao Carlos, Brazil
elisa@icmc.usp.br

Abstract. Continuous software engineering aims at orchestrating engineering knowledge from various disciplines in order to deal with the rapid changes within the ecosystems of which software-based systems are part of. The literature claims that one means to ensure these prompt responses is to incorporate virtual prototypes of the system as early as possible in the development process, such that requirements and architecture decisions are verified early and continuously by means of simulations. Despite the maturity of practices for designing and assessing architectures, as well as for virtual prototyping, it is still not clear how to jointly consider the practices from these disciplines within development processes, in order to address the dynamics imposed by continuous software engineering. In this regard, we discuss in this paper how to orchestrate architecture drivers and design specification techniques with virtual prototypes, to address the demands of continuous software engineering in development processes. Our proposals are based on experiences from research and industry projects in various domains such as automotive, agriculture, construction, and medical devices.

Keywords: Continuous engineering · Architecture drivers
Architecture design · Architecture simulation · Virtual prototypes

1 Introduction

The emerging notion of *Continuous Engineering* [1] refers to orchestrations of practices like *Continuous Integration* (CI) and *Continuous Deployment* (CD) [2], and aims at improving architecture drivers such as *Time-to-Market* (TTM) and reacting faster to market demands that might range from a mobile phone software update to the incorporation of a new feature in a vehicle [2].

© Springer Nature Switzerland AG 2018
C. E. Cuesta et al. (Eds.): ECSA 2018, LNCS 11048, pp. 115–130, 2018.
https://doi.org/10.1007/978-3-030-00761-4_8

In the software engineering world, the so-called *Continuous Software Engineering* is about orchestrating unlocked engineering knowledge to enable continuous verification, and build software products by means of strategic reuse [1–3]. This approach enables a holistic perspective on software production processes, regardless of whether these take place in a unique software organization or in a smart ecosystem [3].

Continuous software engineering practices are already being implemented in the industry. For example, Tesla is efficiently reacting to customer requirements requested on social networks. In a particular case, a Tesla car owner sent a recommendation via Twitter directly to Teslas CEO Elon Musk, suggesting moving the car seat back and raising the steering wheel when the car is parked. Elon Musk answered twenty-four minutes later via Twitter, saying that the feature would be included in the next software update[1]. The requested feature was released by Tesla less than two months later. The implications of this case on the engineering departments are tremendous, and the realization of such immediate responses is only possible by incorporating continuous engineering practices into the development processes, ranging from market and product monitoring to architecture analysis, redesign, verification, and deployment. The literature discusses that, in continuous software engineering, the classical V model is no longer sequential but is rather based on iterative executions of activities onf the left side of the V (Decomposition and Definition) and its on the right side (Integration and Validation) [3]. To enable these dynamics, the existence of executables of the system is necessary as early as possible. This enables to verify the requirements and the correspondent architecture strategies early and continuously [3]. The literature claims that one means to achieve this is to use virtual prototypes [3,4], which correspond to executable architecture models that enable simulations of the architecture against the requirements before the actual system implementation.

Despite these discussions, it is still unclear how to properly orchestrate state-of-the-art and state-of-the-practice techniques for dealing with architecture-significant requirements and architecture design, virtual prototypes, and the particularities imposed by continuous software engineering. In this regard, this paper presents means for realizing this orchestration, which have been continuously developed according to experiences acquired in several research and industry consultancy projects. The remainder of this paper is organized as follows: In Sect. 2 we discuss the state-of-the-art and the state-of-the-practice of continuous software engineering and virtual prototypes from the architecture perspective. In Sect. 3 we present our approach and in Sect. 4 we present an experience report of industrial practices. Finally, we conclude and discuss the future works in Sect. 5.

---

[1] https://www.inc.com/justin-bariso/elon-musk-promises-to-implement-customer-suggestion.html.

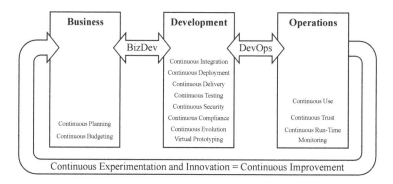

Fig. 1. General overview on continuous engineering activities (adapted from [2]).

2 State-of-the-Art and State-of-the-Practice

2.1 Continuous Software Engineering at a Glance

Continuous engineering emerged because of the need for a more holistic approach for dealing with the rapid changes within an ecosystem that software-based systems are inserted into [2,3]. There is a common misunderstanding that continuous software engineering is a synonym for continuous integration or continuous delivery. However, as discussed by Fitzgerald and Stol [2], these two practices are only two aspects of the continuous software engineering notion. Additionally, continuous software engineering incorporates aspects intrinsically related to business strategy, development and operations. As shown in Fig. 1, these other aspects include continuous planning, continuous deployment, continuous evolution, continuous trust and continuous experimentation. Therefore, they also refer to continuous engineering as *Continuous**. Figure 1 also depicts software engineering trends such as *DevOps* and *BizDev*, whose concepts and practices provide appropriate interfaces between the different groups of activities, like *Business Strategy* and *Development*. The only item depicted in Fig. 1 that is not discussed by Fitzgerald and Stol [2] is *Virtual Prototyping*. The integration of this aspect to properly address architecture activities in continuous engineering is the key aspect discussed in this paper.

2.2 Architecture Practices and Continuous Software Engineering

Architecture activities are not properly considered in the continuous engineering research agenda of Fitzgerald and Stol [2]. The only part where architecture is mentioned is in the description of *Continuous Evolution*. Here it is stated that the architecture activities in continuous software engineering shall be explored more deeply. In this regard, our research has shown that discussions by the scientific communities on how to consider practices from the architecture discipline in the continuous software engineering world are still scarce. The existing works on this topic published in conference proceedings and journals are limited to investigating the appropriateness of architecture styles for continuous delivery such as microservices architectures [5], and do not deal with how to reconsider the architecture practices and methods for continuous software engineering.

A commonly referenced book on continuous software engineering is entitled *Continuous Software Engineering* [1], written by Jan Bosch. It has one chapter on the *Role of Architects in Agile Organizations*. However, the focus is on the agile architecture process, and not on the key aspects that compose continuous software engineering as discussed in Sect. 2.1.

To the best of our knowledge, the book by Cathleen Shamieh, an IBM limited edition on continuous software engineering [3] is the only reference that provides pointers to where the architecture discipline should head for addressing the needs of continuous software engineering. The author claims that the whole dynamics imposed by this new trend demands architecture models that go beyond the mission of systematically representing and communicating the system; it can also be used to be executed against the high volume of requirements before the actual implementation of the system. These models are referenced in the literature as virtual prototypes [4], and have been widely used for continuous system verification not only of software- based systems, but also of heterogeneous models (which comprise electronics, mechanics, and hydraulics), and also software, as will be discussed in Subsect. 2.3.

In this regard, this paper is also motivated by the lack of discussion in the literature on proper methods to deal with architecture activities like specification and evaluation of architecture drivers and design in continuous software engineering.

2.3   Virtual Prototyping

Virtual Prototypes (VPs) are the key for enabling continuous integration for embedded systems, because they allow *Shift Left*, i.e. performing the concurrent development of steps that are usually serial and *Frontloading* of testing, i.e., testing the system already in advance to detect conceptual problems that cannot be foreseen in the planning phase [4]. VPs can range from the simulation of high level models to the detailed simulation of processors and other components in *Electronic Control Units* (ECUs). However, for VPs there exists a challenging trade-off between a fast simulation and accurate simulation, which has to be considered wisely for the beneficial usage in the development flow.

In the remainder of this subsection we will discuss the state-of-the-practice of VPs and the benefits that VPs brings to the engineering of software-based products. In Sect. 3 we will discuss how VPs can be used to enhance architecture activities in continuous software engineering.

Nowadays, companies have to deal with complex hardware architectures such as heterogeneous multi-core systems. For instance, the transition from hundreds of distributed Electronic Control Units (ECUs) to a dozen consolidated domain controllers is a current trend in the automotive domain [6]. Platforms

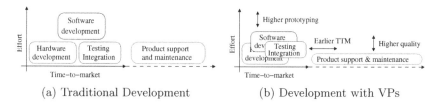

(a) Traditional Development   (b) Development with VPs

Fig. 2. Advantages of virtual prototyping

like Audi's zFAS[2] and NVIDIA's Xavier[3] illustrate how powerful GPUs, custom SoCs, microcontrollers, and FPGAs are integrated on a single domain controller, in order to perform sensor fusion, processing and decision making on a single *Printed Circuit Board* (PCB). Companies are under constant pressure to adapt to these emerging trends and deliver their products quickly because there are many competitors on the market. Traditional design-flow procedures have a performance problem due to the high complexity of modern systems. Therefore, new tools and approaches for system design are needed to fulfill these requirements. For example, in the past, embedded software was developed after the hardware had been provided by a supplier. To master this situation of complex hardware/software and the pressure with respect to time-to-market, cost and engineering efforts, a new idea has emerged over the last years: the idea of parallel development of hardware and embedded software by means of VPs (often denoted as *Shift Left* [4]).

Virtual hardware prototypes are high-speed, fully functional software models of physical hardware systems, which are used for embedded software development before the actual hardware is available. Here, industry focuses mainly on virtual prototypes based on SystemC and *Transaction Level Modeling* (TLM) to have very realisitc hardware models that can be used to develop and test hardware-near software like operating systems or bare-metal firmware. VPs provide visibility and controllability across the entire system which makes the products easier to test: There are helpful and powerful debugging mechanisms for VPs, which are almost inconceivable for a real hardware system. For example, in traditional embedded software development, the programmer is limited to JTAG interfaces or has to use a logic analyzer for debugging. With VPs the hardware, software, tool-chain, and debugging tools are located on the developers desktop PC and the developer can easily observe all internal registers, variables and signals. This leads to a higher quality of the product and a lower supporting effort [4]. Figure 2 shows the fusion of hardware development, software development, and testing which leads to a decreased TTM, less effort, better quality, less costumer support, and, finally, to reduced costs.

Industry reports from Bosch, Hitachi, and General Motors indicate the following advantages and improvements achieved by using virtual prototypes [4]:

---

[2] https://www.tttech.com/markets/automotive/projects-references/audi-zfas/.
[3] https://blogs.nvidia.com/blog/2018/01/07/drive-xavier-processor/.

(i) visibility and controllability across the entire system; (ii) quick correction of specification errors prior to implementation; (iii) early exploration of the architecture design space; (iv) development and collaboration in worldwide locations; (v) no more physical hardware dependency on the supply chain; (vi) improvement of development cycles by 30% to 50%; (vii) reuse of (parts of) the prototype for future work;(viii) start of software development 9 to 12 months before hardware availability; (ix) identification and correction of software bugs with hours rather than days; (x) integration of new software on first silicon within a day; and (xi) delivery of more competitive products up to six months faster. Examples of tools and models for VPs are provided by Synopsys[4], ARM[5], gem5 [7], and DRAMSys [8], and VPs case studies can be found in [9].

The notion of virtual prototypes as discussed in Sect. 3 is a key means for addressing architecture activities in continuous software engineering.

3 Architecture Practices for Continuous Software Engineering of Embedded Systems with Virtual Prototypes

In this section we discuss how architecture VPs shall be considered to enable continuous software engineering of embedded systems[6]. In this regard, this section discusses a restructuring of the traditional V-Model (cf. Sect. 3.1), how to deal with the specifications of architecture drivers (cf. Sect. 3.2) and architecture design (cf. Sect. 3.3), the simulation environments for co-simulations of architecture specification (cf. Sect. 3.4), and what architecture aspects shall be subject to which continuous verification and validation techniques (cf. Sect. 3.5).

3.1 From the V-Model to the II-Model

The whole dynamics imposed by continuous software engineering demands rethinking the *V-Model* as it is (Fig. 3a) [3]. We claim that the V-Model shall no longer correspond to a ordered sequence of activities, but rather enable different possible iterations and even parallel executions of V-Model tasks, as depicted in Fig. 3b. We call this the *II-Model*.

The *II-Model* brings together the left and the right side of the V-Model. The connection of *Specification and Design* with *Integration and Testing* shall happen continuously, and the different *X-in-the-Loop (XiL)* aspects depicted in Fig. 3b correspond to architectural virtual prototypes that enable the continuous and integrated verification of different system properties at the architecture levels (ranging from the overall system functional behavior to hardware specifics like capacity of communication buses). The idea is to reduce the distance between requirements, design, implementation, and maintenance with *XiL* practices.

---

[4] https://www.synopsys.com/verification/virtual-prototyping.html.
[5] https://developer.arm.com/products/system-design/fast-models.
[6] http://www.ovpworld.org/about_continuous_integration.

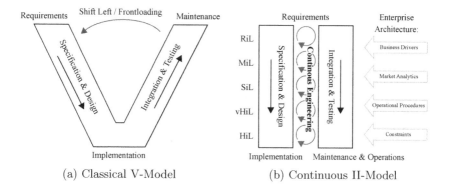

(a) Classical V-Model   (b) Continuous II-Model

Fig. 3. Virtual prototypes enable continuous engineering of embedded systems

Virtual Prototypes Along the II-Model: Architectural virtual prototypes based on *XiL* as depicted in Fig. 3b are key aspects to be considered in continuous software engineering because of the precise and fast feedbacks provided by architecture simulation techniques [4]. More specifically, different simulation techniques should be used for different levels of abstractions of the architecture, as depicted in Fig. 3b, and detailed as follows:

- **RiL (Requirements in the Loop):** aims at verifying system requirements regarding completeness, consistency, and robustness by means of larger simulation scenarios [10]. RiL focuses on quality properties that require the execution of the system or its parts, like functional appropriateness and quality requirements like performance. It demands a rather complete formal specification of the relevant system properties as executable models on an appropriate abstraction level, like the abstract description of the input-output-behavior of a new function in the system. The systematic modeling and the automated model-based evaluation on the requirements level enables the earliest possible detection of specification issues through intensive system validation.
- **MiL (Model in the Loop):** aims at verifying in early stages of the development process whether the architecture strategies described with functional and logical architecture models [11] are adequate for addressing specific requirements. Examples of these are Simulink models. At this stage, no hardware or software elements are taken into consideration, but only the interaction between the functional and logical architecture elements.
- **SiL (Software in the Loop):** aims at verifying to which extent the implemented software realizes the functional and logical architecture specifications. Examples of these are architecture specifications of software components, packages, classes, interfaces, and other elements like the ones proposed by the Fraunhofer Embedded Modeling Profile [11]. One of the challenges with *SiL* verifications in the embedded domain is that, in the case of implementation in the C programming language, for instance, the code is compiled for the host PC instead of the target micro-controller [4]. In this regard, industrial reports from Bosch, Hitachi and General Motors provide evidence that this

may introduce differences in terms of precision, e.g., due to different architecture and data types as well as other problems related to resource limitations on the microcontroller (memory, processing power) [4].

- **vHiL (Virtual Hardware in the Loop):** aims at considering virtual hardware in order to verify the adequacy of software deployment and the functional realization of dedicated hardware functions. vHiL has proven its contribution to the automotive industry in terms of efficacy and efficiency [4]. The evolution in building virtual prototypes of vHiL has led to simulation models for example in SystemC/TLM, that are very close to the real hardware, and enables more and heterogeneous tests to be conducted earlier in the development process.

- **HiL (Hardware in the Loop):** aims at verifying the tests performed in the vHiL on real hardware. In the case of high accurate vHiL virtual prototypes, HiL tests may consume less time, because critical hardware challenges have already been identified.

The execution of these different simulations will enable the achievement of continuous software engineering because precise verification can already be done at the architecture level, considering the existence of architecture models that represent the software and hardware entities composing the product. In the case of systems that comprise mechanical and hydraulic parts, the proper abstraction of these properties will enhance the accuracy of integrated simulations at the architectural level. Actually, the possibility to combine virtual prototypes of different architecture levels makes it possible to build set-ups with completely simulated products in a vHiL, enabling verification and validation without physical hardware. In this regard, considering the existence of robust virtual prototypes of the software and hardware, different tests and deployment strategies can be conducted at the architecture level, which improves not only TTM, but also the quality of the products, which is the key goal of continuous software engineering. Proper simulation at the architecture level might lead to less faulty products, which, in the case of the automotive industry, might decrease the number of recalls. In 2016, for instance, recalls caused a loss of $22.1 billion in claims and warranty accruals by OEM and suppliers[7].

The Enterprise Architecture Inputs for the II-Model: Beyond the XiL activities, it is important to consider the speed at which the market changes, and how the organization shall react to these changes at the enterprise level. Aspects like *Business Drivers*, *Market Analytics*, *Operational Procedures*, and *Constraints*, known as architecture drivers [12], have to be monitored continuously and will continuously feed the engineering process, demanding different interaction possibilities in the *II-Model* in order to address market and enterprise demands faster. These inputs from the enterprise level provide means to jointly exploit assets like engineering data together with reusable components,

---

[7] https://www.cnet.com/roadshow/news/automotive-recalls-cost-22-billion-in-2016/.

depending on the concrete demand, like, for example, quick fixes, position of new products in the market ahead of the competitor, combined analysis of production costs and return on investment, amongst others. It shall also integrate the marketing analytics knowledge aspect, which is fundamental to comprehend and assess the feasibility and urgency to incorporate punctual strategic demands like the request to Tesla using Twitter as discussed in Sect. 1, but also long-term demands.

3.2   Efficient Creation and Maintenance of Architecture Drivers

To enable the proper use of VPs to improve architecture activities in continuous software engineering, the specification of architecture drivers shall be based on techniques that allow these specifications to be created, maintained, and analyzed efficiently. Architecture drivers are requirements that are new to the development organization, risky and expensive [12], and can be categorized as follows: business drivers, key functional and quality requirements, and constraints, which can be organizational, technical and legal in nature [12].

In continuous software engineering, user requests are dynamically captured and are expected to be implemented fast, such as in the Tesla case described in Sect. 1. This demands means for quickly updating architecture drivers. However, in industrial practice, architecture drivers are specified using natural language only. As a consequence, every changed architecture driver will demand a great amount of human labor and effort to manually identify and update each architecture driver impacted by the change. One means for specifying architecture drivers that can be updated faster is to enrich the textual description with semi-formal approaches like traditional UML sequence diagrams or Live Sequence Charts. These diagrams offer means to specify the scenarios in an interactive way to check how the system may, must or must not react to certain events [13]. On live sequence charts, there are also means for generating them from natural language requirements documents using natural language processing [14].

3.3   Specify Architecture Models with Proper Approaches

To enable the dynamics imposed by continuous software engineering as well as fast reactions in the engineering environment, the use of adequate architecture models is fundamental. However, as for the architecture drivers (cf. Sect. 3.2), the models that describe the architecture solutions are, very often, specified informally, e.g., using PowerPoint or Visio diagrams. The adoption of appropriate techniques like the use of modeling languages such as the Embedded Modeling Profile [11], is growing, but it is still far from being the common practice [15].

Another key challenge in this regard is the gap that usually exists between the architecture models and the source code. Modern UML modeling environments address this gap with code generators and executable models. They use C/C++ or Java as action languages to make models executable. Consequently, guards, activities, effects, and actions need to be programmed with these languages. Comparable approaches like Simulink or SCADE also use design models to abstract from concrete code and enable developers to specify algorithms on a higher level of abstraction. The integration of architecture models and realizations is only possible when both are integrated with each other. Testing across levels of abstraction and the gradual movement between architecture and realization levels must be possible to enable the integration of artifacts at development time, and their refinement during the software's lifetime. In this regard, virtual prototypes enable co-simulation of high-level models and code, and are therefore a promising candidate for the gradual transition from architecture to code, when a valid semantic model is being defined. Co-simulation of high-level models and code also enables back-to-back testing between these types of models and therefore supports the maintenance of architecture models after code changes.

3.4   Simulation Environments for Co-simulation of Architecture Specification and Source Code

Architecture specifications describe the structure of a system, the main information flows, and the high-level behavior of important algorithms. Concrete algorithm designs are therefore intentionally not part of architectures. One common problem in industry is that software low-level designs are not linked to the reference behavior specified in architectures. The consequence is that changes in one artifact are, very often, not reflected in the other artifacts. Consequently, the deviation between the reference behavior specified in architectures and the realization implemented in code increase over time which constitues a high risk in continuous engineering approaches.

Modern model-driven-development tools address this issue by enabling the development of executable specifications and code generation. This requires architects to provide low-level specifications like state machine guards and UML activities as executable C code. Specifying system behavior at this low level of abstraction is neither always possible nor desired in early phases of the development process. To address this challenge, we recommend considering the process depicted in Fig. 4 and described in the remainder of this subsection. High-level architectures document important use cases of a system, core components, their abstract behavior, and important interfaces. The detailed architecture defines the functional components of the system under development as blocks as well as information flows between these blocks. The software design refines the functional blocks with behavior models that are, for example, created with development environments like Simulink, Stateflow, ASCET, Dymola, and SCADE. Realizations are either generated automatically from software design models or implemented manually. Depending on the size of the project, these phases are performed once or iteratively, and require the use of one or many tools. Large development projects make early decisions about the tools to use for the development of individual function blocks, develop them individually, and then integrate them during HiL testing. Because these artifacts are developed independently of each other, only defects that become visible during testing get fixed. This includes design models as input for code generation and code, but usually not

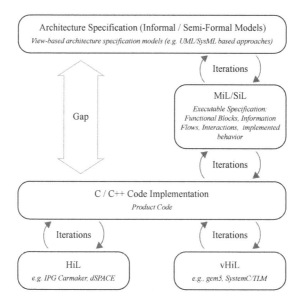

Fig. 4. Usual gap between architecture and source code.

architecture models. Enabling the validation of architecture models requires their integration into both design and validation processes.

In continuous software engineering, it is necessary to overcome this gap. As already outlined previously, it is necessary to have already executable specifications of the architecture drivers in terms of executable scenarios. Together with the structural models of the software architecture, these scenarios can already be simulated in very early design phases. During continuous development, we can then replace abstract executable architecture models with more concrete executable architecture models and finally with real code. To that end, it is neither necessary nor desirable for the models that work together to have the same abstraction level. Actually, it is necessary to have a simulation framework like FERAL [16] that can integrate high-level architecture models such as sequence diagrams or state machines with real code such that iterative refinement can take place during continuous development. Especially in the embedded systems domain, it is also necessary to simulate certain aspects of the underlying hardware like the communication buses needed or the processors used, e.g., whether we use an ARM low-power processor or a high-end Intel core-processor. If this is done properly, the virtual prototypes will cover the implementation, the software, and the hardware architecture specifications independently, and also the integrated holistic view proposed in the II-Model (cf. Sect. 3.1).

3.5   Continuous Verification and Validation in the II-Model

Nowadays, technical systems and their parts are developed by different suppliers and integrated by the manufacturer [6]. Continuous system updates with short release cycles demand high quality of the artifacts being developed and highly efficient quality assurance steps have to be performed. We understand that the three aspects described in the remainder of this subsection are the cornerstones that enable an integrated architecture verification and validation approach in continuous software engineering.

Eco-system and Platform Verification and Validation: The ecosystem has to be prepared to run new features as a reliable and safe platform with defined interfaces, interaction patterns, and integration constraints. This means, on the one hand, that the system interfaces and the extensibility of the system design have to be verified. On the other hand, reliability, performance, and robustness of the ecosystem with its existing and potential new features have to be assured. Dedicated specification models and highly automated in-the-loop test activities with extensive exploitation of simulation make it possible to efficiently run manifold test scenarios in order to assure the required quality properties.

Feature Verification and Validation: The short development cycles and the high quality needs require an efficient and seamless flow of information and cooperation between the specifying and integrating units and the feature developing units. Issues are the information types, notations, and degree of details that are needed to support the design and implementation of the new feature and its integration and acceptance tests on the other side. Existing specification models and automated simulation environments enable a test-driven approach with clear test stopping criteria and continuous testing of feature properties during short cycles. The integration and acceptance test has to assure that (i) the feature provides its intended functionality with the defined quality properties, (ii) the feature is fault-tolerant and robust in case of unintended usage or stimulation, and (iii) there are no safety-related unintended feature interactions in the ecosystem.

Continuous Ecosystem Monitoring: Additionally, continuous monitoring as part of the holistic quality assurance is applied to identify problems and potential future issues at run-time. Monitoring comprises the observation of system and feature states, output data, and error flags. In the case of severe issues, appropriate countermeasures have to be taken such as the partial or complete deactivation of features.

4 Industrial Engagement on Continuous Software Engineering

4.1 Continuous Software Engineering at Tesla, BMW, Jaguar Land Rover, Brockwell Technologies, and Diagnostic Grifols

Tesla is making extensive use of continuous engineering practices and delivering innovations to customers in record times, such as the case discussed in Sect. 1, where features for managing steering wheel and seat position for a parked vehicle, which were requested by a Tesla owner via Twitter, were delivered within less than two months. Beyond that, Tesla is known for delivering incremental build updates including feature extensions in-between two consecutive releases of major firmware versions on a short-time basis. Beyond the continuous monitoring of social networks in order to detect new customer demands, content provided through the *Tesla Firmware Upgrade Tracker*[8] gives evidence that Tesla must truly be applying a continuous engineering process for software build updates with a recurrent life-cycle of builds. This becomes even more evident by looking at the inconsistent number of updated cars observed for each and every build and by the fact that updates of different releases regularly overlap in time. That is, a specific software update is delivered and installed on different cars at different dates for various reasons, some of which seem obvious while others remain subject to Tesla's proprietary deployment strategy. Nonetheless, there are 3 phases that can be observed during a typical build lifecycle. The build release date as the initial short phase when many of Tesla's customers receive the update is followed by a medium-length phase, i.e., a period of just a few days during which the majority of cars get updated. The lifecycle is complemented by a long phase of up to several months with updates being delivered on an almost daily basis.

One known aspect that has been changing directions towards a continuous software engineering approach at BMW regards the safety engineering activities of the development process, as described in [17]. As discussed by Vöst and Wagner, BMW claims that the safety backlog has to be integrated with the functional sprint backlog. The safety backlog will include the architecture drivers centered on safety that must be addressed by architecture decisions described in the functional, software, and/or hardware architecture. In this regard, the use of virtual prototypes provide the necessary means for performing the appropriate verification and validation by means of simulations. An integrated simulation approach comprising the aspects discussed in Sect. 3.1 will enrich the evidences that the safety requirements are properly addressed. Beyond the engineering artifacts, BMW understands that in order to enable the continuous software engineering of safety engineering activities, the developers have to be aware of the impact that their commits will have on safety-critical components. If such an impact is detected, BMW claims that it is necessary to jointly analyze and update the safety analysis, the source code, and the requirements to keep the build running [17].

In addition to the Tesla and BWM examples of the adoption of continuous software engineering, IBM[9] mentions three examples of companies adopting continuous engineering practices and the benefits achieved so far: (i) **Jaguar Land Rover**, which achieved 90% faster software validation for its vehicle infotainment systems after adopting continuous software engineering practices; (ii) **Brockwell Technologies**, a defense systems company, which achieved 40 % faster development cycles; and (iii) **Diagnostic Grifols**, a manufacturer of medical devices, whose time to market became 20% faster.

---

[8] https://ev-fw.com.
[9] http://www.ibmbigdatahub.com/blog/what-continuous-engineering.

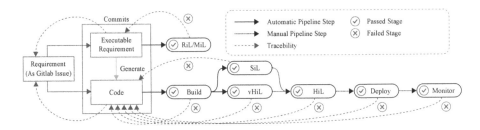

Fig. 5. Possible pipeline setup for GitLab

4.2 A Vison for Supporting the II-Model with CI/CD and DevOps

Thinking of Fitzgerald and Stols *Continuous** [2] in an enterprise or industrial context emphasizes the necessity for a powerful and performant tool environment for every part of the *Continuous-Engineering-Cycle* (CEC). As described in the *II-Model* shown in Fig. 3b a requirement is handled in short iterative cycles which makes implementation, testing, and maintenance nearly parallel processes. This methodology entails the need for a toolchain that empowers all participants to focus on their main tasks but also makes the continuous information flow of the iterative process beneficial to them. In the field, typical tasks that can be found in every cycle, like the build process, checking, testing, deployment, target evaluation, and monitoring, are handled in several *Stages* which are evaluated continuously for every change made in the whole project. By grouping the stages into *Pipelines* where every stage depends on the product or at least the success of its predecessor, the whole pipeline can be evaluated upon every change in requirements, executable requirements, the code, the simulations (RIL, MIL, SIL, (v)HIL), the hardware or even the monitoring results. A state-of-the-art solution for accelerating this procedure is to automate the pipeline with one or more task runners, using, for instance, a tool like *GitLab*. A GitLab runner can execute stages of the pipeline in suitable service environments, for example creating builds for different processor architectures which are then executed in a simulation environment such as a (v)HiL to gather functional or non-functional information (e.g. performance or power-consumption). This enables the process to fill the gap between specification and realization with automated virtual prototypes as well as to stock up the area between pure code and hardware testing with simulations to gather information as early and efficiently as possible in the workflow. In particular, automated mapping of the errors or achievements of every stage to the related requirements and tasks of earlier stages is enabled by grouping tasks into dependent stages. Dependencies between stages in a typical scenario can be seen in Fig. 5. GitLab's CI/CD features[10] can be easily used to manage the tasks of those CECs. It enables the engineer to create one ore more automated jobs for each step of the CEC which can be grouped and executed as a pipeline, as shown in Fig. 5. For that the

---

[10] https://about.gitlab.com/features/gitlab-ci-cd/.

simple markup language YAML[11] is used to specify any desired behavior of the pipeline. By tracking human-generated requirements in GitLab issues the results of pipeline stages (e.g., success or failures and their causes) can be easily mapped back to the requirement descriptions, thereby providing maximum traceability. Even automated gate keeping tasks like merge-requests could be realized easily by checking every change in the code (see *Commits* in Fig. 5) with the corresponding pipeline stages, for example by running the generated tests in massive parallel vHiL simulations, before running the more costly and time-consuming HiL tests. In that way supporting the II-Model process with CI/CD or even Continuous* [2] allows it to fully develop, test, and monitor features in very short sprints of only a few weeks or even days. Also, service providers like GitLab are reacting to those needs by providing scalable products that take the complete continuous engineering process into account including for example DevOps as a particular feature[12].

Our proposed workflow can be imagined in the context of the Tesla example of Sect. 1, where a user voiced a requirement via Twitter. From this so-called crowd-based requirement engineering [18] a requirements engineer could have formulated a GitLab issue. A programmer assigned to this issue would now prototype the requested feature as an executable requirement. After the implementation of this executable specification, a pipeline with RiL or MiL tests would be started automatically. If the tests were successful, the code would then be either generated or implemented by the programmer. Once the code had been committed, another pipeline would be started, which would automatically initiate the build processes, including SiL and vHil simulations. Because the HiL test often needs some interaction from a testing engineer, it is usually a manual step. Once the feature would have been approved by the testing engineer, the pipeline stage would get marked as passed and the code could be handed over to production or deployed to Tesla cars worldwide in order to collect monitoring data about the actual usage of the feature by the customer.

5   Conclusions and Future Works

In this paper we discussed how virtual prototypes should be used to improve architecture specification and assessment in continuous software engineering contexts. We also discussed how different industries are orchestrating techniques to realize the dynamics imposed by continuous software engineering, and how virtual prototypes could improve existing architecture practices. As our next steps, we intend to develop a *domain specific language* to enable the execution of simulations with virtual prototypes from specifications of semi-formal architecture drivers. We also intend to evolve the integration of different X-in-the-Loop virtual prototypes to fully integrate the different aspects of the engineering process, targeting architecture models, implementation, calibration, delivery, and marketing monitoring, all in an automated, continuous, and integrated pipeline. These

---

[11] http://www.yaml.org/start.html.
[12] https://about.gitlab.com/2017/10/04/devops-strategy/.

next steps will be fundamental for delivering the ultimate software at the push of a button.

References

1. Bosch, J.: Continuous Software Engineering. Springer, Heidelberg (2014). https://doi.org/10.1007/978-3-319-11283-1
2. Fitzgerald, B., Stol, K.J.: Continuous software engineering: a roadmap and agenda. J. Syst. Softw. **123**, 176–189 (2017)
3. Shamieh, C.: Continuous Engineering for Dummies. Wiley, Hoboken (2014)
4. De Schutter, T.: Better Software. Faster!: Best Practices in Virtual Prototyping. Synopsys Press, Mountain View (2014)
5. O'Connor, R.V., Elger, P., Clarke, P.M.: Continuous software engineering a microservices architecture perspective. J. Softw.: Evol. Process, **29**(11) (2017) e1866-n/a e1866 JSME-16-0193.R2
6. Reinhardt, D., Kucera, M.: Domain controlled architecture - a new approach for large scale software integrated automotive systems. In: Proceedings of the PECCS2013 - International Conference on Pervasive and Embedded Computing and Communication Systems (2013)
7. Binkert, N., et al.: The gem5 simulator. SIGARCH Comput. Archit. News **39**(2), 1–7 (2011)
8. Jung, M., Weis, C., Wehn, N.: DRAMSys: a flexible DRAM subsystem design space exploration framework. IPSJ Trans. Syst. LSI Des. Methodol. (T-SLDM) **8**, 63–74 (2015)
9. Jung, M., et al.: Virtual development on mixed abstraction levels: an agricultural vehicle case study. In: Synopsys Usergroup Conference (SNUG), June 2015
10. Jeannet, B., Gaucher, F.: Debugging embedded systems requirements with stimulus: an automotive case-study. In: Proceedings of the 8th European Congress on Embedded Real Time Software and Systems (ERTS 2016) (2016)
11. Morgenstern, A., Antonino, P., Kuhn, T., Pschorn, P., Kallweit, B.: Modeling embedded systems using a tailored view framework and architecture modeling constraints. In: Proceedings of the ECSA 2017. ACM, New York (2017)
12. Knodel, J., Naab, M.: Pragmatic Evaluation of Software Architectures, 1st edn. Springer, Heidelberg (2016). https://doi.org/10.1007/978-3-319-34177-4
13. Harel, D., Marelly, R.: Come, Let's Play: Scenario-Based Programming Using LSC's and the Play-Engine. Springer, New York (2003). https://doi.org/10.1007/978-3-642-19029-2
14. Gordon, M., Harel, D.: Generating executable scenarios from natural language. In: Gelbukh, A. (ed.) CICLing 2009. LNCS, vol. 5449, pp. 456–467. Springer, Heidelberg (2009). https://doi.org/10.1007/978-3-642-00382-0_37
15. Antonino, P.O., Morgenstern, A., Kuhn, T.: Embedded-software architects: it's not only about the software. IEEE Softw. **33**(6), 56–62 (2016)
16. Kuhn, T., Forster, T., Braun, T., Gotzhein, R.: Feral - framework for simulator coupling on requirements and architecture level. In: ACM/IEEE MEMOCODE 2013, pp. 11–22 (2013)
17. Vöst, S., Wagner, S.: Keeping continuous deliveries safe. In: Proceedings of the 39th International Conference on Software Engineering Companion, ICSE-C 2017, pp. 259–261. IEEE Press, Piscataway (2017)
18. Groen, E.C., et al.: The crowd in requirements engineering: the landscape and challenges. IEEE Softw. **34**(2), 44–52 (2017)

Abstraction Layered Architecture: Writing Maintainable Embedded Code

John Spray[1] and Roopak Sinha[2(✉)]

[1] Tru-Test Group, Auckland, New Zealand
john.spray@trutest.co.nz
[2] Department of Information Technology and Software Engineering,
Auckland University of Technology, Auckland, New Zealand
roopak.sinha@aut.ac.nz

Abstract. The brisk pace of the growth in embedded technology depends largely on how fast we can write and maintain software contained within embedded devices. Every enterprise seeks to improve its productivity through maintainability. While many avenues for improvement exist, highly maintainable code bases that can stay that way over a long time are rare. This article proposes a reference software architecture for embedded systems aimed at improving long-term maintainability. This reference architecture, called the Abstraction Layered Architecture (ALA), is built on the existing body of knowledge in software architecture and more than two decades of experience in designing embedded software at Tru-Test Group, New Zealand. ALA can be used for almost any object-oriented software project, and strongly supports domain-specific abstractions such as those found in most embedded software.

Keywords: Software architecture · Maintainability · Readability
Reusability · Embedded software · Embedded systems

1 Introduction

Tru-Test Group (henceforth, Tru-Test) is a New Zealand based company which manufactures numerous embedded solutions for livestock management, with many code bases existing for well over 20 years. A closer inspection of these code bases revealed useful insights into how some architectural practices can lead to better maintainability and lower complexity. While many code bases at Tru-Test gradually unravelled into *big balls of mud* [5] and some of these had to be abandoned, a few non-trivial examples thrived despite ongoing long-term maintenance. In fact these software parts had undergone regular maintenance for many years with almost trivial effort. Our perception was that they were two orders of magnitude easier to maintain than our worst code bases. This paper reports our attempt to uncover what makes software more maintainable, and to then integrate our findings into a reference architecture that can be used for future development.

© Springer Nature Switzerland AG 2018
C. E. Cuesta et al. (Eds.): ECSA 2018, LNCS 11048, pp. 131–146, 2018.
https://doi.org/10.1007/978-3-030-00761-4_9

It is said that 90% of commercial software is under maintenance [13], so any improvements here can provide high rewards. Maintainable software is easier to update and extend, which helps a company's profitability by reducing ongoing software development costs. A review of maintainable code bases at Tru-Test found that the many accepted software engineering *best practices* were helpful but not sufficient by themselves. Code-level practices (like clear naming, appropriate commenting, coding conventions, low cyclomatic complexity, etc.), module-level practices (encapsulation, programming to interfaces, etc.) and design-level practices (separation of concerns using design patterns like dependency injection, using object-oriented design, etc.) are all useful. However, individually they concern themselves with relative micro-structures within software code. The more maintainable code bases also featured robust *in-the-large* architectures. This paper focuses on architecture level interventions, which relate to high-level design decisions, structures, and constraints that, if followed, can achieve measurable improvements in maintainability.

For a developer already juggling a large set of requirements, quality attributes and deadlines, coming to a solution that also satisfies a large set of principles is often impossible. We hypothesize that it is possible to emerge a reference architecture that satisfies the principles of maintainable software without knowing the requirements, and that using this reference architecture is significantly easier than trying to satisfy all the maintainability and complexity principles concurrently. This hypothesis was broken into three research questions, as follows, leading to the main contributions of this article:

RQ1 *What are the key system, sub-system and code-level practices that improve maintainability?* This sets the foundation for this work - we reuse and build on existing insights into writing maintainable software and consciously and deliberately avoid inventing new names for known terms. Section 2 provides a summary of these principles for writing maintainable code.

RQ2 *How, and to what extent, can the practices identified in RQ1 be used to emerge a reference architecture?* This part of the research involves the creation of a reference software architecture that optimises maintainability and complexity. The creation of this proposed architecture, called *abstraction layered architecture* (ALA) is covered in Sect. 3.

RQ3 *How can we evaluate the impact of the architecture proposed in RQ2 on maintainability?* We test the impact of ALA on software maintainability through both a re-architecting of the code base of an existing commercial product from Tru-Test, and through the addition of more features to the product. ALA shows measurable improvements in maintainability relating to all its sub-characteristics as listed by ISO/IEC 25010. The evaluation phase is described in Sect. 4.

2   Principles for Writing Maintainable Software

The principles listed in this section may not constitute an exhaustive list, but have been found to be the most important for writing maintainable software.

These principles were identified primarily through an internal review of all code bases at Tru-Test for identifying the key qualities of code-bases that remained robustly maintainable over the long-term. We also carried out a subsequent literature search for identifying design and development techniques and practices useful for writing maintainable code. At the conclusion of these investigations, we identified the following principles, which are listed in no particular order.

P1-The First Few Strokes: Christopher Alexander, the creator of the idea of design patterns in architecture states, "As any designer will tell you, it is the first steps in a design process which count for the most. The first few strokes which create the form, carry within them the destiny of the rest" [1].

The primary criteria for logically decomposing a system into discrete parts is well known to have a high impact on maintainability [10]. An "Iteration Zero" (the first Agile iteration) is needed to create the primary decomposition. It will not emerge from refactoring.

P2-Abstraction: Ultimately the only way of achieving knowledge separation is abstraction [14]. An abstraction is the brain's version of a module. It is the means we use to make sense of an otherwise massively complex world and it is the only means of making sense of any non-trivial software system. A great abstraction makes the two sides completely different worlds. A clock is a great abstraction. On one side is the world of cog wheels. On the other someone trying to be on time in his busy daily schedule. Neither knows anything about the details of the other. SQL is another great abstraction. On one side is the world of fast algorithms. On the other is finding all the orders for a particular customer. How about a domain abstraction, the calculation of loan repayments. On one side, the world of mathematics with the derivation and implementation of a formula. On the other the code is about a person wanting to know if they can afford to buy a house. If abstractions do not separate two different worlds like this, then we are probably just factoring out common code. We need to find the abstraction in that common code, and make it separate out something complicated which is really easy to use, like a clock.

P3-Knowledge Dependencies: The dependencies that matter are "knowledge dependencies" [3], not runtime dependencies [9]. Knowledge dependencies occur at code design-time (code read time, code write time). In order to understand and maintain a module, what knowledge do you need? Run-time dependencies are not important - they can go in any direction, and be circular. Often runtime dependencies in code are implemented as knowledge dependencies, destroying the abstractions.

P4-Zero Coupling: The concepts of coupling and cohesion have been studied extensively in literature [12]. A common misconception is that, because components in a system must interact to do anything useful, they must, at the least, be loosely coupled. The confusion arises from the use of the words 'dependency', or 'uses' for both runtime and design-time (knowledge) dependencies as noted in P3. It is important that runtime dependencies are always implemented completely inside an abstraction. For example, let's say abstractions A and B will exchange data at runtime. There must be an abstraction C that knows about the runtime dependency, and, for example, instantiates A and B and uses dependency injection to connect them. A and B must know zero about each other. Not only do A and B remain mutually zero coupled, the knowledge inside C is also mutually zero coupled with the knowledge inside both A and B. The only coupling remaining is the necessary knowledge coupling inside C on the abstractions A and B.

P5-Composition not Collaboration: In the example in **P4** above, C is a composition of A and B. Ultimately, composition is the only necessary relationship between abstractions of an architecture. Often architectures are described with components and connectors. The connector is often a runtime dependency. Thinking of components A and B as connected will induce us to let A or B have knowledge of each other. If A and B collaborate, however subtly, there will be a detrimental knowledge dependency between them, which will destroy them as abstractions. This is especially problematical when there is only one instance of each component. The lack of reuse makes it less likely to think of them as knowledge independent abstractions. Whenever we draw two components and connect them with a line, we should think of that as shorthand for two composition relationships. The drawing of instances of A and B connected by a line is just code completely contained inside C. From the point of view of A, B and C and all other abstractions in the system, the only relationship between them should be composition.

P6-Layers: Layers provide a framework for controlling dependencies. They should obviously be down the chosen layers, not across or within a layer and certainly not upwards.

Following on from principle **P3**, the only dependencies allowed are knowledge dependencies. This significantly changes how we do layering. Layering should only reflect the design time view. It should not contain layers based on run-time dependencies. Apart from [11], the layering metaphor is frequently used to represent runtime dependencies. For example, layering schemes such as GUI/Business logic/database, 3-tier, the OSI communications model are all based on runtime dependencies. Those dependencies run both ways. For instance, at run-time a database on its own is just as useless as a GUI on its own, and data will flow in both directions. To fit these systems into knowledge layers, they need to be rotated ninety degrees. Now the metaphor for them becomes a chain. Their component abstractions would generally all go into one layer, like A and B in our previous examples. One additional abstraction, like C in our previous example, would go in a higher layer. It would instantiate the required abstractions for a given application, configure them and connect them together.

P7-Stable Dependencies Principle: From $P5$ and $P6$ we have abstractions arranged in layers connected only by composition relationships going down. Ripple effects of change, are now confined to these composition relationships. To reduce the likelihood of the ripple effects, we reduce the likelihood of changing abstractions in lower layers. There is a relationship between abstraction, stability and reuse in that they tend to increase together. The lower layers should have increasing stability, and therefore increasing abstraction and reuse [8]. In higher layers, the abstractions are more specific so that is where the majority of change will be. All knowledge specific to the application requirements or other changeable things such as hardware are put in the highest layer abstractions.

P8-Abstraction Granularity: There is a threshold point that should occur at about 100 to 500 lines of code that relates to our brain's capacity to handle complexity. Abstractions larger than this size may be too complex and need decomposing. If the average size is too small, abstractions will become numerous, again increasing the complexity.

P9-Primary Separation - Requirements from Implementation: The first division line of decomposition is to separate requirements from implementation. This is the same principle used by DSLs. The requirements are expressed, succinctly, in terms of domain abstractions that you invent. Only internal DSLs are used (we don't want the disadvantages that external DSLs entail). The representation of the requirements knows nothing of the implementation and the implementation knows nothing of the requirements. Both depend on abstractions. The representation of requirements may typically take only about 1% of the total code.

P10-Fluent Expression of Requirements: Maintainability is directly proportional to the ease with which new or changed requirements can be implemented into an existing system. More maintainable code bases allow requirements and the top-level application code that expresses them, to have a high degree of one to one correlation.

P11-Diagrams: Architectures must distill out details. We make a distinction between the use of Diagrams and Models (or boxes and lines). Models, as we define them, can leave out details arbitrarily, and these details can turn out to be important at the architectural level. Diagrams, as we define them, can only leave out details inside abstractions. Diagrams are therefore protected from change caused by the details. Diagrams are also executable. Diagrams are true source code.

Models should not be used as documentation of the large-scale structure of our code, as in for example an informal UML model. That would mean that the actual large scale-structure of the code is implicit and distributed in the detailed code. The structure should be explicit and in one place.

Diagrams and text are tools for different situations. Text is better for representing linear chains of relationships, or small tree structures that can be represented through indenting. Diagrams are better in situations where there are arbitrary relationships between the elements, such as in state charts.

The lines on a diagram show the connections and the structure visually. The lines also do it anonymously - without use of identifiers that you would otherwise need to do searches on to find the connections. Diagrams also provide an alternative and much better way to control scope than encapsulation does. Encapsulation is not particularly visible at read-time, and limits scope only to a boundary. A line on a diagram explicitly limits the scope to only those places where it connects.

Existing literature presents architectural tactics to deal with only some of these principles, but we still lack a cohesive reference architecture like ALA for achieving maintainability by design. Standards such as ISO/IEC 25010 define maintainability and its sub-characteristics [6]. Other works, such as the Architecture-Level Modifiability Analysis (ALMA) provide a way to evaluate a given architecture for maintainability [2]. ALMA and ALA both have the same goal. ALMA uses change scenarios to evaluate modifiability of a given architecture. ALA is a reference architecture that is pre-optimized with respect to modifiability. A loose analogy would be solving a mathematical equation. ALMA is analogous to a numerical technique whereas ALA is analogous to a symbolic technique. ALMA requires iteration to find an optimal solution. ALA solves for the optimal solution directly. That solution is the reference architecture. ALMA measures the quantity of interest, modifiability, directly and does so in the context of a domain, so is potentially more accurate (after some iterations). ALA makes the assumption that because the reference architecture satisfies the stated modifiability principles, modifiability is already optimized. The two approaches are complimentary. Compare modifiability with dependability (correctness). The two fundamental techniques here are understandability and testing. The developer first creates code that should be correct by understanding it, and then tests if it is actually correct by testing it. Using one without the other would not work well. Similarly ALA provides an architecture that should be modifiable, but still needs testing that it is actually modifiable.

3   Abstraction Layered Architecture

Abstraction Layered Architecture (ALA) was documented using the Software Architecture Documentation (SAD) process and template [4]. The following subsections follow the structure provided by SAD, and we highlight the key aspects of each part of the overall architecture document.

3.1   Architecture Background and Drivers

ALA is geared towards making embedded code more maintainable. Embedded code bases often contain entities (objects or components) which integrate different programming paradigms like logical, event and navigation flow together. More generally, we consider any object-oriented system written using any language which contains some degree of control or data flow and user interactions. For pure algorithmic problems, like those that essentially carry out sequential and nested function calls, ALA reduces to the well known functional decomposition strategy for functional programs, but adds emphasis on creating functions at discrete abstraction layers. We identify the following *architectural drivers*, based on the sub-characteristics of maintainability as per ISO/IEC 25010 [6]:

- *Modularity* is the degree to which parts of the system are discrete or independent. It depends on the coupling between components, calculated as the ratio between the number of components that do not affect other components and the number of components specified to be independent. It also requires each component to have acceptable cyclomatic complexity.
- *Reusability* relates to the degree to which an asset within one component or system can be used to build other components and/or systems. Reusability depends on the ratio of reusable assets to total assets, as well as the relative number of assets conforming to agreed coding rules.
- *Analysability* is the degree to which we can assess the impact of localized changes within the system to other parts of the system, or identifying individual parts for deficiencies or failures. Analysability depends on the relative numbers of logs in the system, and suitability and proportion of diagnosis functions that meet causal analysis requirements.
- *Modifiability* is the ease at which a part of the system can be modified without degrading existing product quality. It depends on the time taken for modifications themselves, and having measures to check the correctness of implemented modifications within a defined period.
- *Testability* relates to the ability to easily test a system or any part of it. It depends on the proportion of implemented test systems, how independently software can be tested, and how easily tests can be restarted after maintenance.

3.2   Views

We use the *4 + 1* model of documenting a reference software architecture [7]. The *logical view*, which decomposes the overall code base into smaller packages, is the most important aspect of ALA due to its direct impact on maintainability. The other views are also affected and are discussed briefly after we present the logical view.

Logical View. Figure 1 shows a representation of the top layer of ALA. Figure 1(a) shows ALA's focus on the creation of clear interfaces which conform to specific programming paradigms. For instance, we can have explicit, named interfaces for data flow, event flow and navigation flow in a system. Most embedded code bases would benefit from multiple programming paradigms meshed together, and this mapping of interfaces to programming paradigms provides clarity in their use during the creation and maintenance of the application.

Figure 1(b) introduces the concept of a *domain abstraction*. In general, a domain abstraction is a class which explicitly uses named interfaces, selected from the list of available interfaces in Fig. 1(b). A domain abstraction can *accept* an interface, or *provide* an interface, consistent with UML class and component diagrams. Interfaces do not need to be one way. For instance, an interface accepted by a class may not necessarily feed data into the class, and can also receive data. However, the two kinds of interfaces can help in understanding the

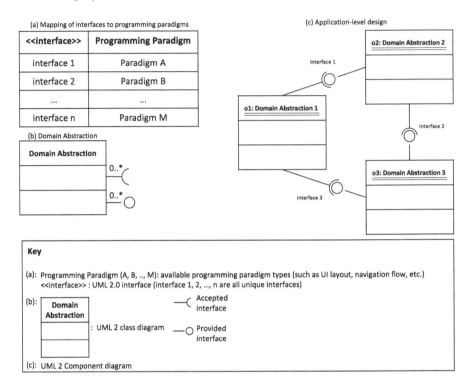

Fig. 1. Primary representation of the logical view in ALA

general flow of data at the application-level (Fig. 1(c)). Another point to note is that domain abstractions can have multiple interfaces and can within themselves use several programming paradigms represented by these interfaces. This is in line with the tight coupling between aspects like event flow and navigation flow in a code base.

Figure 1(c) shows the top-level application code. This is a UML Component diagram containing objects of named domain abstractions, connected or *wired* using compatible interfaces. The idea here is to allow the top-level application design to closely mimic functional requirements. Then, carefully chosen domain abstraction instances can simply be wired or re-wired together as needed. In all, ALA proposes the following four layers, (illustrated in Fig. 2):

1. *Application layer*, as shown in Fig. 1(c), contains knowledge of a specific application, no more and no less. Each requirement or feature of the application is succinctly represented by instantiating and wiring together the objects of domain abstractions defined in the second layer.
2. *Domain Abstractions layer* contains all knowledge specific to the domain, like the domain abstractions shown in Fig. 1. A domain may roughly equate to a company. Its abstractions are reusable across all potential applications in the domain.

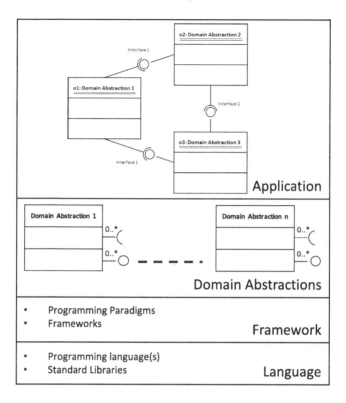

Fig. 2. The four layers in ALA

3. *Framework layer* contains all knowledge of programming paradigms and their associated frameworks and the interfaces shared by domain abstractions. This layer also abstracts out how the Domain Abstraction layer and Application layer execute. For example, a common execution model framework here is 'Event driven'. A common service is a timer service. This layer contains knowledge and services that have potential to be more widely applicable than the domain layer, and consequently are more abstract, stable and reusable than those in the domain layer. We may not have to write anything in this layer ourselves as its ubiquity means that someone else may have already done it. The Applications and Domain Abstractions will only need to change if we change the programming paradigm or service abstractions.

4. *Language layer* contributes the most generic knowledge, that of the programming language(s) and associated libraries. This layer is included for completeness, but it is so generic, reusable and stable that we would never implement it for ourselves. We would always just choose the language(s) suitable for the types of Applications, Domain Abstractions and Frameworks we are going to make. All of those higher three layers will have knowledge dependencies on this language choice, but if the language is stable, those knowledge dependencies should never be a problem.

These layers are adopted from a similar set of layers proposed in [11]. The layers are relatively discrete, meaning that ideally each layer would be roughly an order of magnitude more abstract, more stable and more reusable than the one immediately above it. Having said that, code contained within a layer need not be completely flat. For instance, in the domain abstractions layer, we can have intra-layer hierarchies where abstractions could be built using local compositions.

Four major layers may seem like a small number. But note that the human brain can be built from just six composition layers - (protons, electrons, etc.), atoms, (protein molecules), (cells or neurons), neural net structures, brain. Sometimes an additional layer may be needed. For example, a features layer could be introduced between the Application and Domain layers. A given application is then a composition of features.

Development View. The development view constrains the process of designing and developing a system. ALA requires significant up-front design, in which the domain abstractions are identified from all known functional requirements. The need for some upfront design puts us clearly outside the camp of the agile purists who might say that the design will emerge over time, and clearly in the camp of the iteration zeroists. After this zero-th sprint spent on design, most of the domain abstractions will be known and any remaining architectural design can be done iteratively, but it remains deliberate and emergence is not encouraged. In ALA, the first application design involves taking one requirement at a time and writing it in terms of suitably invented domain abstractions, until all known requirements have been designed. In this respect the Domain Abstractions together with their shared interfaces form a DSL for concisely implementing requirements. The shared interfaces of the domain abstractions define the grammar. In terms of elements, form and rationale, Domain Abstractions are the elements, the shared interfaces give the form, and this paper provides the rational.

ALA requires two skill levels. It needs the skills of a software architect competent with all the principles outlined in this article, for the architectural design and the on-going architectural refactoring. It then requires only average development skills for coding the domain abstractions and interfaces, as these are already stand alone. TDD suddenly starts to work well here as contractors can be used for the development roles, because they need to know only about the abstractions they work on. When they go, they will not take any other knowledge with them.

Most modifications to a mature system usually only affect the top layer. The top layer will typically contain only 1 to 10% of the total code. Addition of new functionality may require introducing or generalizing domain abstractions.

Process View. The process view is concerned with the runtime structure of a code base. ALA supports both single and multi-process/threaded systems due to its emphasis on ensuring that domain abstraction instances are wired through using the right interfaces logically. How these instances and objects bind at run time is a decision that can be taken later.

Physical View. The physical view allows mapping software to resources like available hardware. ALA does not explicitly constrain the physical view, but the application-level design shown in Fig. 1(c) can be modified to annotate where each part of the diagram executes.

4   Evaluating ALA

We carry out two kinds of evaluations for ALA. Firstly, at the architectural level, we identify the mechanisms that ALA provides for supporting each of the quality attributes identified in Sect. 3.1. These mechanisms are listed in Table 1. Overall, as can also be seen in Fig. 1(c), ALA supports our original goal of ensuring functional requirements can be mapped onto the application level in a one-to-one manner (research question RQ2). The second set of evaluations were based on using ALA on a Tru-Test product. These experiments are described in the following subsections.

4.1   Re-architecting an Existing Product

We chose to re-architect the XR5000, shown in Fig. 3, a hand-held embedded device used for managing several activities on a dairy farm. The device features a number of soft-keys for user actions. The user action associated with a soft-key depends on which screen is currently active. The XR5000 is the latest in a family of such devices produced by Tru-Test, and the code base for the product has been maintained and modified over many years. The XR5000 legacy code base represented a common "big ball of mud" scenario. It contained approximately 200 KLOC. It had taken 3 people 4 years to complete. One additional feature (to do with animal treatments) had taken an additional 3 months to complete - indicative of the typical increasing cost of incremental maintenance for a code base of this type.

For re-architecting this product using ALA, we first did an 'Iteration Zero' (two weeks) to represent most of the requirements of the XR5000. This produced an application diagram with around 2000 nodes. Figure 4 shows a part of the application diagram. Table 2 shows the various kinds of interfaces used and their associated programming paradigms as per Fig. 1.

The size of the diagram was interesting in itself. The actual representation of requirements was about 1% of the size of the legacy code. The nodes were instances of around 50 invented domain abstractions. The diagram was not a model in that it was, in theory, executable. Most requirements were surprisingly easy to represent at the application level. There were occasional hiccups that took several hours to resolve, but as more abstractions were brought into play, large areas of functionality would become trivial to represent. This was a positive beginning.

Table 1. ALA's support for maintainability sub-characteristics as per ISO/IEC 25010

QA	ALA mechanisms
Modularity	The solution consists entirely of modules (that are abstractions). No module need be large because it can always be broken up into a composition of other abstractions
	Cyclomatic complexity can be dealt by hierarchical layer-based decompositions
	Cyclomatic complexity is reduced because modules based on abstractions naturally have a single responsibility
	Upfront design ensures high cohesion within domain abstractions
Reusability	Reusability increases typically by an order of magnitude as we go down each layer
	Two layers are dedicated to two levels of reuse, layer 2 for reuse at the domain level, and layer 3 for reuse at the programming paradigm level
	Interfaces and domain abstractions are reusable types
	Domain abstractions conform to coding rules via interfaces
	The interfaces that exist for connecting domain abstractions are at the reuse level (and abstraction level) of the framework layer
Analysability	Any piece of code, being inside an abstraction, is small and coherent in itself, and the only external knowledge dependencies needed to understand it are on abstractions in lower layers. These abstraction dependencies, being composition relationships, are necessary to the meaning of the higher layer abstraction content
Modifiability	The knowledge contained inside abstractions tends to be naturally cohesive and therefore easy to change
	The knowledge contained inside abstractions is zero-coupled with that in all other abstractions - zero ripple effects
	Dependencies are restricted to true knowledge dependencies, so zero ripple effects from run-time dependencies
	All Dependencies are composition relationships on abstractions, (not their contained knowledge) so ripple effects occur only if the nature of the abstraction itself changes
	Abstractions tend to be naturally stable entities - reducing ripple effects
	Abstractions are an order of magnitude more stable in a lower layer, further reducing ripple effects
Testability	All abstractions can be tested individually within a layer because they are already zero coupled with their peers. Testing mocks can easily be wired to them
	Inter-working of domain abstractions can be tested with straightforward integration tests by wiring each possible combination of abstraction
	Higher layer abstractions are generally tested with their composition of lower layer abstractions intact
	Automated acceptance testing via the external interfaces is not significantly easier in ALA as the system appears as a black box to these type of tests. However 'under the skin' acceptance testing can be easier because all I/O abstractions can be replaced by wiring in modified versions that can mock the hardware instead.

4.2   Adding a New Feature

The diagram created during the re-architecting experiment deliberately did not include the aforementioned "treatments" feature. The next experiment was to add this feature to the application. This involved adding database tables, fields to existing tables, a settings screen, a data screen, and event-driven behaviours. The incremental time for the diagram additions was of the order of one hour.

Fig. 3. The XR5000 embedded device

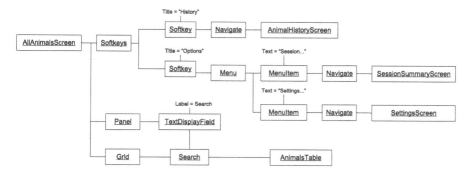

Fig. 4. Sample application-level diagram for a part of the ALA-based XR5000 code base

Obviously testing was needed to be considered also, and the 'Table' abstraction also needed additional work so it could migrate the data in its underlying database, a function the product had not needed up until this point. Although somewhat theoretical, the experiment was evidence to us of a potential order of magnitude improvement in incremental maintenance effort.

The big question now was, could the application diagram be made to actually execute? Fortunately we were allowed to fund a summer undergraduate student for 3 months to try to answer this question. It was a simple matter to translate the application diagram into C++ code that instantiated the abstractions (classes), wire them together using dependency injection setters, configure the instances using some more setters, and use the fluent interface pattern to make all this straightforward and elegant. As an example, the wired code for the diagram sample shown in Fig. 4 is shown in Fig. 5. Thanks to the composability offered by the interfaces of the domain abstractions, wiring instances in code follows exactly the same structure as the application diagram. We have omitted the interface types and kinds (provided or accepted) since we can only

Table 2. Mapping of interfaces to programming paradigms for the XR5000

Interface(s)	Programming paradigm
IUiLayout, IMenuItem	UI layout
IDestination	Navigation flow
IEventHandler	Reactive
ITable	Data flow or stream
iAction	Activity flow

legally connect two instances through compatible interfaces. Also, the distinction between provided and accepted interfaces is more useful when defining the domain abstractions, and not so much during the wiring of their objects because both kinds of interfaces allow bidirectional flow of information.

The student's job was to write the classes for 12 of the 50 abstractions in the application. These 12 were the ones needed to make one of the screens of the device fully functional. The initial brief was to make the new code work alongside the old code, (as would be needed for an incremental legacy rewrite) but the old code was consuming too much time to integrate with so this part was abandoned. The learning curve for the student was managed using daily code inspections, explaining to him where it violated the ALA principles, and asking him to rework that code for the next day. It was his job to invent the methods he needed in the interfaces between his classes to make the system work, but at the same time give no class any knowledge of the classes it was potentially communicating with. It took about one month for him to fully "get" ALA and no longer need the inspections. As a point of interest, as the student completed classes, the implementation of parts of the application other than the one screen we were focused on became trivial. He could not resist making them work. For example, as soon as the 'Screen', 'Softkey' and 'Navigation action' classes were completed, he was able to have all screens displaying with soft-keys for navigating between them, literally within minutes.

The 12 classes were completed in the 3 months, giving the screen almost full functionality - showing and editing data through to an underlying database, searching, context menus, etc. Some of the 12 domain abstractions were among the most difficult needed for the XR5000, and most of the interfaces had to be designed, so there is some validity for extrapolation. Also, performance issues were considered during the implementation. For example, the logical flow of data from a Table to a Grid was actually implemented by passing a list of objects in the opposite direction that describe how the data is transformed along the way. These objects are eventually turned into SQL in a 'Database interface' class within the Table abstraction. We can estimate that the 50 classes may have taken about one man-year to complete for the student. This compares with the 12 man-years to complete the original, conventionally written code. An interesting observation is that the original architecture diagram did not need to change as a result of the implementation of its composite abstractions.

```
#include "Application.h"
...
Application::Application ()
{
    ...//Initialization
    buildAnimalListScreen();
    ...//Run
}
void Application::buildAnimalListScreen()
{
    Softkey* skeyOptions;
    Field* VIDField;
    DisplayField* searchField;
    ColumnOrder* columnOrder;
    Sort* sortAnimal = new Sort();

    m_animalListScreen
        // title bar
        ->wiredTo((new TitleBar())
            ->setTitle(string("Animal > All Animals"))
        )
        // Softkeys
        ->wiredTo((new Softkeys())
            ->wiredTo((new Softkey())
                ->setTitle("History")
                ->wiredTo(new Navigate(m_animalHistoryScreen))
            )
            ->wiredTo((skeyOptions = new Softkey())
                ->setTitle("Options")
                ->wiredTo(new Menu()
                    ->wiredTo(new Navigate("Session...", m_sessionSummaryScreen))
                    ->wiredTo(new Navigate("Settings...", m_settingScreen1))
                    ->wiredTo(new SectionSeparator("Shortcuts"))
                )
            )
        )
        ->wireTo(new Vertical()
            ->wireTo(new Panel()
                ->wiredTo((searchField = new TextDisplayField())
                    ->setLabel("Search")
                    ->setField(VIDField = new Field(COLUMN_VID))
                    ->setPosition(CLIENT_AREA_X, CLIENT_AREA_Y)
                    ->setLabelWidth(200)
                    ->setFieldWidth(CLIENT_AREA_WIDTH - 200)
                )
            )
            ->wiredTo(new Grid()
                ->wiredTo(columnOrder = new ColumnOrder())
                ...
```

Fig. 5. Code snippet relating to Fig. 4

5   Concluding Remarks

Abstraction Layered Architecture or ALA is an attempt to integrate principles that seem to produce code bases that are easy to maintain over a long time. These principles were identified via a review of Tru-Test code bases, both successful or unsuccessful from a maintenance point of view, and supplemented by a review of existing literature on this subject. This set of principles was then used to emerge a reference architecture based on layering of abstractions. We later show how ALA meets the key sub-characteristics of maintainability as per ISO/IEC 25010. More importantly, we show how an existing product at Tru-Test was re-architected and extended using ALA to produce a more maintainable and compact code base in a fraction of the time it took for the original code base.

This paper opens up several exciting directions for future research. We aim to continue developing ALA to incorporate other practices for maintainability, several of which are becoming more apparent as Tru-Test's software operations scale up. Investigating the use of ALA in non-embedded code bases such as for enterprise systems, and gathering empirical data on its effectiveness are some other future directions.

References

1. Alexander, C.: The Nature of Order: The Process of Creating Life. Taylor & Francis, Abingdon (2002)
2. Bengtsson, P., Lassing, N., Bosch, J., van Vliet, H.: Architecture-level modifiability analysis (ALMA). J. Syst. Softw. **69**(1–2), 129–147 (2004)
3. Cataldo, M., Mockus, A., Roberts, J.A., Herbsleb, J.D.: Software dependencies, work dependencies, and their impact on failures. IEEE Trans. Softw. Eng. **35**(6), 864–878 (2009)
4. Clements, P., Garlan, D., Little, R., Nord, R., Stafford, J.: Documenting software architectures: views and beyond. In: Proceedings of the 25th International Conference on Software Engineering, pp. 740–741. IEEE Computer Society (2003)
5. Foote, B., Yoder, J.: Big ball of mud. Pattern Lang. Program Des. **4**, 654–692 (1997)
6. ISO/IEC: ISO/IEC 25010 - Systems and software engineering - systems and software quality requirements and evaluation (SQuaRE) - system and software quality models, Technical report (2011)
7. Kruchten, P.B.: The 4 + 1 view model of architecture. IEEE Softw. **12**(6), 42–50 (1995)
8. Martin, R.C.: Agile Software Development: Principles, Patterns, and Practices. Prentice Hall, Upper Saddle River (2002)
9. Nicolau, A.: Run-time disambiguation: coping with statically unpredictable dependencies. IEEE Trans. Comput. **38**(5), 663–678 (1989)
10. Ossher, H., Tarr, P.: Using multidimensional separation of concerns to (re)shape evolving software. Commun. ACM **44**(10), 43–50 (2001)
11. Page-Jones, M., Constantine, L.L.: Fundamentals of Object-Oriented Design in UML. Addison-Wesley Professional, Boston (2000)
12. Perepletchikov, M., Ryan, C., Frampton, K.: Cohesion metrics for predicting maintainability of service-oriented software. In: 2007 Seventh International Conference on Quality Software, QSIC 2007, pp. 328–335. IEEE (2007)
13. de Souza, S.C.B., Anquetil, N., de Oliveira, K.M.: A study of the documentation essential to software maintenance. In: Proceedings of the 23rd Annual International Conference on Design of Communication: Documenting and Designing for Pervasive Information, pp. 68–75. ACM (2005)
14. Visser, E.: WebDSL: a case study in domain-specific language engineering. In: Lämmel, R., Visser, J., Saraiva, J. (eds.) GTTSE 2007. LNCS, vol. 5235, pp. 291–373. Springer, Heidelberg (2008). https://doi.org/10.1007/978-3-540-88643-3_7

Towards Preserving Information Flow Security on Architectural Composition of Cyber-Physical Systems

Christopher Gerking[1(✉)] and David Schubert[2]

[1] Paderborn University, Heinz Nixdorf Institute, Paderborn, Germany
[2] Fraunhofer IEM, Paderborn, Germany
christopher.gerking@upb.de

Abstract. A key challenge of component-based software engineering is to preserve extra-functional properties such as security when composing the software architecture from individual components. Previous work in this area does not consider specific characteristics of cyber-physical systems like asynchronous message passing, real-time behavior, or so-called *feedback* composition with two-way communication. Thereby, a composition of secure components might lead to insecure architectures with undetected information leaks. In this paper, we address the preservation of information flow security on composition of cyber-physical systems, taking the above characteristics into account. We refine security policies during the architectural decomposition, and outline a compositional verification approach that checks the security of individual components against their refined policies. On composition of secure components, our approach preserves security and thereby enables the design of secure software architectures. We give a proof of concept using a component-based software architecture of a cyber-manufacturing system.

Keywords: Information flow · Composition · Cyber-physical systems

1 Introduction

Due to the distributed and interconnected nature of cyber-physical systems, *component-based software engineering* is widely used for their architectural design [3]. A crucial challenge for software architects is to preserve extra-functional properties of individual components when composing the overall software architecture. For cyber-physical systems, one such key property is *security*. Thus, a composition of secure components should not result in an insecure architecture.

The theory of *information flow security* [9] allows to detect information leaks in the application-level behavior of software systems, giving provable security guarantees at an early design stage. However, information flow security is not necessarily preserved on composition [8] because the communication behavior of components might conflict with crucial assumptions of other components.

© Springer Nature Switzerland AG 2018
C. E. Cuesta et al. (Eds.): ECSA 2018, LNCS 11048, pp. 147–155, 2018.
https://doi.org/10.1007/978-3-030-00761-4_10

The problem that we address in this paper is to preserve information flow security on composition of component-based software architectures for cyber-physical systems. The communication within such systems is special in many regards. First, cyber-physical systems typically communicate by message passing because they are often spatially divided and wirelessly connected. However, asynchronous message passing contradicts the frequent assumption that systems communicate synchronously [8]. Second, the communication must comply with hard real-time constraints imposed by the physical environment. This real-time behavior must be taken into account to detect *timing channels*, i.e., information leaked through the system's response times. Third, the application-level communication protocols used by cyber-physical systems are usually based on a two-way communication. This form of composition, known as *feedback*, is a major limiting factor for the preservation of information flow security [15].

Related work on compositional security does either not take the above characteristics of cyber-physical systems into account [1,5,13,14], or is not based on information flow security and therefore does not give provable security guarantees [2,6,11,16]. In both cases, composing architectures from secure components might lead to undetected information leaks.

In this paper, we extend our previous work [4] by proposing a compositional verification approach for the information flow security of component-based cyber-physical systems. We establish a basis for compositionality of our approach by providing software architects with a set of well-formedness rules for refining security policies during the architectural decomposition of systems. Following these rules allows to refine a global, system-wide security policy into a well-formed set of local security policies for individual components. On this basis, we outline a verification technique to check if the real-time message passing behavior of an individual component complies with its local security policy. On feedback composition, our approach ensures that local security of the individual components implies global security of the overall software architecture. Thereby, we enable software architects to preserve security on architectural composition.

We illustrate our approach based on a cyber-manufacturing system that enables *manufacturing as a service*. To this end, the system communicates both with a service market and a knowledge base. On composition of the system's software architecture from individual components, software architects need to ensure that no sensitive information from the knowledge base is leaked to the public service market.

In summary, this paper makes the following contributions:

- We propose well-formedness rules for refining security policies during decomposition of cyber-physical systems into a component-based architecture.
- We outline a verification technique to preserve the information flow security of individual components on composition of the overall architecture.

Paper Organization: We introduce our underlying component model in Sect. 2, before proposing well-formedness rules for refining security policies in Sect. 3. In Sect. 4, we outline our compositional verification approach. Finally, we discuss related work in Sect. 5, before concluding in Sect. 6.

2 Component Model

We assume a top-down architectural design of component-based systems. Starting with an initial top-level component, a hierarchical software architecture is formed by iterative decomposition into *subcomponents*. The bottom-level components without further subcomponents encapsulate a stateful behavior that drives the communication of a component with other components inside the architecture. Hence, the behavior of composite components results from the composition of their subcomponents. Components communicate asynchronously by passing messages over *ports*. To that end, ports must be linked by a *connector*. A *delegation* is a connector between a component and a subcomponent at the next lower level. In contrast, a connector between two components at the same hierarchy level is called *assembly*. Since the message passing between components is used to realize complex, application-level communication protocols, we assume that every port both receives input messages and sends output messages. This form of composition, underlying a two-way communication, is known as *feedback* [15].

Figure 1 shows the architecture of a Manufacturing-as-a-Service (MaaS) system that provides manufacturing services to a market. The top-level component named Manufacturing System is composed of two subcomponents. Production Control coordinates the execution of an order received from the market. Knowledge Management provides all the information required to execute the order.

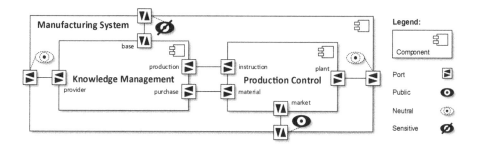

Fig. 1. Example component architecture of a manufacturing-as-a-service system

In the following, we describe the system's behavior without going into details about the communication protocols and the concrete message passing. An order received by the Manufacturing System is delegated to the market port. Subsequently, Production Control requests a material overview and the control instructions for the plant over the material and instruction ports. Knowledge Management answers both requests based on a product specification that is acquired from an internal knowledge base, or alternatively from an external provider. We assume that in both cases the required materials are identical, however, the provider's instructions deviate from the instructions in the knowledge base which are regarded as a business secret. After Production Control receives both information, it orders the materials over the market port and controls the production over the plant port.

Information flow security [9] of the MaaS system requires that no information from the knowledge base is leaked to the market. According to this approach, we distinguish between *public* and *sensitive* information. A system is secure if the public information given by the system does not depend on any sensitive information. To specify such security requirements at the architectural level, we extend each component with a *security policy* by categorizing the component's ports according to their sensitivity. Thus, a security policy is a labelling for each port of a component as either public, sensitive, or *neutral* (i.e., neither public nor sensitive). To comply with its security policy, a component must ensure that its communication behavior over public ports does not depend on information received over sensitive ports. In contrast, an information flow from sensitive to neutral or from neutral to public is not restricted. In our approach, the sensitivity of a message corresponds to the labelling of the port that sends or receives it.

Figure 1 illustrates a security policy for the Manufacturing System. The base port is labelled as sensitive because it provides access to the secret knowledge base, whereas the market port is labelled as public due to its open access. The remaining ports are labelled as neutral. Whether or not the system is secure depends on the communication behavior of its subcomponents. Therefore, in the remainder of this paper, we refine the security policy along with the decomposition into subcomponents (cf. Sect. 3), and apply compositional verification based on the resulting refined security policies (cf. Sect. 4).

3   Refining Security Policies on Decomposition

Based on the initial top-level component of a software architecture, we present an iterative procedure for refining the component's security policy during the architectural decomposition. Thereby, decomposing a component leads to a set of refined security policies, one for each subcomponent. To refine a security policy, software architects need to provide each port of a subcomponent with a sensitivity label. However, a crucial requirement for the refined policies is compositionality, i.e., the composition of refined policies must imply the security policy of the composite component. To ensure compositionality, we provide software architects with a set of well-formedness rules (WFR) that are derived from the validity conditions for compositional security analyses by Mantel [8]. These rules restrict the sensitivity labels for the ports of subcomponents as follows:

(WFR1) Inheritance on Delegation: A port that is connected to a delegation inherits the sensitivity label of the delegating port. This rule ensures that subcomponents do not upgrade or downgrade the sensitivity of ports.

(WFR2) Equivalence on Assembly: Every two ports that are connected by an assembly must share the same sensitivity label. Thereby, we ensure that two assembled components agree on the sensitivity of their connected ports.

(WFR3) Non-Neutrality on Assembly: A port connected by an assembly must not be labelled as neutral. We thereby ensure that neutral ports can not be exploited to indirectly leak information from one subcomponent to the other. Thus, assembled ports must either be public or sensitive.

During decomposition, the sensitivity of all delegated ports follows immediately from WFR1. For example, in Fig. 2a, we depict the inheritance of sensitivities for the neutral provider port and the sensitive base port. In contrast to delegations, assemblies require architects to assess the sensitivity of information exchanged between the assembled components. In accordance with WFR2 and WFR3, Fig. 2b illustrates the labelling of the communication between production and instruction as sensitive, whereas the communication between purchase and material is labelled as public. In general, assessing these sensitivities is a manual effort and requires architects to anticipate the communication behavior of components. In particular, the assessed sensitivities might be subject to change if the specified component behavior can not be made compliant with the resulting security policy. However, the provided well-formedness rules ensure that if the behavior of subcomponents complies with the refined policies, then the policy of the composite component is complied as well.

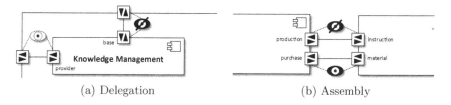

(a) Delegation   (b) Assembly

Fig. 2. Well-formedness of sensitivities on architectural decomposition

4   Preserving Security on Composition

We now present a verification approach to check if the message passing behavior of a bottom-level component complies with its security policy. A crucial requirement for our approach is *compositionality*, i.e., when composing two secure components, the composition must preserve security. To this end, we select a definition of information flow security that is known to be preserved on feedback composition, provided that the underlying communication is asynchronous [15]. The selected definition, named *generalized noninterference* [10], requires that any *perturbation* of sensitive inputs (i.e., adding or deleting received messages) does not alter the public communication of a system. To verify this property, we check that the public communication of a component is equivalent to a perturbed variant of itself that receives a varying set of sensitive input messages.

In Fig. 3, we illustrate our verification approach based on the equivalence of public communication between the Manufacturing System and a corresponding *Perturbed System*. The perturbation applies to all messages received over the sensitive base, production, and instruction ports. To verify the global security policy of the Manufacturing System, we check both Production Control and Knowledge Management against their local security policies, which were refined according to the rules given in Sect. 3. Thus, the verification comprises two equivalence checks between the bottom-level components and their perturbed variants. For restricting the equivalence to public communication, we consider only messages sent or received over the public purchase, material and market ports. Due to the compositionality of generalized noninterference, equivalence for the two bottom-level components implies equivalence for the top-level component. Thus, if both subcomponents comply with their refined security policies, then the Manufacturing System is secure with respect to its security policy as well.

As a vehicle for checking the equivalence of communication, we rely on the notion of *bisimulation* which requires two systems to send and receive equivalent sequences of messages. However, due to the real-time behavior in our approach, the instant of time at which messages are processed needs to be equivalent as well. Deviations in the timing might enable public observers to deduce sensitive information from the system's response times. Thus, in our previous work [4], we detect such timing channels by model checking a time-sensitive variant of bisimulation known as *timed bisimulation*. By reusing this approach, we make our compositional verification accessible to automation using off-the-shelf tools.

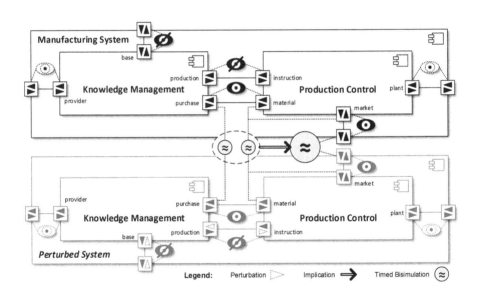

Fig. 3. Compositional verification of the Manufacturing System component

5   Related Work

Research on compositional information flow security has been pioneered by McCullough [10] and led to a uniform theory by Mantel [8]. In this section, we focus on approaches for compositional security at the architectural level.

Gunawan and Herrmann [6] as well as Copet and Sisto [2] provide compositional verification approaches for security properties at design level, similar to our work. However, both approaches are not based on information flow security, lacking provable security guarantees. Said et al. [13], Sun et al. [14] as well as Greiner et al. [5] enable the compositional verification of component-based systems based on information flow security. In contrast to our work, no systematic refinement of security policies during the architectural design is addressed.

By contrast, Zhou and Alves-Foss [16] provide a set of architectural refinement patterns for preserving generic multi-level security properties. Whereas the authors guide the architectural design itself, our aim is to refine security policies during design. Chong and van der Meyden [1] propose a theory of refinement for secure software architectures. The authors deduce global information flow security from the resulting architectural structure and from local security constraints of individual components. In this respect, their work is similar to our approach.

However, none of the aforementioned approaches takes the specific characteristics of cyber-physical systems into account, such as asynchronous communication or real-time behavior. By contrast, Mohammad and Alagar [11] address the verification of multiple trustworthiness properties like access control security in component-based systems. Similar to our approach, real-time behavior of systems is considered, and composition rules are proposed to preserve properties. However, the approach does not take information flow security into account. Li et al. [7] address the compositional verification of information flow security in the presence of message passing. However, their work enforces security of individual processes at program level. Thus, the architectural design and the refinement of security policies are beyond their scope. Rafnsson et al. [12] propose a set of *combinators* to preserve information flow security of processes under composition. The authors consider both time-sensitive behavior and asynchronous communication. However, their approach is limited to discrete time and does not take the refinement of security policies during architectural design into account.

6   Conclusions and Future Work

We proposed a compositional verification approach for the information flow security of component-based cyber-physical systems. We provided a set of well-formedness rules to refine security policies during the architectural decomposition. Furthermore, we sketched a compositional approach to verify generalized noninterference of the overall software architecture. Our approach is based on timed bisimulations to check the real-time message passing behavior of individual components against their refined security policies. On composition of the overall architecture, our approach preserves the security of components.

Our well-formedness rules guide software architects during the architectural decomposition, allowing them to systematically refine security policies alongside. Our verification enables the architects to reason about the security of an architecture only by checking the bottom-level components against their refined security policies. Thereby, we avoid the drawbacks of a monolithic verification.

In future work, we intend to automate our approach using an off-the-shelf model checking tool. Furthermore, we seek to underpin our work by formally proving the soundness of the compositional verification under consideration of real-time behavior. In addition, we intend to weaken our well-formedness rules for the refinement of security policies, providing software architects with a higher degree of freedom during the architectural decomposition. Finally, we also plan to extend our scope towards variable and self-adaptive software architectures.

References

1. Chong, S., van der Meyden, R.: Using architecture to reason about information security. ACM Trans. Inf. Syst. Secur. **18**(2), 8:1–8:30 (2015)
2. Bettassa Copet, P., Sisto, R.: Automated formal verification of application-specific security properties. In: Jürjens, J., Piessens, F., Bielova, N. (eds.) ESSoS 2014. LNCS, vol. 8364, pp. 45–59. Springer, Cham (2014). https://doi.org/10.1007/978-3-319-04897-0_4
3. Crnkovic, I., Malavolta, I., Muccini, H., Sharaf, M.: On the use of component-based principles and practices for architecting cyber-physical systems. In: CBSE 2016, pp. 23–32. IEEE (2016)
4. Gerking, C., Schubert, D., Bodden, E.: Model checking the information flow security of real-time systems. In: Payer, M., Rashid, A., Such, J.M. (eds.) ESSoS 2018. LNCS, vol. 10953, pp. 27–43. Springer, Cham (2018). https://doi.org/10.1007/978-3-319-94496-8_3
5. Greiner, S., Mohr, M., Beckert, B.: Modular verification of information flow security in component-based systems. In: Cimatti, A., Sirjani, M. (eds.) SEFM 2017. LNCS, vol. 10469, pp. 300–315. Springer, Cham (2017). https://doi.org/10.1007/978-3-319-66197-1_19
6. Gunawan, L.A., Herrmann, P.: Compositional verification of application-level security properties. In: Jürjens, J., Livshits, B., Scandariato, R. (eds.) ESSoS 2013. LNCS, vol. 7781, pp. 75–90. Springer, Heidelberg (2013). https://doi.org/10.1007/978-3-642-36563-8_6
7. Li, X., Mantel, H., Tasch, M.: Taming message-passing communication in compositional reasoning about confidentiality. In: Chang, B.-Y.E. (ed.) APLAS 2017. LNCS, vol. 10695, pp. 45–66. Springer, Cham (2017). https://doi.org/10.1007/978-3-319-71237-6_3
8. Mantel, H.: On the composition of secure systems. In: IEEE S&P, pp. 88–101. IEEE (2002)
9. Mantel, H.: Information flow and noninterference. In: van Tilborg, H.C.A., Jajodia, Sushil (eds.) Encyclopedia of Cryptography and Security, pp. 605–607. Springer, Boston (2011). https://doi.org/10.1007/978-1-4419-5906-5
10. McCullough, D.: Noninterference and the composability of security properties. In: IEEE S&P, pp. 177–186. IEEE (1988)
11. Mohammad, M., Alagar, V.S.: A formal approach for the specification and verification of trustworthy component-based systems. J. Syst. Softw. **84**(1), 77–104 (2011)
12. Rafnsson, W., Jia, L., Bauer, L.: Timing-sensitive noninterference through composition. In: Maffei, M., Ryan, M. (eds.) POST 2017. LNCS, vol. 10204, pp. 3–25. Springer, Heidelberg (2017). https://doi.org/10.1007/978-3-662-54455-6_1

13. Ben Said, N., Abdellatif, T., Bensalem, S., Bozga, M.: Model-driven information flow security for component-based systems. In: Bensalem, S., Lakhneck, Y., Legay, A. (eds.) ETAPS 2014. LNCS, vol. 8415, pp. 1–20. Springer, Heidelberg (2014). https://doi.org/10.1007/978-3-642-54848-2_1

14. Sun, C., Xi, N., Li, J., Yao, Q., Ma, J.: Verifying secure interface composition for component-based system designs. In: APSEC 2014, pp. 359–366. IEEE (2014)

15. Zakinthinos, A., Lee, E.S.: How and why feedback composition fails. In: CSFW 1996, pp. 95–101. IEEE (1996)

16. Zhou, J., Alves-Foss, J.: Security policy refinement and enforcement for the design of multi-level secure systems. J. Comput. Secur. **16**(2), 107–131 (2008)

Microservices Architectures

A Quantitative Approach for the Assessment of Microservice Architecture Deployment Alternatives by Automated Performance Testing

Alberto Avritzer[1], Vincenzo Ferme[2], Andrea Janes[3], Barbara Russo[3],
Henning Schulz[4], and André van Hoorn[2(✉)]

[1] EsulabSolutions, Inc., Princeton, NJ, USA
[2] University of Stuttgart, Stuttgart, Germany
van.hoorn@informatik.uni-stuttgart.de
[3] Free University of Bozen-Bolzano, Bolzano, Italy
[4] NovaTec Consulting GmbH, Leinfelden-Echterdingen, Germany

Abstract. Microservices have emerged as an architectural style for developing distributed applications. Assessing the performance of architectural deployment alternatives is challenging and must be aligned with the system usage in the production environment. In this paper, we introduce an approach for using operational profiles to generate load tests to automatically assess scalability pass/fail criteria of several microservices deployment alternatives. We have evaluated our approach with different architecture deployment alternatives using extensive lab studies in a large bare metal host environment and a virtualized environment. The data presented in this paper supports the need to carefully evaluate the impact of increasing the level of computing resources on performance. Specifically, for the case study presented in this paper, we observed that the evaluated performance metric is a non-increasing function of the number of CPU resources for one of the environments under study.

1 Introduction

The microservices architectural style [13] is an approach for creating software applications as a collection of loosely coupled software components. These components are called microservices, and are supposed to be autonomous, automatically and independently deployable, and cohesive [13]. This architecture lends itself to decentralized deployment, and for continuous integration and deployment by developers. Several large companies (e.g., Amazon and Netflix) are reporting significant success with microservice architectures [9].

Currently, several deployment alternatives are possible for microservices deployment, as for example, serverless microservices using lambdas, container-based deployment (e.g., Docker[1]), virtual machines per host, and several hosts.

---

[1] https://www.docker.com/.

© Springer Nature Switzerland AG 2018
C. E. Cuesta et al. (Eds.): ECSA 2018, LNCS 11048, pp. 159–174, 2018.
https://doi.org/10.1007/978-3-030-00761-4_11

Of course, depending on the microservice granularity, a combination of these deployment mechanisms could be used. The available deployment alternatives and their configuration parameters imply a large space of architectural configurations [15] to choose from.

Microservices are supposed to be independent from each other. However, the underlying deployment environment might introduce coupling and impact the overall application performance. Coupling can occur at the load balancer, at the DNS look-up, and at the different hardware and software layers that are shared among the microservices. Ueda et al. [16] report the performance degradation of microservice architectures as compared to an equivalent monolithic deployment model. The authors have analyzed the root cause of performance degradation of microservice deployment alternatives (e.g., due to virtualization associated with Docker) and have proposed performance improvements to overcome such a degradation. Therefore, microservice architects need to focus on the performance implications of architectural deployment alternatives. In addition, the impact of the expected production workloads on the performance of specific microservices deployment configuration needs to be taken into account. The alternatives for microservice architecture deployment considered in this paper are memory allocation, CPU fraction used and number of Docker container replicas assigned to each microservice.

In this paper, we introduce a quantitative approach for the performance assessment of microservice deployment alternatives. The approach uses automated performance testing results and high-level performance modeling to quantitatively assess each architectural configuration in terms of a domain metric introduced in this paper. For performance testing, we focus on load tests based on operational workload situations [10,17], e.g., arrival rates or concurrent number of users.

Our approach for the domain metric evaluation is based on the input domain partition testing strategy [19] and domain-based load testing [5] that was designed for the performance testing of telecommunication systems. In partition testing based on input domains, the input domain is divided into subsets that have equivalent fault-revealing behavior. In domain-based load testing the load testing domain is divided into subsets that have equivalent workload situations [5].

Operational profile data is used to estimate the probability of occurrence of each operational workload situation in production. Each operational situation is reflected by a performance test case that is weighted by its relevance based on the operational profile. Scalability requirements are used to assess each architectural configuration. The resulting quantitative assessment is a measure between 0–1 that assesses the fitness of a certain architecture alternative to perform under a defined workload situation.

The key contributions of this paper are as follows:

- a new quantitative approach for the assessment of microservice deployment alternatives, and
- the experimental validation of the proposed approach.

We have evaluated the introduced domain metric for ten different configurations based on two different memory allocations, two different CPU allocations, and three different values for the number of Docker container replicas. The experiments were executed in two data center environments. We evaluated for each environment the best performing architectural configuration. It is very significant that in both environments, increasing the number of containers for the service being evaluated, or the fraction of CPU allocation did not guarantee better performance. Therefore, we can conclude that it is very important for practitioners to carefully assess expected operational profiles and deployment alternatives of their applications using quantitative assessment approaches, such as the one introduced in this paper.

The remainder of this paper is organized as follows. Section 2 contains a summary of the reviewed literature on microservice architecture challenges and performance assessment. Section 3 contains an overview of the proposed approach for performance assessment of microservice architectures. Section 4 contains the experimental design, while Sect. 5 presents the experimental results obtained by applying the proposed approach. Section 6 contains the threats to validity identified in this research. Section 7 presents our conclusions and suggestions for future research. A reproducibility package is provided online [4].

2   Related Work

In this section we present a summary of the reviewed literature on microservice architecture challenges.

2.1   Microservice Architectural Challenges

Alshuqayran et al. [2] present a comprehensive literature review of microservice architectural challenges. The authors focus on the challenges, the architecture descriptions, and their quality attributes. They have found that most of the current research on microservice architecture quality attributes has focused on scalability, reusability, performance, fast agile development, and maintainability. Pahl and Jamshidi [14] present a systematic survey of the existing research on microservices and their application in cloud environments. They have found that microservices research is still immature and there is a need for additional experimental and empirical evaluation of the application of microservices to cloud environments. Their literature survey has also identified the need to develop microservices tool automation.

Francesco et al. [9] present a characterization of microservice architecture research. The authors' focus was on answering research questions about publication trends, research focus, and likelihood for industrial adoption. They reported that research on microservices is in the initial phases concerning architecture methodologies and technology transfer from academia to industry. Most of the research focus seems to be on architecture recovery and analysis. An important finding of this paper is that most of the literature reviewed is related to the design phase, and only one research did address requirements. They have also found from their literature survey that industrial technology transfer of the architecture methodology is still far-off.

Esposito et al. [7] present design challenges of microservice architectures. The authors have identified security and performance as major challenges resulting from size and complexity. They have proposed to address these challenges by carefully trading-off security and performance.

2.2   Performance Assessment of Microservice Architectures

Kozhirbayev and Sinnott [11] present the performance assessment of microservice architectures in a cloud environment using several container technologies. The authors have reported on the experimental design and on the performance benchmarks that were used for this performance assessment. Casalicchio and Perciballi [6] analyze the impact of using relative and absolute metrics to assess the performance of autoscaling containers. They have concluded that for CPU-dominated workloads, the use of absolute metrics can lead to better scaling decisions.

McGrath and Brenner [12] present an approach for the design of a performance-oriented serverless computing platform. The authors have evaluated the performance of their approach using measurements derived from a prototype. They have also discussed how to achieve increased throughput using their approach.

3   Approach

In this paper, we extend our previous approaches [5, 18] to define a new methodology for the assessment of microservice deployment alternatives—also referred to as *(architectural) configurations*. Our methodology enables an automatic assessment of scalability criteria for architectural configurations and their comparison. For each configuration, this results in a measure—the so-called domain-metric—that quantifies the configuration's ability to satisfy scalability requirements under a given operational profile.

3.1   Summary of Previous Work

In [18], we introduced a metric to evaluate software architecture alternatives with system workload growth. This metric uses the requirement definition, high-level architecture modeling, and system measurement results to assess the system architecture's ability to meet architecture requirements as a function of workload increases.

In [5], we introduced an approach for the assessment of telecommunication systems using Markovian approximations. This approach uses operational data and a resource-based Markov state definition to derive an efficient test suite that is then used as the basis for the domain-based reliability assessment of the

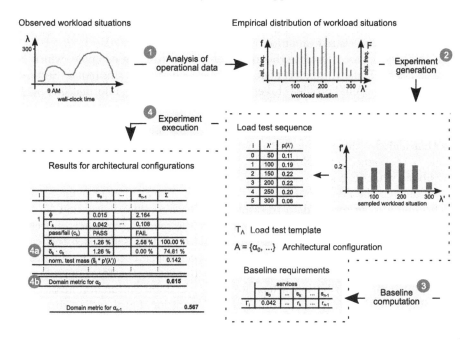

Fig. 1. Overview of the approach

software under test (SUT). The Markovian approximation is used to estimate the steady-state probability of occurrence of each test case. In this way, the test suite can be effectively reduced to focus on the performance test cases that are most-likely to represent production usage. In domain-based load testing, the input domain is the workload, e.g., in terms of the arrival rate or the concurrent number of users. The total workload is divided into subsets that are related to the probability of occurrence of each workload situation [5]. Therefore, we make an implicit assumption that the testing domain can be divided into fault-revealing subsets. Each subset is then mapped to a load test.

3.2   Computation of the Domain-Based Evaluation Metric

The approach introduced in this paper and illustrated in Fig. 1 consists of the following steps: 1. *Analysis of operational data*, i.e., the quantitative estimation of the probability of occurrence of a certain workload situation (e.g., number of concurrent users) based on the analysis of the operational data, 2. *Experiment generation*, i.e., the automated generation of the load test cases for the deployment configurations under evaluation, 3. *Baseline computation*, i.e., the quantitative definition of the scalability requirements that consist of the expected pass/fail criteria for the load tests, e.g., based on a specified threshold of the system response time for the expected workload, 4. *Experiment execution*, i.e., the execution of load test cases for the architectural configurations specified in the experiment generation step, and the computation of the domain-based microservice architecture evaluation metric.

In this section, we illustrate the approach with a running example, which is based on the SUT and the experiments from the evaluation in this paper (Sects. 4 and 5). The operational profile is taken from publicly available information about a video streaming service.

Step 1—Analysis of Operational Data – This step relies on operational data that includes the workload situations Λ observed over time, i.e., each point in time t_k is assigned a workload situation $\lambda_i \in \Lambda$. We make no specific assumptions about what metric is used to represent the workload situation. Example metrics include the number of concurrent users or arrival rates of requests. We use this operational profile data to estimate for each workload situation $\lambda_i \in \Lambda$ its probability of occurrence $p(\lambda_i)$ estimated by the relative frequency of occurrence $f(\lambda_i)$. The probability of occurrence will be used to weigh each test case execution result. This is called probability of occurrence because it provides a test coverage function for each test case with respect to the total operational profile probability distribution, which we denote by *total probability mass*.

To illustrate this step, we first analyze the operational profile data to create a user profile of the frequency of occurrence (i.e., state frequency) of the number of concurrent users (i.e., workload situation) found in the system at a certain time t. The graph of the state frequency distribution is shown in Fig. 1 (result of Step 1). Then, for each workload situation λ_i, we set $p(\lambda_i)$ to the corresponding state frequency. The test suite coverage criteria is based on the values of $p(\lambda_i)$. Then, we use the operational profile obtained from the video streaming service as a proxy for the operational profile of the system being evaluated. We have scaled the number of concurrent users from the operational profile to 0–300.

Step 2—Experiment Generation – This step generates the load test suite to analyze the architectural configurations. The four elements of this step are the load test sequence, the load test template, the architectural deployment configurations, and the baseline requirements (see result of Step 2 in Fig. 1). The load test sequence is obtained by sampling the empirical distribution of workload situations f into a so-called aggregated mass of workload situations f' that are representative for the neighboring workload situations. A value $f'(\lambda')$ represents the aggregated probability of neighboring workload situations of λ in f. The reason for having this aggregated mass based on sampling is that it would not be feasible to execute load tests for every single workload situation due to the huge combinatorial space of configurations. The load test template T_Λ is a load test specification that is parameterized by a workload situation $\lambda_i \in \Lambda$. An instance of this load test template will be executed for each element of the cross product of the set of load test sequences and the architectural configurations. The baseline requirement Γ_i defines for each service s_j provided by the SUT the criteria of a passed/failed test based on a performance measure Φ. We denote the concrete measurements for Φ for a service s_j under a workload situation λ as $x(\lambda)_j$. We make no specific assumption about the performance measure. An example used in this section is the average response time of a service.

Table 1. Scalability requirements based on baseline measurements (in seconds)

s_j	createOrder	basket	getCatalogue	getItem	login	...
$x(\lambda')_j$	0.018	0.008	0.011	0.012	0.033	...
$\sigma(\lambda')_j$	0.008	0.003	0.002	0.009	0.025	...
Γ_j	0.042	0.017	0.017	0.039	0.108	...

Step 3—Baseline Computation, Quantitative Definition of the Scalability Requirements – We now describe the approach that can be used to calculate the fraction of correctly executed services $\hat{s}_i$ for test case i. Initially, a baseline performance test is run for each configuration $\alpha_k \in A$, similarly to the approach used in our previous work [18]. Such baseline is chosen with a starting workload situation $\beta \in \Lambda$. Then, the average response time, $x(\beta)_j$, and the standard deviation, $\sigma(\beta)_j$ for each service s_j, under the baseline workload β are measured.

Using the baseline performance measured for each service s_j, the scalability requirement is defined as $\Gamma_j = x(\beta)_j + 3 \times \sigma(\beta)_j$. Table 1 illustrates the measured results for the baseline measurement workload β, for all services s_j. This is an innovative approach for scalability requirements definition that employs the measured no-load baseline performance to automatically define a specific tolerance for scalability degradation under load.

The proposed approach for setting scalability requirements using a normal distribution follows an existing approach [3], where the normal distribution was shown to be a good approximation for the distribution of a stream of concurrent transactions.

Step 4a—Experiment Execution (Pass/Fail Assessment) – Next, each service s_j is tested under a certain workload $\lambda_i \in \Lambda$ and configuration $\alpha_k \in A$. Each test case execution produces a metric between 0–1 that represents the fraction of the service executions that was assessed as successful by comparison with the scalability requirement.

Each service s_j will be marked as pass for workload λ_i and configuration α_k, if $x(\lambda_i)_j < \Gamma_j$. In this case, $c_j = 1$ will be set to denote that service s_j has passed the test, otherwise $c_j = 0$ will be set.

In the following, we drop λ and the configuration α to simplify the notation, as these computations are repeated for each workload situation and configuration. In addition, as each test case i executes the set of n services $\{s_0, \ldots, s_{n-1}\}$ with activation rates $\{\delta_0, \ldots, \delta_{n-1}\}$, the fraction $\hat{s}_i$ of correctly executed calls to all services can be evaluated as:

$$\hat{s}_i = \sum_{j=0}^{n-1} \delta_j c_j \tag{1}$$

The activation rate δ_j denotes the fraction of calls to the service s_j over the overall number of calls to all services. Table 2 illustrates the pass/fail estimation for one workload situation λ. For this test case, the fraction of correctly executed services was evaluated as $\hat{s}_i = 74.81\%$ (Fig. 1).

Table 2. Pass/fail based on scalability requirements (in seconds) for workload situation λ

s_j	createOrder	basket	...	login	...
Γ_j	0.042	0.017	...	0.108	...
$x(\lambda)_j$	0.015	0.009	...	2.164	...
Pass/fail	pass	pass	...	fail	...
δ_j	1.26%	1.26%	...	2.58%	...

Step 4b—Experiment Execution (Computation of Domain-based Metric) – Finally, the domain-based architecture evaluation metric for the configuration α, with respect to a test suite S, $D(\alpha, S)$ can be evaluated as:

$$D(\alpha, S) = \sum_{i=0}^{z} p(\lambda_i)\hat{s}_i \qquad (2)$$

where $p(\lambda_i)$ is the frequency of occurrence corresponding to workload situation λ_i (as in Step 1). For the running example, as illustrated in Fig. 1, $D(\alpha, S)$ would be evaluated as 0.615. The contribution of the test case case depicted in Fig. 1 is 0.142 ($0.19 \times 74.81\%$). The resulting quantitative assessment is a measure between 0–1 that can be used to assess the performance of different architectural deployment configurations.

4   Experiment Design

In our evaluation, we show how to use our approach as illustrated in Fig. 1 to assess the scalability of an environment for a specific target system and its architectural alternatives by utilizing the domain metric. We use the operational profile from Step 1 (Sect. 3) and apply it to the Sock Shop microservices demo in two different environments. We execute the experiments generated by our Step 2 and compare the results against individual baselines as per Step 3. In doing so, we cannot only show the usage of our approach but also reveal interesting insights on scalability of microservice applications and its adoption in practice.

The remainder of this section describes the precise details of our experiment design. A reproducibility package is provided online [4].

4.1   System Under Test

As system under test (SUT), we utilize the most recent version of the Sock Shop microservices demo (as per March 28, 2018[2]) built by Weaveworks. It represents

---

[2] https://microservices-demo.github.io/.

a sample e-commerce website that sells socks, implemented using 12 microservices, one of which is named *cart*, handling the user's shopping cart. For the implementation, various technologies were used, e.g., Java, .NET, Node.js and Go. The Sock Shop has been found to be a representative microservice application regarding several aspects [1]. For our research, the usage of well-known microservice architectural patterns, the automated deployment in containers and the support for different deployment options were the main criteria for selecting the Sock Shop as the SUT.

4.2   Load Testing Tool

As the load testing tool, we use BenchFlow [8], that is an open-source framework[3] automating the end-to-end process of executing performance testing. BenchFlow reuses and integrates state of the art technologies, such as Docker[4], Faban[5], and Apache Spark[6] to reliably execute load tests, automatically collect performance data, and compute performance metrics and statistics, as well as to validate the reliability of the obtained results.

BenchFlow users define their performance intent relying on a declarative domain-specific language (DSL) for goal-driven load tests by using provided declarative templates for expressing tests' requirements such as the test goals and test types, metrics of interest, stop conditions (e.g., maximum test execution time) and which parameters to vary during the execution of the test. To satisfy the user's goal, the BenchFlow framework implements strategies and processes to be followed that are driven by the user's input specification and current conditions of the SUT during the execution of those processes.

4.3   Testing Infrastructure

We deployed the load testing tool and the SUT to two different infrastructures. The first one supports containerized deployment to bare metal at the Hasso Plattner Institute (HPI) Future SOC (Service-Oriented Computing) Lab. The second one enables containerized deployment in virtual machines on top of the VMware ESXi[7] bare metal hypervisor at the Free University of Bozen-Bolzano (FUB).

The containerized bare metal machines (HPI) have the following characteristics: **Load driver server**—32 GB RAM, 24 cores (2 threads each) at 2300 MHz and **SUT server**—896 GB RAM, 80 cores (2 threads each) at 2300 MHz. Both machines use magnetic disks with 15 000 rpm and are connected using a shared 10 Gbit/s network infrastructure.

The containerized deployment in virtual machines (FUB) has the following characteristics: **Load driver server**—4 GB RAM, 1 core at 2600 MHz and **SUT server**—8 GB RAM, 4 cores at 2600 MHz with SSDs. Both machines use

---

[3] https://github.com/benchflow.
[4] http://docker.com.
[5] http://faban.org.
[6] http://spark.apache.org.
[7] https://www.vmware.com/products/esxi-and-esx.html.

an EMC VNC 5400 series network attached storage solution[8] and are connected using a shared 10 Gbit/s network infrastructure.

We rely on Docker CE v17.12 for the deployment of the containerized application on both infrastructures.

4.4   Architectural Deployment Configurations

By relying on BenchFlow's DSL [8], users can specify performance tests in a declarative manner. In our case, we defined a load test exploring different system configurations, as presented in Table 4 (on p. 12). BenchFlow supports a wide range of variables to be automatically explored during configuration tests, namely: (i) number of simulated users, (ii) amount of RAM/CPU share assigned to each deployed service, (iii) service configurations, through environment variables, (iv) number of replicas for each service.

We rely on BenchFlow's DSL to define all the experiments reported in this section, and on the BenchFlow framework for their automated execution, test execution quality verification, and results retrieval.

Figure 2 depicts an example SUT deployment, showing one Docker container for each of the 11 microservices (i.e., 11 containers) and two Docker containers for the cart service, running on top of a Docker engine, which is deployed as a daemon process on the bare metal server at HPI and hypervisor at FUB. The figure shows that a container can have multiple replicas.

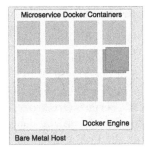

Fig. 2. Docker containers for each microservice (13 containers) running on top of the Docker engine deployed as a daemon process on the bare metal server

4.5   Design of Synthetic User Behavior

Even if we are not focusing on the behavior of an individual user, we need to generate a representative workload on the target system when evaluating its performance. Therefore, we model a synthetic user behavior that is replayed with different numbers of users during the experiments, as per our methodology, representing types of users that could utilize the Sock Shop in reality. We model

---

[8] http://www.emc-storage.co.uk/emc-vnx-5400-emc-vnx5400-vnx5400-storage.

Table 3. Summary of requests and its numbers of occurrence in the user types (V = visitor, B = buyer, O = orders visitor) and actual overall workload mix

Label	Path	Method	V	B	O	Mix (%)
home	/index.html	GET	2	3	2	11.85%
login	/login	GET	0	1	1	3.21%
getCatalogue	/catalogue	GET	2	4	2	12.56%
catalogueSize	/catalogue/size?size={}	GET	1	1	0	3.07%
cataloguePage	/catalogue?page={}& size={}	GET	1	1	0	3.07%
catalogue	/category.html	GET	1	1	0	3.07%
getItem	/catalogue/{}	GET	1	5	1	8.42%
getRelated	/catalogue?sort={}& size={}& tags={}	GET	1	2	0	3.78%
showDetails	/detail.html?id={}	GET	1	2	0	3.78%
tags	/tags	GET	1	1	0	3.07%
getCart	/cart	GET	4	9	3	23.34%
addToCart	/cart	POST	0	1	0	0.71%
basket	/basket.html	GET	0	1	0	0.71%
createOrder	/orders	POST	0	1	0	0.71%
getOrders	/orders	GET	0	1	1	3.21%
viewOrdersPage	/customer-orders.html	GET	0	1	1	3.21%
getCustomer	/customers/{}	GET	2	5	1	10.78%
getCard	/card	GET	0	1	0	0.71%
getAddress	/address	GET	0	1	0	0.71%

the following behavior mix [17]: three types of users with the respective relative frequency, and a maximum allowed 5% deviation for the defined frequency distribution:

- *visitor* (40%): visits the home page, views the catalog and the details of some products.
- *buyer* (30%): visits the home page, logs in, views the catalog and some details, adds a product to the cart, visits the cart, and creates an order.
- *order visitor* (30%): visits the home page, logs in, and views the stored orders.

The summary of all requests sent to the Sock Shop and the occurrence of each requests in the user types are provided in Table 3. We set a workload intensity function [17] with 1 min of ramp-up and 30 min of steady state, to ensure the system reaches the steady state and we collect reliable performance data. We have added a negative exponential think time, which is executed between every two requests, with 0, 1, and 5 s for minimum, mean and maximum think time respectively and an allowed deviation of 5% from the defined time.

4.6 Experiment Runs

We deployed the SUT using ten different architectural configurations per testing infrastructure. The parameters we vary over the different configurations are

Table 4. Domain metric $D(\alpha, S)$ per configuration $\alpha = $ (RAM, CPU, # Cart Replicas) in the two environments (HPI, FUB). The configuration with the highest domain metric is highlighted.

RAM	CPU	# Cart replicas	$D(\alpha, S)$ (HPI)	$D(\alpha, S)$ (FUB)
0.5 GB	0.25	1	0.61499	0.54134
1 GB	**0.25**	**1**	**0.77631**	0.53884
1 GB	0.5	1	0.53559	0.54106
0.5 GB	0.5	1	0.51536	0.54773
0.5 GB	0.5	2	0.50995	0.54111
1 GB	0.25	2	0.74080	0.54785
1 GB	0.5	2	0.53401	0.54106
0.5 GB	*0.5*	*4*	0.50531	*0.54939*
1 GB	0.25	4	0.37162	0.54272
1 GB	0.5	4	0.56718	0.54271

the amount of available RAM, the CPU share, and the replicas for the cart service. We target the cart service, as most of the requests issued by the designed workload (see Sect. 4.5) target the cart service. The different configurations we explore are reported in Table 4. We set the RAM to [0.5 GB, 1 GB], the CPU share to [0.25, 0.5], and the number of replicas to [1, 2, 4].

The remaining resources of the server on which we deploy the SUT are shared among all the other services part of the Sock Shop application and managed by the Docker engine. In order to avoid containers to be "killed" during the execution in case of out-of-memory, we disabled this behaviour on the Docker engine.

By relying on the operational data presented in Sect. 3, we identified the following number of users interacting with the system, resembling aggregated workload situations for the system: 50, 100, 150, 200, 250, 300.

The baseline experiment (Step 3, Sect. 3), which we conduct to set a reference point for our methodology, sets the RAM to 4 GB, the CPU share to 1 and the replicas to 1 for the cart service, and measures the performance when 2 users interact with the system.

In total, we executed 122 experiments with different configurations.

5   Empirical Results

In this section, we describe and analyze the results of our experiments that are described in Sect. 4, as per Step 4 in Sect. 3. All the experiment results are available online [4].

5.1   Results

Figure 3 shows the test masses for the different investigated architectural configurations in relation to the workload situations Λ (numbers of users). The domain

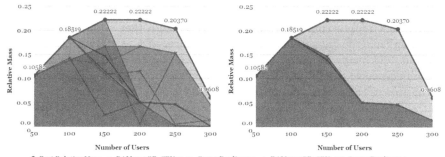

Fig. 3. Relative and best test masses per number of users in the two environments (HPI, FUB)

metrics $D(\alpha_i, S)$ for all configurations $\alpha_i \in A$ are provided in Table 4. The best relative test mass plot represents the theoretical maximum which is reached if all tests pass. It can be seen from Fig. 3 that none of the alternatives reached the best relative mass, because of scalability assessment failures identified. For the HPI environment (bare metal), the configuration with 1 GB of RAM, 0.5 CPU share, and four cart replicas not have failures for up to 150 users. However, the relative mass decreases significantly when the number of users is increased. For the FUB environment (bare metal hypervisor), all configurations do not experience failures up to 100 users. After such load, the performance decreases with a similar rate.

For the HPI (bare metal) experiments, the configuration with 1 GB of RAM, 0.25 CPU share and one cart replica has the highest domain metric $D(\alpha, S) \approx 0.78$, followed by the configuration with 1 GB of RAM, 0.25 CPU share, and two cart replicas having a metric value of about 0.74. The worst configuration with $D(\alpha, S) \approx 0.37$ is 1 GB of RAM, 0.25 CPU share, and four cart replicas. This is an interesting result with significant implications to the assessment of architectural deployment alternatives, since adding additional replicas with the same memory and CPU configuration may decrease the application's performance for the HPI environment.

The results for the FUB experiments (VMware ESXi11 bare metal hypervisor), show a significant performance degradation as assessed by the domain metric, when compared to the HPI experiment. In addition, most of the experiment results are within a narrow domain metric range as can be seen from Fig. 3 where most of the lines overlap. The configuration with 0.5 GB of RAM, 0.5 CPU share, and four cart replicas obtains the highest domain metric for the FUB experiments, with $D(\alpha, S) \approx 0.54$. The worst domain metric for the FUB experiment is for the 1 GB of RAM, 0.25 CPU share and one cart replica configuration. However, this configuration was assessed as the best configuration among the HPI experiments. The difference in the domain metric assessment between the HPI and FUB environments for the 1 GB of RAM, 0.25 CPU share, and one cart replica configuration, seems to indicate that additional architecture factors may be impacting system performance, such as VMware Hypervisor overhead, I/O bandwidth, etc. These findings support the recommendation that practitioners have to evaluate the expected operational profile and deployment alternatives in their own context.

5.2 Analysis

Our results show that determining the best deployment configuration for an application requires the systematic application of quantitative performance engineering approaches.

We have found that adding more CPU power or increasing the number of Docker container replicas may not result in system performance improvement. As listed in Table 4, the best configuration at HPI is 1 GB of RAM, 0.25 CPU share and one cart replica, with the domain metric value of 0.77631. In addition, more cart replicas at HPI results in performance degradation. For example, the configuration with 1 GB of RAM, 0.25 CPU share, and four cart replicas, was assessed as $D(\alpha, S) = 0.37162$, while the configuration with 1 GB of RAM, 0.5 CPU share, and one cart replica, was assessed as $D(\alpha, S) = 0.55356$. At FUB, the domain metric oscillates over a narrow range. Scaling beyond 0.5 GB of RAM, 0.5 CPU share, and 4 cart replicas does not lead to a better performance if the number of users is higher than 150. In addition, the choice of the HPI or the FUB deployments have significant impact on the domain metric as shown in Table 4. These findings suggest that bottleneck analysis and careful performance engineering activities should be executed before additional resources are added to the architecture deployment configuration.

6   Threats to Validity

The following threats to validity to our research were identified:

Operational Pofile Data Analysis. The domain metric introduced in this paper relies on the careful analysis of production usage operational profile data. Many organizations will not have access to accurate operational profile data, which might impact the accuracy of the domain metric assessments. Several approaches can be used to overcome the lack of accurate operational profile data [5], such as: using related systems as proxy for the SUT, conducting user surveys, and analyzing log data from previous versions of the SUT.

Experiment Generation. Experiment generation requires the estimation of each performance test case probability of occurrence, which is based on the operational profile data. When the operational profile data granularity is coarse there is a threat to the accuracy of the estimated operational profile distribution. Some of the suggested approaches to overcome the coarse granularity of the operational profile data are: performing the computation of operational profile data using analytic or simulation models [18], and developing heuristics based on Markovian approximations [5].

Baseline Computation. The suggested approach for the quantitative definition of the scalability requirements proposed in this paper consisted of defining the expected pass/fail criteria for system scalability based on a specified percentile (e.g., 3 σ) of the system response. This approach works well if we assume that a baseline performance for each microservice was validated. However, the approach could provide a worst case scalability requirement, if one of the microservices' baseline performance is already exhibiting significant performance degradation.

Experiment Execution. The proposed approach for automated execution and analysis of the load test cases needs to be assessed for continuous improvement using a declarative approach and automated deployment.

7   Conclusion

In this paper, we have introduced a new four-step approach for the quantitative assessment of microservice architecture deployment alternatives. Our approach consists of operational profile data analysis, experiment generation, baseline requirements computation, and experiment execution. A domain-based metric is computed for each microservice deployment alternative, specified as an architectural configuration. The metric (0–1) reflects the ability of the deployed configuration to meet performance requirements for the expected production usage load.

We have applied our approach to several deployment configurations in a large bare metal host environment, and a virtualized environment. The approach took advantage of automated deployment of Docker containers using a state-of-the-art load test automation tool.

Our approach contributes to the state of the art by automatically deriving baseline performance requirements in a baseline run and assessing pass/fail criteria for the load tests, using a baseline computation of these requirements.

We have found that in auto-scaling cloud environments, careful performance engineering activities shall be executed before additional resources are added to the architecture deployment configuration, because if the bottleneck resource is located downstream from the place where additional resources are added, increased workload at the bottleneck resource may result in a significant performance degradation.

Acknowledgements. This work has been partly supported by EsulabSolutions, Inc., the German Federal Ministry of Education and Research (grant no. 01IS17010, ContinuITy), German Research Foundation (HO 5721/1-1, DECLARE), the GAUSS national research project, which has been funded by the MIUR under the PRIN 2015 program (Contract 2015KWREMX), and by the Swiss National Science Foundation (project no. 178653). The authors would like to thank the HPI Future SOC Lab (period fall 2017) for providing the infrastructure.

References

1. Aderaldo, C.M., Mendona, N.C., Pahl, C., Jamshidi, P.: Benchmark requirements for microservices architecture research. In: Proceedings of ECASE@ICSE, pp. 8–13. IEEE
2. Alshuqayran, N., Ali, N., Evans, R.: A systematic mapping study in microservice architecture. In: Proceedings of SOCA, pp. 44–51 (2016)
3. Avritzer, A., Bondi, A.B., Grottke, M., Trivedi, K.S., Weyuker, E.J.: Performance assurance via software rejuvenation: monitoring, statistics and algorithms. In: Proceedings of DSN, pp. 435–444 (2006)
4. Avritzer, A., Ferme, V., Janes, A., Russo, B., Schulz, H., van Hoorn, A.: Reprodicibility package for "a quantitative approach for the assessment of microservice architecture deployment alternatives using automated performance testing". https://doi.org/10.5281/zenodo.1256467
5. Avritzer, A., Weyuker, E.J.: The automatic generation of load test suites and the assessment of the resulting software. IEEE Trans. Softw. Eng. **21**(9), 705–716 (1995)
6. Casalicchio, E., Perciballi, V.: Auto-scaling of containers: the impact of relative and absolute metrics. In: Proceedings of FAS*W@SASO/ICCAC, pp. 207–214 (2017)
7. Esposito, C., Castiglione, A., Choo, K.K.R.: Challenges in delivering software in the cloud as microservices. IEEE Cloud Comp. **3**(5), 10–14 (2016)
8. Ferme, V., Pautasso, C.: A declarative approach for performance tests execution in continuous software development environments. In: Proceedings of ACM/SPEC ICPE, pp. 261–272 (2018)
9. Francesco, P.D., Malavolta, I., Lago, P.: Research on architecting microservices: trends, focus, and potential for industrial adoption. In: Proceedings of ICSA, pp. 21–30 (2017)
10. Jiang, Z.M., Hassan, A.E.: A survey on load testing of large-scale software systems. IEEE Trans. Softw. Eng. **41**(11), 1091–1118 (2015)
11. Kozhirbayev, Z., Sinnott, R.O.: A performance comparison of container-based technologies for the cloud. Future Gener. Comp. Syst. **68**, 175–182 (2017)
12. McGrath, G., Brenner, P.R.: Serverless computing: design, implementation, and performance. In: Proceedings of ICDCSW, pp. 405–410 (2017)
13. Newman, S.: Building Microservices, 1st edn. O'Reilly Media Inc., Newton (2015)
14. Pahl, C., Jamshidi, P.: Microservices: A systematic mapping study. In: Proceedings of CLOSER, pp. 137–146 (2016)
15. Taylor, R.N., Medvidovic, N., Dashofy, E.M.: Software Architecture: Foundations, Theory and Practice. Wiley, Hoboken (2009)
16. Ueda, T., Nakaike, T., Ohara, M.: Workload characterization for microservices. In: Proceedings of IISWC, pp. 1–10 (2016)
17. Vögele, C., van Hoorn, A., Schulz, E., Hasselbring, W., Krcmar, H.: WESSBAS: extraction of probabilistic workload specifications for load testing and performance prediction–a model-driven approach for session-based application systems. Softw. Syst. Modeling **17**(2), 443–477 (2018)
18. Weyuker, E.J., Avritzer, A.: A metric for predicting the performance of an application under a growing workload. IBM Syst. J. **41**(1), 45–54 (2002)
19. Weyuker, E.J., Jeng, B.: Analyzing partition testing strategies. IEEE Trans. Softw. Eng. **17**(7), 703–711 (1991)

Crunch: Automated Assessment of Microservice Architecture Assignments with Formative Feedback

Henrik Bærbak Christensen[(✉)]

Computer Science, Aarhus University, Aarhus, Denmark
hbc@cs.au.dk

Abstract. Microservice architectures and the DevOps development practices have become essential as companies strive to provide reliable and robust software systems supporting millions of users at the same time as new features are released and defects corrected and deployed in hours rather in months or years. It is therefore relevant to teach the microservice architectural style as well as the DevOps practices to our students. A central tenet of DevOps is *fast feedback* which pose a problem when it comes to providing formative feedback on exercises handed in by students. In this paper, we present the architectural design challenges in assessing student solutions embodying microservice systems as well as our analysis and solutions to them. We present our implementation, Crunch, and present student and instructor evaluation of having this support in a concrete course.

1 Introduction

Over the last decade, practices have been developed to bring agility to not only the software development process itself but all the way into software deployment and production. The rationale is that it serves little purpose to have test driven development, Scrumm, and other practices produce software fast, if the software takes months to be deployed in production. From the development process perspective, one notable practice is DevOps which is *a set of practices that aim to decrease the time between changing a system and transferring that change to the production environment* [2]. From a software architecture perspective, a notable architectural style is microservice architecture which *describes a particular way of designing software applications as suites of independently deployable services, that [...] have common characteristics around organization around business capability, automated deployment, intelligence in the endpoints, and decentralized control of languages and data* [19].

In this paper, we outline a master level course that aims to teach central practices of DevOps as well as to teach architectural tactics for microservice architectures, notably for achieving high availability. As the learning vehicle, the course uses the development of a microservice system as the central case, formulated as a progression of exercises requiring enhancing architectural quality

© Springer Nature Switzerland AG 2018
C. E. Cuesta et al. (Eds.): ECSA 2018, LNCS 11048, pp. 175–190, 2018.
https://doi.org/10.1007/978-3-030-00761-4_12

attributes of the system (improved availability and performance), keeping the system under automated test control, and agile deployment in a production environment. A central pedagogical tenet in the course is to provide fast and continuous feedback to students on their developed architecture and source code implementations. Our automated assessment system, Crunch, was developed to achieve this for a subset of the exercises.

Our main contribution is to present an architectural analysis for automated assessment (AA) of student submissions of microservice architectures with formative feedback. We outline the additional challenges compared to traditional AA of single programs, analyse the design space, and argue for our choices. Second, we present our implementation, Crunch, and demonstrate how it fits in our teaching context, and present student and instructor experiences.

2   Related Work

Recent literature surveys [16,17] have analysed and classified automated assessment (AA) tools from 1976 and onwards. They analysed research papers and tools, and identified seven techniques for assessing submissions and for providing feedback to students, such as model tracing, static analysis, program transformations, automated testing, and others. In their analysis of 74 AA systems, the by far most employed technique is *automated testing* (54 systems)—in its most basic form, the student's program is run and its output compared to the expected. In more elaborate AA systems, student's programs are subjected to instructor written test cases and feedback is the failed tests.

Our tool, Crunch, falls squarely in this automated testing class: It starts the student's services, execute a number of test cases on them, and verify that output is correct. If not, students are presented with common root causes of failures as well as detailed execution traces for failure analysis. All AA systems reported by Kuening et al. handles just a single program or a program fragment. Comparing to other class 2 environments [18] (defined as AA systems focused on exercises that have many potential solutions but a particular solution strategy is suggested) we find related work like Sykes's [22] JIST that focus on Java code fragments for novices, the same for Daly et al.'s [10] RoboProf, Truong et al.'s [23] ELP, and Insa et al.'s [14] ASys: These systems combine several techniques to provide strong feedback to students but only consider a code fragment or single source file, not distributed systems.

Our contribution is to extend test-based AA to student developed distributed system, to production deployments, and to assessing non-functional (architectural quality attribute) requirements of these. To the best of our knowledge, this is the first research to report on these aspects. While there is little research to relate to in the area of AA of distributed systems, we acknowledge that the model and architecture of our AA tool have been inspired by *build pipelines* from continuous delivery [13] and uses technology and practices from DevOps [1,24].

3   Educational Context

The context is a course, *Cloud Computing and Architecture*, which is a 5 ECTS quarter length (7-week) course taught for computer science master level students, at Computer Science, Aarhus University. Students have 3–4 years of programming education and training (including courses in algorithms, object-orientation, design patterns, compilers, and distributed computing), and are thus relatively proficient in developing code that fulfill functional requirements.

The intended learning outcomes (ILO) of the course was therefore to cover developing code for non-functional requirements (quality attribute logic), developing the microservice architecture, developing code for deploying (infrastructure logic), as well as developing automated tests for all introduced code.

3.1   Course Pedagogy and Structure

The course pedagogy was designed to closely align with the values and practices of agile development and DevOps, focus strongly on techniques and tools used in industrial practice, and is detailed by Christensen [9]. We combined elements from constructive alignment [4], cognitive apprenticeship [6] with a story-telling approach [7]. These elements were put into practice by structuring the course on these premises:

- Learning activities were primarily quality attribute and infrastructure logic programming assignments on a large DevOps project in which students evolve a functionally correct but simple distributed system (called *SkyCave*) into a cloud based, highly available and fault tolerant, scalable multi-user system. Each exercise added increments of complexity over the previous ones, focusing on enhancing availability, scalability, or performance to the SkyCave system; and testing, deploying, and monitoring it.
- Submissions were in the form of their developed programs and systems. We avoided requesting written reports.
- The final course grade was directly based on the amount and quality of exercises solved. Each exercise has a point score, each solved exercise increased the total score, and this was the foundation for the final grade.

3.2   Learning Vehicle: SkyCave

Students are given a functionally complete "worked example" [6] system, *SkyCave* that provides the scaffolding for their learning activities. SkyCave is inspired by the first adventure game, Colossal Cave Adventure [15]; however, game elements have been removed and replaced by social networking and massive multi-user aspects: Friends can log into the SkyCave, meet in specific rooms, post and read messages on that room's wall, and extend the cave by creating new rooms. A simple interaction is shown below (user commands after the > prompt):

```
== Welcome to SkyCave, player Joe ==
Entering command loop, type "q" to quit, "h" for help.
> look
You are standing at the end of a road before a small brick building.
There are exits in directions:
  NORTH   EAST    WEST    UP
You see other players in this room:
  [0] Joe [1] Carla [2] Peter
> north
You moved NORTH
You are in open forest, with a deep valley to one side.
```

A non-web based interface may seem odd nowadays, but it kept the code base small, in a single programming language (no JavaScript, html, nor css), allowed us to introduce message queues as client-server communication middleware, and user interface issues were not a learning goal of the course.

SkyCave is a classic client-server architecture with students extending and enhancing both the server part (called "daemon" in SkyCave) as well as a text based client part (called "cmd"). Furthermore, the daemon is designed to connect to several external services, such as NoSQL database, a centralized user authorization server, and more, thus forming a microservice architecture.

The initially provided SkyCave uses simple socket-based client-server communication, a JSON based protocol, and a Broker pattern (RPC/RMI) based architecture. It uses a Java8, Ant, Ivy, and JaCoCo toolstack and the code base handed out to students is about 2,300 SLOC implementation and 1,900 SLOC JUnit test code in 78/29 files. It "functionally works" but crashes in case of internal failures, network issues, high load, high latency, etc. It only implements a single-threaded, single server solution, and all external services are only provided by fake-object implementations [20]: for instance, the database interface is implemented by an in-memory hash map—not a real database; etc.

The course had 38 exercises, available at [8], of which 13 were assessed by Crunch, the rest by manual source code review by instructors. To give an impression, example exercises are (a) develop code to interface external REST based authentication service, (b) develop code to store data in external MongoDB NoSQL database server, (c) implement availability patterns like Timeout and Circuit Breaker [21], (d) develop code to handle horizontal scaling of "daemon" using session caching in external Memcached, (e) setting up MongoDB redundancy using passive replication, (f) develop code to use RabbitMQ as message broker between "cmd" and "daemon", and (g) deploy services to DigitalOcean cloud platform. Many exercises were doubled in the sense that one exercise required students to implement code in their "cmd" and "daemon", while the follow-up exercise required students to develop automated tests to validate correct behavior of the developed production code.

Solving all exercises in the course will make student's SkyCave a horizontally scalable system with geographically redundant, sharded, NoSQL databases, session cache servers, gracefully degrading in face of all types of network loss or slow external services, deployed at commercial cloud providers, and required more than 20 correctly configured servers to operate.

3.3   Technological Platform

DevOps practices require that it is fast and automated to establish development and staging environments for testing a set of collaborating services. In current industrial practice, *container technology* plays a central role and was thus a central learning goal of the course. Containers are lightweight virtual machines that are operated from the command-line, and can be controlled from scripts/infrastructure logic. We adopted Linux based Docker [1,11] as it is versatile and well supported. Exercises in the set required students to write *Dockerfiles* which are infrastructure logic code in a Docker defined domain specific language. A dockerfile describes how to build a Docker image that includes the students' services built from their codebase, and defines how to start their services.

Furthermore, Docker allows students to release their solution proposals for exercises by uploading their image with their SkyCave code on Docker Hub[1] which is a cloud based online repository. These images were private and with course instructors given read permission, to avoid plagiarism.

Thus, in addition to be a learning goal, it allows instructors to start student's services, notably the "daemon" service, easily by issuing the docker run command, like:

```
docker run -d css-17:skycave ant daemon -Dcpf=exercise.cpf
```

which translated to "download and next run a container from the docker hub image named 'css-17:skycave' ('css17' is the student group's account name, 'skycave' their image name) by executing `ant daemon -Dcpf=exercise.cpf`; 'ant' invokes the ant build management tool, 'daemon' is the predefined target, and the final part specifies a configuration file specific to the exercise to be tested (See Sect. 5.2 later).

4   Example of Crunch Assessment

In this section, we outline an exercise named 'weather-timeout' whose intended learning outcome is development of quality attribute logic code to increase availability, detail how Crunch assesses it, and finally shows the type of formative feedback presented to the students. It serves as a concrete context to base the later architectural discussion on.

4.1   Assignment 'Weather-Timeout'

One of the commands in the SkyCave client is 'weather' which will print the current weather situation at the student's registered hometown.

---

[1] https://hub.docker.com/.

```
> weather
The weather at: AARHUS
The weather in AARHUS is Cloudy, temperature 12.4C (feelslike 12.1C).
Wind: 4.1 m/s, direction West.
This report is dated: Mon, 29 May 2017 10:38:37 +0200.
```

Architecturally, the "cmd" sends a weather request to its "daemon" server, which in turn must contact an external microservice, a course provided HTTP based weather service, retrieve current weather information, format it, and pass it back to the "cmd". In a previous exercise, named 'weather', students have added code to their SkyCave "cmd" and "daemon" code base to achieve this, but have not considered external weather service failure situations.

The 'weather-timeout' exercise extends upon this exercise and require students to implement a safe failure mode using the *timeout* pattern [21] in case their "daemon" cannot contact the external weather service due to connection errors, or in case the weather service is too slow to respond. The availability requirement is that the 'weather' command never takes more than 8 s to complete, and output details about the cause like e.g.:

```
> weather
The weather service failed with message: *** Weather service not available.
  Slow response. Try again later. ***
```

4.2   Assignment Submission

Students submit an assignment for assessment by Crunch using a webpage which also serves to show an overview of submitted assignments, point score, and formative output (see Fig. 1). The submission process is simple as it only records that the assignment from this group should be assessed by Crunch on its next run. The source code must be released by the students to their docker hub image using the image name that Crunch has recorded for this group.

4.3   Crunch Assessment

Crunch is a batch program which runs at scheduled intervals, and performs an assessment of all submitted exercises for all groups. In our course, Crunch ran every second hour of the day.

For each group, Crunch assesses if the student's latest published image on docker hub fulfills the tests associated with the submitted exercises in a sequence defined by progressive complexity in the assignments: easier first and most complex last. Upon the first failing solution, it skips the assessment of the rest, which also means no points are awarded! This aligns strictly to the agile doctrine: *All tests pass, always.* We will return to this in Sect. 7.

Crunch's internal algorithm is similar to the pipeline architecture in continuous integration servers [13]: A given group's image is subjected to a build pipeline, in which each assignment assessment is similar to a *stage* consisting of a series of *steps* to be performed. In the case of the *assess if group's codebase solves assignment 'weather-timeout'* stage, Crunch will execute these steps:

1. Pull students' image from docker hub.
2. Start a slow responding weather service on address `slowweatherservice:`
   `9876`. It will accept connections but replies are 15 s delayed.
3. Start "daemon" from student's image RECONFIGURED to connect to slow
   responding weather service at `slowweatherservice:9876`.
4. Start "cmd" and issue the 'weather' command.
5. Verify that "cmd" output contains *** *Weather service not available. Slow*
   response. Try again later. ***
6. Verify the time taken between issuing the 'weather' command and the answer
   received is no more than 8 s.
7. Stop "daemon", "cmd", and weather service.

A stage with similar steps was also executed to test for a non-existing weather
service.

4.4   Formative Feedback

A failure is clearly marked in the student group's overview page as shown on
Fig. 1: The 'weather-timeout' entry in the list is red and its status is "Failed".
To get formative feedback, students must follow the "Link to Detailed Result"
link. Figure 2 shows the upper and middle part of the formative feedback to our
student group. The left side of the figure shows the group name, a time stamp, the
name of the docker image used for the scenario run, and the conclusion "Failure".
Next follows the "Steps exercised" section. This lists all actions Crunch made up
until the failing step, similar to our stage outline in Sect. 4.3. Here step 14 failed
"Executing 'ant cmd' and issuing commands to validate assignment 'weather-
timeout' ". Thus the students already know that their server/"daemon" has been
started correctly, as step 13 succeeded.

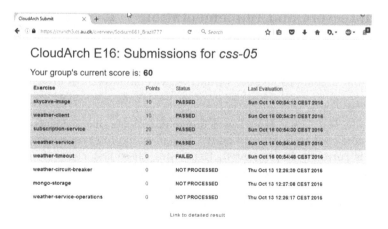

Fig. 1. Assessment page for failed submission

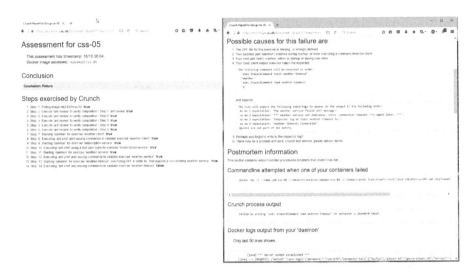

Fig. 2. Feedback - part I (left), and part II (right)

The section named "Possible causes for this failure are", right part of Fig. 2, is formative feedback in which Crunch lists potential sources of the error. This section encodes the instructors' accumulated knowledge of recurring issues in the student's code bases, as well as details the exact test case steps executed and expected output.

Finally, the actual log output from both 'daemon' and 'cmd' are provided for very detailed post mortem analysis by the students. The upper part "Docker logs output from your daemon" is visible in the bottom in the right part of Fig. 2.

5   Architecture and Implementation

Our main contribution is to push the boundary of automated testing AA systems from single programs to distributed, robust, microservice architectures deployed in production. Testing robustness of microservice architectures presents several challenges:

- *Expressing Test Cases.* Exercises define requirements that students must produce source code to fulfill, and an AA tool must express test cases that verify that it is correctly implemented. Expressing these test cases of course rely on a mutual agreement on the interface as the instructor developed test code must call services developed by the students. However, an interface dictated by the AA tool may limit the design space of the students, if not careful.
- *Distribution Challenge.* Microservice architectures are distributed systems and thus not only a single program needs to be executed, but a set of services must be deployed, started, and correctly configured to communicate and collaborate as a cohesive system on a network.

- *Quality Attribute Evaluation.* Our course puts emphasis on enhancing quality attributes, notably increasing availability, or performance of the SkyCave system, through coding appropriate tactics and patterns [3, 21], implement caching, or deploying and configuring redundant services.
- *Operations.* The point of DevOps is putting software into its final operational environment fast—so it can provide value to customers. Thus a central part of assessment is not only that the student's microservices work—but that they are indeed available to the end users.

5.1   Expressing Test Cases

Regarding how to *express test cases*, there are two options:

Internal Test Case Deployment: In the case of Java programs, the obvious choice is using the JUnit[2] testing framework. Though tedious, we would be able to write JUnit test cases in a Java test class, copy this test class into the student's code base in the docker image, and compile, and execute it from within their container: thus test cases are deployed internally in their virtual machine. This allows the unit-under-test (UUT) to be very fine-grained (testing at unit level), like testing a single method in a single class, by the test case code instantiating the class, invoke the method, and verify its output.

External Test Case Deployment: Write test cases that execute in its own container, instantiate student's services (like daemon or cmd or both) in separate containers and execute tests by interacting over the network or some other defined interface: test cases are deployed externally. The UUT is then coursegrained (testing at integration/system level), like sending commands to their 'cmd' command line interface and let it interact with the 'daemon', or sending network packages to the student's daemons in the marshalling format of method calls.

The internal deployment scheme has the decisive liability that it puts much too strong limitations on the student's design space: To compile our test case code as part of their code base, the Java interface, method name, parameter lists, and package had to be dictated as part of the exercise description. This would limit their design space, and also hint much too strongly at a solution, to be desirable at master level.

We therefore adopted to use *external test case deployment*, which treats the student's developed system as a service that our AA tool interacts with as part of the assessment. This is also in line with the course goals of teaching microservices as *independently deployable services.*

The next issue is then to define the interface between an AA tool and the student's "daemon". Again we face two options:

Network Messages: The communication between the "cmd" and "daemon" is in the SkyCave codebase designed using the Broker pattern [5], and implemented

---

[2] www.junit.org.

in the delivered code, using JSON marshalling. It is thus possible to create correctly formatted network messages and send them to, say, the daemon, receive the reply message and demarshall it for verification. Note however, that validating "cmd" behaviour is not possible using this scheme, as "cmd" output goes to the console, and thus no networks messages are interceptable.

User Interface Input/Output: The "cmd" is a command line user interface, with users typing commands (Sect. 4.1) and reading output. Docker allows connecting stdin and stdout of a running container and we can thus programmatically provide input and read output from a student's running "cmd" service and define our test case this way.

We chose the *user interface input/output* scheme for two reason. First, choosing the network message format would delimit the student's design space and ability to change and enhance the network protocol. Indeed one of the later exercises dealt with enhancing performance by changing the protocol. In contrast, the external user interface of the text UI "cmd" was defined once and for all by the assignments. Second, requirements in exercises were stated in terms of UI output which is in line with what to expect in a real development project. And third, it allows validating exercises whose focus is development of code in the "cmd" itself.

Generalizing this to other AA systems for testing student's solution including a web or graphical user interface, would require the provide code base architecture to include a *Window Driver* pattern [12,13], to let the AA mimic user interaction.

The liability is of course that this system level testing is rather coarse-grained and can to some extend be cheated (tests pass, but no real solution coded). To mitigate this, we added a internal inspection tool to the SkyCave code base: basically a dedicated log file that Crunch could read. Exercises had requirements dictating what to write into this specialized log under given circumstances. For instance, one exercise required students to implement the Circuit Breaker pattern [21] which is a state machine. All state transitions had to be written to the inspector log. Crunch would then configure a service that should force their circuit breaker through all state transitions, and then verify that all proper state transitions were written to their inspector log. This allowed Crunch to assess internal state in their system, not visible from a normal system testing level, and thus represents the *specialized interfaces* testability tactic [3].

5.2   Distribution

The *distribution challenge* actually encompass several challenges as seen from an AA viewpoint.

- *Starting and stopping services.* AA relies on scripted executions of students' executables, and in our context this means we have to start and stop microservices developed by them from our AA program.
- *Configuring services for collaboration.* Starting the student's "daemon" is not enough, as it depends on an ever growing number of external services, such

as MongoDB database, MemCached cache servers, external services, etc. In a microservice architecture context, these dependencies are defined by TCP/IP hostnames and port numbers. For most of our AA tests, we need to reconfigure some or all of these bindings.

Regarding the *start and stop services* issue, many virtual machine system (like VMWare and VirtualBox) use graphical user interfaces, which is difficult to operate from an AA test case. We considered Vagrant and Chef, but choose Docker as it suits both our learning goals as well as it is a command-line tool (See Sect. 3.3), making it easy to put under programmatic control. In addition, Docker images are generally small which reduces the time spent on downloading images.

Regarding the *configuring service* issue, it is similar to dependency injection of test doubles [20], like test stubs or mocks, which is normal practice when developing unit tests. However, as our test cases are at the service interface level, the challenge is to reconfigure the student's service to communicate with Crunch defined services, tailored to test a specific scenario. For instance, the 'weather-timeout' assessment in Sect. 4.3 required Crunch to reconfigure the student's "daemon" to interact with a slow responding weather service. For this end, we developed a simple dependency injection framework, *Chained Property File (CPF)*, which is basically property files that define key-value pairs, such as SKYCAVE_WEATHERSERVER = `localhost:8182`. Our exercises required students to specify their configuration in CPF files named after the exercise. So, the interface between Crunch and the student's codebase was that they had to create a CPF file name 'weater-timeout.cpf' for that particular exercise. What sets CPF apart from ordinary property files is that our AA tool could chain itself into it, and overwrite specific properties, much like cascading stylesheets (CSS). Thus to reconfigure their "daemon" to use Crunch's slow responding weather service, Crunch used a special CPF for this exercise, and would start their "daemon" using it `ant daemon -Dcpf=wt-exercise.cpf`. The `wt-exercise.cpf` uses the chaining feature `< (cpf)`:

```
< weather-timeout.cpf
SKYCAVE_WEATHERSERVER = slowweatherservice:9876
```

This CPF file translates to *read and set properties according to the (chained) student CPF "weather-timeout.cpf", and next overwrite the value of key* SKYCAVE_WEATHERSERVER.

5.3   Quality Attribute Evaluation

Assessment of quality attributes using a test based approach pose challenges that range from easy to difficult. For instance, performance testing would require specialised tools, like JMeter, and long-running processes to measure correctly. Crunch is in its first release, and focus on the availability quality attribute which is relatively easy to measure: if safe failure modes are in place, the "daemon" will survive calls to broken external services and produce the proper output;

otherwise it will crash which is easily detected by Crunch. In addition, it is simple to test the timing requirements, like the maximal 8 s delay in 'weather-timeout'.

Table 1. Classification of supported Assignments

Assignment	ILO	Environment
Skycave-image	Deployment	Staging
Weather-client	Functional	Staging
Wall	Functional	Staging
Subscription-service	Microservice	Staging
Weather-service	Microservice	Staging
Weather-timeout	Availability	Staging
Weather-circuit-breaker	Availability	Staging
Mongo-storage	Microservice	Staging
Mongo-storage-wall	Microservice	Staging
Rabbitmq-request-handler	Microservice	Staging
Operations	Operations	Operations
Weather-service-operations	Operations	Operations
Rabbitmq-operations	Operations	Operations

5.4   Operations

Finally, the *operations* aspect was assessed by introducing a set of exercises that required students to deploy their "daemon" on a cloud provider of their choice. Our Crunch AA tests consisted of connecting to their production system every second hour of the day, and exercise a simple user story. The assessment criteria was just that the services were available (servers running and operational) and thus rather weak. However, as Crunch was testing an externally deployed system, it of course had no way of reconfiguring its service bindings.

6   Evaluation

The exercise set contained a total of 38 exercises of which 13 were mandatory to solve (total of 385 points), while 25 were optional (total of 645 points). The full set of exercises can be found in [8]. Table 1 outlines the 13 assignments that Crunch can assess. The table lists the assignment name, the intended learning outcome (ILO), and the environment set up for assessment. Regarding the intended learning outcome column, exercises marked "Microservice" are focused upon extending SkyCave to interact with and deploy new/external services; "Availability" are focused on increasing availability of the "daemon" in failure situations; "Operations" assesses their deployed production system, while "Functional" and "Deployment" are feature adding or deployment related exercises.

The Environment column shows the execution context that Crunch sets up, either a staging environment providing services, or directly in the operational environment in the cloud.

Over the seven weeks of the course, a total of 369 exercises from 32 groups (mean: 11.5 exercises per group) were submitted. Thus at the end of the course Crunch evaluated 369 exercises every two hours.

6.1   Questionnaire

After the course instance in which Crunch was used, a questionnaire was given with seven course related question on a Likert scale from 'Strongly agree' to 'Strongly disagree' plus free text option on all; and a final free text question asking for recommendations for improvement. Two of the questions were regarding the use of Crunch in the course. In all 23 students filled out the questionnaire. The questions regarding Crunch were:

– Question 2 (Q2): "The automated marking by Crunch is better than manual/human review for assignments focusing on functionality"
– Question 3 (Q3): "The automated feedback from Crunch was detailed enough to help me find the cause of failing the test"

The resulting score was more than 95% agreed or strongly agreed on the Q2 statement; while 91% on the Q3 statement. The results are of course encouraging, with more than 90% of the students being happy about the support given by Crunch. Especially encouraging is the about 91% agreement that the formative feedback given by Crunch is adequate for the student's ability to reproduce and ultimately remove defects from their systems. This is also supported by the most common critique in the free text feedback, namely that Crunch should run more often than the two hour interval we had set it for. As one student noted: *"However, why not run Crunch on a more frequent basis (and during night-time it's out!)? I sometimes had to eagerly wait for a long time to see if I had successfully squashed a bug."*

7   Discussion

We have run the course twice with an almost identical exercise set. In the first instance, all assessments were made manually, while Crunch was introduced in the second instance, which allows a comparison. Overall, our experience of using Crunch in the course is positive. Our main motivation was to provide the fast feedback cycle of agile and DevOps development—while some students complained about the "long" two hour cycle, it should be contrasted to manual, instructor provided, feedback that may take days to arrive. A second motivation was the emphasis on regression testing—adding new features should never invalidate existing functionality. We saw that happening on numerous occasions in our first instance of the course using only manual review and testing, while after introducing Crunch no student group would be able to pass the course if this happened. The final motivation, of course, was taking a burden off our shoulders as reviewers. Introducing Crunch meant more time was available to review their design, architecture, and deployment code, without spending a lot of time setting up a staging environment for execution to verify functional behaviour.

We observed one interesting difference between the two instances of the course, namely that the average grade level was significantly lower the second time we ran it: 7.8 versus 9.8 (just above grade C compared to just below grade B)[3]. While there are many reasons for this, we attribute at least some of it to the regression testing nature of Crunch: student's had to keep existing behaviour running.

Crunch is in its first release, and was admittedly developed under an inherent assumption of "good behaviour" from the students, which thus pose a source of error, and also pose a risk of direct cheating. One such issue we discovered was that we assumed the Ant build script in the student's code was unaltered from what we have handed out, and we used a particular Ant target to build and execute their own tests as part of the initial Crunch test 'skycave-image'. After the exam, we discovered at least one group that had changed this target in such a way that it only built their production code but did not run their own tests, and thus not in line with the learning goals. Still, Crunch does validate external production behaviour correctly.

Regarding direct cheating by, say, just writing required "cmd" output instead of implementing real behaviour, we judge the chance as minimal. First, Crunch assesses a piece of behaviour in several ways, for instance, the 'weather' command is first assessed configured with a working service (functional test), next configured to a non-existing service (availability test), and finally configured to a slow responding one (availability). As the students' daemon is shut down and restarted between each test, it cannot maintain state and thus "count how many times it has been assessed, and respond accordingly". Secondly, most of the exercises in the course set were manually review of their produced code (by retrieving the exact same images as Crunch used), so such cheating would have been spotted.

Agile and DevOps development is based on developing strong automated test suites before or as part of production code development, and this was a clearly defined learning goal of the course. However, one may argue that Crunch's tests represent an a priori oracle which allows students to ignore their own test development. We have indications that at least one group used this loophole, but perhaps the complaints from several groups that the "two hour cycle is too long" points in the direction, that others did as well.

---

[3] In Denmark, grades A–E are mapped to a numerical scale, A = 12, B = 10; C = 7, D = 4, and E = 2).

8 Conclusion

In this paper, we have presented Crunch which is a tool to perform automated assessments of microservice assignments while providing formative feedback to the students both in terms of accumulated score but more importantly by providing feedback in order to diagnose why a particular assignment solution fails. We have discussed the learning context, a course on DevOps and microservice architecture, which puts strong emphasis on agile processes which makes it natural that also the feedback cycle on submitted assignments is fast and agile.

Automated assessment of programming exercises is hard, and assessment of client-server systems relying on many external services (client, server, replicated databases, caching services, message queues, credential servers, etc.) are even harder, as the solution space is vast, and setting up the proper execution context for a particular test case is complex. To the best of our knowledge, our contribution is the first reported attempt to tackle this problem.

We have analysed the challenges facing microservice system validation and discussed our design choices: external test case deployment using container technology, validation through user interface input/output, service configuration through chained property files, and finally fine-grained inspection through a special logging mechanism. Common to the first three design solutions are that they operate on service boundaries and not on object boundaries and are thus course-grained. This fits the content of our course well as it is oriented towards microservice architectures, but more importantly it does not limit the solution space much for the students, providing room for student's imagination and freedom of implementation. The fine-grained inspection facility was introduced to enhance Crunch's ability to inspect internal state while leaving the design space open. We find that these design choices are viable and may serve as guidelines for further experimentation and research in the area of automated assessment.

Finally, we have provided data from evaluating Crunch in our teaching context. Though our data is limited, they are still encouraging and points towards the benefits of test-based automated assessment of distributed systems.

Acknowledgements. Daniel Damgaard contributed to the architectural analysis.

References

1. Anderson, Charles: Docker. IEEE Software, pp. 102–105 (2015)
2. Balalaie, A., Heydarnoori, A., Jamshidi, P.: Microservices architecture enables DevOps: migration to a cloud-native architecture. IEEE Softw. **33**(3), 42–52 (2016)
3. Bass, L., Clements, P., Kazman, R.: Software Architecture in Practice, 2nd edn. Addison-Wesley, Boston (2012)
4. Biggs, J., Tang, C.: Teaching for Quality Learning at University. Open University Press, McGraw-Hill, New York City (2007)
5. Buschmann, F., Henney, K., Schmidt, D.C.: Pattern Oriented Software, vol. 4. Wiley, Hoboken (2007)

6. Caspersen, M.E., Bennedsen, J.: Instructional design of a programming course: a learning theoretic approach. In: Proceedings of the Third International Workshop on Computing Education Research, ICER 2007, pp. 111–122. ACM, New York (2007)
7. Christensen, H.B.: A story-telling approach for a software engineering course design. In: Proceedings of the 14th Annual ACM SIGCSE Conference on Innovation and Technology in Computer Science Education, ITiCSE 2009, pp. 60–64. ACM, New York (2009)
8. Christensen, H.B.: Cloud Computing and Architecture, E16 Website. (2016). http://users-cs.au.dk/baerbak/c/cloud-e16/menu1.html
9. Christensen, H.B.: Teaching DevOps and cloud computing using a cognitive apprenticeship and story-telling approach. In: Proceedings of the 2016 ACM Conference on Innovation and Technology in Computer Science Education, ITiCSE 2016, pp. 174–179. ACM, New York (2016)
10. Daly, C., Horgan, J.M.: An automated learning system for Java programming. IEEE Trans. Educ. **47**(1), 10–17 (2004)
11. Docker. Docker web site (2017). www.docker.com
12. Fowler, M.: Window driver (2004). https://www.martinfowler.com/eaaDev/WindowDriver.html
13. Humble, J., Farley, D.: Continuous Delivery: Reliable Software Releases through Build, Test, and Deployment Automation. Addison-Wesley, Boston (2010)
14. Insa, D., Silva, J.: Semi-automatic assessment of unrestrained Java code: a library, a DSL, and a workbench to assess exams and exercises. In: Proceedings of the 2015 ACM Conference on Innovation and Technology in Computer Science Education, ITiCSE 2015, pp. 39–44. ACM, New York (2015)
15. Jerz, D.G.: Somewhere nearby is Colossal cave: examining will crowther's original "Adventure" in Code and in Kentucky. Digit. Humanities Q. **1**(2), 2 (2007)
16. Keuning, H., Jeuring, J., Heeren, B.: Towards a systematic review of automated feedback generation for programming exercises. In: Proceedings of the 2016 ACM Conference on Innovation and Technology in Computer Science Education, ITiCSE 2016, pp. 41–46. ACM, New York (2016)
17. Keuning, H., Jeuring, J., Heeren, B.: Towards a systematic review of automated feedback generation for programming exercises - extended version. Technical report, Department of Information and Computing Sciences, Utrecht, The Netherlands, March 2016
18. Le, N.-T., Pinkwart, N.: Towards a classification for programming exercises. In: Workshop on AI-supported Education for Computer Science, pp. 51–60 (2014)
19. Lewis, J., Fowler, M.: Microservices (2014). https://www.martinfowler.com/articles/microservices.html
20. Meszaros, G.: xUnit Test Patterns: Refactoring Test Code. Addison-Wesley, Boston (2007)
21. Nygard, M.T.: Release It! Design and Deploy Production-Ready Software, 2nd edn. Pragmatic Bookshelf (2018). https://pragprog.com/
22. Sykes, E.R.: Qualitative evaluation of the Java intelligent tutoring system. J. Syst. Cybern. Inform. **3**(5), 49–60 (2006)
23. Truong, N., Roe, P., Bancroft, P.: Static analysis of students' Java programs. In: Proceedings of the Sixth Australasian Conference on Computing Education - Volume 30, ACE 2004, pp. 317–325. Australian Computer Society, Inc., Darlinghurst (2004)
24. Wikipedia. DevOps (2016). www.wikipedia.org. Accessed Jan 2016

Beethoven: An Event-Driven Lightweight Platform for Microservice Orchestration

Davi Monteiro[1]([⊠]), Rômulo Gadelha[1], Paulo Henrique M. Maia[1], Lincoln S. Rocha[2], and Nabor C. Mendonça[3]

[1] State University of Ceará (UECE), Fortaleza, CE, Brazil
{davi.monteiro,romulo.gadelha}@aluno.uece.br, pauloh.maia@uece.br
[2] Federal University of Ceará (UFC), Fortaleza, CE, Brazil
lincoln@dc.ufc.br
[3] University of Fortaleza (UNIFOR), Fortaleza, CE, Brazil
nabor@unifor.br

Abstract. The microservice architecture provides an efficient manner to allocate computational resources since each microservice can be individually scaled. Despite its benefits, there are still challenges regarding the cooperation among different microservices in order to provide elaborated business processes. In this paper, we propose Beethoven, an event-driven lightweight platform for microservice orchestration that eases the creation of complex applications that use microservice data flows. The platform is composed of a reference architecture and an orchestration language. The reference architecture has been instantiated by using the Spring Cloud Netflix ecosystem. To demonstrate the feasibility of the Beethoven platform, an example application has been developed. All artifacts produced as part of this work are available.

Keywords: Event-driven architecture · Reference architecture
Microservice composition · Orchestration

1 Introduction

Microservice Architecture (MSA) arises as a novel architectural style to develop a single application as a collection of independent, well-defined, and intercommunicating services [3]. Microservices are autonomous and communicate with each other through lightweight mechanisms, often an HTTP resource API [2]. In addition, MSA proposes a solution for efficiently scaling computational resources and solving other problems present in a monolithic architecture. Since microservices can be individually scaled, they provide an efficient manner to allocate computational resources, enabling flexible horizontal scaling in cloud environments.

Despite providing numerous benefits, MSA brings costs such as difficulties in explicitly defining collaborations between microservices. Although accessing a microservice through its API using a communication protocol is straightforward,

© Springer Nature Switzerland AG 2018
C. E. Cuesta et al. (Eds.): ECSA 2018, LNCS 11048, pp. 191–199, 2018.
https://doi.org/10.1007/978-3-030-00761-4_13

there are issues to manage business processes that stretch across the boundaries of an individual microservice as the overall software complexity increases [4]. MSA faces challenges such as the cooperation among different microservices in order to provide complex and elaborated business processes. To address this issue, there are two approaches that may be used for microservices composition: orchestration and choreography. The former refers to a centralized business process that coordinates a series of service invocations, while the latter represents decentralized and cooperative service coordination [4].

Although there exist some recent approaches for microservice orchestration [5,6], those solutions have limitations in dealing with the microservices dynamic location since the solutions require a previous registration of the microservices, which compromises the scalability in case of new microservices need to be composed at runtime. Moreover, those solutions are not available for both industry and academic communities, which may compromise their reusability, extensibility, and experimental reproducibility.

To fill that gap, this paper proposes Beethoven, a lightweight platform for microservice composition that eases the creation of complex applications that use microservice data flows. The platform is composed of a reference architecture and an orchestration Domain Specific Language (DSL) that enables software engineers to express microservice orchestration. The reference architecture follows an event-driven design approach and has been instantiated by using the actor model and the ecosystem provided by Spring Cloud Netflix. In order to demonstrate the feasibility of the Beethoven platform, an example application has been developed.

The remainder of this paper is organized as follows. Section 2 presents the theoretical background of this work and discusses relevant existing work related to our proposal. Section 3 describes the Beethoven platform (reference architecture and orchestration DSL). Section 4 outlines the concrete architecture that implements the reference architecture using the ecosystem provided by Spring Cloud Netflix. Section 5 demonstrates the use of Beethoven by means of an example application. Finally, Sect. 6 provides some final considerations.

2 Background and Related Work

For some researchers, MSA is a subset of SOA or a special approach to constrain any SOA-based application to be successful. Although there is no formal definition of the microservices architectural style, Lewis and Fowler [2] describe microservices using the following set of principles: (i) componentization via services; (ii) organized around business capability; (iii) products not projects; (iv) smart endpoints and dumb pipes; and (v) decentralized data management and governance. In addition, in order to address common problems presented in distributed systems, a MSA-based application should implement the following patterns: (i) **Circuit Breaker Pattern:** an effective mechanism to tackle long timeouts and cascading failures; (ii) **Service Discovery Pattern:** a solution used to determine the location of a microservice instance at runtime by using a service registry; and (iii) **Client Side Load Balancer Pattern:** a load balancer that is performed on the client side for routing requests across servers.

The works more closely related to ours are Medley and Microflows. The former, proposed by Yahia et al. [6], is an event-driven platform for service composition based on a DSL for describing orchestration. Before defining a composition, Medley requires to register the information (e.g. endpoints, operations, data types) about each microservice that will be used during the orchestration. Microflows [5] is an approach for microservices orchestration using BDI agents that requires three activities: describing information (e.g. endpoints, supported operations, inputs, and outputs) about a microservice using a JSON-based service description; specifying goals for a particular microservice composition; and defining constraints for the microservice compositions.

As a consequence of the dynamic aspect of a microservice that can be deployed, replicated or reallocated during the application execution, it is not possible to determine the microservice endpoint at design time. For instance, in order to orchestrate microservices using Medley or Microflows, it is required to previously describe and register each microservice that will be part of the orchestration. This means that, if new microservices need to be composed with the existing ones, a software engineer needs to describe and register the new microservices and then restart the orchestration platform.

Therefore, differently from the aforementioned works, Beethoven does not utilize service descriptors for describing and registering microservices, but rather relies on the Service Discovery Pattern to determine the location of a microservice instance during orchestrations, thus making the composition more dynamic and scalable.

3   Beethoven

3.1   Reference Architecture

A reference architecture is a special type of software architecture that provides abstractions and guidelines for the specification of concrete architectures in a certain domain [1]. Figure 1 depicts the general representation of the Beethoven reference architecture using a block diagram (modules). This is a 4-layer architecture composed by API, Service, Database Abstraction, and Orchestration Engine layers, which are described below.

API Layer—provides a uniform interface and endpoints to standardize the access to the Service Layer. Such interface and endpoints are specified following the RESTful standard and conventions, being technology-agnostic.

Service Layer—provides a controlled access point to the other two layers in the reference architecture (i.e., Database Abstraction and Orchestration layers). This layer implements all services that are consumed by the API layer. In addition, the services offered by this layer can be used to build applications for managing, monitoring, and visualizing the workflow execution.

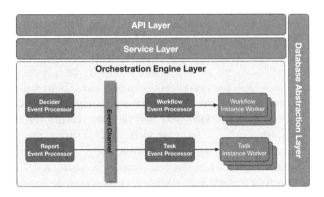

Fig. 1. Beethoven's reference architecture

Database Abstraction Layer—used to store the workflow, task, and event handler definitions. The Database Abstraction Layer is also responsible for recording information about the execution of workflow instances, such as resource utilization, throughput, and execution time. Such information can be used in subsequent analysis to identify, for instance, the existence of bottlenecks or failures when performing certain tasks.

Orchestration Engine Layer—it is the architecture core layer and follows the event-driven architectural style to provide a workflow execution mechanism in a decoupled and scalable manner. This layer is composed of three main architectural components: Event Channel, Event Processor (Decider, Report, Workflow, and Task), and Instance Work (Task and Workflow). The *Event Channel* component is used as an event bus to exchange messages among Event Processor components and can be implemented as message queues, message topics, or a combination of both. The *Event Processor* component is responsible for processing a specific type of event and notifying a successful or failure execution by publishing another event in the Event Channel. An Event Processor component can be bound to a set of *Instance Worker* components, which are responsible for performing a specific activity (e.g., decision, reporting, workflow, or task) demanded by the Event Processor component to which it is bound.

The Orchestration Engine, as shown in Fig. 1, is composed by an event channel, used to transfer event messages among event processors, which can be of four types: Decider Event Processor, Report Event Processor, Workflow Event Processor, and Task Event Processor. Specifically, in the event process context, there are two types of events: an *event* (occurrence of a particular action) and a *command* (an action to be performed). In the Orchestration Engine, each event processor can send or receive events and commands to or from another event processor using the Event Channel.

The Workflow Event Processor sends events (e.g., scheduled, started, or completed) during execution of workflow instances and receives commands (e.g., start, stop, or cancel) to manage the execution of a workflow instance. After receiving the command to start a workflow, the Workflow Event Processor creates a workflow instance and a worker (Workflow Instance Worker) for handling all events and commands related to the workflow instance that has been created. In this way, multiple workflow instances can be executed in parallel. The Task Event Processor sends events during the execution of tasks and receives commands to execute tasks.

The Decider Event Processor receives events generated by the Task Event Processor and Workflow Event Processor in order to decide which action (command) should be performed. To this end, the Decider Event Processor evaluate event handlers definitions.

The Report Event Processor receives all events that are generated during the execution of workflow instances and their respective tasks to record metrics (e.g., execution time, throughput, and errors). Furthermore, additional information about failures or timeouts during the task execution is also written from the events received by this processor.

3.2 Orchestration DSL

This section introduces a textual DSL named Partitur, available on GitHub[1], for expressing microservices orchestration in Beethoven. Partitur is built using Xtext[2], a tool based on the Eclipse Modeling Framework for the development of programming languages and DSLs. In the following subsections, we present the main Partitur elements: Workflow, Task, and Event Handler.

Workflow—A workflow is an abstraction of a business process that is executed in a distributed manner among different microservices. A workflow is composed of a set of activities that may eventually be executed and a set of constraints that must be obeyed. In this way, the definition of a workflow is designed to ensure that all activities performed during a business process are in accordance with the business constraints that have been specified. A Partitur workflow is composed of: (i) a **unique identifier** that represents the workflow name; (ii) a **set of tasks** that represent each business task or activity that is possible to be performed during a business process execution; and (iii) a **set of event handlers** that enclose all the business constraints that must be satisfied.

Task—In Partitur, a task is an atomic and asynchronous operation responsible for performing an action that manages a microservice. A Partitur task is composed of: (i) a **unique identifier** that represents the task name and (ii) an **HTTP request**, which is composed of the main four HTTP methods (i.e., DELETE, GET, POST, and PUT).

Event Handler—Partitur event handlers are based on Event-Condition-Action (ECA) rules that form the following structure: on *Event* if *Condition* do *Action*. Partitur event handlers are composed of the following structure: (i) a **unique identifier** that represents the event handler name; (ii) an **event identifier** that

---

[1] https://github.com/davimonteiro/partitur.
[2] https://www.eclipse.org/Xtext/.

is used to define which event must be listened and captured during the workflow execution; (iii) a set of **conditions** representing boolean parameters that must be true in order to process an event; and (iv) a set of **commands** defining the actions that should be performed on the occurrence of an event that satisfies the specified conditions.

4   Spring Cloud Beethoven

Aiming at observing the viability of the reference architecture, a concrete architecture, named Spring Cloud Beethoven[3], has been implemented using the actor model and the following technologies: Java, Spring Cloud Netflix[4], and Akka[5].

Since the concrete architecture is based on the Spring Cloud Netflix ecosystem, it provides integration with Spring Boot applications using auto-configuration and binding to Spring Cloud Netflix components, such as Spring Cloud Eureka, Spring Cloud Ribbon, and Spring Cloud Hystrix. Therefore, in order to address dynamic microservices location, Spring Cloud Beethoven relies on Spring Cloud Eureka for service discovery and Spring Cloud Ribbon for client-side load balancer. As consequence, there is no need to describe previously and register each microservice that will be part of the orchestration. Thus, new microservices that are added to a microservices-based application can be used during the microservice composition.

In the actor model, actors are essentially independent of concurrent processes that encapsulate their state and behavior and communicate exclusively by exchanging messages. To implement the orchestration engine of the reference architecture, each event processor has been instantiated in the concrete architecture as an actor. Next, each actor implemented in the concrete architecture is detailed in terms of internal state, sent or received messages, and behavior.

WorkflowActor—The *WorkflowActor* has been implemented following the Workflow Event Processor specification. For this reason, it is able to receive and process commands to manage workflow instances. In practice, the *WorkflowActor* receives commands and creates child actors to manage the workflow instances. Specifically, the *WorkflowActor* works as a supervisory actor who receives commands to manage a workflow instance and delegates that responsibility to a *WorkflowInstanceActor* (*WorkflowActor*'s child). Each *WorkflowInstanceActor* receives commands from the *WorkflowActor* and updates the state of the workflow instance. As a result, all work that the *WorkflowActor* receives is delegated to a *WorkflowInstanceActor*. This approach provides a mechanism to isolate a workflow execution with no shared data among the concurrent actors.

TaskActor—The *TaskActor* receives only the command to start tasks and sends success or failure events during a task execution. To execute a task, *TaskActor* uses the services provided by the *TaskService* to perform HTTP requests

---

[3] https://github.com/davimonteiro/beethoven.
[4] https://cloud.spring.io/spring-cloud-netflix/.
[5] https://akka.io/.

asynchronously. For example, when executing an HTTP request, one callback is recorded for success and another callback for failure. Each callback triggers an event on the task response. After receiving a command to start a task, the *TaskActor* performs an HTTP request and registers the request callbacks. In this way, different tasks can be performed asynchronously in parallel with no external interference.

ReportActor—The *ReportActor* is responsible for listening to all events triggered by the execution of a workflow and its task. Thus, it can record information about the execution of each task in a workflow. As an internal state, the *ReportActor* stores information about all workflow instances. At the end of a workflow instance execution, the information is stored in a database for further analysis of the application engineers.

DeciderActor—Finally, the *DeciderActor* receives events triggered by the actors *WorkflowInstanceActor* and *TaskActor* to decide, as specified by the event handlers, which command (e.g. start a workflow or a task) should be sent and to whom. The *DeciderActor* does not store state information and behaves in a reactive fashion.

5   Example Application

In order to demonstrate the feasibility of the Beethoven platform, an example application has been developed. The example application, available on GitHub[6], is a Customer Relationship Management (CRM) system based on MSA for an investment bank. The application is composed of the following microservices:

costumer-service   manages the costumer registry;
profile-service   analyses costumers' history to define retention strategies;
email-service   sends welcome, promotion, and informational emails;
package-service   sends personalized packages to customers;
account-service   sends credit/debit card, and letter within card password;
discovery-service maintains a registry of service information;
beethoven-service manages and performing Partitur workflows.

In the CRM application, there is a business process for new customers that is started after registering a new customer using the *costumer-service*. Next, the *profile-service* analyzes the new customer profile to define which retention strategies should be used. In this process, new customers should receive a welcome email (*email-service*), a personalized package (*account-service*), and a letter that contains the card's password and the account's card (*account-service*). Each business process step is performed by a specific microservice.

In order to use the Beethoven platform in a MSA-based application, it is necessary to create a microservice based on the Spring Cloud Netflix ecosystem and to add the Beethoven dependency in the project classpath. In this way,

---

[6] https://github.com/davimonteiro/crm-msa-example.

it is possible to initialize the Beethoven platform. Listing 1.1 depicts a part of Partitur specification for the new consumers process. Line 1 declares the workflow definition with the keyword **workflow** and *newConsumersProcess* as workflow name. Lines 2–6 define a task for creating a new consumer. Lines 7–11 define an event handler that specifies when the workflow named *newConsumersProcess* has been scheduled, then the task named *createNewConsumer* must be started.

```
1  workflow newConsumerProcess {
2      task createNewConsumer {
3        post("http://consumer-service/consumers")
4              .header("Content-Type", "application/json")
5              .body("${createNewConsumer.input}")
6      }
7      handler h1 {
8          on WORKFLOW_SCHEDULED
9          when workflowNameEqualsTo("newConsumerProcess")
10         then startTask("createNewConsumer")
11     }
12 }
```

Listing 13.1. Partitur specification for the new cosumer process.

6   Conclusion and Future Work

In this paper, we have presented a platform for microservice orchestration that eases the creation of complex microservice data flows. The main contributions of this work are threefold: (i) an event-driven platform, named Beethoven, for microservice orchestration and an DSL, named Partitur, for expressing microservice orchestration; (ii) a concrete implementation of the reference architecture, called Spring Cloud Beethoven; and (iii) an example application to demonstrate how the proposed platform can be used in a real example. As limitations, failures that may occur during the execution of workflow instances must be handled by using the orchestration DSL. As future work, we will concentrate on improving the reliability, flexibility, and resilience of the proposed platform by using self-adaptation mechanisms. In addition, we plan to perform empirical evaluations to validate the proposed platform. At last, we expect to receive feedback from both academic and industrial communities that can be used to improve the platform.

References

1. Angelov, S., Grefen, P., Greefhorst, D.: A framework for analysis and design of software reference architectures. Inf. Softw. Technol. **54**(4), 417–431 (2012)
2. Lewis, J., Fowler, M.: Microservices. http://www.martinfowler.com/articles/microservices.html (2014)
3. Nadareishvili, I., Mitra, R., McLarty, M., Amundsen, M.: Microservice Architecture: Aligning Principles, Practices, and Culture. O'Reilly Media, Inc., Sebastopol (2016)

4. Newman, S.: Building Microservices. O'Reilly Media, Sebastopol (2015)
5. Oberhauser, R.: Microflows: automated planning and enactment of dynamic workflows comprising semantically-annotated microservices. In: Shishkov, B. (ed.) BMSD 2016. LNBIP, vol. 275, pp. 183–199. Springer, Cham (2017). https://doi.org/10.1007/978-3-319-57222-2_9
6. Ben Hadj Yahia, E., Réveillère, L., Bromberg, Y.-D., Chevalier, R., Cadot, A.: Medley: an event-driven lightweight platform for service composition. In: Bozzon, A., Cudre-Maroux, P., Pautasso, C. (eds.) ICWE 2016. LNCS, vol. 9671, pp. 3–20. Springer, Cham (2016). https://doi.org/10.1007/978-3-319-38791-8_1

Service-Oriented Architectures

A Platform for the Automated Provisioning of Architecture Information for Large-Scale Service-Oriented Software Systems

Georg Buchgeher[1]([⊠]), Rainer Weinreich[2], and Heinz Huber[3]

[1] Software Competence Center Hagenberg GmbH, Hagenberg im Mühlkreis, Austria
georg.buchgeher@scch.at
[2] Johannes Kepler University, Linz, Austria
rainer.weinreich@jku.at
[3] Raiffeisen Software GmbH, Linz, Austria
heinz.huber@r-software.at

Abstract. Providing valid architecture information to stakeholders remains a challenge, as the effort required for documenting and maintaining this information over a longer period of time is very high. Automatically and continuously extracting architecture information from the system implementation makes it possible to document and keep architecture information up-to-date. In large software systems, architecture extraction has to deal with the continuous and efficient extraction of architectural information from very large code bases. In cooperation with a company from the financial sector, we have developed over several years a platform for the automatic extraction and provision of architectural information for large-scale service-oriented software systems. The platform was evaluated in a real industrial environment. The results of this evaluation show that it can provide up-to-date architectural information for large code bases on a daily basis. It also provides information on the trustworthiness of the extracted information and how it can be improved.

Keywords: Software architecture knowledge
Architecture documentation · Architecture model
Architecture extraction · Service-based systems · Code analysis
Software analytics

1 Introduction

(Ultra) large-scale software systems, are characterized by their (ultra-)large size on dimensions such as lines of code (LoC), number of people developing and operating such systems, the amount of data stored, accessed, manipulated and refined, the number of software connections and interdependencies among software components, and the number of hardware elements [8]. The large scale

© Springer Nature Switzerland AG 2018
C. E. Cuesta et al. (Eds.): ECSA 2018, LNCS 11048, pp. 203–218, 2018.
https://doi.org/10.1007/978-3-030-00761-4_14

dimension also applies to the architectural information that is required by many different stakeholders contributing to the development and operation of large-scale systems.

In such a context it is required that architecture information is made explicit, i.e., that it is documented, to facilitate the sharing and reusing of architecture information across team and organizational boundaries [7]. Otherwise, architecture information needs to be re-discovered from the system implementation whenever this information is required by a particular stakeholder, which is tedious and time-consuming and it slows down development and release cycles.

Another challenge is the continuous system evolution of large-scale systems in response to changing requirements and the migration to new implementation technologies, which requires that explicit architecture information is updated accordingly [4]. Stakeholders require trustworthy architecture information, i.e., architecture information that is complete and up-to-date. Providing this information for large-scale systems - ideally on a daily basis - is likely to exceed the available resources for architecture documentation, at least if documenting has to be performed manually. Automating the creation of documentation can help. However, this means that approaches for automated architecture information extraction and documentation are capable of (1) extracting architecture information at the abstraction level required by stakeholders and (2) dealing with the size of large-scale systems and the resulting amount of data that needs to be processed for documentation generation.

In this paper we present a platform for automatically provisioning architecture information of large-scale service-oriented systems. The platform extends a project's development infrastructure and provides architecture information to different stakeholders and tools. The platform has been developed as part of a long lasting research-industry cooperation with Raiffeisen Software GmbH (RSG), a provider of IT solutions for the finance domain in Austria with the goal to improve software architecture management at RSG.

The contributions of this paper are twofold: (1) We present a platform for the automated provisioning of up-to-date architecture information for large-scale software systems. (2) We analyze the developed platform in terms of performance, scalability, and trustworthiness of the extracted information in an industrial case study with RSG, where it has been used in a real production setting.

The remainder of this paper is organized as follows: In Sect. 2 we describe the industrial context of our work, we outline the industrial research approach, and we refer to previous work we have performed in this area. Section 3 discusses challenges and requirements for provisioning architecture information. In Sect. 4 we present our platform, i.e., the provisioned architecture information, how this information is extracted from the implementation, and how we address the identified challenges and requirements. Section 5 describes how we have validated our work. In Sect. 6 we discuss related work. Section 7 concludes the paper with a summary and outlook on future work.

2 Industrial Context, Research Approach, and Previous Work

Raiffeisen Software GmbH (RSG) is developing a large-scale enterprise service oriented architecture (SOA) for the financial domain in Austria including software for end users (i.e., internet banking applications and portals), and software for employees in banks (front and back office applications). RSG has ∼800 employees at 7 international development sites located in Austria and other European countries. The applications are operated in multiple computing centers at different locations in Austria. RSG is currently in the process of migrating its SOA towards microservices in order to speed up development and release cycles. RSG has a long lasting research cooperation with the Software Competence Center Hagenberg (SCCH) and the Johannes Kepler University (JKU) Linz with the goal to innovate development practices at RSG. In this research cooperation we are following a model for technology transfer from research to practice proposed by Gorschek et al. [6]. This seven step model begins with the identification of potential improvement areas in an industrial context (step 1), and the definition of a prioritized research agenda based on these needs (step 2). Next, a candidate solution is formulated (step 3), which is then validated at different levels beginning with evaluation in experimental laboratory settings (step 4), followed by a presentation of the candidate solution to practitioners and management from industry to collect feedback (step 5). Further validation is done in piloting projects in companies permitting realistic validation (step 6), before the solution is finally released (step 7).

In our case, RSG has identified architecture information extraction as important improvement area. Architecture information is vital for system development and SOA governance activities. RSG considers the system implementation as the only trustworthy source of information since manually created documentation is typically not maintained during system evolution. Beginning in 2011 we developed an approach for extracting architecture information from the system implementation via static code analysis along with enriching the system implementation with dedicated metadata facilitating architecture extraction [12]. We also developed an approach for automatically analyzing the extracted architecture information for compatibility with RSG reference architectures [11]. The approach has been validated using selected subsystems at RSG, first in a laboratory setting for concept and tooling refinement, later directly at RSG in order to get feedback from a real world industrial setting. Feedback from applying our approach in an industrial setting showed that the developed concepts for architecture extraction and analysis were perceived as valuable at RSG, which also contributed to our long-term research collaboration. Our approach gained the attention of additional stakeholders at RSG, which saw the potential of supporting their daily work with the automatic provisioning of architecture information. Additionally, the development practices evolved at RSG with a stronger focus on automation and continuous delivery. These factors imposed additional requirements on the implementation of our approach in terms of performance and scalability, but also stakeholder accessibility.

Originally, we started to implement our approach for architecture extraction as an extension for integrated development environments (IDEs) since we initially targeted mainly solution architects and developers with our approach. Additional stakeholder interest lead as first to implement the approach on the basis of a client/server architecture and to decouple it from the IDE. The change of development practices and the interest from additional stakeholders made it evident that our approach needed to further evolve to be integrated into a continuous delivery process. This also meant that we now had to continuously extract and analyze not only the architecture of single subsystems but of the entire large-scale SOA. Additionally, we had to support not only the current version of the overall system, but multiple versions in the light of continuous systems evolution. These new and challenging requirements and use cases lead us to completely redevelop our approach for architecture extraction in 2016. While our approach remained the same from a conceptual point of view, we reimplemented it from a technical point of view to deal with the aforementioned requirements.

3   Challenges and Requirements

The following challenges and requirements have been identified at RSG for our architecture information platform:

- *Standardized Architecture Information*: Software development at RSG is performed by over 800 employees organized in multiple teams, including a software architecture management team, several development teams, a test management team, a release management team, and an operations team. This large number of employees requires means for standardizing architecture information, i.e., for using the same terminology and also for creating standardized documentation.
- *Up-to-date Architecture Information*: Stakeholders require that the provided architecture information is up-to-date. This means that the extracted information reflects the state of the currently implemented system so that the stakeholders do not perform their work based invalid data.
- *Support for Large-scale Systems*: Architecture information needs to be provided for the entire system, which is considerably large. Analysis of the whole system is required for SOA governance activities, as well as for analyzing service dependencies across subsystem boundaries.
- *Support for System Evolution*: RSG also needs to analyze the evolution of architecture information over time, i.e., across multiple versions of the system. Evolution analysis is, for instance, required by software testers to focus testing activities on modified system parts, or by release managers for the planning of new releases as well as identifying old service versions that are already replaced by new versions and thus can be retired.
- *Full Automation*: Provisioning of architecture information needs to be fully automated - except for initial setup steps that have to be performed only once. Automation is considered by RSG as a fundamental prerequisite for the successful establishment of the architecture information platform.

4   An Architecture Information Provisioning Platform

In this section, we present our platform for automated provisioning of architecture information. First, we present the *RSG Component Model*, a conceptual model that identifies the main architectural elements (information) required by RSG for system development. Then we describe how this conceptual model is automatically extracted from the system implementation and how it is provided to different stakeholders and tools. Finally, we discuss how the platform addresses the challenges and requirements described in Sect. 3.

4.1   RSG Component Model

The *RSG component model* is used for describing systems at a conceptual level and at a high level of abstraction, where systems are discussed among different technical stakeholders like solution architects, designers, test managers, release managers, as well as non-technical stakeholders like product managers and domain experts. The component model is part of an RSG-specific reference architecture and was derived by the architecture management group by analyzing system development and SOA governance processes and by identifying the main architectural entities and their dependencies.

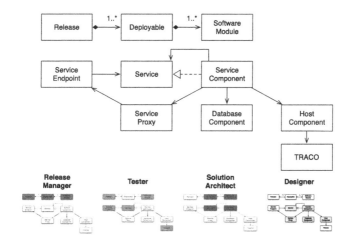

Fig. 1. RSG component model

The main elements of the RSG component model are shown in Fig. 1:

Release: *Releases* are collections of *deployables* defined by a release manager for a joint release.
Deployable: *Deployables* are software units (i.e., docker images) that are deployed/released to a platform as a service (PaaS) infrastructure. A *deployable* contains one or more *software modules*.
Software Module: A *software module* represents a single application providing one or more *services*. *Software modules* are versioned and contain *services*,

service endpoints, service components, service proxies, database and *host com-ponents*. (We have omitted these containment relationships in Fig. 1.)

Service: *Services* define business functionality in terms of service operations that can be used by applications.

Service Components: A *service component* implements the business function-ality defined by a *service*. Internally, a *service component* uses *database* and *host components*, as well as functionality provided by other *services*. If other *services* are located in the same *software module*, *services* are directly invoked using local procedure calls. If *services* are located in another *software module*, *services* are used via *service proxies* that encapsulate remote communication.

Service Endpoints: *Service endpoints* are technology-specific access points for providing *services* via dedicated communication technologies like REST or SOAP.

Service Proxies: *Service proxies* are - typically automatically generated - service client implementations encapsulating the remote access of a *service* located outside of a software module.

Database Components: *Database components* are components for reading and writing data from/to database management systems (DBMS).

Host Components: *Host components* are components that are using function-ality provided by host programs that are executed at a mainframe.

TRACOS: Transaction Codes (TRACOS) are identifiers of host programs executed at a mainframe, which are used by host components. *TRACOS* are an important concept for communication between service development teams and host development teams. Further they are also important for software testers for developing service tests for a particular *TRACO*.

The conceptual model also had an impact on the definition of the current reference architecture and technology stack used by RSG. As part of the current technology stack the architecture management team has defined how the concep-tual model can be extracted from the system implementation (see also Sect. 4.2). Each element of the conceptual component model can be derived from an imple-mentation artifact like source files, and build and configuration files. *Deployables* and *software modules* can be identified based on the Maven Project Object Model (POM) files that define packaging information for deployables and software mod-ules. *Services, service components, service endpoints, service proxies, database* and *host components* are identified by adding metadata (code-level annotations) to dedicated Java classes and interfaces representing these elements. RSG follows a model-based approach for the high level design of software modules that auto-matically generates implementation stubs for many elements of the component model including corresponding metadata - this eliminates the need to specify metadata manually. *TRACOS* are not directly contained in host components but in separate so-called record mapping files (XML files). Identifying the used *TRACOS* of a host component requires a look up of human-readable operation names used in host components to find the corresponding 4 character short iden-tifier of the corresponding host program at the mainframe. Only *releases* cannot be extracted from the system implementation - they are defined by a release manager via a dedicated release management tool.

Additionally to identifying the elements of the RSG component model, also the relationships between these elements can be extracted directly from the system implementation using call graph analysis for determining component and service usage.

The *RSG component model* represents a union set of architectural entities - not all stakeholders are interested in all elements of the component model. This is shown at the bottom of Fig. 1 where for selected stakeholders relevant elements are highlighted. For instance, release managers are mainly interested in *deployables* and *software modules* and their required dependencies for verifying the completeness of releases. Testers are writing tests at the service level, thus they are interested in which *service endpoints* they have to test for a particular *service*. Further, in order to test host transactions they have to determine by which service a particular host transaction (*TRACO*) is being called. Solution architects are concerned with the high-level design of *deployables* and *software modules*, i.e., the design of *services* and service dependencies, while designers are responsible with the internal detailed design of a *software module* in terms of internal components like *database* and *host components*.

4.2   Platform Overview

In the following, we describe how the *RSG component model* is automatically extracted from the system implementation, and how the extracted architecture information is then provided (shared) to stakeholders and tools for further usage. An overview of the platform is depicted in Fig. 2. The platform is implemented as a set of microservices providing different kinds of analyses at different levels of abstraction. These services are used by a set of tools.

Extracting and providing architecture information is a three step process. In the first step we provide a set of code-level analyses, in the second step we are extracting and verifying architecture information using code-level analysis, finally in the third step architecture information is visualized and used by different tools and stakeholders.

Code Analysis: We have implemented an approach for source code analysis based on graph databases, i.e., Neo4j[1]. This approach differs from typical code analysis approaches where analysis is implemented via abstract syntax tree (AST) visitors for deriving information from the system implementation. The use of a database permits working with large codebases as well as analyzing the evolution of such codebases without the need to fetch different version from a version control systems (VCS). A graph database is a natural fit since source code in terms of an AST is already a graph-based structure. We duplicate the system implementation stored in a VCS in a graph database since VCS provide no means for analysis - this is also not the intended use case of an VCS. The system implementation in the graph database is updated as part of cyclic build processes. During the build process the system implementation (i.e., source, XML,

---

[1] https://neo4j.com/.

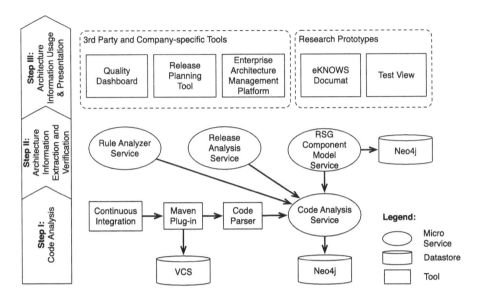

Fig. 2. Architecture information platform

and Manifest files) are fetched from the VCS, are converted to a graph model via dedicated parsers, and written to the graph database via the *Code Analysis Service*. It was decided to store the complete AST in the graph database and not only information currently required for architecture extraction. This will permit implementing additional kinds of analyses in the future without the need of extending parsers and underlying datamodels. All elements stored in the database are versioned to facilitate evolution analysis. While the version of the current development iteration (snapshot build) is overwritten when a new build is triggered, all release builds (increase of version) are kept in the database.

The *Code Analysis Service* provides a set of code analyses to be used by other higher-level services:

- Search for type and interface declarations of a specified module.
- Search for type, field, and method declarations with specified metadata.
- Search for extended types and implemented interfaces of a specified type declaration, search for all type declarations derived from a specified type, and search for all type declarations implementing a specified interface.
- Search for import relationships of a specified module, and search for modules importing a specified module.
- Search for method declarations of types and interfaces.
- Calculation of call graphs for specified method declarations
- Search for XML documents and elements and attributes of XML documents

These analyses are implemented by means of Cypher[2] queries - the query language provided by Neo4j. While some analyses can be formulated as single

---

[2] https://neo4j.com/cypher-graph-query-language/.

queries, other analyses are implemented as a combination of multiple subsequent queries. Source code analysis with database queries provides several advantages: The creation of ASTs by parser infrastructures is time-intensive - especially when an AST needs to be created multiple times for a large number of source files due to different kinds of analyses; Analyses can span module and version boundaries; Finally, new analyses can be provided by simply adding new queries instead of modifying existing AST visitors performing different kinds of analyses.

Architecture Information Extraction and Verification: In this step the *RSG component model* is extracted from the system implementation using analysis functionality provided by the *Code Analysis Service*. Architecture information extraction is triggered at the end of cyclic build processes after the system implementation has been updated in the *Code Analysis Service*. Extraction processes are performed whenever a new version of a *software module* is built. As part of the extraction process the following steps are performed:

1. Find or create the corresponding *deployable* for a *software module* by analyzing its Maven POM file.
2. Find Imported Modules: Find all module dependencies of the *software module* that need to be analyzed.
3. Delete any existing elements of the RSG component model for the current *software module* version that might no longer be up-to-date.
4. Find and create *services, service endpoints, service components, database components, host components*, and *service proxies* by searching for types with corresponding marker interfaces in their implementation. For all these elements we store a mapping from the element of the RSG component model to the corresponding implementation type.
5. For all *host components* determine the used *traco codes* by analyzing metadata of method declarations and by looking up *traco codes* in XML-based record mapping files.
6. The final step of the extraction process is determining usage/call dependencies between the different elements of the *RSG component model*. This is done by walking the call graph for all operations (methods) defined in *services* at the code level and checking if a called methods belong to a type that has a corresponding element in the *RSG component model*. In this case a dependency in between these two elements is created.

Next to extracting architecture information from the system implementation, two additional services are verifying the consistency and completeness of the architecture information.

The *Rule Analyzer Service* is analyzing the system implementation, i.e., it searches for types with missing and incomplete metadata that cause the architecture extraction to be incomplete. For example, it searches for *services* not implemented by a *service component* or *service components* without a corresponding *service*. Further issues can be detected by analyzing the use of 3rd party metadata, i.e., defined by the Java EE [3] standard. In many cases the use

---

[3] http://www.oracle.com/technetwork/java/javaee/overview/index.html.

of Java EE metadata also requires the use of RSG-specific metadata. While this means that some elements of the *RSG component model* could also be identified without RSG-specific metadata, it was an explicit design decision of RSG to require the use of RSG-specific metadata. The motivation behind this decision was that RSG-specific metadata reflecting the elements of the *RSG component model* are more stable than technology-specific metadata that might change over time due to the move to new technologies and frameworks.

The *Release Analysis Service* analyzes the integrity of planned releases. The service verifies that a release comprised of a set of *deployables* is (1) complete, i.e., that it contains all dependent *deployables*, and (2) that the versions of all *software modules* belonging to the release are compatible with each other.

Architecture Information Usage and Presentation: Extracted architecture information is provided to a set of different tools (3rd party and company-specific tools as well as research prototypes) used at RSG acting as front-end for providing architecture information to different stakeholders:

Quality Dashboard: RSG uses a quality dashboard (SonarQube[4]) for the monitoring of all quality issues. A dedicated plug-in creates issues for violations detected by the *Rule Analysis Service*, i.e., missing code-level annotations causing the extracted information to be incomplete.

Release Planning Tool: RSG is using a dedicated release planning tool (XL Release[5]) for orchestrating, visualizing, and automating release pipelines. RSG has extended this tools via a dedicated release verification step that shows the results of *Release Analysis Service* for each release. Only if a release has been successfully verified, i.e., a release is complete and all version dependencies are satisfied, further - partially manual - release activities are carried out.

Enterprise Architecture Management Platform: The enterprise architecture management platform (EAMP) is a RSG-developed tool for analyzing and managing service dependencies. EAMP was developed supporting SOA governance activities. Information provided in EAMP is provided by the *RSG Component Model Service*.

eKNOWS Documat: *eKNOWS Documat* is a research prototype for automatically generating viewpoint-based architecture documentation. In addition to general purpose viewpoints like module and code viewpoints, the *eKNOWS Documat* also provides RSG-specific viewpoints for generating documentation for *deployables*, *software modules*, and selected *services*.

Test View: *Test View* [3] is a research prototype supporting software testers in focusing their testing activities, i.e., by detecting modified services that have to be retested, and by identifying hot spots like frequently used services and services used by many different services.

---

[4] https://www.sonarqube.org/.
[5] https://xebialabs.com/products/xl-release/.

4.3   Support for Challenges and Requirements

In the following, we describe how we addressed the challenges and requirements presented in Sect. 3.

Standardized Architecture Information: Standardization is achieved by establishing a company-wide conceptual model that defines a terminology that is consistently used among all stakeholders. Also automated extraction of architecture information from the system implementation and providing this information to different tools contributes the standardization of architecture information within RSG.

Up-to-Date Architecture Information: By automatically updating architecture information as part of cyclic build processes it is ensured that requested architecture information is kept up-to-date. Further a dedicated analysis service detects issues like missing metadata and reports quality issues to a centralized quality dashboard.

Support for Large Codebases: Support for large codebases was one of the main drivers behind the re-engineering of our work based on new implementation technologies. Foundation for addressing performance and scalability requirements was the use of a graph database (Neo4j) for storing and analyzing large amounts of data. Also implementing the platform as a set of microservices addresses performance requirements, since single services can be independently scaled in case of increasing performance and scalability requirements. Also Neo4j is scalable via clustering.

Consider System Evolution: Storing both - system implementation and architecture information - in a graph database permits analyzing this information across version boundaries as it is for instance needed for documenting incremental system changes.

Automation: Fully automated provisioning of architecture information was a long term effort at RSG. Foundation for automation lies in the RSG specific technology stack, the reference architecture and the *RSG component model*, which define how architecture information can be extracted from the system implementation. For the development of our platform complete automation without any human intervention was a fundamental requirement.

5   Evaluation

We have evaluated our platform in an industrial case study at RSG.

5.1   Case Study Design

Objective: In the case study we analyzed the performance and scalability of the platform, as well as the trustworthiness of the extracted architecture information. It was our goal to perform validation under real conditions. Therefore we investigated the following research questions (RQs):

RQ1: Does the platform scale to real world industrial use cases?
RQ2: Is the extracted architecture information trustworthy?

Unit(s) of Analysis: We have used the platform for extracting architecture information for the entire online banking system of RSG that was released early 2018. The online banking solution consists of 296 *software modules* plus 5 framework projects defining the technology stack for the system. The 296 *software modules* are grouped into 89 *deployables*.

Data Collection: For answering the research questions we have used runtime monitoring and static code analysis. Further, we discussed the results with experts at RSG.

For answering RQ1, we have measured the required build time for each of the 89 *deployables* at RSG's build infrastructure. Build processes include a dedicated build step where the system implementation is parsed and transferred to the *Code Analysis Service*. We have analyzed the log files of the continuous integration infrastructure at RSG and measured the duration of cyclic build processes with and without the parsing process enabled to determine the overhead during the build process. We have analyzed the duration of build processes over a period of two weeks.

For each of the 296 *software modules* we measured the duration for extracting architecture information, i.e., the RSG component model from the system implementation, via the *RSG Component Model Service*. Therefore we analyzed the logfiles of the *RSG Component Model Service*, which provided dedicated log entries.

For answering RQ2, we have analyzed the results of the *Rule Analyzer Service*, i.e., the found problems of each *software module* to make statements regarding the completeness of the extracted architecture information. To ensure the integrity of collected data, the data was verified by the software architecture management group at RSG.

5.2   Quantitative Analysis

At the time of analysis, the Neo4j database of the *Code Analysis Service* has stored 44.48 millions lines of code (LoC) from 8288 Maven modules. 4653 modules were 3rd parts libraries, while 3635 modules (3.17 millions LoC) were source modules developed by RSG. Some of the source modules existed in multiple versions in the database because during the analyzed time span multiple releases of modules occurred. In sum, 2331 distinct source modules existed in the database.

The build duration of a quality assurance (QA) build of the entire online banking solution (94 build jobs) at RSG lasted in average 4.6 h. If parsing to the *Code Analysis Service* is enabled, the build process lasts 7.4 h, which is an increase of 62%. We should note that these build jobs are performed in parallel. The average duration for a single build process of a *deployable* goes up from 2.9 min to 4.8 min. The required overhead of the parsing process varied between 9% and 156% and depends on different factors like the number of concurrently executed build processes and the resulting server load, or the size of the parsed *deployables*.

Extraction of architecture information via the *RSG Component Model Service* was measured for 296 distinct *software modules*. We only considered the latest version of each *software module*. In average, the extraction of architecture information took 14.72 s per *software module*. Architecture extraction for all *software modules* lasted in average for 72.6 min.

Analysis of the implementation with the *Rule Analyzer Service* has revealed 254 problems, where architecture information was not extracted correctly. Problems were found in 112 *software modules* (38%), while 184 modules (62%) had no problems. Of the 254 problems, 237 problems indicated missing elements of the *RSG component model*. Two *software modules* contained more than 10 problems - one module contained 48 problems, the other module contained 19 problems. Another five modules contained more than 5 problems. Most modules with problems contained between one or two problems.

5.3   Qualitative Analysis and Answers to the Research Questions

RQ1: Does the platform scale to real world industrial use cases? Analysis of the performance data shows that extracting architectural information, i.e., the *RSG component model* via the *Code Analysis Service* does scale well - even for a large-scale software systems, like the online banking solution of RSG. More resource-intensive is the parsing process where the system implementation is written as graph structures to the Neo4j database. This adds a significant overhead to cyclic build processes. Despite this overhead it was still possible to provide architecture information on a daily basis. Currently, RSG neither had to scale the services nor the Neo4j database to meet RSG's performance and scalability requirements.

RQ2: Is the extracted architecture information trustworthy? Validation showed that the extracted architecture information was valid for almost 2/3 (62%) of all analyzed *software modules*, while in 1/3 (38%) of all *software modules* problems were detected. While the number of *software modules* with problems is still high, it needs to be considered that this is the result of a first-time analysis of the quality of the extracted architecture information. Further, most *software modules* with problems contained only between 1 and 2 problems that can be resolved with minimal efforts, i.e., by adding dedicated metadata in the source code. Regarding the 7 *software modules* containing more than 5 problems, it turned out that these modules were not developed following a model-based approach where metadata was automatically added to the system implementation, but where metadata has to be defined manually. In summary, RSG is optimistic that the quality of the extracted architecture information can be improved with reasonable efforts. Nevertheless, analysis results show that is necessary also to provide means for assessing the quality of the extracted architecture information. Further, RSG is also planning to introduce a dedicated quality control step as part of their service development process where solution architects will manually have to assess the validity of extracted architecture information.

5.4   Threats to Validity

Internal Validity: We have applied the platform to RSG's online banking system, which encompasses about 1/3 of the applications developed by RSG. The large size of the analyzed systems and the validation directly in the production environment at RSG make us confident that the platform will also scale to the additional systems developed at RSG since the remaining applications are built based on the same technology stack. Regarding the trustworthiness of the extracted information it still remains to be seen if the quality of the extracted information can be increased in the future by means of automated verification combined with manual quality control steps.

External Validity: Although the platform has been developed for one specific company our work can also be adapted for other domains. Large parts (i.e., 19.5 kLoC of 29.3 kLoC) of the platform are not company-specific, i.e., the *Code Analysis Service* as well as the code parsers (see Sect. 4.2), and are therefore reusable. Also the *RSG Component Model* - although developed for a particular company - can at least partially be reused and adapted to other domains since most of its elements describe general concepts of service-based systems.

6   Related Work

Our platform for automated provisioning of architecture information is related to work from different areas, i.e., source code analysis, architecture recovery approaches, approaches for architecture documentation, and architecture knowledge sharing platforms.

Performing code analysis with graph databases was already proposed by Urma and Mycroft in [10]. They have developed a system on top of Neo4j for source code querying, call graph, and data flow analysis in a similar way as our *Code Analysis Service.* Urma and Mycroft have developed their system supporting program comprehension and programming language evolution research, while we use code analysis as foundation for extracting and analyzing architectural information. We also took different steps for validating our work. While Urma and Mycroft have analyzed twelve open source java projects in a laboratory setting, we performed validation in an industrial setting. Further, we included in our validation also the process of storing and updating the system implementation in Neo4j as part of cyclic build processes which is an important aspect in the light of continuous quality control that requires a significant amount of resources. Urma and Mycroft focused their validation only on analyzing the query performance. The only information they provide regarding writing data to Neo4j is that *"pre-processing the source code and loading into Neo4j as a transaction took between two and ten times longer than compiling it using javac".* We can confirm their findings that code analysis with graph database queries scales to large-scale codebases.

Our approach differs from architecture recovery approaches that RSG requires an approach for the reliable extraction of architecture information, which is a problem of existing architecture recovery approaches [5].

Our extracted architecture information (the *RSG component model*) is related to the C4 model proposed by Brown [2]. I.e., *deployables* of the RSG component model correspond to *containers* in the Container Diagram in C4. Other elements of the RSG component model (components and services) can be mapped to *components* in C4 with corresponding tags indicating the different kinds of components and services of our model. Despite these commonalities, the *RSG component model* contains a larger number of different elements since this model has been developed for a domain-specific use case, while C4 is a generic approach. Diagrams of the C4 model can be generated via the Structurizr[6] tool where diagrams are defined directly in code. This permits linking of diagram elements to implementation artifacts, which ensures that diagram elements are - at least partially - updated automatically on implementation changes. For RSG, expressing architecture models in code as intended by the Structurizr tool would require too much resources for maintaining these models over time. Further, RSG not only needs diagrams but needs to provide architecture information to different visualization and analysis tools.

ArchiMedes [1] is a Wiki-based architecture knowledge management platform. The platform can connect to architecture model repositories and visualize, document, and analyze enterprise architecture models written in the ArchiMate language[7]. While our platform also provides means for visualizing and analyzing architecture models, a central aspect of our work is to automatically extract architecture models from the system implementation and to keep architecture information up-to-date on a daily basis.

7   Conclusion

Architecture information is vital for many software development activities. This applies especially for large-scale software systems being developed by hundreds of developers. We have presented a platform for automated provisioning of architecture information. Architecture information is extracted from the system implementation, automatically analyzed and verified, and provided to different stakeholders and tools. Validation in an industrial setting showed that the platform is capable of providing architectural information for large-scale software systems on a daily basis. However, trustworthiness of the extracted information still needs to be improved by establishing dedicated quality control activities.

As part of future work we plan to extend our work to support not only architecture solution structures but also other kinds of architectural knowledge, i.e. architectural design decisions (ADD) and their rationale. We plan to investigate the capturing of ADDs in the system implementation proposed by Oliver and Zimmermann [9] and the integration with our work on an architecture knowledge base, which uses community-driven processes for architecture knowledge management.

---

[6] https://structurizr.com/.
[7] http://www.opengroup.org/subjectareas/enterprise/archimate-overview.

Acknowledgements. The research reported in this paper was supported by the Austrian Ministry for Transport, Innovation and Technology, the Federal Ministry for Digital and Economic Affairs, and the Province of Upper Austria in the frame of the COMET center SCCH.

References

1. de Boer, R.C.: Archimedes publication and integration of architectural knowledge. In: 2017 IEEE International Conference on Software Architecture Workshops (ICSAW), pp. 268–271. IEEE (2017)
2. Brown, S.: Software Architecture for Developers - Volume 2: Visualise, document and explore your software architecture. Leanpub, Victoria, British Columbia, Canada (2018)
3. Buchgeher, G., Klammer, C., Heider, W., Schüetz, M., Huber, H.: Improving testing in an enterprise SOA with an architecture-based approach. In: 2016 13th Working IEEE/IFIP Conference on Software Architecture (WICSA), pp. 231–240. IEEE (2016)
4. Feilkas, M., Ratiu, D., Jurgens, E.: The loss of architectural knowledge during system evolution: an industrial case study. In: IEEE 17th International Conference on Program Comprehension, ICPC 2009, pp. 188–197. IEEE (2009)
5. Garcia, J., Ivkovic, I., Medvidovic, N.: A comparative analysis of software architecture recovery techniques. In: Proceedings of the 28th IEEE/ACM International Conference on Automated Software Engineering, pp. 486–496. IEEE Press (2013)
6. Gorschek, T., Garre, P., Larsson, S., Wohlin, C.: A model for technology transfer in practice. IEEE Softw. **23**(6), 88–95 (2006)
7. Lago, P., Avgeriou, P., Capilla, R., Kruchten, P.: Wishes and boundaries for a software architecture knowledge community. In: Seventh Working IEEE/IFIP Conference on Software Architecture, WICSA 2008, pp. 271–274. IEEE (2008)
8. Northrop, L., Feiler, P., Gabriel, R.P., Goodenough, J., Linger, R., Longstaff, T., Kazman, R., Klein, M., Schmidt, D., Sullivan, K., et al.: Ultra-large-scale systems: the software challenge of the future. Carnegie-Mellon University, Pittsburgh, PA, Software Engineering Institute, Technical report (2006)
9. Oliver, K., Zimmermann, O.: Capturing design decision rationale in program-level aspects (tool demo). In: 2016 13th Working IEEE/IFIP Conference on Software Architecture (WICSA) (2016)
10. Urma, R.G., Mycroft, A.: Source-code queries with graph databases–with application to programming language usage and evolution. Sci. Comput. Program. **97**, 127–134 (2015)
11. Weinreich, R., Buchgeher, G.: Automatic reference architecture conformance checking for SOA-based software systems. In: 2014 IEEE/IFIP Conference on Software Architecture (WICSA), pp. 95–104. IEEE (2014)
12. Weinreich, R., Miesbauer, C., Buchgeher, G., Kriechbaum, T.: Extracting and facilitating architecture in service-oriented software systems. In: 2012 Joint Working IEEE/IFIP Conference on Software Architecture (WICSA) and European Conference on Software Architecture (ECSA), pp. 81–90. IEEE (2012)

Providing Context as a Service Using Service-Oriented Mobile Indie Fog and Opportunistic Computing

Chii Chang[✉] and Satish Narayana Srirama

Mobile & Cloud Lab, Institute of Computer Science, University of Tartu,
Tartu, Estonia
chii.chang@acm.org

Abstract. The increasing number of sensor-embedded mobile devices has motivated the research of mobile Sensing as a Service in which mobile devices can host Web servers to serve sensory data to the Internet of Things systems, urban crowd sensing systems and big data acquisition systems. Further, the improved processing power of modern mobile devices indicates the mobile devices are not only capable of serving sensory data but also capable of providing Context as a Service (CaaS) based on requesters' own interpretation algorithms. In order to demonstrate mobile CaaS, this paper proposes a service-oriented mobile Indie Fog server architecture, which enables dynamic algorithm execution and also supports distributed CaaS processing among mobile devices. Moreover, in order to optimise the process distribution, the proposed framework also encompasses a resource-aware process assignment scheme known as MIRA. Finally, the authors have implemented and evaluated the proposed framework on a number of real devices. Accordingly, the evaluation results show that the MIRA scheme can improve the process assignment in the collaborative mobile CaaS environment.

1 Introduction

Ericsson Research [3] forecasts the global mobile Internet subscription will reach 9.2 billion in the year 2020 in which 6.1 billion subscription derives from smartphones. Explicitly, this phenomenon has motivated the research in utilising smartphones, tablets and phablets (i.e. large size smartphones), which consist of various embedded sensors, as a part of Internet of Things (IoT) [5] to support crowd sensing [21], urban sensing [2] and big data acquisition [8]. Further, as the computational power of mobile devices continues evolved, they are now capable of providing mobile Context- [4] as a Service (CaaS) [20].

Different to Sensing as a Service (S2aaS) [17], which provides raw sensory data from the mobile device-hosted Web servers [7], CaaS-based mobile servers are capable of extracting meaningful information from the batch of raw sensory data that is of interest to the requester. For example, a CaaS-based mobile server can inform the remote urban big data server that currently the X-district of the

© Springer Nature Switzerland AG 2018
C. E. Cuesta et al. (Eds.): ECSA 2018, LNCS 11048, pp. 219–235, 2018.
https://doi.org/10.1007/978-3-030-00761-4_15

Y-city is crowdy based on the interpretation of the raw sensory data collected by the mobile server.

Although a mobile server can provide mobile CaaS (mCaaS) by simply associating context reasoning mechanisms with the sensory data it collects, consider that context can be subjective [14], different individuals have their own interpretation of the context from the same data. Hence, the pre-defined context reasoning methods on mobile servers will face difficulty to fulfil the requesters' needs. Alternatively, the mobile server can allow the requesters submit their own context reasoning algorithm and use the requesters' algorithm to interpret the sensory data for the requesters. In order to achieve this mechanism, a promising solution is to apply Indie Fog [6] model.

An Indie Fog-enabled mobile server, which is called mobile Indie Fog (MIF) server, provides a process execution engine that allows the mobile server dynamically execute CaaS requesters' context reasoning algorithms. Further, MIF servers can establish distributed computing environment among themselves when they encounter each other opportunistically. Specifically, we term such a distributed computing environment—mobile fog computing (MFC). In particular, MFC allows the participated mobile servers to share their computational and networking resources for certain tasks collaboratively, which reduces the resource usage of single nodes and ideally can improve the overall processing speed. Below, we use an example to express the MFC for CaaS.

In Fig. 1, the MIF server that provides CaaS (CaaSMIF) has registered to Indie Fog registry with its Service Description Metadata (SDM).

An IoT-based big data server intends to orchestrate a large number of mobile S2aaS servers in an urban area in order to produce real-time spatiotemporal information. Consider that retrieving and processing raw sensory data from all the mobile servers will cause bottleneck issue and also can be costly for mobile servers' Internet bandwidth, the big data server decided to request MIF servers, which can pre-process the raw sensory data for the big data server before

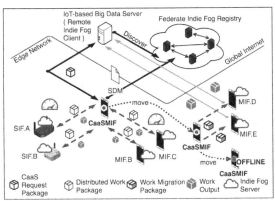

Fig. 1. Overview of mobile Indie Fog for providing context as a service and distributed context interpretation processing.

they reply the requests. As the figure shows, the big data server discovered the CaaSMIF and then sent a CaaS request package to the CaaSMIF. Afterwards, the CaaSMIF deploys the algorithm and starts the context reasoning processes.

While the CaaSMIF is performing the context reasoning, due to the size of the involved data and the complexity of the algorithm, the CaaSMIF has reached its resource allowance threshold. Hence, it seeks the help of proximal stationary and mobile Indie Fog servers by distributing processes to them. Consider that the CaaSMIF is a moving object, it may not stay connected with the other Indie Fog server. Therefore, the distributed process package should contain all the involved files such as the algorithm, the dependencies of the algorithm method and also a portion of sensory data.

In case that the CaaSMIF is unable to complete all the context reasoning processing and is unable to maintain the communication channel with the requester, it can migrate all the remaining works to the other Indie Fog servers by specifying its request as *process migration*. In particular, a *process migration* request specifies the process handler should route the final result to a specific node, which in this example is the big data server.

Above overview briefly summarises the mechanisms provided by Indie Fog for mCaaS. However, it also raises a question:

How does the CaaSMIF partition the workload of the context reasoning processes in MFC environment while all the participants are heterogeneous?

In order to support the adaptive process distribution in MFC environment, we propose **M**obile **I**ndie fog **R**esource-aware process **A**ssignment (**MIRA**) scheme. Further, in order to validate MIRA scheme in MFC environment, we developed a service-oriented mobile Indie Fog server architecture.

This paper is structured as follows. Section 2 describes the proposed system architecture and the main components of the MIF server. Section 3 describes the proposed MIRA scheme. Section 4 provides the prototype implementation details and the evaluation results. Section 5 reviews and compares the related works with the proposed framework. This paper is concluded in Sect. 6 together with future research directions.

2   System Design

This section firstly describes the proposed service-oriented mobile Indie Fog server architecture for CaaS. Afterwards, we explain how the server handles CaaS request, how it performs distributed processes with the other MIF servers in proximity and how it migrates its processes to the other MIF servers.

2.1   System Architecture

Figure 2 illustrates the proposed server architecture, which consists of the following main components.

Controller—is the core of the MIF server that is responsible for three primary tasks:

– *Request routing.* When a component needs to access the data or the function of another component, the request needs to route through the Controller for security and privacy control.

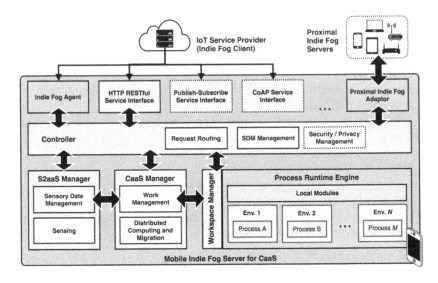

Fig. 2. Architecture of mobile Indie Fog server for CaaS.

– *SDM Management.* The Controller needs to maintain an up-to-date Service Description Metadata (SDM) of the MIF server. Specifically, the SDM should describe the following information.
  - Hardware specification (e.g. device model ID, CPU name and architecture, RAM model etc.), performance (e.g. processing *compute-score*, SD-Card read/write speed, Wi-Fi signal strength etc.) and current usage of resources such as CPU load, RAM usage, network throughput etc.
  - Currently supported services, such as sensory services for environmental pictures, data brokering service (i.e. deliver the data to a specific networked server) or the context interpretation service, which interprets the raw sensory data using the methods from the requesters. Further, if the server currently supports CaaS, then the SDM should also contain the information regarding the Runtime Engine specification and states.
  - Supported process runtime environments. This information lets MIF clients understand what types of code or script the server is capable of executing. Based on this information, the MIF client can prepare their algorithm in the corresponding program code or script.

  As suggested by the Indie Fog architecture [6], SDM is expected to be written in OData (www.odata.org/) format.
– *Security and Privacy Management* is a component that handles the security and privacy settings. In general, the owner of MIF server can manually configure the available services such as which S2aaS are available, what type of secure program deployment protocol is available (e.g. public key based SSH). Since this is more practical-related, we consider it as a future work.

Indie Fog Agent—is a core component derived from the Indie Fog architecture [6], which registers the Mobile Indie Fog (MIF) server to the global registry and it enables the communication between the MIF server and Indie Fog clients.

Service Interfaces (HTTP RESTful Service Interface, Publish-Subscribe Service Interface and CoAP Service Interface etc.) are the protocols to enable different types of service provision by the MIF server. In general, RESTful is the basic protocol for providing S2aaS and CaaS based on HTTP request/response.

Proximal Indie Fog Adaptor—is a component that allows the MIF server to communicate with proximal Indie Fog servers. In general, we expect the environment consists of various mobile and stationary Indie Fog providers.

S2aaS Manager—is a local service that has two main mechanisms: (1) *Sensory Data Management*, which allows other components to request S2aaS Manager for the sensory data that has been collected previously; (2) *Sensing* mechanism allows other components to request S2aaS Manager to perform on-demand sensory data acquisition using the device's internal sensors via the underline OS-provided Application Programming Interfaces (APIs).

CaaS Manager—is a local service that handles CaaS requests. Specifically, it has two main mechanisms—Work Management and Distributed Computing and Migration. The details of how CaaS Manager handles its request will be described in the next section.

Workspace Manager—is the component that handles program deployment on Process Runtime Engine. In particular, different to the regular stationary Indie Fog servers that do not have much constraint, MIF servers' operation environments are highly dynamic and constraint due to the limitation of available resources (i.e. available processing power and battery life). Therefore, MIF servers may not host the general Virtual Machine or Containers Engine for executing the requesters' program. However, MIF servers can still provide isolated runtime environments that allow dynamic code execution. For example, an Android OS device can utilise Termux (termux.com) to build a Process Runtime Engine that can configure multiple runtime environments (application instances) which supports different programming languages (NodeJS, Python, Perl, Ruby etc.) for each program execution. Certainly, the supported runtime environments depend on the pre-installed libraries by the MIF server and the corresponding information should be included in SDM. The example shown on Fig. 2 illustrates that the Process Runtime Engine is currently operating N number of isolated runtime environments for N number of different requesters.

Due to the privacy concern, the other components of MIF server do not have permission to access the data of Process Instances in the runtime environments. Further, the Workspace Manager will remove a Process Instance entirely (including the data and repository) when the process is completed, which indicates that if a MIF client intends to perform a process repeatedly, the client needs to configure it from the program code. Otherwise, the MIF client has to upload the request package to the MIF server again.

2.2 CaaS Request Handling

Here, we provide the details of how CaaS Manager handles its requests. Specifically, we use Business Process Modelling Notations to express the workflows.

Figure 3a illustrates the process deployment workflow. When CaaS Manager receives a request package, it first requests the corresponding raw sensory data from S2aaS Manager. Second, it prepares the work package, which contains the content of the request package together with the raw sensory data, then CaaS Manager sends the work package to Workspace Manager, who will extract the work package and place the files in a workspace in the Process Runtime Engine. Once the workspace is ready, Workspace Manager will execute the CaaS process in Process Runtime Engine as an isolated Process Instance and establish a communication channel between itself and the Process Instance to receive output. Afterwards, the Workspace Manager will pass the output(s) to CaaS Manager and CaaS Manager will pack the output(s) to a response package and relay it to the corresponding component.

The *process distribution* and *process migration* mechanisms share numerous common tasks. Therefore, we use a single figure to explain their activities.

Figure 3b illustrates the interaction between a MIF server who received the initial CaaS request (denoted by delegator) and another MIF server (worker) who has agreed to participate in *process distribution* or *process migration*.

The workflow starts with the task of creating work package. Here, a work package consists of the corresponding raw sensory data files, the context reasoning algorithm program code and all the dependencies of the program. In general, it is possible to request the worker to download the dependencies via the Internet. However, it will increase the cost of the worker and it may not reduce the overall timespan because

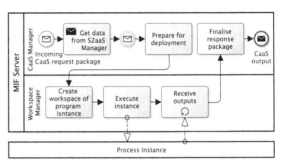

(a) CaaS process deployment.

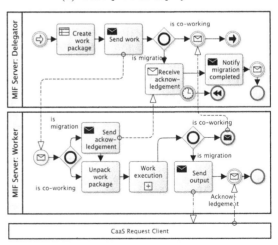

(b) CaaS process distribution and migration.

Fig. 3. CaaS process workflows.

the delegator and worker are communicated locally either via LAN or Wi-Fi Direct. Alternatively, based on the SDM of the worker, if the worker has all the dependencies in the local modules of its Process Runtime Engine, the work package does not need to include the dependencies.

The main difference between *process distribution* and *process migration* is the receiver of the final output. Essentially, the objective of *process distribution* is to co-working on a set of works. For example, the delegator needs to process 30 raw sensory data for CaaS, it may partition the workload to two parts with 15 raw sensory data per each part, then request a worker to handle one of the work packages. Afterwards, the delegator will wait to receive the output from the worker, then the delegator can pack the output from the worker together with the output from its local processes to a single output package and send it back to the CaaS requester. In contrast, if the objective is *process migration*, the delegator may pack all the raw sensory data together with the CaaS request package as one single work package and send it to the worker. When the worker receives the work package as a *process migration* request (e.g. based on the RESTful request parameter), it will immediately notify the delegator that it has received the work package successfully and the delegator can notify the CaaS requester that it has successfully migrated the CaaS process to another server. However, if the delegator does not receive the acknowledgement from the worker in a period of time, it will try to find another worker to handle the process migration. Once the worker completes the work, it will directly send the output package to the initial CaaS requester.

Note that in certain cases, the program and the related data can be privacy-sensitive. Hence, the CaaS requester should clarify it in the request message in order to prevent the MIF server distributing or migrating the program and the data to other servers.

3   Mobile Indie Fog Resource-Aware Process Assignment Scheme

In this section, we describe the proposed Mobile Indie fog Resource-aware process Assignment (MIRA) scheme for adaptive *process distribution* and *process migration* in MFC environment.

A naïve approach to partition the workload may consider only the processing performance among all the participants. For example, let $P = \{p_i : 1 \leq i \leq N\}$ be a set of MIF servers and let $comp_i$ be the computational performance of MIF server—p_i. Therefore, the workload shared by one of the MIF servers—p_x will be $|W| \times \frac{comp_x}{\sum_{i \in |P|} comp_i}$, where $comp_x$ is the computational performance of $p_x \in P$ and W is the set of works.

However, in MFC environment, such an approach is infeasible because the dynamic factors such as the network latency caused by signal interruption, the runtime hardware resource usage including CPU load, RAM usage, read/write storage status, the network bandwidth availability are influenced by the device

user's activities. Therefore, we designed MIRA scheme based on the consideration of the dynamic factors.

To proceed with MIRA scheme, the delegator needs to collect the following
information from—SDM of worker and the local record of CaaS processing.

The information from the workers SDM are:

- Compute-score of the worker based on a common measuring tool such as
  GeekBench, which is a cross platform benchmark tool and its database
  contains a broad range of benchmark results contributed by the society
  (browser.geekbench.com). Note that MIRA scheme uses compute-score based
  on the CPU usage. For example, if a device, which has compute-score as 3000
  and its current CPU usage is 20%, then MIRA scheme considers the compute-
  score of the device as $3000 - 3000 \times 20\% = 2400$.
- Average CPU and RAM usage in recent time (i.e. 1, 5 and 15 min).
- The CPU architecture (e.g. ARM, x86 etc.).

The delegator should have performed the context reasoning process for a
number of times locally and record the following values before it intends to perform *process distribution*. In contrast, if the delegator has never proceed with the
processes, it can only perform the naïve *process distribution* described previously.

- The timespan for processing one data object using the requester's algorithm
  with one CPU core.
- The total process timespan for N number of data objects using M number of
  CPU core(s) in which N must be greater than M. Specifically, these records
  will help MIRA to calculate the *base variety* value of the process timespan
  varied by M number of CPU core(s).

With the *base variety* value (denoted by bv_m^y, m is the number of cores, y is
the type of data), MIRA can measure the timespan of processing a data batch
that contains N number of data objects of a given type. In detail, bv_m^y derives
from the following formula:

$bv_{d,m}^y = \frac{\Delta \alpha_d^y}{\frac{1}{n} \Delta t_{d,n,m}^y} = \frac{\Delta \alpha_d^y \times n}{\Delta t_{d,n,m}^y}$ where n is the number of data objects.

$\Delta t_{d,n,m}^y$ is the timespan for delegator—d to process n number of data using
m number of CPU core.

$\Delta \alpha_d^y$ is the timespan for delegator—d to process one y type data object using
1 CPU core.

Example of using $bv_{d,m}^y$ to measure the timespan for d to process a data batch
(D; denoted by $\Delta t_{d,m}(D)$) is as follow:

$$\Delta t_{d,m}(D) = \frac{\Delta \alpha_d^y}{bv_{d,m}^y} \times |D| \tag{1}$$

In order to measure the optimal partition of the workload for *process distribution* or *process migration*, we need to measure the comparable timespan when
the worker is handling the work package. Specifically, $\Delta t_{d,x}^\omega$ denotes the distributed processing timespan when delegator—d relies on worker—x to handle

all the works. Note that MIRA scheme uses the maximum workload to measure the timespan of each distributed processing. Below illustrates all the elements involved in the measurement of $\Delta t_{d,x}^{\omega}$:

$$\Delta t_{d,x}^{\omega} = \Delta t_{d,x}^{pk_{\omega}} + \Delta t_{d,x}^{po_{\omega}} + \Delta t_{x}^{npk_{\omega}} + \Delta t_{x}^{pc_{\omega}} + \Delta t_{x}^{pk_O} + \Delta t_{x,r}^{po_O} + \Delta t_{r}^{npk_O} \qquad (2)$$

where:

- ω is the work package. ω consists of three elements—dependency modules used in the algorithm (mdl), algorithm program code (alg) and a set of raw sensory data R, where $R = \{rsd_k : 1 \le k \le N\}$.
- $\Delta t_{d,x}^{pk_{\omega}}$ is the work package packing time. It consists of:
  - $\Delta t_{d}^{pk_{mdl}}$ is the measured timespan to pack the modules.
  - $\Delta t_{d}^{pk_{alg}}$ is the timespan to pack the algorithm program code.
  - $\Delta t_{d}^{pk_R} = \Delta t_{d}^{pk_{rsd}} \times |R|$ is the timespan to pack $|R|$ number of $rsd \in R$ where R is all the rsd in queue. Note that MIRA scheme analyses the optimal assignment based on the measured latency and the comparable computational performance score. For example, suppose a delegator has compute score of 3000 and it can complete 20 works of a batch in 30 s. Further, the delegator found a worker that has compute score of 7000. In order to measure the performance of the process distribution, MIRA needs to use the same number of works (20 works) and also considering the other factors (i.e. packing, unpacking, network transmission etc.) when 20 works will be distributed to the worker.
- $\Delta t_{d,x}^{po_{\omega}}$ is the timespan to post ω from d to x. It consist of the following elements:
  - $\Delta t_{d,x}^{po_{mdl}} = \frac{Mb_{mdl}}{cMb_{d,x}}$ is the measured timespan to post mdl, where Mb_{mdl} is the size of mdl in Megabit and cMb is the network transmission speed between d and x in Megabit. The transmission speed between d and x is known when d requests SDM from x.
  - $\Delta t_{d,x}^{po_{alg}} = \frac{Mb_{alg}}{cMb_{d,x}}$ is the measured timespan to post alg, where Mb_{alg} is the size of alg in Megabit.
  - $\Delta t_{d,x}^{po_R} = \frac{Mb_R}{cMb_{d,x}}$ is the measured timespan to post R, where Mb_R is the size of R in Megabit.
- $\Delta t_{x}^{npk_{\omega}}$ is the timespan to unpack and deploy ω on the worker. It consists of the following elements:
  - $\Delta t_{x}^{npk_{mdl}} = \frac{\Delta t_{d}^{npk_{mdl}}}{\varrho(d,x)}$ is the measured timespan to deploy mdl. $\Delta t_{d}^{npk_{mdl}}$ is an known value since d has previous unpacked the modules when it received the initial CaaS request.
  - $\Delta t_{x}^{npk_{alg}} = \frac{\Delta t_{d}^{npk_{alg}}}{\varrho(d,x)}$ is the measured timespan to deploy alg. $\Delta t_{d}^{npk_{alg}}$ is an known value since d has previous unpacked the modules when it received the initial CaaS request.
  - $\Delta t_{x}^{npk_R} = \frac{\Delta t_{d}^{npk_{rsd}}}{\varrho(d,x)} \times |R|$ is the measured timespan to deploy R. $\Delta t_{d}^{npk_{rsd}}$ is a value obtained by performing and recording one packing and unpacking

an rsd on d. $\varrho(d,x) = \frac{cs_x}{cs_d}$ is the computational performance rate between the two nodes d and x, where cs_x is the compute score of x and cs_d is the compute score of d.

- $\Delta t_x^{pc_\omega} = \frac{\Delta t_d^{pc_{rsd}} \times |R|}{\varrho(d,x)}$ is the measured timespan to process ω on x.

- $\Delta t_x^{pk_O} = \frac{\Delta t_d^{pk_o} \times |O|}{\varrho(d,x)}$ is the measured timespan to pack the process outputs, where $O = \{o_l : 1 \le l \le N\}$ is a set of outputs. $\Delta t_d^{pk_o}$ is a value obtained by performing and recording one packing and unpacking an o on d.

- $\Delta t_{x,r}^{po_O} = \frac{Mb_O}{cMb_{x,r}}$ is the measured timespan to post the outputs to receiver. The receiver is unnecessary to be the delegator itself. In case of process migration, the receiver could be the initial CaaS requester.

- $\Delta t_r^{npk_O} = \frac{\Delta t_d^{npk_o} \times |O|}{\varrho(d,r)}$ is the measured timespan for receiver to unpack the output package, where $\varrho(d,r) = \frac{cs_r}{cs_d}$ is the computational performance rate of r and d based on their *compute-score* and current CPU usages.

Once we obtain the above values, we can calculate the non-normalised score of a participant—z (including the delegator):

$$\nu_z(\omega) = 1 - \frac{\Delta t_{d,z}^\omega}{\sum_{i \in |\Omega|} \Delta t_{d,i}^\omega} \tag{3}$$

where $\Omega = \{\omega_i : 1 \le i \le N\}$ denotes N number of work packages created for participants. Note that in here, if the z is the delegator, its $\Delta t_{d,z}^\omega$ does not involve the latencies described in previous formulations.

The normalised score of a participant—z will be:

$$n\nu_z(\omega) = \frac{\nu_z(\omega)}{\sum_{i \in |\Omega|} \nu_i(\omega)} \tag{4}$$

and the workload shared by the participant—z will be:

$$sh(R, z) = \|n\nu_z \times \#R\| \tag{5}$$

4   Evaluation

The goal of the evaluation is to test the performance of the proposed framework and the MIRA scheme. We have implemented the proposed framework in real devices. The configuration of the testing environment is described as below:
    We implemented the MIF server on three mobile devices:

- Asus Zenfone 3, as the delegator node, which has $8 \times 2\,\text{GHz}$ CPU, $3\,\text{GB}$ RAM, operated by Android 7.
- Nokia 8, as a worker, which has $4 \times 2.5\,\text{GHz}$ CPU and $4 \times 1.8\,\text{GHz}$ CPU, $4\,\text{GB}$ RAM, operated by Android 8.
- Asus Zenpad 3S, as a worker, which has $2 \times 2.1\,\text{GHz} + 4 \times 1.7\,\text{GHz}$ CPU, $4\,\text{GB}$ RAM, operated by Android 7.

The MIF server and its Process Runtime Engine were built on top of Termux and the current prototype supports NodeJS-based process instance. We consider to include the other types of instances as future work.

Here, we assume the CaaS requester intends to interpret context information from image-based sensory data.

The raw sensory data used for the testing was a number of full colour 1453 × 2560 pixel JPEG images files with 1.8 Megabyte in file size. The context reasoning program was mainly processing the image files and generate fixed size output data files.

4.1 Solo Process Performance

In order to demonstrate the factors influenced by the available computational resources, we firstly tested the CaaS process on the delegator device solely.

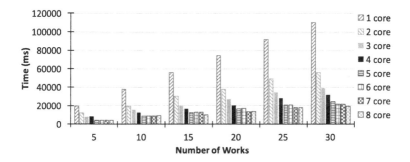

Fig. 4. Solo CaaS process performance.

Figure 4 illustrates the performance test results by the delegator device solely. The X-axis denotes the number of raw sensory data objects involved in the process and the Y-axis denotes the average processing timespan in millisecond. As the results show, when the device is capable of using 2 cores, the process timespan can be greatly reduced comparing to single core-based processing. Further, 3 and 4 core-based processes could also improve the performance but not as explicitly as the comparison between single core and dual core. When we assign the process with more cores, the performance was unable to improve much, it is because the device itself has been using significant processor resources for the operating systems activities. Note that, although we have successfully performed the testing on 8 cores, the operating system was unable to maintain the CPU resource for the other background applications, and hence, the HTTP server of MIF has been forced to terminate.

4.2 Distributed Processing

Figure 5 shows the results of the performance testing among 8 cases. To enumerate, the first 4 cases are solo processing using different number of CPU on the delegator device (denoted by Solo 1 core, Solo 2 core, Solo 3 core and Solo 4 core); the next 2 cases are equal process distribution with 1 MIF worker (Nokia 8) while the delegator was using single core (1c 1w equal) or dual CPU cores (2c 1w equal); the last 2 cases illustrate the results in which the process distribution have applied the proposed MIRA scheme (1c 1w adaptive and 2c 1w adaptive).

As expected, when the number of raw sensory data in the batch is small (i.e. 6 works), the process distribution did not provide much improvement to the overall speed. Explicitly, packing and unpacking the work packages have caused significant overhead. Moreover, when the delegator is capable of allocating more CPU cores to the process, it can outperform the distributed processes. On the other hand, allocating more cores on CaaS processes also means that the device is reducing the resources allocated from the other applications, which could affect the device users regular activities.

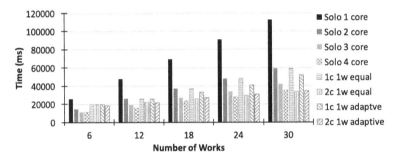

Fig. 5. Performance comparison among cases of multi-core processing, equal process distribution and adaptive process distribution with one MIF worker.

As the results are shown, utilising distributed processing with the MIF worker, if the workload was equally distributed among the delegator and worker, the performance is similar to the performance of dual core solely processing on the delegator when the number of works were over 12. Further, if the system applied the proposed MIRA scheme, the speed can be further improved. Specifically, as the results are shown when there were 30 works, applying MIRA scheme can almost achieve the similar speed as the cases of solely processing using 3 cores on the delegator, which indicates that the delegator can save 2 cores CPU resource usage by utilising MIRA-based distributed processing.

Note that the results of case (2c 1w equal) and case (2c 1w adaptive) were very similar because the analysis result from MIRA was similar to equal partitioning.

As Fig. 6 shows, when the workload is small (e.g. 6 works), process distribution is unable to improve the overall processing speed, especially if the delegator was capable of allocating two or more cores for the processes. On the other hand, when the amount of works in the batch is large (e.g. 30 works), distributing the works to two workers can significantly improve the overall speed. Further, when

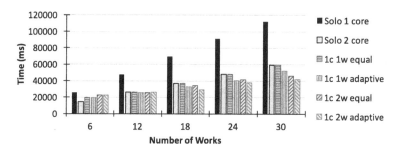

Fig. 6. Performance comparison among solo, single worker-based and two workers-based process distribution.

the system applied MIRA scheme, the system can further improve the speed. However, similar to the previous testing results, the improvement granted by MIRA is not clear when the workload is small (i.e. 6 or 12 works) because the work distribution analysis results from MIRA were the same as equal distribution.

4.3   Process Migration Performance

Figure 7 shows three cases of migration. Migrate all the processes with the rest of unprocessed raw sensory data to one single worker (Nokia 8). The 2nd case is equally partition the number of unprocessed raw sensory data into each migration package then migrate the processes to two workers (Nokia 8 and Zenpad 3). The 3rd case was also migrate processes to the two workers but with the proposed MIRA scheme to decide how to distributed the works in each migration package.

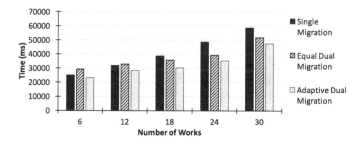

Fig. 7. Process migration performance.

As the result shows, utilising MIRA scheme can also improve the overall speed (around 11% to 15%) when the works need to be migrated to multiple nodes.

4.4   Discussion

Overall, the evaluation results show that *process distribution* does not improve much performance in MFC environment when the data batch size is small because there was much overhead involved. However, the results also show that the performance of MIRA-enabled *process distribution* with one worker is almost equivalent to the performance of utilising 2 to 4 CPU cores on the delegator (depending on the worker's processing power), which indicates the resource conservation the proposed framework can provide. Further, one may argue that since the processing timespan was quite long, why not simply retrieve the raw sensory data from the mobile server then process the data in the cloud? The answer highly depends on the mobile Internet availability and the cost in the countries. Consider that if the mobile server receives a number of requests that involve 100 MB sensory data per each request, it can be very costly for the mobile server and hence, it may discourage the device owner to provide the service. Definitely, the results of the experiments have raised a new research direction in proposing an adaptive process distribution and migration in a cross-layered cloud-fog-edge environment.

5   Related Works

The framework proposed in this paper involves two research fields—mobile sensing services and mobile ad hoc distributed computing. Hence, in this section, we review a number of related works and justify the differences between the proposed framework and the related works.

Mobile Sensing—In last decade, researchers have proposed numerous mobile sensing approaches. To enumerate, effSense [21] introduced cost-efficient mobile crowd sensing solution which lets mobile devices collaboratively route the collected sensory data among the participative nodes towards reducing the mobile Internet transmission costs; COROMM [18] is a context-aware cost-efficient real-time mobile crowdsensing framework that can dynamically adjust the data collection process in order to reduce the bandwidth and energy consumption from mobile devices. Further, there exist a number of related approaches in mobile phone sensing [1,9,13,15], where, the mobile sensing data is uploaded to a central repository. Different to these works, Sarma et al. [16] proposed a multi-layer architecture for mobile sensing in which the devices can form an edge group in proximity and utilise the resource richer broker peers to communicate with other groups and the global repository. Hence, remote clients can either communicate with the edge broker or the global central server to retrieve the sensory data.

The major difference between the proposed framework in this paper and the past related works is that the proposed framework supports CaaS directly from the mobile devices. To the best of our knowledge, this is the first framework proposed for providing CaaS from mobile devices based on extending Indie Fog architecture.

Mobile Ad Hoc Distributed Computing—Hyrax [12] is a framework that aims to apply MapReduce to the grid computing environment formed by a group of mobile devices. The result of Hyrax shows that the approach is too heavy-weight. Honeybee [10] is a framework that aims the same purpose as Hyrax. However, instead of utilising the heavyweight MapReduce, Honeybee applied the active work stealing scheme in which participants in mobile grid computing environment will actively be taking the work (e.g. processing image files) from the other nodes who have more works.

The extension of Honeybee results in [11] as mobile crowd computing using work stealing model. The idea is each worker will take one work from the delegator. The connected 2nd tier node of the worker will influence the 1st tier worker taking how many works from the delegator. For example, if a 1st tier worker has a 2nd tier worker, then the 1st tier worker will 'steal' two works from the delegator. One for itself and one for its connected 2nd tier worker. The extension of [11] proposed by Soo et al. [19] using proactive resource-aware work-stealing scheme, which optimise the number of works stolen by workers based on the workers' current computational and networking states. The work in [19] was proposed for fog computing environment with static Fog nodes and mobile delegator.

The proposed framework in this paper is different to all the above works. First, the collaboration does not assume the workers are stationary like in [19]. Second, we do not assume workers are stably connected like in Hyrax. Third, we do not assume workers already have the same program code installed for processing the data like the assumption made in Honeybee and Mobile Crowd Computing [11]. Therefore, our work requires a different strategy which has not been addressed by the past related works.

6   Conclusion

This paper proposed a framework for providing Context-as-a-Service (CaaS) from mobile-embedded servers based on extending the service-oriented Indie Fog architecture. Further, in order to effectively achieve the distributed computing mechanism of Indie Fog in mobile ad hoc environment, we proposed MIRA scheme, which can optimise the work partitions based on resource-aware dynamic factors in mobile environments. Finally, we have implemented the prototype of mobile Indie Fog on real world devices and used the prototype to validate the proposed MIRA scheme. Overall, MIRA scheme has proved that it can improve the overall performance of the distributed processes.

In the future, we plan to extend the proposed framework with the following mechanisms.

1. Blockchain-based incentive model. In order to encourage the MIF providers to contribute more computational resources, a distributed incentive model will be used to credit the contributors of MIF.
2. We also plan to extend and to validate the MIRA scheme in a more complex environment which consists of heterogeneous Fog nodes (e.g. industrial integrated routers, single-board computers, fan-less low power PCs) and geo-distributed cloud servers.

References

1. Agarwal, V., Banerjee, N., Chakraborty, D., Mittal, S.: Usense-a smartphone middleware for community sensing. In: 2013 IEEE 14th International Conference on Mobile Data Management (MDM), vol. 1, pp. 56–65. IEEE (2013)
2. Arkian, H.R., Diyanat, A., Pourkhalili, A.: Mist: fog-based data analytics scheme with cost-efficient resource provisioning for IoT crowdsensing applications. J. Netw. Comput. Appl. **82**, 152–165 (2017)
3. Barboutov, K.: Ericsson mobility report. Technical report, Ericsson, June 2017. https://www.ericsson.com/assets/local/mobility-report/documents/2017/ericsson-mobility-report-june-2017.pdf
4. Capra, L.: Mobile computing middleware for context-aware applications. In: 2002 Proceedings of the 24th International Conference on Software Engineering, ICSE 2002, pp. 723–724. IEEE (2002)
5. Chang, C., Srirama, S.N., Buyya, R.: Mobile cloud business process management system for the internet of things: a survey. ACM Comput. Surv. **49**(4), 70:1–70:42 (2016). https://doi.org/10.1145/3012000
6. Chang, C., Srirama, S.N., Buyya, R.: Indie fog: an efficient fog-computing infrastructure for the internet of things. Computer **50**(9), 92–98 (2017)
7. Chang, C., Srirama, S.N., Liyanage, M.: A service-oriented mobile cloud middleware framework for provisioning mobile sensing as a service. In: The 21st International Conference on Parallel and Distributed Systems, pp. 124–131. IEEE (2015)
8. Cheng, X., Fang, L., Hong, X., Yang, L.: Exploiting mobile big data: Sources, features, and applications. IEEE Netw. **31**(1), 72–79 (2017)
9. Das, T., Mohan, P., Padmanabhan, V.N., Ramjee, R., Sharma, A.: PRISM: platform for remote sensing using smartphones. In: Proceedings of the 8th International Conference on Mobile Systems, Applications, and Services, pp. 63–76. ACM (2010)
10. Fernando, N., Loke, S.W., Rahayu, W.: Honeybee: a programming framework for mobile crowd computing. In: Zheng, K., Li, M., Jiang, H. (eds.) MobiQuitous 2012. LNICST, vol. 120, pp. 224–236. Springer, Heidelberg (2013). https://doi.org/10.1007/978-3-642-40238-8_19
11. Loke, S.W., Napier, K., Alali, A., Fernando, N., Rahayu, W.: Mobile computations with surrounding devices: proximity sensing and multilayered work stealing. ACM Trans. Embed. Comput. Syst. **14**(2), 22:1–22:25 (2015)
12. Marinelli, E.E.: Hyrax: cloud computing on mobile devices using MapReduce. Carnegie-mellon univ Pittsburgh PA school of computer science, Technical report (2009)
13. Ngai, E.C.H., Huang, H., Liu, J., Srivastava, M.B.: Oppsense: information sharing for mobile phones in sensing field with data repositories. In: 2011 8th Annual IEEE Communications Society Conference on Sensor, Mesh and Ad Hoc Communications and Networks (SECON), pp. 107–115. IEEE (2011)
14. Penco, C.: Objective and cognitive context. In: Bouquet, P., Benerecetti, M., Serafini, L., Brézillon, P., Castellani, F. (eds.) CONTEXT 1999. LNCS (LNAI), vol. 1688, pp. 270–283. Springer, Heidelberg (1999). https://doi.org/10.1007/3-540-48315-2_21
15. Philipp, D., Durr, F., Rothermel, K.: A sensor network abstraction for flexible public sensing systems. In: 2011 IEEE 8th International Conference on Mobile Adhoc and Sensor Systems (MASS), pp. 460–469. IEEE (2011)
16. Sarma, S., Venkatasubramanian, N., Dutt, N.: Sense-making from distributed and mobile sensing data: a middleware perspective. In: Proceedings of the 51st Annual Design Automation Conference, pp. 1–6. ACM (2014)

17. Sheng, X., Tang, J., Xiao, X., Xue, G.: Sensing as a service: challenges, solutions and future directions. IEEE Sens. J. **13**(10), 3733–3741 (2013)
18. Sherchan, W., Jayaraman, P.P., Krishnaswamy, S., Zaslavsky, A., Loke, S., Sinha, A.: Using on-the-move mining for mobile crowdsensing. In: IEEE 13th International Conference on Mobile Data Management, pp. 115–124. IEEE (2012)
19. Soo, S., Chang, C., Loke, S.W., Srirama, S.N.: Proactive mobile fog computing using work stealing: data processing at the edge. Int. J. Mobile Comput. Multimedia Commun. (IJMCMC) **8**(4), 1–19 (2017)
20. Wagner, M.: Context as a service. In: Proceedings of the 12th International Conference Adjunct Papers on Ubiquitous Computing-adjunct, pp. 489–492. ACM (2010)
21. Wang, L., Zhang, D., Xiong, H.: effSense: energy-efficient and cost-effective data uploading in mobile crowdsensing. In: The 2013 ACM Conference on Pervasive and Ubiquitous Computing Adjunct Publication, pp. 1075–1086. ACM (2013)

Spotlighting Use Case Specific Architectures

Mohamed Lamine Kerdoudi[1,2(✉)], Chouki Tibermacine[2], and Salah Sadou[3]

[1] Computer Science Department, University of Biskra, Biskra, Algeria
lamine.kerdoudi@gmail.com
[2] LIRMM, CNRS and Montpellier University, Montpellier, France
Chouki.Tibermacine@lirmm.fr
[3] IRISA-University of South Brittany, Vannes, France
Salah.Sadou@irisa.fr

Abstract. Most of the time a large software system implies a complex architecture. However, at some point of the system's execution, its components are not necessarily all running. Indeed, some components may not be concerned by a given use case, and therefore they do not consume/use or register the declared services. Thus, these architectural elements (components and their services) represent a "noise" in the architecture model of the system. Their elimination from the architecture model may greatly reduce its complexity, and consequently helps developers in their maintenance tasks. In our work, we argue that a large service-oriented system has, not only one, but several architectures, which are specific to its runtime use cases. Indeed, each architecture reflects the services, and thereby the components, which are really useful for a given use case. In this paper, we present an approach for recovering such use case specific architectures of service-oriented systems. Architectures are recovered both through a source code analysis and by querying the runtime environment and the service registry. The first built architecture (the core architecture) is composed of the components that are present in all the use cases. Then, depending on a particular use case, this core architecture will be enriched with only the needed components.

1 Introduction

The context of this work is the architecture of large-sized service-oriented software systems. By large-sized systems, we mean systems that are composed of hundreds to thousands of components, registering and consuming hundreds of services. Architectures of systems in general are important to be explicitly modeled, and this is particularly critical for large systems. When such architecture models are not explicit, it becomes important to recover them from the system's artifacts (e.g., source code). Architecture recovery is a challenging problem, and several works in the literature have already proposed contributions to solve it (e.g., works cited in [8,13,15]). Architectures recovered from large systems are however complex and difficult to "grasp". Indeed, architectures of large systems

C. E. Cuesta et al. (Eds.): ECSA 2018, LNCS 11048, pp. 236–244, 2018.
https://doi.org/10.1007/978-3-030-00761-4_16

model a lot of components, their contracts (required and provided interfaces) and their numerous and tangled interconnections. If we add, to these architecture elements, services that are registered and consumed by components (which enrich their contracts), these architectures can be easily assimilated to "spaghetti" code.

We noticed that at some point in the execution of such large systems, not all their components are running/active. Components that are not running and their properties (services and their connections) represent a "noise" in a recovered (complex – "spaghetti") architecture. Their elimination reduces thereby the complexity of this architecture and helps the developers in their maintenance tasks. In this work, we argue that large systems do not have a single large and complex architecture, but rather several architectures depending on the use context. In this paper, we present an approach (Sect. 2) which enables to recover the architecture of a service-oriented system, depending on a particular use case. This approach contributes with a process that analyzes the source code of the system and interacts with the runtime environment, including the service registry, to build a first core architecture modeling the components of the system that always run. Then, this core architecture is enriched with new elements that reify the runtime entities involved in a particular use case, of interest for the developer (in which a bug occured, for instance). Simplifying architecture models in this way enables developers to make like a quick "inventory" of what is concretely running, among all what composes their system, at a particular execution time. They can easily identify which component is consuming a particular failing service, for instance. In the literature there is no efficient process for recovering these dynamic use case architectures from running systems (see Sect. 5).

We implemented the proposed process for the OSGi platform (see Sect. 3) and we experimented it on a set of real-world Eclipse-based applications (see Sect. 4). At the end of the paper, we highlight the interests and limitations of the proposed process, as well as some future directions of this work (Sect. 6).

2   General Approach

The problem with traditional architectural models of a software system is that they describe all involved components and their potential dependencies. The proposed process (see Fig. 1) enables to produce an architecture model that can be used by the developer to solve a maintenance problem related to a given use case. First, we create the core architecture, which represents only components that exist in the system whatever the executed application's use case. In the second step, we use traces obtained by executing scenarios corresponding to the application's use cases to identify what we call "use case"-specific (or use-case) architectures. The latter are built around the core architecture with variants (adding new components, services, etc.) concerning the executed use case.

Recovering the Core Architecture: To create the core architecture, we use first a static analysis to collect all the components involved at the system's

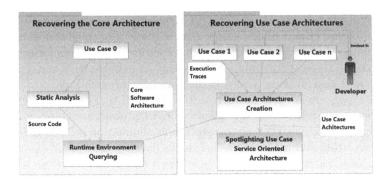

Fig. 1. Proposed approach

starting time. The core architecture will be comprehensive once the dynamic elements are identified. Indeed, some dependencies exist only through requests for services made during execution time. To identify these dependencies, we launch the application without applying a use case ("Use Case 0" in Fig. 1).

Recovering Use Case Architectures: During a maintenance activity, the developer focuses on a given use case of the application. Thus, we ask a developer to execute a set of use cases and we capture all traces produced by the involved components. After that, we parse the code of the newly activated components in order to identify their dependencies. The collected information is used to enrich the core architecture in order to build the "use case"-specific architecture.

3   Implementation of the Approach: Case of OSGi

We implemented our approach for OSGi-based systems. OSGi is a specification that defines a component model and a framework for creating highly modular Java systems [16]. An OSGi component is known as a bundle that packages a subset of the Java classes, and a manifest file. The OSGi framework introduces a service-oriented programming model. Indeed, a bundle (provider) can publish its services into a Service Registry, while another bundle searches the registry to use available services. We take as a running example an Eclipse-based application that runs on top of Equinox, which is the reference implementation of the OSGi specification. We used the release: Eclipse JEE for Web Developers, Oxygen.2[1].

3.1   Recovering the Eclipse Core Architecture

In order to recover the core architecture of the Eclipse-based application, we first perform a static analysis of the source code and the manifest files of the bundles that are needed to start this application. These bundles refer to components

---

[1] Downloaded from repository: https://lc.cx/P2Qw.

that have the state "ACTIVE". They are recognized by querying the runtime environment. Indeed, we have added listeners in the Eclipse plugin which implements the proposed process. We rely on SCA[2] for the modeling of the obtained architecture. SCA has been chosen because of its simplicity and the existence of good tools support for the graphical visualization. First, each bundle is modeled as an SCA component which has as a name the bundle's symbolic name. Then, by parsing the manifest files, we identify the dependencies between components. Indeed, we consider each declared interface in the exported package as a provided interface and the declared interfaces in the imported packages are considered as required interfaces. The SCA Wires are used to represent the connections. After that, we hide the required interfaces that are not concretely used in code.

Besides, in the context of OSGi components, services are defined by dedicated classes that are instantiated and registered with the OSGi Service Registry either programmatically or declaratively (i.e., using the OSGi DS framework). Services declared with DS framework are identified by parsing the "*OSGI − INF/component.xml*" files. For the programmatically registered services, we parse the following two statements: `<context>.registerService(..)` and `<context>.getServiceReference(..)`. Then, the core architecture is enriched by dynamic features. Indeed, we query at runtime the execution environment and Service Registry to identify what are the concretely registered dynamic services and consumed services. Therefore, we hide the static information.

3.2 Recovering Eclipse Use Case Architectures

Once the core architecture is recovered, we ask the developer to execute a set of scenarios corresponding to use cases. New components related to each scenario can be activated and new services can be registered. These components and services, are identified by querying at runtime the execution environment and the Service Registry. As consequence, for each scenario, we generate a runtime use case architecture by adding to the core architecture the newly activated components, interfaces, and services. For instance, after executing the following use case: "Accessing the Toolbar Menu, Opening Help− >Install New Software...", 11 new components are activated. Figure 2 shows an excerpt of the recovered use case architecture for this scenario. We show in this figure the new activated components (surrounded by bold lines) which are connected to the core architecture components. For reasons of readability, we show only some core architecture elements that are directly connected to the newly activated components.

Besides, we offer also to the developers a way to refine the recovered use case architecture and spotlight the implicit service-oriented architecture (pure SOA), which contains only services (without interfaces) and the active components that register or consume services. In this way, we enable them to focus only on services-based dependencies, which simplify greatly the architecture model.

---

[2] SCA is a set of specifications which describe SOA systems: https://lc.cx/AEP3.

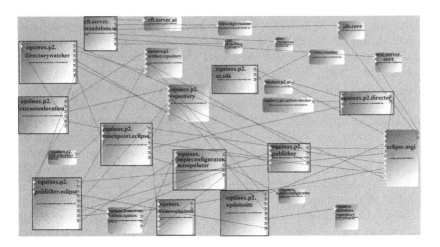

Fig. 2. A "Use Case"-specific architecture

4   Empirical Evaluation

We evaluated our approach starting from two Eclipse-based applications of different sizes. The aim is to measure the gain in the reduction of complexity of the recovered runtime use case architectures. Indeed, we have compared the complexity of the architecture that is obtained by a static code analysis of all the system components with the complexity of the recovered use case architectures. Table 1 describes the chosen systems[3]. For each system, we executed 4 use cases related to the installed projects. In order to measure the complexity of the recovered architectures, we have used a complexity metric (CM) proposed in [10]: $CM = \frac{AC}{AC_w}$, where, AC is Absolute Complexity of a use case architecture and AC_w is the worst architecture complexity which corresponds to the static architecture complexity. To estimate AC, we create an adjacency matrix from the architecture and we calculate the influence degree of each component on the rest of the system.

Table 1. Selected eclipse-based applications

S. Id.	Description	Installed projects	# of bundles	# of classes	SLOC
1	Eclipse JEE for Web Developers Oxygen.2	WTP, BPEL, Axis Tools.	1040	131282	4.11M
2	Eclipse Modeling Tools Oxygen.2	ArchStudio, Papyrus, BPMN2.	1502	151471	4.90M

4.1   Complexity Measurement Results

The obtained results are presented in Table 2. As we can see in column 2, the static architectures of the two candidate systems are very complex and this is

---

[3] They have been downloaded from the following repository: https://lc.cx/m77k.

particularly true for the largest application. Column 4 presents the number of actions on the graphical user interface in order to describe quantitatively each use case. We can see (in Column 5) that the complexity of all the obtained use case architectures is greatly less than the complexity of the static architectures (AC_w). This confirms our intuition that focusing on the runtime use case architectures greatly reduces the complexity of the architecture compared to the static one. Second, the obtained CM values (Column 6) are good for all the recovered use case architectures. However, we noticed that these values decrease when we increase the size of the system. If we take UC2 in the two systems, which have almost equal number of GUI actions, we can see that CM value in the second system is less than in the first system (0.25 vs. 0.31). This because, the AC_w increases with the system size, while the AC vary in a stable interval. Third, we can observe in column 7 that the average number of newly activated components is equal to 50 components per use case. This can be considered as a good value for a system that contains more than a thousand components. Developers recover and understand the core architecture once (it is common to all use cases), which is considered as the initial overhead of our approach. After that, they can focus only on the newly activated components for a use case. At the end, we can observe the high correlation between the number of GUI actions and CM values (correlation coefficient equal to 0.86 for System 1 and 0.88 for System 2). The more the GUI actions we do, the greater CM values we obtain. But CM values remain very low, AC is thereby kept far below AC_w.

Table 2. Experiment Results

S. Id.	AC_w	Use Case	# of GUI Actions	AC	CM	# of Active Components
1	5637	UC 0	0	1076	0.19	163
		UC 1	11	1195	0.21	174
		UC 2	28	1777	0.31	242
		UC 3	35	1907	0.33	248
		UC 4	55	1941	0.34	259
2	9014	UC 0	0	2153	0.23	392
		UC 1	4	2197	0.24	394
		UC 2	27	2330	0.25	413
		UC 3	30	2429	0.26	425
		UC 4	49	2885	0.32	473

4.2 Performance Measurement

We evaluated the performance of our approach by estimating the time for recovering each architecture. We ran our experiments in a machine with a CPU 4.20 GHz Intel Core i7-7700K, with 8 logical cores, 4 physical cores, and 32

GB of memory. The recovering of the static architectures takes 4 h for the first System and 9 for the second System. Besides, the average time for recovering a use case architecture is 45 min for the first System and 2 h for the second System. Therefore, this results demonstrate the efficiency our approach.

4.3   Threats to Validity

This experiment may suffer from some threats to the validity of its results:

Internal Validity. In order to evaluate the accuracy of our approach, we need to compare the recovered architectures with "ground-truth" use case architectures. A "ground-truth" architecture is an architecture that has been verified as accurate by the architects [9]. Obtaining this architecture is challenging. To mitigate this threat, we have verified manually the component dependencies of large parts of the recovered use case architectures by analyzing and checking manually source code and the manifest files of the candidate components.

External Validity. Our evaluation is based on set of OSGi systems which limits our study's generalizability to other kind of systems. To mitigate this threat, we selected systems providing different functionalities (BPMN, BPEL,...) and sizes.

5   Related Work

A framework comprising a set of principles and processes for recovering systems' ground-truth architectures has been proposed in [9,13]. The authors in [15] provide a review of the hierarchical clustering techniques which seeks to build a hierarchy of clusters starting from implementation level entities. In our work, we focus on runtime use case architectures, instead of recovering whole static architectures. However, if the recovered use case architectures remain complex for a human analysis, we can use of one of the existing clustring methods for abstracting those architectures. The works in [3–5,21] focused on extracting component-based architectures from existing object-oriented systems. Seriai et al. in [20] used FCA to identify the component interfaces. Unlike these works, in our work, we deal with reducing the size of the recovered architecture by focusing on particular use cases, and we include dynamic features in this architecture.

Besides, several SOA recovery approaches have been proposed in the literature as part of the process of migrating systems to SOA solutions [18]. Most of these approaches are based on static code analysis of the target system. Examples of these works are [2,11,17]. A number of works such as [7,12,22] have been proposed to detect SOA patterns from service oriented applications. Our approach focused on the recovery of pure SOAs. Using SOA design patterns may be a good complement to our approach for a better understanding of the recovered architecture. More particularly, this helps in better understanding the design decisions made during the modeling of the analyzed system.

Managing complex architectures of large software systems became a topic of interest of several research works. Some authors proposed to organize architectural information using a Dependency Structure Matrix [14, 19]. The authors in [6] have proposed an architectural slicing and abstraction approach for reducing the model complexity. Abi-Antoun et al. [1] proposed a technique to statically extract a hierarchical runtime architecture from object-oriented code. In our approach, we deal with architectures at a higher level of granularity (component ones) and not low level ones (at object-oriented program level).

6   Conclusion and Future Work

In this work, we noticed that recovering the whole architecture of a large system produces models that are not tractable for developers due to their size and complexity. In this paper, we proposed a process for recovering the architecture of large component-/service-oriented systems. Since services in these systems are not provided and consumed all together, in a given use case, and components are not all active in the same time, we defined in this process a method to reduce the size and the complexity of the architecture. Thanks to a runtime analysis and taking into consideration only specific use cases of interest for the developer (related to a bug occurrence, for instance), we spotlight the active elements (components and services) in the recovered architecture. We benefited from the OSGi framework capabilities to implement such a process, and we experimented it on a set of Eclipse-based applications. The results showed the potential of the approach in recovering the architectures of these large systems, while reducing their complexity by spotlighting essential elements.

As a future work, we plan to make the recovered architecture models dynamic: they evolve (elements are shown and hidden) while the system is running by following debugger-like behaviors. In this way, we help the developer to monitor and evolve her/his system directly via its architecture. In addition, we want to make them interactive, by enabling developers to control components and services just by clicking, dragging and dropping the visualized elements.

References

1. Abi-Antoun, M., Aldrich, J.: Static extraction and conformance analysis of hierarchical runtime architectural structure using annotations. In: Proceedings of the ACM OOPSLA (2009)
2. Alahmari, S., Zaluska, E., De Roure, D.: A service identification framework for legacy system migration into SOA. In: Proceedings of the IEEE SCC 2010. IEEE (2010)
3. Allier, S., Sadou, S., Sahraoui, H.A., Fleurquin, R.: From object-oriented applications to component-oriented applications via component- oriented architecture. In: Proceedings of WICSA, Colorado, USA. IEEE (2011)
4. Allier, S., Sahraoui, H.A., Sadou, S., Vaucher, S.: Restructuring object-oriented applications into component-oriented applications by using consistency with execution traces. In: Grunske, L., Reussner, R., Plasil, F. (eds.) CBSE 2010. LNCS, vol. 6092, pp. 216–231. Springer, Heidelberg (2010). https://doi.org/10.1007/978-3-642-13238-4_13

5. Chardigny, S., Seriai, A., Oussalah, M., Tamzalit, D.: Extraction of component-based architecture from object-oriented systems. In: Proceedings of WICSA. IEEE (2008)

6. Colangelo, D., Compare, D., Inverardi, P., Pelliccione, P.: Reducing software architecture models complexity: a slicing and abstraction approach. In: Najm, E., Pradat-Peyre, J.-F., Donzeau-Gouge, V.V. (eds.) FORTE 2006. LNCS, vol. 4229, pp. 243–258. Springer, Heidelberg (2006). https://doi.org/10.1007/11888116_19

7. Demange, A., Moha, N., Tremblay, G.: Detection of SOA patterns. In: Basu, S., Pautasso, C., Zhang, L., Fu, X. (eds.) ICSOC 2013. LNCS, vol. 8274, pp. 114–130. Springer, Heidelberg (2013). https://doi.org/10.1007/978-3-642-45005-1_9

8. Ducasse, S., Pollet, D.: Software architecture reconstruction: a process-oriented taxonomy. IEEE TSE **35**(4), 573–591 (2009)

9. Garcia, J., Ivkovic, I., Medvidovic, N.: A comparative analysis of software architecture recovery techniques. In: Proceedings of IEEE/ACM ASE (2013)

10. Jiao, F., Hu, C., Zhao, C.: A software complexity metric for SCA specification. In: Proceedings of the CSSE. IEEE (2008)

11. Kerdoudi, M.L., Tibermacine, C., Sadou, S.: Opening web applications for third-party development: a service-oriented solution. J. SOCA **10**(4), 437–463 (2016)

12. Liang, Q.A., Chung, J.Y., Miller, S., Ouyang, Y.: Service pattern discovery of web service mining in web service registry-repository. In: Proceedings of ICEBE 2006 (2006)

13. Lutellier, T., Chollak, D., Garcia, J., Tan, L., Rayside, D., Medvidovic, N., Kroeger, R.: Measuring the impact of code dependencies on software architecture recovery techniques. IEEE TSE **44**(2), 159–181 (2018)

14. MacCormack, A., Rusnak, J., Baldwin, C.Y.: Exploring the structure of complex software designs: an empirical study of open source and proprietary code. Manag. Sci. **52**(7), 1015–1030 (2006)

15. Maqbool, O., Babri, H.: Hierarchical clustering for software architecture recovery. IEEE TSE **33**(11), 759–780 (2007)

16. McAffer, J., VanderLei, P., Archer, S.: OSGi and Equinox: Creating Highly Modular Java Systems. Addison-Wesley Professional, Boston (2010)

17. O'Brien, L., Smith, D., Lewis, G.: Supporting migration to services using software architecture reconstruction. In: Proceedings of STEP. IEEE (2005)

18. Razavian, M., Lago, P.: A systematic literature review on SOA migration. J. Softw.: Evol. Process. **27**(5), 337–372 (2015)

19. Sangal, N., Jordan, E., Sinha, V., Jackson, D.: Using dependency models to manage complex software architecture. In: Proceedings of the ACM OOPSLA. ACM (2005)

20. Seriai, A., Sadou, S., Sahraoui, H., Hamza, S.: Deriving component interfaces after a restructuring of a legacy system. In: Proceedings of WICSA. IEEE (2014)

21. Seriai, A., Sadou, S., Sahraoui, H.A.: Enactment of components extracted from an object-oriented application. In: Avgeriou, P., Zdun, U. (eds.) ECSA 2014. LNCS, vol. 8627, pp. 234–249. Springer, Cham (2014). https://doi.org/10.1007/978-3-319-09970-5_22

22. Upadhyaya, B., Tang, R., Zou, Y.: An approach for mining service composition patterns from execution logs. J. Softw.: Evol. Process. **25**(8), 841–870 (2013)

Architectural Design Decisions

Empirical Insights into the Evolving Role of Architects in Decision-Making in an Agile Context

Femke Heijenk[1], Martin van den Berg[2(✉)], Henrik Leopold[1],
Hans van Vliet[1], and Raymond Slot[3]

[1] Department of Computer Science, VU University,
Amsterdam, The Netherlands
femke@heijenk.nl, h.leopold@vu.nl, hans@cs.vu.nl
[2] Department of ICT, De Nederlandsche Bank, Amsterdam, The Netherlands
m.j.b.k.van.den.berg@dnb.nl
[3] Information Systems Architecture Research Group,
University of Applied Sciences Utrecht, Utrecht, The Netherlands
raymond.slot@hu.nl

Abstract. The transition to agile software development changes the decision-making power in organizations. This study aims to provide researchers and practitioners with empirical insights into how the participation in decision-making by enterprise, solution and system architects evolves due to this transition. For this purpose, a case study was conducted to examine the participation of and challenges for architects in decision-making in agile projects. A mixed-method research approach was used comprising observations, conversations, interviews, literature study and a survey. We found that 101 decision types are used prior to and in agile iterations, in which architects and stakeholders collaborate to make these decisions. The projection of these types of decisions over 25 different actors in the case study organization demonstrates that decision-making is a group effort in which solution and system architects are highly involved. Architecture and agility can indeed co-exist. Another finding of this case study is that stakeholders in agile teams perceive less architecture involvement in decision-making and expect less design decisions up front. Architects are challenged to become team players, to make design decisions only when they are necessary, and finally, to document, communicate, and share design decisions more effectively.

Keywords: Enterprise architecture · Solution architecture
System architecture · Agile decision-making · Agile software development
Agile teams

1 Introduction

The adoption of agile software development has become mainstream [1, 2]. The transition to agile, however, is still a challenge in the areas of people, organization, project and process [3]. One of the consequences of this transition is that agile gives more decision-making power to teams and developers [4, 5]. This implies that some

© Springer Nature Switzerland AG 2018
C. E. Cuesta et al. (Eds.): ECSA 2018, LNCS 11048, pp. 247–264, 2018.
https://doi.org/10.1007/978-3-030-00761-4_17

other actors see a reduction in their decision-making power. Architects are one of the actors in an agile context, so the question is how their decision-making power changes due to the agile transition: are they involved in more or less decisions, do they have to find different ways to collaborate in decision-making, and how do stakeholders[1] perceive the role of architects in decision-making? Several publications describe an adapted role for architects in agile software development, albeit from a more theoretical perspective [6–11]. In this research, we intend to empirically explore the involvement of architects in all kinds of decisions in agile projects and their collaboration with stakeholders. Just as stakeholders of architecture may be involved in design decisions, architects may participate in other types of decisions, like management decisions [12]. The main research question of this study is therefore:

What is the impact of the agile transition on the role of architects in decision-making prior to and in agile iterations?

To answer the main research question we divided it into the following sub-questions:

- *RQ-1: What types of decisions are used prior to and in agile iterations?*
- *RQ-2: What is the involvement of architects in these types of decisions?*
- *RQ-3: What is the perception of stakeholders about the way architects participate in decision-making prior to and in agile iterations?*

To answer the research questions, a case study was conducted. In this case study, we used a mixed method research approach comprising observations, conversations, interviews, literature study and a survey. The transition to agile is still ongoing [10, 13]. Case studies can therefore provide useful insights to research. The case study was conducted in an organization that has an architecture practice for eight years, and has applied agile in software development for two years.

The results of this case study demonstrate that 101 different types of decisions are used prior to and during agile iterations. The projection of these types of decisions over 25 different actors in the case study organization demonstrates that decision-making is a group effort in which solution and system architects are highly involved. Stakeholders in agile teams perceive less architecture involvement and expect less comprehensive documents. Architects are challenged to become team players, to make design decisions only when they are necessary, and finally, to document, communicate, and share design decisions more effectively.

This study is important for a number of reasons. First, it provides architecture practitioners and researchers with empirical insights into how the role of architects in decision-making evolves due to agile software development. These insights are useful to confirm and extend existing theories, as well as to improve architecture practices. Second, it provides insights into what types of decisions are made in an agile context. These insights may enable organizations to assess and improve themselves.

This paper is structured as follows: in Sect. 2 we discuss related work. The research method is explained in Sect. 3. In Sect. 4 we present the results of this case study. In Sect. 5 we discuss results and in Sect. 6 threats to validity and limitations. Section 7 contains the conclusion.

---

[1] We consider stakeholders as the actors other than architects who participate in decision-making

2 Related Work

To answer our main research question we first need to know what decisions are made in an agile context. Drury studied the decision-making process in agile teams extensively [14–16]. In one of her studies Drury identified various decision types that are used during software development [15]. Drury's study focuses on the decisions generally made by agile teams during the iteration. These decisions are divided over four phases. In the first phase, the iteration planning, the team plans the upcoming iteration. They assign story points to a user story and divide tasks. In the execution phase, the team works on developing the actual product. In the review phase, the stakeholders get the opportunity to give feedback to the team and review progress. They determine if the requirements are met and which user stories need to be more detailed or debugged and taken to the next iteration. In the final phase, the iteration retrospective, the team members give feedback on the iteration [15]. We used Drury's decision types as a starting point to identify different types of decisions.

With regard to the role of architects in decision-making two aspects play a role. First, decision-making is described as one of the major tasks of architects and key design decisions are seen as the main artifact of architects [17, 18]. Traditionally, the main task for architects is to make decisions that would be costly and risky to change mid-project [19, 20]. These decisions are made prior to or in the early stages of a project, and therefore architects are linked to big design up front planning and decision-making [20]. Second, architecting is conducted on different organizational levels. That means that there are different levels on which key design decisions are made. All these levels are relevant when studying the impact of agile on the role of architects. TOGAF makes the distinction between enterprise, segment and solution architects. The enterprise architect operates at the enterprise level, the segment architect operates in a given domain, and the solution architect has its focus on system technology solutions [21]. SAFe makes the distinction between enterprise, solution and system architects. Enterprise architects act at the portfolio level and solution/system architects at the program and large solution level [6].

The impact of agile on architecture has been studied by different scholars [10, 22, 23]. Architecture has traditionally a top-down approach, while agile works bottom-up. Architects are plan and documentation-driven, while agile works with a trial-and-error approach and documentation is of less importance. The question is whether these two will complement each other, or if there is an unbridgeable gap [9, 10, 22]. In the early days of agile, there was doubt whether agility and architecture could co-exist [24]. Contemporary frameworks and approaches demonstrate that agility and architecture can co-exist [5, 6]. This research aims to provide empirical insight into the challenges for architects in the way they participate in decision-making in an agile context and compare these insights with existing theories.

3 Research Approach

3.1 Research Method

We regard the way different actors are involved in decision-making in an agile context a complex social phenomena. The case study approach is suitable to understand such phenomena [25, 26]. As part of this case study, we used a mixed method research approach comprising observations, conversations, interviews, literature study and a survey. Figure 1 visualizes the research design. As the unit of analysis, we chose the architect [26]. The architect, and more specifically, the enterprise, solution or system architect, is one of the actors who is involved in decision-making in the case study organization.

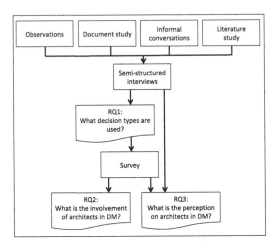

Fig. 1. Research design

3.2 Case Study Organization

The case study organization is a Dutch government body, with approximately 1,800 employees and which operates in the financial sector. The organization has applied the agile approach for software development for two years and is generally aware that architecture and agile teams need to be aligned. The challenge for the organization is to find a way to connect the more bottom-up agile software development approach and the more top-down organizational governance approaches like business planning and portfolio management. In this study, we focus on the decisions that are required prior to and during the agile iterations and what the role of architects is in these decisions. The case study organization employs six enterprise architects, who operate at the enterprise and the domain (portfolio) level, and twelve solution architects who act at the program and project level. Regularly, solution architects work for two or three agile teams. In the domain where this research was conducted, two system architects operate as part of an agile team. The main architecture artifacts are: architecture criteria at the enterprise level, future-state architectures (FSA) at the domain and program level, and project-start architectures (PSA) at the project level. Architecture criteria consist of principles, policies, and standards. An FSA describes the future state of a domain or program in terms of business, application, and technical architecture. A PSA contains the relevant principles, policies and standards for a project, as well as the current and future state of a project in terms of the business, application, and technical architecture. Figure 2 illustrates the different levels, associated artifacts and positioning of architecture roles in the case study organization. For example, in the development of a new payment system, an enterprise architect created an FSA containing the target organization and processes, the relevant architecture criteria, and the high level requirements for the system. A solution architect and a system architect created a PSA containing the software architecture and the required infrastructure for the system. During the development of the system, two system architects were involved as part of two agile teams. These system architects were also acting as developer.

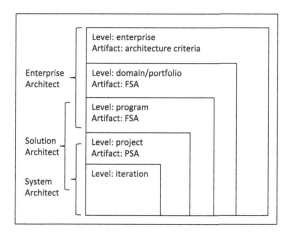

Fig. 2. Organization of architecture function in case study organization

3.3   Data Collection

As a first step, ethnographic methods were applied to gain an understanding in the way of working of the case study organization [25]. The first insights were obtained during observations while attending agile team meetings. In addition to these observations, informal conversations were held with practitioners to expand and clarify observations. Furthermore, documents of the case study organization were studied, in particular architecture documents like FSAs and PSAs. Lastly, a literature study was conducted to gain an understanding of relevant literature. Four databases (Google Scholar, IEEE Xplore Digital Library, Springer Link, and the digital library of the VU University) were searched based on the following keywords: "Enterprise Architecture", "Architecture", "Decision-making Agile projects", "Agile and Architecture", and "Architecture Decision-making Agile". The literature with the most relevance for the research questions, is included in the related work section. Based on the information gathered to date, semi-structured interviews were held in the last quarter of 2016. The goal of these interviews was to create a list of decision types that were used prior to and in agile iterations. As a starting point we used Drury's list of decision types [15]. In the interviews different decisions were explored in which each respondent participated. These decisions were summarized at the end of each interview. The respondent had the opportunity to confirm or reject a captured decision. A list of the decision types made by the respondent was obtained on the basis of each interview. These decision types were added to Drury's original decision list. A project leader, a product owner, and an enterprise architect validated the complete list of decision types. As a result, duplicate and unclear decision types were removed. The final decision list reflects the decision types of an organization in an agile transition. The interviewees were also asked for their perception about the role of architects in decision-making. Table 1 shows the number of participants per role in the interviews, as well as in the subsequent survey. The average number of years of experience of all participants with agile software development is 4.7. Six agile teams were included in this research. These teams worked on a variety of systems: a customer relationship management system, a portal, a data collection system, a payment system (two teams), and a contribution collection system: all larger systems (>1 million Euros).

Table 1. Number of participants involved in case study

Role	Interview	Survey
Enterprise architect	2	3
Solution architect	1	3
System architect	2	2
Developer		2
Head of section		2
Information manager		1
Portfolio manager		1
Information analyst		1
Project manager		1
Project leader	2	2
Product owner	3	4
Scrum master		3
Total	**10**	**25**

As a next step, we used a survey to gain insight into the participation in decision-making according to respondents. The decision list we created in the previous step was used as the basis for the survey. Initially we asked 35 people to participate in the survey. These people all play a role related to the six agile teams. Ultimately 25 people participated between December 2016 and January 2017. The respondents can be categorized into two groups: the architects' perspective of their participation in decision-making and the stakeholders' perspective of the architects' and their own participation in decision-making. The architects were asked to identify the decision types in which they participate. By participation, we mean active participation in the sense of having a say in decisions of that type. The stakeholder group consists of all the other participants in the survey. The stakeholders have each a different concern, regarding agile iterations and have different perspectives on decision-making. The stakeholder group was asked to identify participation of the different roles of architects in the different decision types and to identify the decision types in which they participate themselves. As a final step in this research, the results of the interviews and survey were analyzed and discussed among the researchers.

4   Results

4.1   Decision Types

Based on the outcome of the interviews, a list was created with 101 decision types[2] divided over five different phases and three perspectives as shown in Table 2. The first phase is the initiating phase with decision types that are made prior to the agile iterations. Decisions made in this phase provide the context for the agile iterations. The second phase is the operational one with decision types used at the start of each agile iteration. The third phase contains types of decisions used during the execution of the iteration. We then have the review phase that contains end-of-iteration decision types. The final phase contains decision types on the retrospective. Compared to Drury's list of decision types, 72 decision types were added, and one decision type was removed. Drury did not take the initiating phase into account; so all decision types in this phase were added. The decision type removed during validation was "who is the owner of the user story". The three persons validating the decision list interpreted this decision type differently. Furthermore, they remarked that "everyone is the owner of a user story", and therefore "what is the decision here meant to be?" We also classified the decision types according to different perspectives. The management perspective contains decision types regarding planning, estimation, resourcing, and prioritization. The user perspective includes decision types on topics like requirements and acceptance. The third and last perspective is the design perspective with decision types on design and engineering. The decision list provides a snapshot of the decision types identified at the time of this research when the architects in this organization followed a rather traditional, document driven approach. That is why decision types were added like "Decide on the content of the FSA" and "Decide on the content of the PSA" and "Decide if the PSA is final".

Table 2. Number of decision types per phase and per perspective

Phase	Management	User	Design	Total
Initiating	10	3	9	22
Operational	28	5	4	37
Execution	8	0	13	21
Review	4	8	2	14
Retrospective	7	0	0	7
Total	**57**	**16**	**28**	**101**

4.2   Involvement in Decision-Making

We first wanted to know who participates in which decision types. Figure 3 shows the absolute number of decision types in which the 25 respondents of the survey

---

[2] The complete list can be found on https://bergmart.wordpress.com/2018/04/02/research-into-the-evolving-role-of-architects-in-decision-making-in-an-agile-context/

considered themselves to participate. One of the findings from Fig. 3 is that agile decision-making in this organization is a collaborative group effort. Different actors participate actively in the same decision types. On average, eleven actors participate actively in one decision type. Over 50% of all decision types involved all solution and system architects, product owners, the information analyst, one of the enterprise architects, one of the developers and one of the project leaders. Under 30% of decision types involved the scrum masters, the heads of section, the portfolio manager, the project manager, two of the enterprise architects, one of the developers, and one of the project leaders. One enterprise architect participates in far more decision types than the other two. Such a big difference also appears with the developers where one of them participates in 56 decision types and the other one in only three. The heads of section and the project leaders demonstrate considerable, but fewer major differences. With regard to the participation of architects, the system and solution architects are the ones that are most involved. They participate strongly in all phases and there is considerable overlap in the decision types they participate. In 29 decision types, all system and solution architects indicated their participation.

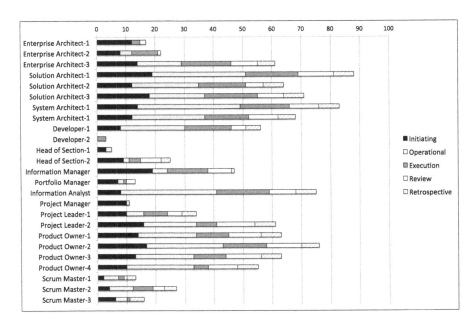

Fig. 3. Absolute number of decision types per phase per actor

Secondly, we wanted to find out who participates in design decision types and whether architects participate in other kind of decisions. Figure 4 demonstrates that most actors have a say in decision types of all three perspectives. E.g., product owners not only decide on user-related topics, but also on management and design related topics. Solution and system architects not only participate in design decision types, but also in user and management related decision types. Conversely, scrum masters are

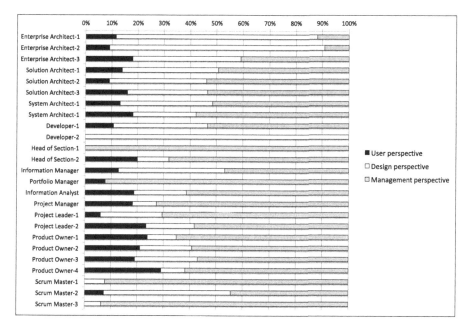

Fig. 4. Relative division of decision types over perspectives per actor

mostly focused on management decision types. The perspective with which architects are most familiar, the design perspective, is certainly not the domain of the architects alone. As can be seen in Fig. 4, different stakeholders participate in design decision types.

The finding that decision-making is a group effort, is further underpinned by looking at the participation in individual decision types. Table 3 contains the decision types that respondents consider have the most simultaneous participation. The decision type on the non-functional requirements attracts the most participation. In total 18 of the 25 respondents indicated that they participate actively in decisions of this type. Five of the 12 decision types with the highest participation relate to the initiating phase and another five to the retrospective phase. The first and last phase show the highest participation across the different participants. It is notable that both system and solution architects are heavily involved in almost all decision types. Furthermore, Table 3 demonstrates that 10 of 12 decision types have a management perspective.

In order to provide a balanced view, we also wanted to chart the decision types with the least simultaneous participation. Table 4 contains these decision types, all of which have a management perspective. Table 4 shows that these decision types require fewer participants than the decision types in Table 3. What stands out, is that system and solution architects play a role in some of the decision types with a management perspective. We already saw in Fig. 3 and Table 3 that system and solution architects are quite heavily involved in decision-making compared to stakeholders.

4.3   Perception about Architectural Participation in Decision-Making

Finally, we were interested in stakeholders' perception of the participation of architects, so that we could derive the challenges for architects. Table 5 contains the number of decision types in which architects participate according to stakeholders. We considered there to be participation of an architecture role if over 50% of the stakeholders were of the opinion that this architecture role participated. For comparison reasons, we also included the scores of the eight architects themselves. As can be seen, stakeholders have a different perception than architects. Especially in the operational and review phases, stakeholders perceive less participation than system and solution architects. Table 6 is similar to Table 5, although the decision types are clustered per perspective instead of per phase. Architects and stakeholders agree on the participation of architects in design decisions. The big differences are in the user and management perspective where solution and system architects participate in much more decision types than stakeholders perceive. Our next analysis addresses which architecture role is dominant in which decision phase according to stakeholders. An architecture role is dominant in a decision type when it has the highest percentage of participation according to stakeholders, and when this percentage is higher than 50%. As is shown in Table 7, stakeholders perceive the system architect overall as the dominant architecture role in the iterations compared to the other two architecture roles. The enterprise and solution architects play a more dominant role in the initiating phase only. This differs from the perception of solution architects themselves (see Table 5), who are of the opinion that they are strongly involved in all phases.

The interviewees commented on the role of architects and their way of working with agile teams. They acknowledged the role of architects but questioned the way in which architects contribute. According to a product owner: "*Architects are not so important during iterations. However, I recognize their value during the initiating phase. The FSA provides us with a framework within which we work and with the rationales of the decisions that were made early on. The PSA is also a good starting point in terms of how applications interact and what tools to use. Our system architect has the PSA in his head. We do not use the document, the system architect works accordingly. I think that the FSA and PSA could be shorter. One should not go into too much detail in the beginning.*" One of the enterprise architects remarked: "*To make sure that the architecture framework becomes part of the team's DNA, you need stable teams. When this is the case you do not need a PSA or any big up front documentation. The most important task of an architect is to talk and talk.*" One of the solution architects thought that the FSA and PSA were overly detailed. He also commented on the role of the enterprise architect versus the solution architect: "*Enterprise architecture is about the ideal world. As a solution architect I'm part of the real world. I have to deal with resource and budget constraints. These constraints determine the architecture to a large extent. I value the FSA, although it is too detailed. I personally make many decisions, and I agree that these decisions should be documented and motivated. We need to find a better way instead of creating a PSA.*"

Table 3. Decision types with most participants

No	Decision	Phase	Pers	Ent Arch	Sol Arch	Sys Arch	Dev	Head Sec	Inf Mng	Portf Mng	Inf Ana	PM	PL	PO	Scr Mas	Total
19	Decide on non-functional requirements	Init	User	3	3	2	1	1	1	–	1	1	1	4	–	18
16	Decide who is suitable for the team	Init	Man	–	2	2	1	2	1	1	1	1	2	2	2	17
95	Decide what to improve during the next iteration	Retro	Man	1	3	2	1	–	–	–	1	–	2	4	3	17
97	Decide what new things the team will try in next iteration	Retro	Man	1	3	2	1	1	–	–	1	–	2	4	2	17
17	Decide for someone (extern or intern) to join the team during the project	Init	Man	–	2	2	–	2	1	–	1	1	2	3	2	16
33	Decide if a user story meets the scope (time, budget, minimal viable product)	Oper	Man	–	3	2	1	–	–	–	1	1	2	4	2	16
67	Decide if a functional direction or solution is too comprehensive	Exec	Des	2	3	2	1	–	1	–	1	–	2	4	–	16
98	Decide root cause if team did not meet its iteration goal	Retro	Man	1	3	2	1	–	–	–	1	–	2	4	2	16
100	Decide issues that will most influence team success	Retro	Man	1	3	2	1	1	–	–	1	–	2	4	1	16
6	Decide on the time scope of a project	Init	Man	1	2	1	–	–	1	1	1	1	2	4	1	15
21	Decide the roadmap of the project	Init	Man	3	2	–	–	1	1	1	1	1	1	4	–	15
96	Decide what went well to continue during next iteration	Retro	Man	1	3	2	1	–	–	–	1	–	1	4	2	15

Table 4. Decision types with least participants

No	Decision	Phase	Pers	Ent Arch	Sol Arch	Sys Arch	Dev	Head Sec	Inf Mng	Portf Mng	Inf Ana	PM	PL	PO	Scr Mas	Total
64	Decide who will pair together for paired programming	Exec	Man	1	1	1										3
50	Decide task estimates	Oper	Man	2	1	1										4
28	Decide capacity for team members	Init	Man					2					2		1	5
26	Decide which people will be available	Init	Man					2	1				2		1	6
57	Decide if a task fits in the scope of the project	Oper	Man	2	2					1				1		6

Table 5. Number of decision types in which architects participate according to themselves and to stakeholders, per phase

	Enterprise architect				Solution architect				System architect		
Phase	Stakeh	EA-1	EA-2	EA-3	Stakeh	Sol-1	Sol-2	Sol-3	Stakeh	Sys-1	Sys-2
Initiating	11	12	8	14	13	19	13	18	10	14	12
Operational	1	0	4	15	8	32	23	19	19	35	25
Execution	5	3	9	17	14	18	16	18	17	17	15
Review	2	2	1	9	2	12	6	9	5	10	10
Retrospective	0	0	0	6	6	7	7	7	7	7	6
Total	**19**	**17**	**22**	**61**	**43**	**88**	**65**	**71**	**58**	**83**	**68**

Table 6. Number of decision types in which architects participate according to themselves and to stakeholders, per perspective

	Enterprise architect				Solution architect				System architect		
Perspective	Stakeh	EA-1	EA-2	EA-3	Stakeh	Sol-1	Sol-2	Sol-3	Stakeh	Sys-1	Sys-2
Design	14	13	18	25	24	27	24	26	24	20	24
User	1	2	2	11	1	14	6	10	4	15	9
Management	4	2	2	25	18	47	35	35	30	48	35
Total	**19**	**17**	**22**	**61**	**43**	**88**	**65**	**71**	**58**	**83**	**68**

Table 7. Number of decision types where a certain architecture role is dominant according to stakeholders

Phase	Enterprise architect	Solution architect	System architect
Initiating	8	8	5
Operational	0	2	18
Execution	1	5	14
Review	2	0	4
Retrospective	0	0	7
Total	**11**	**15**	**48**

5 Discussion

The list with decision types shows a mixed picture. On the one hand, it contains decision types that are typical for an agile process, on the other hand, it includes decision types that belong to a more traditional way of working. Especially, the design decision types in the initiating phase fit to a traditional way of working with decision types on FSA and PSA. This case study shows a snapshot of an organization that applies software development in an agile manner, while at the same time applying architecting in a rather traditional fashion with artifacts like FSAs and PSAs. Two interesting observations can be made. First, despite the rather old-fashioned architecture artifacts, the value of architecture is not questioned by the stakeholders, and according to architects themselves, they participate strongly in decision-making. This is in line with literature that architecture and agility can co-exist [5, 6]. Second, the architects that participated in the interviews are aware of the changes that are needed, i.e., that architecture artifacts like FSAs and PSAs are at some point no longer appropriate. Remember that one of the enterprise architects explained that once agile teams are stable, a PSA or any big documentation is not needed. When we took our snapshot, that stable situation was not yet reached. The agile teams in this study were formed less than two years ago and had many external employees. So it was reasonably obvious for architects to continue creating FSAs and PSAs while at the same time being aware of the necessary transition in the architecture function. From this case study we learn that changes in the way of working of architects lag the changes in the way of working in software development.

This study also confirms that decision-making in an agile context is a collaborative group effort [4, 27]. On average, eleven actors (of a maximum of 25) participate actively in the decisions of one decision type. The actors most involved are the solution architect, system architect, product owner, and information analyst. We also found that solution and system architects just as much participate in management and user-related decision types as product owners participate in design decision types. Where architects in the past had the authority to make design decisions on their own, they now collaborate with other stakeholders [15]. This case study also demonstrates that architects have a say in other types of decisions. Another finding from this study is that all solution and system architects, and one of the enterprise architects, are heavily involved in all decision phases. However, stakeholders have the perception that the involvement of enterprise and solution architects can be limited to the initiating phase.

This case study raised various challenges for architects with regard to their role in decision-making in an agile context. Table 8 summarizes these challenges and discusses possible actions for architects.

Table 8. Challenges for architects in decision-making in an agile context

Topic	Challenge for architects	Action for architects
Who to involve in design decisions and make sure these decisions are adopted by teams?	Stakeholders expect to be involved in design decisions. Architects can no longer make design decisions on their own and impose these decisions to teams. Imposing design decisions to a team is a situation that does not really motivate teams, particularly agile teams. "Teams, in general, have the potential to make more effective decisions than individuals because teams can pool knowledge and information, which helps them to make a good decision" [15].	Architects must become team players who are able to discuss and explain decisions to stakeholders and colleague architects. They need to focus on effective communication and collaboration and be able to compromise and negotiate decisions with stakeholders [7, 9, 28]. Architects have to find ways to intervene effectively: • Learn from organization theory: "effective interventions are based on valid information about the organization's functioning; they provide organization members with opportunities to make free and informed choices; and they gain members' internal commitment to those choices. Free and informed choice suggests that members are actively involved in making decisions about the changes that will affect them" [29]. • Apply nudge theory, which is "a concept in behavioral science, political theory and economics which argues that positive reinforcement and indirect suggestions to try to achieve non-forced compliance can influence the motives, incentives and decision-making of groups and individuals, at least as effectively if not more effectively, than direct instruction, legislation, or enforcement" [5, 30].

(continued)

Table 8. (*continued*)

Topic	Challenge for architects	Action for architects
When to make design decisions?	Stakeholders expect architects not to go into much detail in the beginning.	Architects should try to create a minimal set of design decisions at the level on which they operate, be it a system, solution, domain, or the enterprise as a whole. Architects must try to delay design decisions until they are absolutely necessary [5]. This can be done by applying a risk and cost driven approach to architecting [19, 29]. Such an approach supports architects to identify the key concerns at the right level to address in their decision-making.
How to document design decisions?	Stakeholders do not expect thick documents like FSAs and PSAs. Delivering these types of standard documents can become a goal in itself, which is a common pitfall of architects (not only because of agile) [31].	Architects must find a more integrated way of documenting and communicating design decisions instead of creating documents with design decisions on each organizational level, and passing these documents to the next organizational level. Different authors identified and described the required change from documents to key decisions [7, 8]. The implementation of this change is not straightforward and requires further research.
With whom to share design decisions?	Stakeholders expect design decisions to be shared along the lines of different organizational levels. The simultaneous participation of different architecture roles in the same decision types (like in the case study organization) may seem inefficient, especially in the eyes of stakeholders, but is very valuable from a knowledge-sharing perspective.	Ultimately, design decisions at different levels need to be coordinated. How design decisions can be coordinated and knowledge can be shared across different organizational levels like enterprise, domain, and software system, is an area for future research.

6 Threats to Validity and Limitations

According to Yin, four different threats to validity may occur in case studies: construct validity, internal validity, external validity, and reliability [26]. The following countermeasures were taken against these threats. Construct validity was counteracted by having the list of decision types validated by three different roles in the case study organization. Furthermore, the case study report was drafted by one of the authors and reviewed by two of the other authors. Nevertheless, we do not exclude misinterpretation of survey questions. The results of the survey show some large differences between respondents in the same role. Internal validity is not applicable since this is an exploratory study. Regarding external validity, we argue that the findings of this case study are of interest to other practitioners and researchers outside the case study organization. Although we focused on a single domain in only one organization, the results correspond with contemporary research and confirm earlier defined theories. Reliability was established by creating a case study protocol and a database in MS Excel where the results were stored [26]. Another approach we used was that two authors conducted the data analysis to reduce the threat of bias. This was done partly in parallel, and partly sequential.

A limitation of this study is that we did not include implicit decisions. In an agile approach most of decision-making is done in daily stand-ups, sprint-planning or pre-refinement sessions and documented to a bare minimum. This is an area for future research. The decision list in this study can be used as a point of departure to study what decisions in agile projects are implicit or explicit. Another limitation is that the decision list reflects the decision types identified at some point during an agile transition of just one organization. The findings of this study are thus based on decision types that may change over time. Compared to Drury we found much more different types of decisions [15]. One explanation is that we included the decision types used prior to an agile iteration, where Drury only had the agile iteration in scope. Another explanation is that our list was created based on interviews with architects, project leaders, and product owners, where Drury collected the decisions during a focus group meeting with mainly agile practitioners. A third limitation is the ambiguity of architectural roles. Different respondents of the survey may have had a different understanding of a particular architectural role. A final limitation is that we did not study the interaction between different actors. This is also an area for future research. Social network analysis is a good starting point [32]. Using the lens of social network analysis could help to explain why participants in the same role differ so much in their participation in decisions.

7   Conclusion

This research focused on the role of architects in decision-making in agile projects. The purpose was to provide insights in decision-making participation of architects, especially enterprise, solution, and system architects, and to align the empirical insights with a theoretical perspective. At first a list was created covering all the decision types made in various phases prior to and in agile iterations. From this list we concluded that architecture and agility indeed can co-exist and that changes in the way of working of architects lag the changes in the way of working in software development. The decision list was taken as a starting point for a survey that was designed to receive insights in the architects' and stakeholders' participation in decision types in practice. The results of our study reveal a mixed participation of different actors including architects in all decision types. On average, eleven actors (of a maximum of 25) participate actively in the decisions of one decision type, confirming that decision-making in an agile context is a collaborative group effort. Another finding from this study is that stakeholders in agile teams perceive less architecture involvement and expect less comprehensive documents. Architects are challenged to become team players, to make design decisions only when they are necessary, and finally, to document, communicate, and share design decisions more effectively.

References

1. VersionOne: The 11th Annual State of Agile Report. http://stateofagile.versionone.com/
2. Stavru, S.: A critical examination of recent industrial surveys on agile method usage. J. Syst. Softw. **94**, 87–97 (2014)
3. Hoda, R., Noble, J.: Becoming agile: a grounded theory of agile transitions in practice. In: Proceedings of the 39th International Conference on Software Engineering, IEEE Press, pp. 141–151 (2017)
4. Williams, L., Cockburn, A.: Guest editors' introduction: agile software development: it's about feedback and change. Computer **36**(6), 39–43 (2003)
5. Erder, M., Pureur, P.: Continuous Architecture: Sustainable Architecture in an Agile and Cloud-Centric World. Morgan Kaufmann, Waltham (2015)
6. Leffingwell, D.: SAFe® 4.0 Reference Guide: Scaled Agile Framework® for Lean Software and Systems Engineering. Addison-Wesley Professional, Boston (2016)
7. Woods, E.: Aligning architecture work with agile teams. IEEE Softw. **32**(5), 24–26 (2015)
8. Poort, E.R.: Driving agile architecting with cost and risk. IEEE Softw. **31**(5), 20–23 (2014)
9. Erder, M., Pureur, P.: What's the architect's role in an agile, cloud-centric world? IEEE Softw. **33**(5), 30–33 (2016)
10. Hanschke, S., Ernsting, J., Kuchen, H.: Integrating agile software development and enterprise architecture management. In: Proceedings of the 48th Hawaii International Conference on System Sciences, pp. 4099–4108 (2015)
11. Brown, S.: Software Architecture for Developers. Coding the Architecture. Best Sellers, Pasadena (2016)
12. Riempp, G., Gieffers-Ankel, S.: Application portfolio management: a decision-oriented view of enterprise architecture. Inf. Syst. E-Bus. Manag. **5**(4), 359–378 (2007)
13. Ågerfalk, P.J., Fitzgerald, B., Slaughter, S.A.: Introduction to the special issue: flexible and distributed information systems development: state of the art and research challenges. Inf. Syst. Res. **20**(3), 317–328 (2009)
14. Drury, M., McHugh, O.: Factors that influence the decision-making process in agile project teams using scrum practices. In: Proceedings of the 6th International Research Workshop on Information Technology Project Management, pp. 29–40 (2011)
15. Drury, M., Conboy, K., Power, K.: Obstacles to decision making in agile software development teams. J. Syst. Softw. **85**(6), 1239–1254 (2012)
16. Drury-Grogan, M.L., O'Dwyer, O.: An investigation of the decision-making process in Agile teams. Int. J. Inf. Technol. Decis. Making **12**(6), 1097–1120 (2013)
17. Kruchten, P., Capilla, R., Dueñas, J.C.: The decision view's role in software architecture practice. IEEE Softw. **26**(2), 36–42 (2009)
18. Poort, E.R., van Vliet, H.: RCDA: architecting as a risk-and cost management discipline. J. Syst. Softw. **85**(9), 1995–2013 (2012)

19. Hohpe, G., Ozkaya, I., Zdun, U., Zimmermann, O.: The software architect's role in the digital age. IEEE Softw. **33**(6), 30–39 (2016)
20. Woods, E.: Return of the pragmatic architect. IEEE Softw. **31**(3), 10–13 (2014)
21. Hornford, D., Paider, T., Forde, C., Josey, A., Doherty, G., Fox, C.: TOGAF Version 9.1. Van Haren Publishing, Zaltbommel (2011)
22. Marić, M., Tumbas, P.: The role of the software architect in agile development processes. Int. J. Strateg. Manag. Decis. Support Syst. Strateg. Manag. **21**(1), 16–22 (2016)
23. Hauder, M., Roth, S., Schulz, C., Matthes, F.: Agile enterprise architecture management: an analysis on the application of agile principles. In: Proceedings of the 4th International Symposium on Business Modeling and Software Design (2014)
24. Abrahamsson, P., Babar, M.A., Kruchten, P.: Guest editors' introduction: agility and architecture: can they coexist? IEEE Softw. **27**(2), 16–22 (2010)
25. Runeson, P., Host, M.: Guidelines for conducting and reporting case study research. software engineering. Empirical Softw. Eng. **14**, 131–164 (2009)
26. Yin, R.: Case Study Research, Design and Methods, 5th edn. Sage Publications, Los Angeles (2014)
27. Nerur, S., Mahapatra, R., Mangalaraj, G.: Challenges of migrating to agile methodologies. Commun. ACM **48**(5), 72–78 (2005)
28. Knoernschild, K.: 10 Essential Skills of the Modern Software Architect. Gartner Research Note G00338593 (2017)
29. Cummings, T.G., Worley, C.G.: Organization development and change. Cengage learning, Stamford (2014)
30. Thaler, R., Sunstein, C.: Nudge: Improving Decisions About Health, Wealth and Happiness. Yale University Press, New Haven (2008)
31. Van den Berg, M., van Steenbergen, M.: Building an Enterprise Architecture Practice. Springer, Dordrecht (2007). https://doi.org/10.1007/978-1-4020-5606-2
32. Manteli, C., van Vliet, H., van den Hooff, B.: Adopting a social network perspective in global software development. In: Proceedings IEEE 7th International Conference on Global Software Engineering, pp. 124–133 (2012)

Using Informal Knowledge for Improving Software Quality Trade-Off Decisions

Yves Schneider, Axel Busch[(⊠)], and Anne Koziolek

Karlsruhe Institute of Technology, Karlsruhe, Germany
{yves.schneider,busch,koziolek}@kit.edu

Abstract. To deliver high-quality software, in a software development process a variety of quality attributes must be considered such as performance, usability or security. In particular, quality attributes such as security and usability are difficult to analyze quantitatively. Knowledge about such quality attributes is often only informally available and therefore cannot be processed in structured and formalized decision-making approaches to optimize the software architecture. In this paper, we have defined a framework in order to make use of informally available knowledge in automated design decision support processes. We connect qualitative reasoning models with models for quantitative quality estimation to optimize software architectures regarding both knowledge representation models together. By our approach quality attributes for which no quantitative evaluation model is available can now be used in automated software architecture optimization approaches. For evaluating our approach, we demonstrate its benefits using a real-world case study and an example that is related to a real-world system.

Keywords: Software · Architecture · Model · Reuse · Solutions
Design decision · Qualitative reasoning · Quality

1 Introduction

Todays increasingly complex software systems have many responsibilities and often implement a large number of features. In addition to the core business features, the systems often also support a variety of features designed to operationalize quality requirements, that are intended to improve a certain quality attribute (QA). From the viewpoint of the quality performance alone, any additional functionality with the same hardware configuration can be an influencing factor.

Performance is not even the only quality that is influenced by new features. In the case of user authentication, other QAs such as usability are also influenced. The software architect would like to know these effects as early as possible in the design phase, in order to avoid expensive refactoring later in the project.

Software architects often have implicit knowledge about such effects on QAs of different software components. However, this knowledge is often only informally available and cannot be used in automated analysis and decision processes.

© Springer Nature Switzerland AG 2018
C. E. Cuesta et al. (Eds.): ECSA 2018, LNCS 11048, pp. 265–283, 2018.
https://doi.org/10.1007/978-3-030-00761-4_18

Moreover, QAs such as security or usability often lack applicable analysis techniques. In approaches for design time quality prediction such QAs often remain unconsidered due to missing quantification and analysis techniques, although they are often crucial for the success of a project. Due to the lack of possibilities for considering informal knowledge in systematic decision support approaches, important trade-off decisions between performance and other quality requirements cannot be analyzed sufficiently.

The Palladio [19] approach together with PerOpteryx [12] is one example for design-time quality prediction and decision support for component-based software architectures. With the help of Palladio software architects can evaluate their design decisions with the focus on QAs such as performance, reliability, and maintainability at design time. On the basis of Palladio's analysis engine, PerOpteryx evaluates architecture candidates resulting in the Pareto-optimal solutions. However, the analysis is limited to quantified QAs such as performance. In our previous work [5], we have extended the PerOpteryx approach so that not-quantified QAs can be analyzed in a very simple manner. However, this extension and also other existing approaches, such as ArcheE [2], or ArcheOpteryx [1], can not analyze complex relationships between modeled knowledge such as the mutual effect between usability and security. Therefore, when using approaches that rely on quantified QAs to analyze the software architecture quality, informal knowledge remains unconsidered.

In this paper, we address the aforementioned issues by extending Palladio and PerOpteryx for improving software architecture design decisions by modeling informal knowledge explicitly and include the knowledge in PerOpteryx' automated decision support process. Our approach offers tools to annotate knowledge about QAs of software components and to model mutual effects on QAs from and to other components. The aim of our approach is to create a framework for evaluating architectural design options, which uses both quantitative and qualitative methods to estimate the relative merits of quality attributes in an architectural design. The contribution of this paper is an approach that can be used to analyze QAs for which no adequate quantification methodology is available or the quantification is too expensive even for complex mutual effects. The results can then be used to analyze the impact of decisions on the performance of the system and to make trade-off decisions. At the end, this helps software architects to consider informal knowledge in systematic processes together with quantified knowledge, in order to improve their software architecture design decisions.

2   Background

For our approach, we use two approaches namely Palladio and PerOpteryx for software quality analysis and optimization as a basis and extended it in order to consider interferences of not-quantified QAs in the design space optimization.

2.1   Architecture Model: Palladio Component Model

Palladio is an approach for the definition of software architectures with focus on performance QAs [19]. Several parts of this introductory section are taken from [10].

As our running example let us consider the *Business Reporting System* (BRS) model. The BRS allows users to retrieve statistical analysis of business processes. For this purpose, the system allows the user to generate graphical and online reports. The system is roughly based on a real system [22]. The architecture model specified by the software architect consists of nine software components deployed on four different hardware nodes. The software components contain cost annotations, while the hardware nodes are annotated with performance units (processing rates) and cost (fixed and variable cost for example in EUR) units.

For each software component service, the component developers provide an abstract behavioral description called service effect specification (SEFF). SEFFs model the abstract control flow through a component service in terms of internal actions (i.e., resource demands accessing the underlying hardware) and external calls (i.e., accessing connected components). SEFFs are composed automatically to determine the system-wide behavior. Modeling each component behavior with separate SEFFs enables us to quickly exchange component specifications without the need to manually change system-wide behavior specifications (as required in e.g. UML sequence diagrams).

For performance annotations, component developers can use the extended resource-demanding service effect specifications (RDSEFFs). Using RDSEFFs, developers specify resource demands for their components (e.g., in terms of CPU instructions to be executed).

A software architect composes component specifications modeled by various component developers to create a system model. The performance simulation finally is performed by solving such a model analytically or simulation-based. In this paper, we use the transformation from PCM to Layered Queueing Networks [7].

2.2   Design Space Exploration: PerOpteryx

The PCM separates parameterized component performance models from the composition models and resource models. The PCM thus naturally supports many architectural degrees of freedom (DoF), such as replacing components, changing the component assignment, and so on. The PerOpteryx approach explores these given DoF and thus supports to make well-informed trade-off decisions for performance, reliability, and cost. Several parts of this introductory section are taken from [10].

For the exploration, PerOpteryx makes use of DoF of the software architecture that can either be predefined and derived automatically from the architecture model or be modeled manually by the architect.

On the basis of our running example we can derive two types of DoF: For instance we could change the component allocation and the server configuration.

For the allocation degree, we could have several servers, each having different possible processing rates. As an example of a manually-modeled DoF, let us consider that some of the architecture's components offer standard functionality for which other implementations (i.e. other components) are available. Here, an alternative component for several components could be used in the BRS as for example the `Scheduler` component. This component could be replaced by a functional fully equivalent `QuickScheduler` component. Assuming that `QuickScheduler` has less resource demand but is also more expensive than `Scheduler`, the resulting architecture model has a lower response time but higher cost.

The resulting DoFs span a design space which can be explored automatically. Together, they define a set of possible architecture candidate models. Each of these candidate architecture models is defined by choosing one design option for each DoF. The set of all possible candidate models corresponds to the set of all possible combinations of the design options, the *design space*.

Using the quantitative quality evaluation provided by Palladio, PerOpteryx determines performance, reliability, and cost metrics for each candidate model.

Based on the DoFs (as optimization variables) and the quality evaluation functions (as optimization objectives), PerOpteryx uses genetic algorithms and problem-specific heuristics to approximate the Pareto-front of optimal candidates. Details on the optimization are not required for the discussion in this paper, but can be found in [10,11].

In our previous work [5] we proposed an extension to include not-quantified QAs on different levels of measurement in a decision support engine together with quantified QAs such as performance, reliability, and cost. To do so, we extended the analysis engine of PerOpteryx to obtain a combined analysis of quantified and not-quantified QAs. This makes it possible to balance between mutually influencing quantified QAs and not-quantified QAs. For example, if a more secure alternative component would have less performance, the component with better performance would always be preferred without taking the not-quantified QAs into account. The combined analysis results in Pareto-optimal values of all QAs. As a result, software architects can analyze the impact of simple design decisions on other QAs (e.g. performance, cost) when including for instance a security related feature.

In its previous version as described in this section, PerOpteryx does not support the complex effect of decisions on other, informally modeled QAs that is common for QAs such as usability or security. For example, no influence of fault tolerance on usability can be modeled. The main effects of design decisions on informal modeled QA would remain unconsidered and may not be fully evaluated with the previous version of PerOpteryx.

2.3   Qualitative Reasoning

Qualitative Reasoning (QR) is a research field of Artificial Intelligence (AI) that expresses conceptual knowledge. QR creates models for continuous aspects of the physical world (e.g. quantity, space, time), which supports a reasoning with little information. Qualitative reasoning also has practical benefits in industry, focusing on scientific and engineering domains [3]. QR is suitable for modeling and simulating such conceptual models. In QR, the quantities describing the dynamic characteristics of a system contain qualitative information about the current size and the direction of possible changes. Usually, an interval scale is modeled by an ordered set of variables. These ordinal scaled variables contain nominal information as well as information about the order of the variable values. Such a set of variables is referred to as the *quantity space*. QR models represent a trade-off between the ability of modeling informal knowledge generated by humans, but at the same time sufficient formal specification of properties to enable automatic evaluation.

3   Approach

Our approach explicitly models informal knowledge and uses that knowledge together with quantified values in order to improve automated software architecture optimization mechanics. This shall improve the tools of a software architect to make better decisions in a software architecture design process.

We developed a meta model and analysis techniques to define informal knowledge about mutual effects between quality attributes of components. This model includes a description of the characteristics of QAs of the system's components and rules that describe how these QAs are influenced by other components. As usual in component-based approaches, these characteristics are composed together with the corresponding software components. Thus, the modeled knowledge fits seamlessly into the component unit. This allows to reuse knowledge by the natural reuse mechanisms of software components.

In order to be able to evaluate the models using informal knowledge, we also describe our reasoning algorithm in the second part. This algorithm automatically evaluates the qualities with their effects for a system model. The results can then be used to make trade-off decisions between a variety of quality attributes. PerOpteryx allows the specification of the QAs to be analyzed. By this, the architect can then select the QAs that are relevant for the requirements. Not relevant QAs can be skipped by the analysis engine.

3.1   Qualitative Reasoning Model

Figure 1 shows the meta model of our approach, with the relevant classes and attributes. At the core of our approach, a *Not-quantified Quality Attribute* (NQA) is used to express a level of quality (i.e. the informal knowledge) of a component, while a *Mapping Rule Set* (MRS) defines how this level of quality is influenced by the quality of other components.

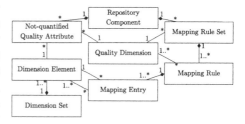

Fig. 1. Schematic representation of our Qualitative Reasoning meta model

A software architect could annotate a component with the NQA (*Accessibility*, +) to express "somewhat good accessibility". Table 1 shows more examples of NQAs. Additionally, the software architect can annotate the component with a MRS as shown in Table 2 to express that the reliability of this component is affected by the fault tolerance and the recoverability of other components.

Dimension Set and Dimension Element. The quantity space, with all its elements and their order, is modeled by the `Dimension Set`.

A dimension set defines the range of all possible values that can be specified within a dimension. Each definition of a dimension set D also contains a strict total order relation $<$, denoted $< \subseteq D \times D$. For two dimension elements $e_1, e_2 \in D$, $e_1 < e_2$ means that e_1 represents a worse quality than e_2.

For our case studies, we model a dimension set with five different dimension elements $\{--, -, 0, +, ++\}$ and define the order $<$ so that $-- < - < 0 < + < ++$.

Table 1. An example NQA set with three example NQAs

NQA set
NQA: (*Accessibility*, +)
NQA: (*Installability*, 0)
NQA: (*Privacy*, -)

Table 2. MRS modeling the dependency from reliability to fault tolerance and recoverability

MRS: Reliability				
MR: Fault tolerance				
IN:	++	+	-	--
OUT:	++	+	--	--
MR: Recoverability				
IN:	++	+	0	-	--
OUT:	++	+	-	-	--

Quality Dimension. A quality dimension q is an attribute that could be analyzed and evaluated by our QR approach. This may be a software quality, such as security, but also any other attribute of software components, such as their manufacturer. For example, such a quality dimension could be denoted as *Usability* or *Recoverability*.

Not-Quantified Quality Attribute. A NQA represents a relevant quality property of a software component. It is represented by a pair (q, e) that is comprised of the quality dimension q and the corresponding dimension element e. Let us assume that the architect wants to express that a component A has comparatively "good" usability. To do so, the architect models an NQA (*Usability*, +) and annotates it to component A.

Mapping Rule Set. A Mapping Rule Set (MRS) is the core of the symbolic non-numerical calculation of the model elements. The MRS defines how a particular quality dimension of a component is affected by another particular quality dimension of other components. For this purpose, a MRS is comprised of several mapping rules (r_n) and a quality dimension d on which the rules apply, i.e. $MRS := (d, (r_n))$. The MRS results in an NQA whose dimension element were calculated according to its rules.

Table 2 shows an example MRS for the quality dimension `Reliability`. This MRS shows how fault tolerance and recoverability of other components affect the reliability of a given component. For example, if another component that affects our given component is annotated with the NQA (*Recoverability*, 0), the example MRS would result in the NQA (*Reliability*, -) for our given component. Details on the evaluation of a MRS is explained in Sect. 3.3. If the quality of a component is affected by multiple other components, the different quality values are averaged (cf. Sect. 3.3).

Mapping Entry. A Mapping Entry E represents the pair $E := \left((k_n)_{n \in \mathbb{N}_+}, v \right)$, while $(k_n)_{n \in \mathbb{N}_+}$ represents the sequence of input elements and v represents the resulting affected element. A Mapping Entry E assigns a sequence of input dimension elements (k_n) to a dimension element v, i.e. $E: (k_n) \mapsto v$. All elements $(k_n), v$ of a mapping entry must be contained in the same dimension set D, i.e. $(k_n), v \in D$. Two input elements $\left(k_n^1 \right), \left(k_m^2 \right)$ are equal if they agree in their length n, m, their elements, while they occur in the same order, i.e. $\left(k_n^1 \right) = \left(k_m^2 \right) \Leftrightarrow n = m \wedge \forall (i)_{i=1}^n \left(k_i^1 = k_i^2 \right)$.

Table 3. Assignment of one NQA to an affected element

MR: Privacy			
IN: ++	+	0	-
OUT: +	0	-	--

Table 4. An example assignment that assigns two NQAs to a resulting element

MRS: Privacy				
MR	Accessibility			
IN	++	+	-	--
++	++	++	+	0
+	+	+	-	0
0	0	+	-	-
-	-	0	--	--
--	-	-	--	--

The first column of the MRS in Table 3 is a mapping entry: An input privacy value of ++, is mapped to the output privacy value (second column) of +. More formally, this mapping entry can defined as follows: ((++), +). An example of several input dimension elements is shown in Table 4. It defines that the privacy of a given component depends on the privacy and accessibility of other components. An example mapping entry is for instance ((++, +), ++). It expresses that a "very good" privacy of other components combined with "good" accessibility of other components result in a "good" privacy of our given component.

Mapping Rule. A mapping rule R calculates the resulting dimension element r for a set of NQAs. It is defined as a pair of a sequence of quality dimensions (q_n) and a set of mapping entries $\{e_m\}$, i.e. $R := ((q_n), \{((k_n), v)_m\})$. For all mapping entries in a mapping rule $e_m \in R$, each sequence of input elements has to be unique. Thus, each sequence of input elements is uniquely assigned to a dimension element.

If there is no NQA input, the mapping rule does not have a resulting element and therefore has no influence on further calculations. This behavior allows the simultaneous use of different modeling granularities. Differently deeply modeled knowledge can be analyzed simultaneously without missing information affecting the analysis result. The formal rules of the mapping will be described in more detail in Sect. 3.3.

The NQA set in Table 1 could be mapped to the element -- according to the mapping rule in Table 3, and according to the mapping rule in Table 4 to the element -. For the first mapping rule, it must only be considered the NQA element (*Privacy*, *+*) of the NQA set. The remaining elements do not influence the result of the first mapping. In the second mapping rule, the relevant subset is the subset {(*Privacy*, *+*), (*Accessibility*, *-*)}.

3.2   Model Creation

Software architects can extend their architecture models by enriching their components by NQAs. More concrete, a component can be annotated with NQAs for the quality attributes security and maintainability. Developers can also use MRS to model dependencies between different quality dimensions. This mechanism could be used, if for example the fault tolerance of particular component affects the reliability of another component. For this purpose, prefabricated dimension sets from Palladio can be reused or new dimensions can be defined.

The NQAs and MRS for particular components are then specified by developers and experts. The values for these NQAs and MRS can be derived from the informal knowledge of the developers and domain experts. Alternatively, the knowledge can be derived from other sources such as related documentation or other technical reports. On that basis software architects can then model implicit knowledge and make it available to the other software architects in component repositories.

3.3   Qualitative Reasoning Process

This section describes the evaluation process of our approach. We describe the process of the model evaluation so that they can be used for the design space exploration. Our QR process allows the evaluation of the informal knowledge of an entire system, which was previously limited for individual components.

The following two notations apply to the pseudo code of the following algorithms: The symbol ← describes the assignment of a value to a variable. The symbol ⊕ describes the append operation on lists.

Candidate Evaluation. PerOpteryx generates the candidate model based on the DoFs. For such a candidate model, our approach provides the NQAEVALUATION function to evaluate our QR models.

Algorithm 1 shows our QR function for a candidate model. The input parameter of this function is a candidate model. This candidate includes all models required for the quality evaluation: The structure information of the system, the connectors of the interfaces, and the annotation of the components with the associated NQA and MRS. After the actual QR about

---

Algorithm 1. Function for evaluating an architectural candidate

> **function** NQAEVALUATION(*candidate*)
>   *nqas* ← [ ]
>   (*c_n*) ← TOPOLOGICALSORT(*candidate*)
>   **for all** *c* **in** (*c_n*) **do**
>   *nqa* ⊕ QUALITATIVEREASONING(*c*)
>   **end for**
>   **return** REDUCE(*nqas*)
> **end function**

informal knowledge has been evaluated in this function, the PerOpteryx processes the results in the ongoing optimization process.

In the first step of Algorithm 1, we create a list that contains the results of the QR. The evaluated NQAs of the candidate model are added to this list.

Second, all components of the candidate model are sorted topologically by their dependencies. To do this, the TOPOLOGICALSORT function extracts all components from the given candidate model, followed by a topologically sort, and returns this resulting list of components. The topological sorting, orders all components in a system in a linear order that their existing dependencies are still fulfilled. The dependencies are predetermined by the interface connections from the components. This allows to iterate linearity over all components and evaluate our QR models for each single component. Through this sorting, all dependencies and mutual influences are retained in our QR evaluation. If a component needs to be evaluated by the QUALITATIVEREASONING function, the topological sorting ensures that all components which affect others have already been evaluated.

The QUALITATIVEREASONING function evaluates the given component and returns its resulting NQAs. This function uses the MRSs of a component to determine the influence of other components on the component's own NQAs. Afterwards, we insert the evaluated NQAs into the result list. After the QR evaluation, the NQAEVALUATION function returns the reduced list of all evaluated NQAs. For this purpose, the REDUCE function reduces multiple different NQAs, so that this multiple NQA can be used by PerOpteryx.

This function accepts a list of different NQAs and returns a list of unique NQAs. For all NQAs with the same quality dimension, the multiple dimension elements are reduced to a unique dimension element. This process often results in different NQAs for the same quality dimension. To consider these ambiguities, we map the different elements for a QA to one unique element. This unique element comes from the same dimension set as the others and is the median of these multiple units. The order relations from a dimension set make it possible to determine the median for a

---

Algorithm 2. Function for quality reasoning on one component

---

   function QUALITATIVEREASONING($comp$)
      $nqas \leftarrow []$
      $(c_n) \leftarrow$ REQUIRED($comp$)
      for all c **in** (c_n) **do**
         $nqas \oplus$ GETNQAS(c)
      end for
      $req \leftarrow$ REDUCE($nqas$)
      for all mrs **in** GETMRSS($comp$) **do**
         $nqas \oplus$ SOLVE(mrs, req)
      end for
      $nqas \oplus$ GETNQAS($comp$)
      $nqas \leftarrow$ REDUCE($nqas$)
      SETNQAS($comp$, $nqas$)
      return $nqas$
   end function

---

list of elements from this set. This step increases the stability, as several different dimension elements for the same quality dimension are mapped to one unique dimension element.

In the first loop, we form the frequency distribution over all NQAs. The classes correspond to the NQA dimensions. A list of the several dimension elements is assigned to each unique class. The DIMENSION and ELEMENT function return the respective parts from a value. This frequency distribution is then reduced in the second loop to unique NQAs. For the multiple dimension elements of a same quality dimension, the median for a list of dimension elements is determined and assigned back to the quality dimension. This new NQA will be added to the result list.

Component Evaluation. The Algorithm 2 shows the QUALITATIVEREASONING function for our QR evaluation for a single component. The function evaluates the influences of other components on the qualities of the component passed as an input parameter. As a result, this function returns the NQAs of the passed component that are influenced by the MRSs, bundled with the NQAs of the components.

First, all NQAs of the required components are collected in the first loop. Thus, all required components are iterated in this loop. Thus, the REQUIRED function returns the components which with their provided interfaces fulfill the required interfaces of the passed components. These required components directly influence the requested components through their provided services. The topological sorting ensures that the MRSs of the required components have already been evaluated. The GETNQAS function returns the NQAs of the component as a parameter. These resulting NQAs are then reduced so that each quality dimension is represented by a unique NQA. Subsequently, the influence of these NQAs on the MRSs is evaluated in the second loop. To do this, the GETMRSS function returns the MRSs of the component as a parameter. All the MRS of a component are evaluated using the SOLVE function. The SOLVE function gets one MRS and several NQAs as input parameters. The function returns a new NQA that results from the evaluation of the passed MRS. This result is marked for reduction. Subsequently, the NQAs of the required components, the results from the MRS and the NQAs of the evaluated components are reduced. We use this result as temporary NQAs for the previously evaluated component.

The SOLVE function in Algorithm 3 calculates for a given MRS how the defined quality dimension is influenced by a given NQA. This function requires a MRS which defines the influenced quality dimension and the mapping rules which define the concrete rules of influence. As second input, the function requires the NQAs that exert the influence. Finally, the function returns an NQA of the affected quality dimension and the evaluated dimension element.

The algorithm works as follows: First, we create a list that contains the evaluated dimension elements (from the mapping rules). These elements are used to determine the dimension element for the NQA. The first loop is used here to iterate over all mapping rules of the given MRS.

Subsequently, in the first inner loop, we iterate over the quality

---

Algorithm 3. Function for solving a MRS

---
function SOLVE(mrs, $nqas$)
  $elements \leftarrow [\,]$
  for all mr **in** mrs **do**
    $key \leftarrow [\,]$
    $(q_n) \leftarrow$ DIMENSIONS(mr)
    for all q **in** (q_n) **do**
      for all nqa **in** $nqas$ **do**
        if DIMENSION(nqa) $==$ q **then**
          $key \oplus$ ELEMENT(nqa)
        end if
      end for
    end for
    for all me **in** mr **do**
      if KEY(me) $==$ key **then**
        $elements \oplus$ VALUE(me)
      end if
    end for
  end for
  $element \leftarrow$ MEDIAN($elements$)
  return (DIMENSION(mrs), $element$)
end function

---

dimensions of the current mapping rule. This is done by the DIMENSIONS function that returns the quality dimension of the mapping rule. The next loop is used to iterate over the given NQAs to find the required dimension element from the NQAs. The resulting dimension elements are stored in the corresponding list. In the second inner loop, the mapping entries of the mapping rule are iterated to determine the resulting dimension element for the previously determined list. This is done by the KEY function that returns the sequence of the input dimension elements of the passed mapping rule. Next, we check for each mapping entry whether the key of a mapping entry corresponds to the list. If yes, the corresponding dimension element is stored in the list. At the end of the function, we calculate the median of all the dimension elements determined by the mapping rules and return it together with the quality dimension of the MRS as NQA.

4   Evaluation

We have applied our approach to two different case studies for considering the following research questions: 1. What new insights can be gained through the additional use of informal knowledge in a decision support process? 2. Are the modeling elements sufficient to enrich real world systems with common knowledge from the domain of information systems?

We have carried out the following case studies to answer the research questions. First, we applied our approach to the previously introduced BRS. The second case study shows the application of our approach to a real-world system namely the Remote Diagnostic Solutions (RDS) [8]. The RDS is used by industrial systems to submit their diagnostic status information.

Both of our case studies follow a three-step design: 1. We create all the models required for the optimization as described in the previous sections. 2. We extend the PCM components by NQAs and MRSs. 3. The design space optimization is carried out to determine the Pareto-optimal candidates.

4.1   Case Study I: Business Reporting System

The BRS allows users to retrieve statistical analysis from running a business process from a database. As the system interacts directly with the user, an important requirement is to include a usability dimension and consider the dimension in the optimization process. Further, the system stores data, thus it is important to include the dimensions reliability and recoverability.

System Configuration. The initial configuration of the BRS is a 4-tiered system that is comprised of a web server, two servers for the business logic, and a database server. In order to generate a graphical report or online view of the raw data, the user submits a request to the web server component. These user requests are delegated to the scheduler component by the web server component. Depending on the type of request, the scheduler component either delegates the request to the graphical reporting component or to the online reporting component. Both components require the database component. To reduce the database load, data that has already been loaded or generated, is cached in the cache component. For user administration, the scheduler first calls the UserManagement component for session handling.

Table 5. MRS modeling the positive influence of recoverability to backupability

MRS: Recoverability					
MR: Backupability					
IN:	++	+	0	-	--
OUT:	++	++	+	0	-

Table 6. MRS modeling the influence of recoverability to usability

MRS: Usability					
MR: Recoverability					
IN:	++	+	0	-	--
OUT:	++	++	+	0	-

In this case, we regard the performance as well as the cost of the system as quantified QAs. To model the performance of the system, we use the RDSEFF mechanism of Palladio. To evaluate the performance, we transform the model into Layered Queuing Networks and use the Solver of [7]. To model the second part of the performance model, we model the hardware context of the BRS.

Experimental Procedure. For this case study, we have chosen a component selection scenario. Therefore, we include several new components in our repository, that serve as architecture alternatives. All of these alternatives are functionally equivalent, but their software quality differs. This in turn influences the software quality of the overall software architecture. First, we added three additional components to our repository: the Database, CoreOnlineEngine, and Web server components.

To enrich the model by informal knowledge, we first define all necessary basic elements for our QR model. The first model element is the dimension set $DS = \{--, -, 0, +, ++\}$. The element $++$ is the best-valued, and the element $--$ is the worst-valued value (ordered set).

An architect might have the choice between two concrete database systems namely the *Oracle Database 12c* and the *IBM DB2 10.5*. For decision-making, the architect reviews several technical reports, including [17]. This report proposes that the backupability of the Oracle database can be rated as better than the backupability of the second database. This information is enriched to the two alternative components by NQA elements. The IBM database is annotated with $(\textbf{\textit{Backupability}}, 0)$ while the Oracle database is annotated with $(\textbf{\textit{Backupability}}, +)$. We expect that measurements show that the Oracle database consumes 1.5-times more CPU resources than the other database and is twice as expensive.

When having a second CoreOnlineEngine component available, this second CoreOnlineEngine component might have 20% lower CPU resource demand and 80% less costs. We define this component less fault tolerant as the original component. From Microsoft's TechNet report we can derive a correlation between database backups and the recoverability of a database [14]. We express that information as an MRS. For this, we annotate both components with the MRS that is described in Table 5. The MRS

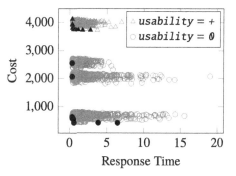

Fig. 2. BRS results: response time, cost, and usability

model defines that if a required component defines a certain backupability, this directly impacts the recoverability of the CoreOnlineEngine component. The ability to recover quickly after a system failure depends, among other things, on current data backups. Consequently, backups of databases are crucial for the system's overall recoverability.

Another important dimension is the usability. A Web server component being more user-friendly would increase the overall usability quality. We expect this component to have a doubled CPU resource demand at the same price. In [16] describe that the usability of user interfaces depends on how easily the users can recover from errors. In this case, the usability is positively influenced by the recoverability of the required components. Thus, we annotate both components with the MRS shown in Table 6. All three new alternative components are included into the repository of our original PCM model. Because these three new alternative components are identical in terms of their provided and required interfaces to the original components, they are automatically used by PerOpteryx as alternatives for the design space exploration. This extended model for QR assertions for not-quantified QAs can now be used in combination with the architectural model to be optimized in PerOpteryx. The analysis is carried out with a constant usage profile for the performance simulations. The resulting Pareto-optimal candidates are described in the following section.

Results. We have evaluated in total 200 iterations, each with 30 candidates per iteration. The optimization resulted in a total of 6015 valid architectural candidates while 22 of them were Pareto-optimal results. The architecture candidates are shown in Fig. 2, the Pareto-optimal candidates are shown black filled.

The two components that have higher quality are more expensive. Accordingly, the candidates which include both better components are comparatively expensive. Furthermore, the evaluation shows that if money is invested for buying more expensive components, this will improve usability, but would not significantly improve the performance. If performance is to be improved further, this must be achieved, for example, by improving processor performance. The evaluation also shows how the Pareto-optimal candidates changes when other QAs such as usability are considered. Without the evaluation of these, some Pareto-optimal candidates with better usability but worst performance would not have been considered. By the help of our results, an architect now gained more information for the decision which architecture candidate to choose in accordance with performance, cost, and usability. If the specific project requirements are based on a better usability of the overall system, the software architect would have to select the more expensive components. However, the results show that performance does not have to be decreased significantly. If performance is less important, money can be saved by investing only in the implementation. Another interesting finding is that the use of only one component with a better usability (instead of both components) does not lead to a noticeable improvement of the overall usability.

4.2   Case Study II: Remote Diagnostic Solution

The Remote Diagnostic Solution (RDS) represents a system used in the industry. It records equipment information, failures and other status information from industrial systems such as power plants. The RDS mainly offers two different services. First, industrial devices can access the system and upload diagnostics status information. Second, in the case of an abnormal behavior, the devices store further error information, which can be analyzed by the operators. Service engineers can then access the system through a website to generate reports on the status of the devices. Additionally, in the case of an atypical behavior, these may send commands for reconfiguring the devices.

System Configuration. The RDS system is designed as a 3-tier system. It consists of: The Peripheral Network Server on which the RDSConnectionPoint runs for remote access of the industrial devices. The application server with the central business logic. The database server with the database component. The business logic consists of: a `deviceData` component, which processes and forwards data. A `parser` component that processes inputs when a status report is uploaded. A `dataMiningAndPrediction` component that performs the data analysis. A `dataAccess` component that handles communication with the database component. The user interface to access the status reports is implemented by the `serviceEngineerWebsite` component. We determine the performance and costs of the system, as in the first case study, as quantified QAs.

Experimental Procedure. Systems often offer different configuration options. The database of the RDS namely the *Microsoft SQL Server* offers the possibility to use the recoverability either in *simple* or *full* mode. For the decision-making, the architect might review technical reports, as for instance the Microsoft recovery model report [13]. This report describes that the backupability of the *full* model is higher, but this is associated with worse performance. The two different operating modes are modeled as two alternatives, so they are automatically used by PerOpteryx to create architecture alternatives.

We model this knowledge by NQA elements and apply them to corresponding components. The *full* recovery model database is annotated with (`Backupability`, +) while the *simple* recovery model database is annotated with (`Backupability`, 0). We expect that the *full* recovery model database has a 4.0-fold increase in CPU resource demands compared to the *simple* mode.

The dataAccess component is responsible for accessing the data. Thus, we apply the MRS shown in Table 7. The MRS models the informal knowledge of the correlation between database backups and the recoverability of the data accessed by this component. Since the serviceEngineerWebsite component can be used to access the database data, it is annotated with the MRS shown in Table 8. By this, we model the informal knowledge about the positive influence of the recoverability to the usability.

Table 7. MRS modeling the influence between backupability and recoverability

MRS: Recoverability				
MR: Backupability				
IN:	++	+	0	-	--
OUT:	++	+	0	-	--

Table 8. MRS modeling the influence of recoverability to usability

MRS: Usability				
MR: Recoverability				
IN:	++	+	0	-	--
OUT:	++	+	0	-	--

In addition to the two alternative recovery models of the database, PerOpteryx has five different additional servers available to distribute possible (additional) load. As in the previous case study, the not-quantified quality (usability) as well as the quantified qualities (performance and costs) are considered. The MRS model used here models properties that affect the usability of the overall system.

Results. We evaluated in total 200 iterations, each with 20 candidates per iteration. The optimization resulted in 2030 valid architecture candidates, while 9 of them were Pareto-optimal. The architectural candidates are shown in Fig. 3, the Pareto-optimal candidates are shown black filled.

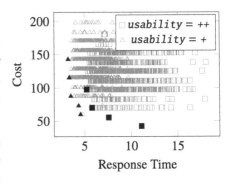

Fig. 3. RDS results: response time, cost, and usability

The configuration mode with the higher recoverability QA also has the higher resource demand. Accordingly, the Pareto-optimal candidates, which include the component with this mode, are also significantly slower than the others.

The experiment also shows how transitive effects of informal knowledge can be evaluated in a system. A usability NQA has not been modeled for any component, but a usability NQA is obtained by evaluating several MRS. This shows how existing dependencies in a system are recognized, which were not directly modeled for the individual components before.

The evaluation shows that the approach can also be applied in real-world scenarios and shows which trade-off decisions still need to be clarified by a software architect. Architects can use this results to deepen their understanding of the interplay of the components in the system. Furthermore, the results show that the system with higher usability does not necessarily have to be more expensive. However, improved usability goes hand in hand with higher response times. Nevertheless, the higher response times should be possible to be compensated by more powerful hardware (which would then result in higher cost).

4.3 Discussion

Both case studies show how informal knowledge can be modeled independently for individual components and then combined in an automated design space exploration together with quantified QAs such as performance. Case study I shows how our approach helps to understand more complex inter-dependencies between different QAs. Through the results of the exploration, an architect can decide whether the better usability justifies the higher cost. Case study II shows how informal knowledge can be combined with quantified QAs applied to a real-world system in an automated design space exploration.

In the case studies we have shown how experts can model the characteristics and influences of qualities for their components and how these independent models can be assembled to evaluate the overall quality of a system. We have also shown that our approach can be used to model and evaluate more complex contexts such as the transitive effects of qualities on each other. This can lead to the detection of existing dependencies that were not previously detected. If these effects are not considered, PerOpteryx would only determine the optimal candidates based on the quantified performance and cost values. The two case studies show how the evaluation of these effects influences the Pareto-optimal candidates.

Creating the initial QR model that models the architectural knowledge may be comparatively time-consuming. However, creating the models only needs to be created once. Wide parts of the models can be reused (except for project-specific modifications). The reuse of the architecture knowledge and the optimization is comparable to the reuse of the component itself or the optimization of the software architecture and can therefore be carried out with comparatively little effort. By using the additional knowledge, however, the software architect can now gain new insights into the interaction of the components and effects of individual architectural decisions that were previously neither explicitly visible nor could be optimized.

5 Related Work

In their comparative survey [6], Falessi et al. have reviewed and compared different methods used in software architecture decision-making. However, most methods focus more on identifying quality attributes and alternatives and are not specified for an automated decision-making approaches to optimize the software architecture, which is the interest of this approach.

Svahnberg and Wohlin presented in [21] an approach that supports the evaluation of different architectural candidates based on the considered quality requirements by means of a multi-criteria decision-making methods. Using multiple architecture candidates and quality requirements, their approach can be used to identify the best architecture candidate according to the requirements. For this, their approach uses the analytical hierarchy process *AHP* to pair-evaluate architecture candidates. Regnell et al. proposed in [18] the quality performance model *QUPER*, an approach to estimate non-functional requirements. Their approach can be used to reason about quality in terms of cost and value. Kazman et al. presented in [9] a qualitative method for architectural trade-off analyzing that takes into account multiple QAs and identifies trade-offs between them. However, *QUPER* and the *AHP*-based approach are manual processes that require quality to be broken down to cost, while the last requires a manual navigation in the design space. Therefore the mentioned approaches are comparatively time-consuming when evaluating many architectural candidates.

The *Garp3* workbench was proposed in [4] and allows to model, simulate, and analyze qualitative models of system behavior. The approach supports domain experts articulating and capturing their conceptual knowledge. The resulting models are not linked to components on architecture level and thus do not enable an automatic improvement of architecture models.

The *NFR* (Non-Functional Requirements) framework was proposed in [15] and focuses on the modeling and analysis of non-functional requirements. NFR models allow good visibility to all relevant non-functional requirements and their interdependencies, and they document design decisions and rationales in addition to providing. The *RE-Tools* was proposed in [20] and is an open-source requirements modeling toolkit. The toolkit supports among others NFR with SIG as a notation for requirements. On the basis of a SIG, the toolkit uses Qualitative Reasoning to evaluate the goal achievement.

The aforementioned approaches model QAs at a higher level of abstraction than in our approach. In contrast to our approach, due to the higher abstraction the reusability of the modeled knowledge is limited.

6   Conclusion

In this paper we presented an approach to model software architecture knowledge to automatically optimize software architectures. Existing quantitative modeling approaches can be combined with our newly developed modeling and evaluation concept that is based on qualitative reasoning. With our newly developed approach, it is therefore possible to take into account qualitative modeled informal knowledge, together with quantitative evaluation processes. Decision support processes gain new dimensions that can be used for optimization and thus increase their benefit. Software architects can thus gain new insights into the mutual influence of components on important QAs that were not previously visible due to a lack of knowledge modeling and optimization possibilities.

We have performed two case studies, to demonstrate the applicability and benefits of our approach on real-world software systems. The case studies have shown how informal knowledge can be modeled and can be used to evaluate software architecture design decisions during the design phase. Based on the case studies we have shown which conclusions can be derived from the results of the optimizations.

References

1. Aleti, A., et al.: ArcheOpterix: an extendable tool for architecture optimization of AADL models. In: MOMPES 2009. IEEE (2009)
2. Bachmann, F., et al.: Designing software architectures to achieve quality attribute requirements. IEE Proc. Softw. **152**(4) (2005)
3. Bredeweg, B., Struss, P.: Current topics in qualitative reasoning. AI Mag. (2003)
4. Bredeweg, B.: Garp3-workbench for qualitative modelling and simulation. Ecol. Inform. **4**(5), 263–281 (2009)
5. Busch, A., Koziolek, A.: Considering not-quantified quality attributes in an automated design space exploration. In: QoSA. ACM (2016)
6. Falessi, D., et al.: Decision-making techniques for software architecture design: a comparative survey. ACM Comput. Surv. (CSUR) (2011)
7. Franks, G., et al.: Enhanced modeling and solution of layered queueing networks. IEEE Trans. SE (2009)
8. de Gooijer, T., et al.: An industrial case study of performance and cost design space exploration. In: ICPE 2012 (2012)
9. Kazman, R., et al.: The architecture tradeoff analysis method. In: ICECCS (1998)
10. Koziolek, A.: Automated improvement of software architecture models for performance and other quality attributes. KIT Sci. Publishing (2014)

11. Koziolek, A., Koziolek, H., Reussner, R.: PerOpteryx: automated application of tactics in multi-objective software architecture optimization. In: QoSA. ACM (2011)
12. Martens, A., et al.: Automatically improve software models for performance, reliability and cost using genetic algorithms. In: WOSP/SIPEW 2010 (2010)
13. Microsoft Docs: Recovery Models (2016). https://docs.microsoft.com/en-us/sql/relational-databases/backup-restore/recovery-models-sql-server
14. Microsoft TechNet: Recoverability(2009). https://technet.microsoft.com/en-us/library/bb418967.aspx
15. Mylopoulos, J., Chung, L., Nixon, B.: Representing and using nonfunctional requirements: a process-oriented approach. IEEE Trans. SE (1992)
16. Nielsen, J.: Usability 101: Introduction to usability (2012). https://www.nngroup.com/articles/usability-101-introduction-to-usability/
17. Oracle HA Product Management: Technical comparison oracle database 12c vs. IBM DB2 10.5: focus on high availability. Technical report, Oracle Corporation (2013)
18. Regnell, B., Svensson, R.B., Olsson, T.: Supporting roadmapping of quality requirements. IEEE Softw. **25**(2) (2008)
19. Reussner, R.H.: Modeling and Simulating Software Architectures: The Palladio Approach. MIT Press, Cambridge (2016)
20. Supakkul, S., Chung, L.: The RE-tools: a multi-notational requirements modeling toolkit. In: RE. IEEE (2012)
21. Svahnberg, M., Wohlin, C.: An investigation of a method for identifying a software architecture candidate with respect to quality attributes. Empir. SE **10**(2) (2005)
22. Wu, X., Woodside, M.: Performance modeling from software components. In: SE Notes, vol. 29. ACM (2004)

Understanding Architecture Decisions in Context

An Industry Case Study of Architects' Decision-Making Context

Ken Power[1]([⊠]) [iD] and Rebecca Wirfs-Brock[2]

[1] Cisco Systems, Inc., Galway, Ireland
ken.power@gmail.com
[2] Wirfs-Brock Associates, Sherwood, OR, USA
rebecca@wirfs-brock.com

Abstract. Many organizations struggle with efficient architecture decision-making approaches. Often, the decision-making approaches are not articulated or understood. This problem is particularly evident in large, globally distributed organizations with multiple large products and systems. The significant architecture decisions of a system are a critical organization knowledge asset, as well as a determinant of success. However, the environment in which decisions get made, recorded, and followed-up on often confounds rather than helps articulation and execution of architecture decisions. This paper looks at aspects of architecture decision-making, drawing from an industry-based case study. The data represents findings from a qualitative case study involving a survey and three focus groups across multiple organizations in a global technology company. Architects in this organization are responsible for multiple products and systems, where individual products can include up to 50+ teams. The impact is not just on others in the system; architecture decisions also impact other decisions and other architects. The findings suggest recommendations for organizations to improve how they make and manage architecture decisions. In particular, this paper notes the relevance of group decision-making, decision scope, and social factors such as trust in effective architecture decision-making.

Keywords: Architecture · Architecture decisions · Decision making
Decision makers · Decision impact · Trust · Roles · Documentation
Agile

1 Introduction

Architecture decisions can significantly affect architects and other roles. Realizing this, a vital component of any architectural approach is having a process that promotes follow through and feedback on architecture decisions. This paper presents a case study of a large technology organization with multiple business units and product lines. This study examines approaches to architecture decision-making and seeks to understand in more depth the reasons for the decision-making approaches employed by architects, as

© Springer Nature Switzerland AG 2018
C. E. Cuesta et al. (Eds.): ECSA 2018, LNCS 11048, pp. 284–299, 2018.
https://doi.org/10.1007/978-3-030-00761-4_19

well as the challenges and context that architects must deal with. In addition, this study attempts to understand the impact of architecture decisions. The remainder of this paper describes the study.

Section 2 places this study in context through a review of relevant literature from software architecture decision-making. This study employs a survey and three focus groups as part of a larger case study into architecture decision-making. Section 3 describes the research approach used in this study and includes the research questions that this study sets out to answer. Section 4 presents the findings from the survey and focus groups. Section 5 is a discussion of the findings. Finally, Sect. 6 presents the summary and conclusions from this study, including a set of recommendations based on the findings, and a discussion of future research that builds on this study.

2 Literature Review

This section presents a review of the relevant architecture and decision-making literature that informs this study and helps to shape its research objectives. Bass, Clements and Kazman [1] define architecture as, *"the structure or structures of the system, which comprise software elements, the externally visible properties of those elements, and the relationships among them."* Traditionally, an architecture may be described using one or more relevant views [2]. Recognizing that some architecture decisions have a broad impact Kruchten, Capilla and Dueñas [3] propose that a "decision view" be added to existing architecture views, superimposing the design rationale which underlies and motivates the selection of design options realized in the architecture. Kruchten, Lago and Van Vliet [4] suggest that *"Architecture Knowledge = Design Decisions + Design"*. Jansen and Bosch [5] go even further to assert that a system's architecture should be viewed as the composition of a set of architectural design decisions. This paper takes the position that it is a distraction to argue whether decisions should drive the selection of relevant views as do Tyree and Akerman [6], or whether selecting relevant views should drive important decisions [7]. Both the architecture and the relevant views that represent it embody design decisions. Both are important to communicate. Important to understanding any architecture are the cumulative decisions that influenced it as well as an appreciation for how those decisions were made.

Although several formal architecture decision-making approaches have been published, software engineering researchers find few to be used in practice. This may be because many published decision-making approaches describe processes for making reasoned tradeoffs between several competing options, while decision making researchers observe that many complex real-world decisions are not about making tradeoffs, but instead about finding a reasonable decision that satisfices the current situation and allows for action [8]. Rekha V. and Muccini [9] also found that none of the published methods account for differences in expertise required to make informed decisions nor do they have provisions for resolving conflicts or differences of opinion. Surveys of architects have found that over 85% of decisions made are group decisions [9, 10]. During group discussions, both shared and unshared (e.g. unknown to all members of the group) information is brought out and examined.

Tyree and Akerman [6] proposed elevating architecture decisions to first-class architectural artifacts suggesting that documented decisions can provide concrete direction for implementation and serve as an effective tool for communicating to customers and management. It is unclear whether practicing architects often take their advice. In a survey by Dasanayake, Markkula, Aaramaa and Oivo [11], architects reported that 90% of their decisions were made and communicated informally. And while these architects were mostly satisfied with their informal decision-making processes, they also recognized some challenges with revisiting design rationale, communicating decisions to customers, and in knowledge gaps between engineers and architects. In our research we also found that decisions were communicated informally through a number of media, including slide decks, wikis, and meeting recordings.

Kruchten [12] proposes the following taxonomy for architecture decisions: *Existence decisions* state that some element or artifact will show up in the system's design or implementation. *Bans* or *non-existence decisions* are statements of things to not do. Kruchten [12] suggests that it is especially important to precisely document *bans* because there isn't a place for them in conventional architecture documentation. *Property decisions* affect the overall qualities of the system and may be represented by design rules or constraints. *Executive decisions* are driven by the business environment and may affect the development process or choices of technology and tools. Although they may place constraints on the architecture, Kruchten [12] asserts that executive-level decisions are often not captured or appear in documents usually not associated with the architecture. Kruchten's model, while one of the few decision categorization models that we can find in software architecture, is insufficient for handling decisions in the type of environment we are studying and for classifying the types of decisions we are uncovering.

While Miesbauer and Weinreich [13] found that architecture decisions could be mapped to Kruchten's taxonomy [12], they noted that architects themselves talk about decisions they make according to level. They proposed classifying architecture decisions according to these levels: Management typically makes *organization-level* decisions with advice from software architects. Once made these decisions are rarely revisited. Project managers, architects, and customers tend to make *project-level decisions* at the beginning of a project. Software architects or team leads typically make *architecture-level* decisions after discussion in a group. Finally, *implementation-level* decisions are made independently by developers and typically not documented. Miesbauer and Weinreich [13] suggest further investigation into whether the levels they identify are adequate to partition the decision space. A weakness in the framework of Miesbauer and Weinreich [13] is it suggests that impact is contained to a specific level. In our research, we found it fruitful to characterize decisions along multiple dimensions, including impact and scope. We also found examples where implementation-level decisions had system-wide impacts on architectural qualities.

3   Research Approach

This section presents the research questions addressed through this paper. This section then states the epistemological stance employed by the study, and how that influences the study and the choice of research methods. This study uses a case study of a large, global technology organization. A survey and three focus groups are used to answer the research questions. This section describes these methods, and how they contribute to the study. Finally, this section describes the data collection and analysis methods.

3.1   Research Questions

With regard to architecture decision-making, the topics of interest to this study relate to approaches, challenges, context, and impact. This paper aims to contribute to the body of knowledge on architecture decision-making by answering the following research questions:

- RQ1: **Approaches:** What are some examples of decision-making approaches used by architects, and how those decisions are made?
- RQ2: **Challenges:** What challenges do architects encounter associated with the current architecture decision-making approaches?
- RQ3: **Context:** How does the context influence decisions made by architects?
- RQ4: **Impact:** How do decisions made by architects impact other people?

Findings related to these questions are presented in Sect. 4.

3.2   Research Method

Any study is shaped by the social and theoretical perspectives adopted by the researchers [14]. This study adopts an interpretivist, constructivist philosophical stance. Interpretivist research acknowledges that people have potentially widely-varying perceptions of the same phenomenon, and that knowledge is a social product [15].

This study uses a case study to "*understand complex social phenomena*" related to how architects make decisions. Case studies are well suited to research in software development because they study contemporary phenomena in their natural setting [16, 17]. This study is concerned with how and why architects make the decisions they do, and how those decisions impact others. Case studies can "*uncover subtle distinctions and provide a richness of understanding and multiple perspectives*" [18]. This research includes perspectives from multiple stakeholders, not just architects. Yin [19] notes that case studies are suitable when "*the boundaries between phenomenon and context may not be clearly evident.*" The primary unit of analysis is a Business Group, BG1, one of the largest business groups in the company consisting of approximately 5,000 people in different sites around the world. BG1 has multiple business units, each of which is responsible for multiple product lines in a particular domain. The initial survey targeted architects across BG1. The researchers decided to conduct a focus group with participants from each of three product lines. We targeted one product line per business unit in order to get a representative sample of perspectives on the topic of architecture decision-making. The case study consists of one survey from BG1 and three focus groups, FG1, FG2, and FG3.

These four units of analysis combine to provide a comprehensive picture of architecture decision-making. Initially, the researchers conducted a survey of 62 architects located across a business group with sites in North America, Europe, Israel, and India. We wanted to broadly understand how architects perceived their role and interactions with others and more specifically what they found to be challenging and rewarding aspects of their work. In addition to demographic information, the survey asked about their role and interactions with other architects, engineers, product owners and product management. The survey participants were highly experienced, as shown in Table 1. The majority (90%) had architect, technical lead, or principal or distinguished engineer in their job title. The remaining respondents were engineers or managers. Different kinds of architects were represented including customer, solutions, systems, and Scrum (team lead) architects. Following on from the survey, we conducted three focus groups specifically on the topic of architecture decision-making.

Table 1. Survey respondents' years of experience as architects

# years experience as an architect	% of respondents
10+ years	47%
6–10 years	23%
4–5 years	15%
1–3 years	13%
<1 year	2%
No response	10%

Morgan [20] defines focus groups as "*a research technique that collects data through group interaction on a topic determined by the researcher*". Yin [21], on the other hand, says the groups are focused because they share some common experience or views. These two perspectives are complimentary for the purpose of this study. The unit of analysis is the group itself, not the individuals within the group, so each focus group is one data collection unit [21] (Table 2).

Table 2. Summary of focus groups conducted as part of this study

Focus group	FG1	FG2	FG3
Focus	Architecture Decision Making	Architecture Decision Making	Architecture Decision Making
# Participants	10	11	12
Location	Israel	USA	India
Domain	Security Products	Video Technology	Networking Technology
Roles	Architects, Program Managers	Architects, Engineers	Architects, Engineers, Program Managers, Engineering Managers

The survey data was collected using a Web-based survey tool. The focus groups were recorded and then transcribed. The authors analyzed the survey data and focus group data independently and reviewed the analyses together through multiple iterations.

3.3   Threats to Validity

This section discusses potential threats to the validity of this research study.

- **External Validity.** The researchers do not claim that these findings are universally applicable. They are representative of a number of business units in a specific, large global technology organization. They serve as illustrative examples that others may learn from.
- **Construct Validity.** To mitigate this threat, data was collected from multiple sources. The researchers used triangulation between the survey data and the three focus groups, thereby converging evidence from four distinct data sources. The researchers compared results across multiple groups, where the data was collected at different points in time and in different geographic locations.
- **Reliability.** Relating to the repeatability of the study, the survey instrument and focus group questions were designed over several iterations and involved other subject matter experts and architects to review these and provide feedback. Using respondent validation [21] the researchers reviewed the data with a small group of architects from BG1 to help ensure validity of the data and the findings
- **Internal validity.** This study does not attempt to establish any causal relationships, so no internal validity threats are described [17].

4   Research Findings

4.1   Survey Results

The top 6 activities surveyed architects reported in order of frequency mentioned were architecture design, 98%; collaborating with development teams, 87%; product and solution requirements specification, 84%; knowledge sharing, 82%; document review, 65%; and program and product planning, 50%. Only 18% reported coding and 15% testing. Most, 82%, interacted daily with engineering and development teams; 13% did so weekly. Frequency of interactions with product owners and management was less with 44% reporting interacting daily, 37% weekly, and 10% monthly.

When asked what impacted their effectiveness, architects identified the dissipation of knowledge, the large number of people involved in making decisions, finding reliable or up to date documentation and information, misalignment with the development team and other architects, organizational changes, time zone differences, time pressures, and overlapping/unclear roles and responsibilities.

For the most part, architects perceived that they were effective in their various roles. 77% rated their effectiveness positively. 79% rated their communications with engineering as successful. Slightly less, 60%, rated their communications with product management as successful. However, some architects, were unsure whether others in the organization considered their work valuable or necessary. Architects wanted to be heard, understood, and recognized as making valued contributions.

Surveyed architects found working with engineers to be extremely rewarding. They were gratified to receive pragmatic, concrete feedback on the architecture and the decisions they made; to see the final solution as implemented and its evolving design; to answer questions, mentor engineers, and bring information about customers and broader issues to the team; to feel part of a team working on a common goal; and to be engaged in collaborative decision-making and mutual learning. They wanted engineers to be more involved earlier in the definition of the product as well as to be more involved themselves during implementation. Learning was perceived as bi-directional: while engineers have broader view of technology and trends in the industry, architects know about customer needs, product requirements, and more broadly about the existing architecture.

Architects expressed frustrations when engineers misunderstood their designs or when engineers lacked product knowledge. Other architects expressed frustration with engineers' seemingly short-term focus or focus on functionality to the exclusion of system qualities. It was also frustrating when engineers didn't contribute to or value architecture documentation, or when the code was viewed as "the only source of truth" about the design.

When asked one thing they would like change to make their practice of architecture more effective when working with engineering, several themes emerged: better knowledge sharing, improved documentation including documentation of decisions, and improved feedback and review of the architecture and its implementation.

Surveyed architects who regularly engaged with product owners or product management (not all did, and some architects were also in the role of product owner) were mixed in their perceptions. Some architects found it rewarding that they could influence product management's understanding of significant architecture requirements, clarify or remove unnecessary requirements, and influence product features and their delivery roadmap. They found it rewarding to get deeper insights into the customer and the product provided by product management.

Architects were frustrated by conflicting requirements or when product owners changed requirements or priorities too rapidly. Another frustration was inflexible product managers who didn't listen. Other architects expressed frustration with product owners' lack of current product or customer knowledge or when they made architecture decisions without asking their advice. They were also frustrated when those decisions seemed shortsighted or overly focused on satisfying a single customer.

When asked one thing they would like change to make the practice of architecture more effective working with product management, architects on the whole wanted to improve communications, increase collaboration, increase their visibility into and influence on the overall product strategy and backlog, and be involved in joint decision-making on architecture.

4.2 Examples of Decisions

Focus group participants were asked to share their experiences with recent architecture decisions. Examples of decisions are sown in Table 3.

The researchers found it difficult to classify these decisions according Miesbauer and Weinreich [13] levels or to line them up with Kruchten's taxonomy [13]. Consequently, we characterized decisions as being technology, design guidelines, infrastructure, or product implementation level decisions. Analysis revealed that technology, design guidelines, and infrastructure decisions were viewed positively, while product implementation decisions were not. The data in Table 3 relates the decision examples

Table 3. Examples of decisions identified in focus groups, and their context

Category	Example from this study	Scope	Impact	Source
Technology	Investing in microservices frameworks	System	Business unit	FG2
Technology	Moving to containers and microservices	System	Business unit	FG2
Technology	Moving to open standards	System	Business group	FG2
Design guideline	Defining a standard for defining and publishing APIs	System	Business group	FG2
Product implementation	Using incompatible technology	Product	Business unit	FG2
Product implementation	Deciding to use platform native encryption components	Product	Business unit	FG2
Product implementation	Taking a short-sighted, simple decision due to client pressure	Component	Business group	FG1
Product implementation	Taking a decision quickly instead of analyzing new information brought up in a meeting	Component	Business unit	FG1
Product implementation	Designing a backwards incompatible end-to-end solution	Component	Business unit	FG1
Product implementation	Extending an existing solution, trying to fit a design to an incompatible platform	Product	Product line team	FG3
Product implementation	Repeatedly bringing up a design problem due to lack of understanding of an existing solution	Component	Product line team	FG3
Infrastructure	Investing in a separate infrastructure group	System	Business unit	FG2

to the case study. The scope of decisions relates to a component, a product (composed of many components), or a system (composed of many products). The decision impact is expressed in terms of whether the decision impacts the product team, the business unit, or the business group. Table 3 also notes the source focus group for the example.

4.3   Approaches to Decision Making

Architects described their decision making as mostly informal, e.g. the right people get in a room or on a phone call and discuss. While decision-making can be informal, it can also be political. One respondent in FG1 recounted a situation where those who dissented were removed from further discussion. Another observed that conversations, and persuasion and interpersonal relationships often drive decisions, and that this was not always positive. Depending on the decision, certain people had veto power, and for some decisions, it was agreed that product management rightfully should make them, although architects would like to be consulted.

The survey raised several questions about who made decisions about the architecture. One respondent noted that in some cases project managers and product managers make technical decisions without consulting architects. A different respondent expressed a desire for "*more formal tracking of decisions*" to help collaboration with product managers and product owners.

4.4   Challenges with Current Approaches to Decision Making

Architects were not always involved in architecture-related decisions. Survey respondents indicated that architects did not always have the influence that they thought they should have: "*significant decisions are completely centralized within the senior leadership team and architects/POs/PMs have less influence than they should.*" This was echoed by another respondent who noted, "*Not all the information is shared with architects which could affect some architecture decisions in the initial phase of the project*". There was no indication that the lack of information sharing or centralizing of decision-making was designed to deliberately to exclude architects, but several architects certainly felt the impact.

Focus group participants cited several challenges that they associated with current decision-making approaches. Decisions are often made without considering the technical feasibility of implementing the solution, and the long-term consequences associated with that. An example cited by one architect related to a build vs buy decision. In the system he worked on, there were several instances where the team decided to build the required functionality, rather than buy a commercial solution. This had the effect of adding to the system's technical debt.

Participants in FG2 noted that it is difficult to reverse poor decisions, and when decisions are reversed or changed, it does not happen quickly enough. Participants in FG1 noted an unwillingness to change decisions: "*the first decision is accepted as the final one and the project leader doesn't adjust or change direction when problems or new information is found*".

The survey highlighted several examples where architects felt decisions were not followed through. In one case, an architect felt that people do not follow through on implementing architecture decisions because they are unaware of them, or they do not trust the decision. One architect noted that architects are often out of the loop during development and that decisions and feedback would be improved if the team were to "*...involve architects on the problems raised during the implementation*".

4.5   Context in Which Architects Make Decisions

Architects didn't directly share many thoughts on why decisions were made the way they were. But some decisions seemed to be made under time pressure. In those cases, decision makers had to make tradeoffs between short-term project considerations and longer-term architecture sustainability. Decisions sometimes were made in the narrow context of delivering the next feature; in this case expediency drove the decision-making process. People got together, discussed, and made a decision. One participant in FG1 noted that it was difficult to make longer-term decisions, so he didn't: "*It's too hard to get enough convergence or consensus or agreement around a long term decision, so I often find that I'm making a small, local decision that serves a particular local need and that is locally optimized, and I'm not able to take any long term wide-ranging considerations into account".* At other times when it was important to gain consensus, it took time to make decisions. One architect in FG2 noted that, *"Because we're focused on getting consensus over multiple engineering teams and architecture teams all over the place, the process has just gotten more complicated."*

A large number of distributed teams is also an important part of the decision-making context. The participants in FG2 are part of a group of 50+ teams working on a single product. Geographic distribution between teams and multiple time zones adds to the difficulty of their context. As one architect from FG2 stated, *"we're not compartmentalized enough that we can make these decisions in one timezone, or even a couple of timezones".*

The distribution among multiple countries, time zones, and teams results in it taking a long time to make "big" decisions. Participants cited situations where consensus-based decisions were necessary and referred to "big" and "consensus" as attributes of decisions that take a particularly long time. As one architect noted about working with teams spread over 5 countries, it takes a long time *"... to sell the idea, right? You have to build consensus around that, and that does take a lot of time".*

Trust is also a factor in decision-making contexts. Focus group participants agreed that decision-making is *"more productive"* when there is a higher level of trust between the people directly involved. Participants cited situations where trust is not present. One example is where there are *"pockets of ... technical feudalism"* where an architect is making decisions in isolation.

The agile development process is also a factor. One surveyed architect noted, *"Agile development as currently practiced ... does not have a place for Architecture. So this needs to be fixed before we can have a meaningful discussion about how developers and architects interact."* Another expressed frustration about the way decisions are changed, *"The thing that frustrates me more is when the implementation doesn't match the design because there is a misunderstanding and the developers make their own decisions without checking with the architect. I'm all for letting the development teams as much freedom as possible but the architect needs to be consulted."*

4.6   Effect of Architecture Decisions on Architects and Other People

There are examples where architecture decisions are not followed through. In one system discussed by participants in FG2, architects defined a high-level architecture (HLA) for several subsystems. The perception of architects is that the teams responsible for implementing that HLA exhibited *"passive aggressive non-compliance"*. They did not challenge the HLA decisions directly. Instead, they disregarded the decisions in the HLA. The perception of the architects was that *"people on various scrum teams ... decide they know better"*. Participants related this problem to the context of operating within a "giant" multi-country, multi-time zone project with 50+ teams. This context added to a lack of visibility by architects into what teams are actually building.

While verbal communication related to follow-through on architecture decisions happens, it is unpredictable. One architect expressed in the survey their desire for engineers to contribute more to design documentation, noting *"I wish engineers would have contributed more to the knowledge sharing via documentation (and not only verbally, which they do very happily)".*

Lack of information related to past decisions have a significant effect on architects currently working on the product. The need for a trail of decisions and their context came through as architects noted challenges associated with joining a product team where the architecture already has a long history, e.g., *"the very long history of the project and the decisions that were taken before I joined the project".*

Engineers don't always have enough context about the architecture. Sometimes engineers encounter cases where the architecture does not seem to support what they need to do. One architect noted in some cases *"they don't care too much about the design; if it seems it doesn't work, they may "adapt" the implementation, not in line with the design (that may well be wrong or incomplete) but without necessarily telling the architects or updating the documentation".* A further risk here is that if architects don't get this feedback, then any architecture decisions recorded earlier become out of date without an appropriate feedback loop.

5 Discussion

The geographic and time zone challenges reflected by FG2 indicates that the organization in question did not give enough consideration to the impact of these factors on architecture decision making.

5.1 Perceptions of Agile Development on Architecture Decisions

Agile development emerged as a particularly strong theme from survey results and the focus group data. The organizations that these groups were part of made decisions and assumptions about what it meant for agile and architecture to co-exist. Architects tend to bring up longer-term perspectives on the architecture. Some feel that shortsighted decisions are made when the decision makers focus only on feature delivery at the expense of architecture integrity or increased maintenance costs. An architect in FG2 noted, *"We do have this type of organization problem. I think it's because a combination of agile and I'm not sure the journey to Agile Architecture is... It's still a journey ... We haven't quite figured it out."*

Several survey respondents and focus group participants echoed a common theme around agile methods contributing to a loss of a paper trail. One survey respondent noted, in connection with the adoption of agile methods, *"we seem to have forgotten that paper-trail is important for adequate product maintenance".*

5.2 Feedback

Architects desire more feedback on their decisions and want more follow through with engineering. One architect in the survey stated, *"In my book software architecture implies that you have to work with the engineers and also be part of the development teams...[It] helps validate the design ideas you have as an architect."*

Some architects want more defined processes: "*I believe the lack of formal development lifecycle processes leaves the architect with a design that no one has to comply with*". "*The 'old way' of architecture process is gone and we don't really have a new one yet*". Another architect offers that one way to improve feedback "...*is for the architect to be a "virtual" member of the development team, going to some of the stand-ups, user story reviews, retrospectives, etc.*"

5.3   Group Decisions

The findings revealed that groups often make architecture decisions informally. Often decisions are not recorded and so the nuances behind the decisions are lost or become tacit knowledge held only by those initially involved with the decisions. Decisions coming from several sources impact the architecture. Product management, with or without architects' involvement, sometimes makes architecture decisions. Still other architecture decisions are "strategic" and made by senior management. Architects wanted more involvement in all these decisions.

5.4   The Roles of Architects and Their Decision-Making Scope

The roles of architects and their scope of decision-making are not always clearly defined. There are different types of architects, ranging from those embedded in development teams (Scrum Architect) to customer and end-to-end solutions architects. Some architects are also Product Owners, which means they define features as well as product architecture. Architects are communicators, and often are the bridge between customer needs and engineering. However, decision-making responsibilities are not always clear. Responsibilities of various architect roles sometimes overlap. Architects would like more clearly defined roles that were better understood and agreed to.

5.5   Scope and Impact of Decisions

The data shown in Sect. 4.2 indicates that the impact of decisions is generally quite high. Relating the decisions examples to the organization structure, 16.7% impact the product line team. 58.3% impact the business unit responsible for the product line. 25% impact the business group responsible for the business units. The majority of examples that impact the business group are architecture decisions that have a system scope, while one decision example has a component scope. This illustrates that, from an architecture perspective, a decision made at the component level can have a wide-reaching impact well beyond the team. Of the example decisions shown in Sect. 4.2, the architecture decisions at the product scope impact either the product line team or the business unit. The architecture decisions at the system scope impact either the business unit or the business group.

5.6   Characterizing Decisions

During the data analysis we realized that none of the decision frameworks discussed in the literature review adequately captured certain dimensions of a decision. During the coding process we identified decision categories, which we noted as "Technology",

"Product", etc. It also proved useful to identify the level of abstraction that a decision related to or impacted, i.e., systems, sub-system, component, etc.

We find it more useful to characterize decisions along multiple dimensions rather than try to fit them in to a single taxonomy. Our approach was to start with the data, and identify suitable characterizations for the data, rather than start with a framework and force-fit the data to the framework. This approach helped us, and the participants in our study, to gain a deeper understanding of the decisions and their context.

6 Summary and Conclusions

This section presents a summary of the research findings. Section 6.1 shows how the research questions have been addressed. Section 6.2 provides a set of recommendations for architects and organizations based on the research findings. Section 6.3 presents conclusions from the research. Finally, Sect. 6.4 outlines directions for future research by the authors that builds on the topics and findings in this paper.

6.1 Answering the Research Questions

This paper sought to address four specific research questions, as outlined in Sect. 3.1. This section summarizes how each research question has been addressed.

- RQ1: **Approaches.** Sections 4.2 and 4.3 presented findings that show examples of current decision-making approaches used by architects. The findings identified a range of approaches, notably the prevalence of informal, group-based decisions. There are also examples of scenarios where architects are not involved in architecture decisions which were made by product management or management, or where they had insufficient information to make an informed decision.
- RQ2: **Challenges.** Section 4.4 articulated challenges encountered by architects related to decision-making approaches. The findings identified some architecture decisions were made without considering the technical feasibility or longer-term consequences and other decisions were made without adequate information.
- RQ3: **Context.** Section 4.5 described some conditions within which architects make decisions. The findings identified that architects worked with large, distributed teams to make decisions which often required consensus building and gaining trust. Architects did not directly offer explanations for their decision-making approaches. Some decisions are made more quickly under time pressures while "bigger" decisions take more time and involve gaining group consensus.
- RQ4: **Impact.** Section 4.6 showed how decisions made by architects, and their decision-making approach, impact other people. The findings suggest that decision-making was viewed as more effective when architects followed through with engineering or decisions were made collaboratively.

6.2 Recommendations

The following recommendations are drawn from the survey and focus group findings:

1. Consider the space-time separation of teams, and how that impacts architecture decisions. When dealing with teams who are separated in space (through multiple

geographies) and time (through multiple time zones), make an effort to compartmentalize the scope of responsibility of teams such that coherent architecture decisions can be made in each location.

2. Establish clear decision-making boundaries. Articulate who is responsible for which type of decisions. This can be based on scope of decision (product, system, component, etc.), nature of decision (product, technology, etc.), or something else.

3. If your organization is using an agile development approach, then take the time to articulate how architecture fits.

4. Understand who is impacted by decisions made by architects. Establish a feedback loop so that architects understand that impact in a timely manner.

5. Start with why. Architects in this study expressed a much higher degree of success in decision adoption when other people understood why a decision is being taken. This is an important part of the context of architecture decisions.

6. Take the time to foster trust among architects and those impacted by decisions.

7. Consider how architecture decisions are retained and communicated. We see a need for retaining and communicating architecture decisions and their rationale, especially when decisions have broad impact. Documenting decisions, to be effective, should fit into existing processes.

8. Some decisions are necessarily made for short-term expediency, e.g. to address an immediate customer need. Perhaps there needs to be some mechanism to flag these types of decisions and manage them, perhaps in a product debt backlog (especially those that will incur architecture debt) for periodic review.

6.3   Conclusions

Having multiple dimensions that help characterize different decisions, as shown in Sect. 4.2, provides deeper insights into the types of decisions architects are dealing with. Architects are generally experienced decision makers operating in an environment characterized by time pressure, insufficient information, poorly defined or nonexistent procedures, and a need for coordination across hundreds of people in multiple global teams. Their perception is they are most effective in making decisions where they have formal and direct collaboration with engineering and product management. The findings showed several examples that help the researchers understand how architects approach decision-making, and the challenges, context and impact of those decisions. The findings did not reveal sufficient data about the reasons why architects choose the decision-making approaches they employ.

6.4   Future Research

Future research based on this study will focus on the following:

• Understanding how architecture decisions constrain other decisions. It is hard for developers who get involved later, long after a decision is made, to understand the initial design context. This research points to the potential need for a cumulative history of decisions.

- Understanding the trade-offs and benefits between documenting decisions, and other aspects of the architecture. In particular, is it more important to document decisions than it is other aspects of the architecture?

The authors also intend to reproduce this study with additional organizations to understand how approaches to architecture decision making vary in different contexts.

References

1. Bass, L., Clements, P., Kazman, R.: Software Architecture in Practice. Addison-Wesley, Upper Saddle River (2013)
2. Rozanski, N., Woods, E.: Software Systems Architecture: Working with Stakeholders Using Viewpoints and Perspectives. Addison-Wesley, Upper Saddle River (2012)
3. Kruchten, P., Capilla, R., Dueñas, J.C.: The decision view's role in software architecture practice. IEEE Softw. **26**, 36–42 (2009)
4. Kruchten, P., Lago, P., van Vliet, H.: Building up and reasoning about architectural knowledge. In: Hofmeister, C., Crnkovic, I., Reussner, R. (eds.) QoSA 2006. LNCS, vol. 4214, pp. 43–58. Springer, Heidelberg (2006). https://doi.org/10.1007/11921998_8
5. Jansen, A., Bosch, J.: Software architecture as a set of architectural design decisions. In: 5th Working IEEE/IFIP Conference on Software Architecture, WICSA 2005, pp. 109–120. IEEE (2005)
6. Tyree, J., Akerman, A.: Architecture Decisions: Demystifying Architecture. IEEE Softw. (2005)
7. Clements, P., Ivers, J., Little, R., Nord, R., Stafford, J.: Documenting Software Architectures in an Agile World. Software Engineering Institute (2003)
8. Klein, G.A.: Sources of Power: How People Make Decisions. MIT Press, Cambridge (2017)
9. Rekha, V.S., Muccini, H.: Suitability of software architecture decision making methods for group decisions. In: Avgeriou, P., Zdun, U. (eds.) ECSA 2014. LNCS, vol. 8627, pp. 17–32. Springer, Cham (2014). https://doi.org/10.1007/978-3-319-09970-5_2
10. Tofan, D., Galster, M., Avgeriou, P.: Difficulty of architectural decisions – a survey with professional architects. In: Drira, K. (ed.) ECSA 2013. LNCS, vol. 7957, pp. 192–199. Springer, Heidelberg (2013). https://doi.org/10.1007/978-3-642-39031-9_17
11. Dasanayake, S., Markkula, J., Aaramaa, S., Oivo, M.: Software architecture decision-making practices and challenges: an industrial case study. In: 24th Australasian Software Engineering Conference (ASWEC), pp. 88–97. IEEE (2015)
12. Kruchten, P.: Documentation of software architecture from a knowledge management perspective – design representation. In: Ali Babar, M., Dingsøyr, T., Lago, P., van Vliet, H. (eds.) Software Architecture Knowledge Management, pp. 39–57. Springer, Heidelberg (2009). https://doi.org/10.1007/978-3-642-02374-3_3
13. Miesbauer, C., Weinreich, R.: Classification of design decisions – an expert survey in practice. In: Drira, K. (ed.) ECSA 2013. LNCS, vol. 7957, pp. 130–145. Springer, Heidelberg (2013). https://doi.org/10.1007/978-3-642-39031-9_12
14. Maxwell, J.A.: Qualitative Research Design: An Interactive Approach. SAGE Publications Inc., Thousand Oaks (2013)
15. Miles, M.B., Huberman, A.M., Saldana, J.: Qualitative data Analysis: A Methods Sourcebook. Sage, Thousand Oaks (2014)
16. Runeson, P., Höst, M., Rainer, A., Regnell, B.: Case Study Research in Software Engineering: Guidelines and Examples. Wiley, Hoboken (2012)

17. Runeson, P., Höst, M.: Guidelines for conducting and reporting case study research in software engineering. Empir. Softw. Eng. **14**, 131–164 (2008)
18. Kohn, L.T.: Methods in Case Study Analysis. Technical Publication, Center for Studying Health System Change (1997)
19. Yin, R.K.: Case Study Research: Design and Methods, 5th edn. SAGE, London (2014)
20. Morgan, D.L.: Focus Groups as Qualitative Reearch. Sage Publications, Thousand Oaks (1997)
21. Yin, R.K.: Qualitative Research from Start to Finish. The Guildford Press, New York (2016)

Software Architecture in Practice

Software Architecture Measurement—Experiences from a Multinational Company

Wensheng Wu[1], Yuanfang Cai[2], Rick Kazman[3]([⊠]), Ran Mo[2], Zhipeng Liu[1], Rongbiao Chen[1], Yingan Ge[1], Weicai Liu[1], and Junhui Zhang[1]

[1] Huawei Technologies Co., Ltd., Shenzhen, Guangdong, China
{wuwensheng,zhipeng.liu,chenrongbiao,geyingan,
liuweicai,zhangjunhui3}@huawei.com
[2] Drexel University, Philadelphia, PA, USA
{yc349,rm859}@drexel.edu
[3] University of Hawaii, Honolulu, HI, USA
kazman@hawaii.edu

Abstract. In this paper, we present our 4-year experience of creating, evolving, and validating an automated software architecture measurement system within Huawei. This system is centered around a comprehensive scale called the *Standard Architecture Index* (SAI), which is composed of a number of measures, each reflecting a recurring architecture problem. Development teams use this as a guide to figure out how to achieve a better score by addressing the underlying problems. The measurement practice thus motivates desired behaviors and outcomes. In this paper, we present our experience of creating and validating SAI 1.0 and 2.0, which has been adopted as the enterprise-wide standard, and our directions towards SAI 3.0. We will describe how we got the development teams to accept and apply SAI through pilot studies, constantly adjusting the formula based on feedback, and correlating SAI scores with productivity measures. Our experience shows that it is critical to guide development teams to focus on the underlying problems behind each measure within SAI, rather than on the score itself. It is also critical to introduce state-of-the-art technologies to the development teams. In doing so they can leverage these technologies to pinpoint and quantify architecture problems so that better SAI scores can be achieved, along with better quality and productivity.

Keywords: Software measurement · Software architecture Software quality

1 Introduction

In this paper, we present our 4-year long experience within Huawei to evaluate, measure, and improve the architectures of their software products. As a multinational company, Huawei is constantly seeking to improve product quality and

C. E. Cuesta et al. (Eds.): ECSA 2018, LNCS 11048, pp. 303–319, 2018.
https://doi.org/10.1007/978-3-030-00761-4_20

maintain rapid feature delivery. As with all software systems, as they age and evolve, more and more effort is spent on maintenance. Recognizing the profound influence of software architecture in accommodating a rapidly-changing market environment, improving productivity and efficiency, and shortening the Time-to-Market (TTM) cycle, in 2013, Huawei embarked on a software architecture improvement program.

Research on software measurement has a long history. From McCabe's canonical Cyclomatic complexity [15] to C&K [6], LK [13], and MOOD metrics suites [8] for object-oriented programs, research on code-level metrics continuously evolves. System and architectural level metrics have been proposed as well. For example, Coleman's maintainability index [7] combines multiple measures into a single scale. Quality assessment tools, such as SonarQube, also provide metrics and maintainability ratings[1].

Huawei practitioners, however, found that existing metrics and indexes could not provide sufficient insight into their architectures. First, there is insufficient evidence that these metrics can be used to compare and contrast projects so that management could reliably discern which projects were suffering maintenance problems. Nor could they rely on these metrics to monitor the evolution of a project so that architecture degradation could be detected early. Second, if a system obtained a sub-optimal score, it was not clear what the underlying problems were and hence what should be done to fix these problems so as to achieve a better score. Finally, our understanding of software architecture and evolution advances over time. New concepts, such as code smells and anti-patterns, have been widely accepted but were not reflected in legacy metrics.

To address these shortcomings, Huawei's Research and Development group proposed to institutionalize a standard software architecture measurement system, to uniformly monitor hundreds of products. For this purpose, we conducted extensive research on architecture design, architecture measurement theory, tooling and practice. Since several software architecture measurement tools were already in use by some product teams within Huawei, we also conducted internal research to collect their experiences, which showed that the most commonly applied metrics are at the source code level, and there are few widely used metrics at the design/architectural level. In addition, many of the adopted metrics were based on the experience and intuition of the development teams, without rigorous theoretical foundations.

Based on these early insights, we created the first version of our software architecture measurement standard, SAI 1.0, which adopted multiple software architecture measurement practices, and used the ISO/IEC 25010 software measurement model as a reference. We first used SAI 1.0 to measure open source projects to benchmark and adjust the model, and then conducted internal pilot studies to collect feedback. After two rounds of pilot studies, we evolved the standard to SAI 2.0. This version provided more precise guidance on where the architecture problems are, and the scope of their impact. During this process we were searching for and adopting state-of-the-art technologies to pinpoint,

---

[1] https://docs.sonarqube.org/display/SONAR/Metric+Definitions.

visualize, and quantify the underlying architectural problems. This way, the teams could actually achieve a better score by fixing these problems. Throughout this process we have validated SAI quantitatively by correlating its scores with productivity measures, and qualitatively by interviewing practitioners. SAI 2.0 is now widely accepted within Huawei and we are working towards the creation of SAI 3.0.

Although our objective is to comprehensively measure software architecture, including both code and models, in reality, source files are the only reliable artifacts available. In this paper, we focus on *architecture* as module structures that can be inferred from source files [2], and our *architecture assessment* focuses on relations among files. Our contributions from this experience are as follows:

(1) First, a successful architecture measurement system should be able to support quantitative comparison of different projects, and to monitor architecture degradation over time. The quantitative score should be supported by quality and productivity data continuously collected through the development process. Most importantly, the components of the score should indicate the existence of flaws in code, design or architecture, so that development teams can understand where improvement is needed.

(2) Second, product teams should be equipped with state-of-the-art tools and conduct key activities to pinpoint, quantify, and visualize architectural debts. Using the overall architecture score as the guidance, the teams could use these tools to identify and remove the underlying flaws, and improve quality and productivity, which in turn, will improve the score. These tools and activities are critical for the teams to take actions based on architecture measurement.

(3) Finally, an effectively way to convince practitioners to adopt such a measurement system is to demonstrate concrete improvement in terms of quality and productivity through pilot studies, and closely work with practitioners, taking their opinions into consideration and adjust the model accordingly. Once the practitioners experienced the benefits of applying this framework, they are not only willing to measure their systems on a daily basis, but also to leverage and improve these technologies in innovative ways.

2   Objective, Challenges, and Strategies

Our objective in creating a standard architecture measurement system is to improve the quality and productivity of Huawei's software products. The challenge is to have this measure accepted by both management and development teams, and to demonstrate the benefits to both parties. To achieve these objectives, the designers of SAI needed to answer the following questions:

Q1. How to create a software measurement system that adds value and provides practical benefits to development teams?

The measurement system must be based on solid theoretical foundations, and provide clear guidance and benchmarks. An improved score should be associated with improved quality and productivity, and vice versa.

Q2. Is it possible to accurately measure software architecture quantitatively?
The measurement system must be quantitative so that the users can understand to what extent a system has been improved or degraded. If a system is known to have a healthy architecture and has been successful, or if the development team is suffering from maintenance difficulties, then the score should faithfully reflect these conditions.

Q3. How to convince developers to accept and use these measures? If architecture measurement is just an extra task that cannot be integrated into the regular development process, then it will become a burden to the development team. Thus we not only needed to answer the first question satisfactorily, but we also had to convince the development teams to integrate the standard into their development process. If the standard is to be accepted in the long run, developers must see that the application of the standard leads to improved productivity and efficiency.

Q4. How to make these measures actionable? That is, can the development team figure out what to do to get a better score?
Since the ultimate purpose of the measurement system is to improve software quality and productivity, the development team should be able to figure out where and how the software should be improved.

To address these challenges, the designers of SAI, under the leadership of the first author, have applied the following strategies, not only to create a theoretically sound and practically beneficial index, but also to prove its benefits to development teams, thus promoting its acceptance:

1. *Conducting internal and external research.* Since 2013, Huawei has established collaborations with researchers around the world, and conducted extensive research on architecture design, measurement theory, technology, tooling, and practice. We also conducted research internally to understand the different emphases and priorities of teams, and the advantages and limitations of SAI. SAI is thus the result of internal and external research, based on both theory and practice.

2. *Conducting pilot studies and rigorous evaluation.* After each version of SAI was designed, and before it was applied to Huawei projects, we first used the index to measure open source systems to conduct initial evaluations and make adjustments. After that, we solicited Huawei development teams to conduct pilot studies to evaluate the measurement system. The evaluation process integrated interviews to assess if the measures faithfully reflect the practitioners' intuitions, and quantitative analysis to see if the variation of measures had a strong correlation with productivity.

3. *Augmenting measurement with tools and key activities.* To help the developers understand where and how to improve their architecture quality, and hence their measurement score, we provided several tools, including a graphical view of the components of their SAI scores, an architecture guarding tool called UADP, design structure matrix (DSM) [1,23,24] tools, and the associated architectural debt quantification methods [12,25], which we will elaborate in the next few sections.

3   The First Version of SAI

Figure 1 depicts the theoretical structure of our architecture measurement system. As shown in the figure, the ultimate objective of SAI is to improve a suite of quality attributes, including maintainability, reliability, security, performance, etc. [2]. For each quality attribute, we measure the software from three dimensions: (1) structural measures that assess the structural relations among files, modules, and components; (2) class/function measures that assess implementation quality and styles within each source file; and (3) global measures that focus on design and implementation choices with global impacts, such as the density of global variables and the rate of unused APIs. Based on these measures, we defined a comprehensive index, which we call *Product SAI* or *Project SAI*. The higher the SAI, the lower the quality of the product architecture; the lower the SAI, the better the quality. In this section, we present the components of the first version of SAI, its supporting tools, and our pilot study results.

3.1   Computational Model and Benchmarks

Considering the availability of architecture measurement technology and tools, as well as the potential applicability and benefits to software development practice, SAI 1.0 was created to focus on maintainability measurement. Table 1 lists all the measures integrated into SAI 1.0, which shows that we intend

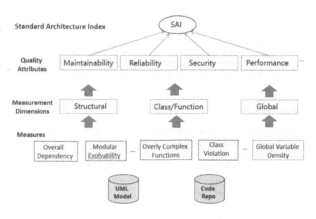

Fig. 1. SAI overview

to measure both source code and software models. In reality, however, high-level models are usually not available. Even if they are available, their accuracy is questionable. Although we have not been able to quantify all dimensions of all quality attributes today, SAI was designed to be extensible to accommodate additional dimensions and metrics in the future.

The metrics listed in Table 1 are either derived from existing metrics, or proposed by our collaborators or senior architects. Following are a few examples:

- *Class disorder rate*: measures if a class takes too many responsibilities, or accesses other class's data, derived from code smells such as Feature Envy [10], and anti-patterns, such as divergent changes [9].

Table 1. Metrics in SAI 1.0

	Structure measures	Class/func. measures	Global measures
Model	Overall dependency level	Average class inheritance depth	Global variable density
	Module independent evolvability	Average class inheritance width	
	Logical architecture coupling		
	Logical architecture cohesion		
	Activity diagram complexity		
	Sequence diagram complexity		
	Module cyclic dependency rate		
Code	Overall dependency level	Average class inheritance depth	Global Variable Density
	Module independent evolvability	Average class inheritance width	Code duplication rate
	Module disorder rate	Class disorder rate	Design pattern defects
	Module cyclic dependency rate	Class violation rate	Redefined symbol rate
	Unstable dependency module	Overly complex class	Unused API rate
	Header file cyclical dependency	Overly complex function	Extra header file rate
	Modularity violation rate	Overly deep function	
	Overly complex module	Overly long function	

- *Class violation rate*: measures how often classes are changed for similar reasons, such as code clone [10].
- *Average class inheritance depth*: derived from the well-known C&K metrics [6] for object-oriented code.
- *Modularity violation rate*: measures how often files belonging to structurally independent modules change together frequently, as recorded in the revision history, following the work of Wong et al. [21].

Most of these measures can be extracted automatically from a project's source code and revision history, but for some of them, we are still exploring practical methods to quantify them, such as *Module Independent Evolvability* that aims to measure the extent to which modules can evolve independently from each other [16]. We keep these measures in our framework so that they can be quantified in the future.

To promote the comprehensive architecture quality index, we must address the following two challenges: (1) how to ensure that the measurement is consistent with the developers' intuition and faithfully reflects architecture quality? (2) How to set thresholds of each measure for projects with different programming languages, ages, scales, markets etc., so that their intrinsic characteristics can be revealed? For example, what should be the threshold to determine if a function is "*overly complex*"? Shall we provide different thresholds for Java and C?

To address the first challenge, we proposed the concept of *Architectural Bad Smells*, which extends the original definition of *code smells* [10], which has been widely accepted in Huawei. Defining the architectural counterpart of *smells* makes SAI more convincing and acceptable to developers. We thus associated each architecture measure with a type of architecture smell (or *defect*), so that each measure is backed up by a group of specific architecture defects. For example, the *Module Disorder Rate* is associated with the *module disorder* architectural smell, that is, modules that take multiple responsibilities and cause divergent changes. The more modules are detected as being disordered, the higher the measure. This mapping has effectively reduced suspicions within development teams towards SAI. After trade-off analysis and careful comparison, the first version of SAI was created as *a sum of weighted architecture smells*:

$$SAI = \Sigma(weight_i * \#ArchitectureSmell_i)/KLOC$$

where $i = 0 \dots n$, and n is the total number of architectural smells.

To address the second challenge of setting reasonable and justifiable thresholds and weights for each architectural smell, we took the following steps:

First, referring to existing architecture measurement practices, we assigned the initial thresholds and weights so that the development teams that were already practicing their own measurement could continue with little disruption. For example, for *Overly Complex function*, the threshold is set as "*CyclomaticComplexity* > 15"; *Duplicated Code* is defined as two units of code with more than 10 lines of similar code, etc. These thresholds were already being used by some product lines for a long time. Furthermore, we assigned slightly different thresholds and weights for C, C++ and Java.

Second, we assigned thresholds and weights for each measure according to the severity of the associated architectural issues. For example, the thresholds and weights of *Underused API* were determined by our architects and measurement experts based on their experiences. Third, we collected opinions from our development teams, and assigned more weight to architectural smells with significant impact on development efficiency, such as *Divergent Changes*. Finally, we collected subjective judgement and rankings of the impact of each architectural smell on development productivity and efficiency. We ranked the results accordingly and adjusted the weight of each architecture measure and smell, so that it was consistent with the intuition of the architects and development teams.

Different teams may have different opinions about how the thresholds and weights should be assigned. To avoid potential arguments and disagreement, we decided not to publicize the weight of each architectural smells. For the three mainstream programming languages used in Huawei—C, C++ and Java—we selected a set of *successful* open source projects and obtained their average SAI scores. Here we consider an open source project to be *successful* if it has evolved for a very long period of time, supports distributed development by a large number of contributors, and has a large number of uses. We used their scores as the benchmark for our software products using the same languages, which we called SAI-benchmark.

These benchmarks, on one hand, enabled the development teams to understand their architecture quality in a straightforward way, and to assess the need to improve their architectures. On the other hand, it conveyed a clear message: if the SAI of a software product is higher than that of successful open source software systems, it means that product may have room for improvement.

3.2 Supporting Tools

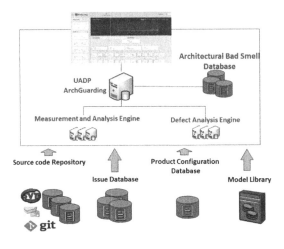

Fig. 2. UADP overview

To improve the application of SAI, we provided a suite of tools and recommended to development teams that they improve their SAI scores, such as guarding their architecture in real time. We created a tool called *UADP ArchGuarding* ("UADP" for short), that comprehensively supported the measurement of all the components of SAI, and could be rapidly deployed in the development environment of our products. Figure 2 depicts the structure of UADP, which collects information from the code repository, issue database, product configuration database, and model library, measures and detects architectural smells, saves the defects into an architectural smell database, and presents the results in a graphical user interface as shown in Fig. 3. Using this interface, a product team can conveniently monitor not only their SAI scores, but also the architectural smells associated with the scores. If the score is not satisfactory, they can figure out which architecture smells are causing the problems, and how to improve the score by fixing the underlying architecture problems.

3.3 Pilot Studies and Results

To test the effectiveness of SAI 1.0, we first collected data from six products, covering the major product domains within Huawei. After that, we reported the architecture measuring and guarding solutions (SAI and UADP), as well as the pilot study plan to management and obtained their approval. Six months later, we organized a teleconference, when all product teams participated in the pilot study presented their progress. The midterm reports were widely circulated within Huawei. At that time we also started the 2nd round of the pilot study, extending the scope to more than 30 products.

After one year of pilot study, by the end of 2014, the data shows that the architecture quality of the pilot products, as measured by SAI 1.0, improved 23.51% on average. As an example, guided by the architectural assessment score, Product A fixed 500+ architecture smells, reduced coupling among subsystems by 30%, increased modularity within subsystems, improved SAI score by 29.71%, and improved development efficiency, measured by the number of person-month per 1000 LOC, by 30%. One subsystem was refactored and reduced LOC from 471k to 199k, by removing a large amount of duplicated code. In this case, the *Divergent Change* architecture smell was reduced substantially.

As another example, the SAI of product B improved 64.2%, coupling among modules was reduced by 20%, 2K LOC were removed, and maintenance effort decreased by 20%. Correspondingly, the ability to conduct parallel development improved significantly, the efficiency of feature delivery improved 18.8%, and efficiency of validation and verification also improved. A manager of the pilot product commented: *"Architecture guardian is an innovative and excellent practice within Huawei, and has produced profound and long-lasting impacts with excellent results"*.

At the beginning of 2015, we summarized our application of SAI to Huawei R&D management, and decided to promote SAI to all products within Huawei. As the number of projects increased, issues concerning its design were reported. The following are some representative examples: *"Should* Overly Complex Class *be considered an architecture smell?"*, "Unstable Dependency Module *lacks theoretical support*

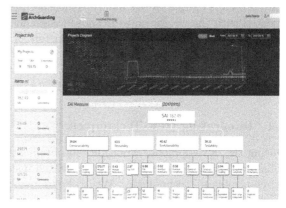

Fig. 3. UADP GUI

and can be ambiguous", etc. We improved the model and UADP tool accordingly.

4   The Second Version of SAI

Based on the feedback we received, we improved the model and released SAI 2.0 in the middle of 2015. In SAI 2.0, we improved the computational model and incorporated new technologies to facilitate architecture quality improvement.

4.1   Improved Computational Model

The most prominent changes of SAI 2.0 include the explicit mapping of architectural smells to quality attributes, and the categorization of architectural smells based on their scope: global, system, component, module, file, and function. The broader the scope of a smell, the more weight assigned to the corresponding measures. The overall SAI score becomes the sum of SAI scores for all quality attributions being considered. Each quality attribute, in turn, is mapped to multiple *architecture factors*, such as repeatability, system coupling, module balance, etc. These factors were either from ISO 25010, or proposed by Huawei senior architects. Each architecture factor is further mapped to a number of architecture smells that may negatively affect the factor. Each architecture smell, in turn, is weighted to reflect its impact scope, e.g., a clique involving 3 modules has a smaller impact scope factor than a clique covering 10 modules.

Our principles for setting the weight of each measure are as follows: (1) the broader the impact scope of an architectural smell, the higher the weight; (2) the higher level of abstraction of an architectural smell, the higher the weight; (3) the more contribution to architecture complexity of a smell, the higher the weight, and (4) the more impact on development and maintenance efficiency, the higher the weight. We conducted interviews with key architects and refined the weights based on the above principles.

The adjustment of SAI 2.0 was non-trivial. To minimize the impact to software products caused by architecture measurement standard changes, we experimented with the weight and threshold assignment so that the scores and trends obtained from SAI 2.0 were largely consistent with those of SAI 1.0. The benefit of using SAI 2.0 was to provide development teams with more fine-grained information about which aspects of the architecture needed improvement and which architecture attributes could be affected.

4.2   Integrating New Techniques

During the development, evolution, and application of SAI, we also established collaborations with universities and research institutes, to learn of state-of-the-art concepts and technologies. We explored a suite of new metrics and measurement techniques, including *independence level* [19], *propagation cost*(PC) [14], *decoupling Level* (DL) [16], *module balance* [3], architectural debt [12,25], etc., and a suite of new technologies that can be used by the development teams to enrich the automatic architecture measuring and guarding solutions. Next we introduce 3 technologies that have been adopted by Huawei development teams.

1. Design Structure Matrix and DSM-based Metrics. Collaborating with Drexel University and the University of Hawaii, in 2013, we introduced the Design Structure Matrix (DSM) [1] representation to Huawei development teams to model the dependency structures of their products. A DSM is square matrix in which the columns and rows are labeled with the same set of elements in the same order, and a marked cell indicates that the elements on the row depends on the elements on the column. We found that DSM modeling is useful in two ways. First, we can model design elements at any level of granularity: files, classes, packages, or the self-defined modules. Figure 4 shows relations among modules in a Huawei product. This DSM shows that the first 4 modules form a strongly connected graph, and none of them depend on Module E. It also reveals the number of dependencies between each pair of the modules.

Second and more importantly, a DSM can model history and structural relations simultaneously. For example, in Fig. 5, each cell is marked with the number of structural dependences between each module pair, and the number of times files within these modules are changed together. For example, the cell in the first row and second column is labeled

	A	B	C	D	E
Module A	(1)	18	52	34	
Module B	144	(2)	68	132	
Module C	576	32	(3)	417	
Module D	283	82	27	(4)	
Module E	36	19	42	3	(5)

Fig. 4. Design structure matrix

"68, 992", meaning that there are 68 structural dependencies from Module A to Module B, and the files within these modules were changed together 992 times. This DSM shows that not only do these modules form cyclical dependencies, but that these cycles are expensive to maintain because files within them have been changed together hundreds of times, presenting compelling evidence that this product needs to be refactored. The DSM-based analysis was enthusiastically adopted by development teams.

Along with DSM modeling, we also adopted a suite of associated metrics, including *independence level* (IL) [19], *decoupling level*(DL) [16], and *propagation cost*(PC) [14]. These metrics complement with one another. PC was designed to measure how tightly source files within a system are *coupled* with each other. The idea is to calculate the transitive closure of a DSM until no more dependencies can be added, and then calculate percentage of non-empty cells to the total number of cells. The higher the PC, the tighter the system is coupled.

	A	B	C	D	E
Module A	(1)	68,992	132,585	0,141	144,222
Module B	32,992	(2)	417,1915	0,246	576,378
Module C	82,858	270,1915	(3)	0,130	283,240
Module D	19,141	42,246	30,130	(4)	36,53
Module E	18,202	52,378	34,240	0,53	(5)

Fig. 5. DSM with history

Both DL and IL are based on the *Design Rule Hierarchy* (DRH) [23] algorithm that clusters a DSM into a hierarchical structure in which the most influential files are at the top of the hierarchy, and files in the lower layers depend on files in higher layers. Most importantly, the files within each layer are clustered into mutually independent modules. Accordingly, the modules at the bottom layer of a DRH are truly

	A	B	C	D	E	F	G	H	I
Module A	(1)								
Module B	13	(2)	2	2	1	1	15		
Module C	11	6	(3)		4		9		
Module D	5		1	(4)			3		
Module E	9	1	4		(5)	4	19		
Module F	6	2	2	2	2	(6)	39		
Module G	216	129	57	16	18	31	(7)		
Module H	3	4	32	417				(8)	
Module I	3	3	2	2	2	1	26		(9)

Fig. 6. DSM after refactoring

independent since they can be revised or replaced without influencing other parts of the system. The metric Independence Level (IL) [19] measures the portion of files that are clustered into the lowest layer of a DRH, that is, the portion of files that can be implemented and changed independently. The larger the IL, the more modules in the system can be changed independently. A new metric, Decoupling Level (DL) [16], evolved from IL to take into account the size of each modules, the number of independent modules in all layers, and the dependency relations among modules. The more independent modules, the smaller each module, and the less coupled they are, the higher the DL.

One of the product teams leveraged DRH clustering in an innovative way to guide their refactoring activities, and obtained impressive results. The DSM in Fig. 5 depicts the initial structure of their product, which made it clear that the original structure of the system was poorly modularized. The product teams thus used the modules clustered by the DRH algorithm as the *de facto* modular structure and refactored the system accordingly. By doing so, they increased the DL of the system by 250%. As a result, the SAI of the subsystem improved by 40%, much better than the open source benchmark. The DSM after refactoring is depicted in Fig. 6. This figure shows that, even though the cycles were not completely removed, the number of dependencies among modules was significantly reduced. Given the excellent results of DSM analysis and the associated metrics, we have integrated them into architectural measurement and guarding solution, SAI standard, and recommended key activities.

2. Architectural Debt Quantification. We explored architectural debt analysis techniques in 2015 and 2016, completed an architectural debt quantification prototype, and conducted a pilot study using Project M, which had experienced difficulty maintaining

Table 2. Product M architectural debt analysis

	Person month	Debt ratio (%)
Module A	166.71	120.45 (72%)
Module B	375.55	281.65 (75%)

their product for a long time. Table 2. The table shows that, of the 166.71 person-months spent in Module A, 120.45 (72%) person-month were extra maintenance costs caused by the severe architecture debt. The percentage of debt in Module B is 75%. These numbers were acknowledged by the development team, and provided a foundation for their decision to conduct refactoring. We plan to further integrate this technology into our architecture automatic measuring and guarding solutions, and make it a key activity to motivate architectural refactoring. This will allow our development teams to quantify their debts and visualize architecture problems using DSMs, so that they can justify refactoring and pinpoint the focus of refactoring.

4.3   Pilot Study and Results

In late 2015, we measured 20 products using SAI 1.0. After that we deployed SAI 2.0 and started a trial assessment in 2016. After 9 months of trial and adjustment, Huawei products switched to SAI 2.0. Since our ultimate purpose is to use SAI as a measure to improve software productivity and efficiency, we collected data from multiple versions of 29 products that have applied SAI 2.0. For each project, we collected both the SAI measures for each release, and productivity measures during the process. In Huawei, we measure productivity using person-months per 1000 LOC. These data were collected continuously over the past two years. As shown in Fig. 7, for 24 out of 29 projects, SAI measures are shown to have positive correlation with productivity. For about 1/3 of the projects, their productively is strongly correlated with their SAI scores.

For some of the projects, the number of data points is not enough to obtain statistically meaningful results. For projects whose SAI scores are shown to be negatively correlated with their productivity, we are investigating the reasons and will continue collecting the

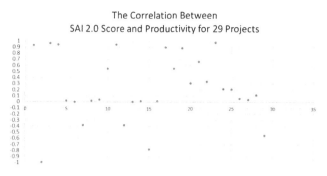

The Correlation Between
SAI 2.0 Score and Productivity for 29 Projects

Fig. 7. SAI and productivity

data and monitoring their variation over time. For the second project whose productivity appeared to be opposite to its SAI score, we found out that it is because the system was undergoing major repository merging and the productivity data was not correctly collected. We will filter out such data in the future.

5 Lessons Learned and Results

Results. SAI has now been widely deployed and accepted within Huawei: it has now been used in more than 100 products. Thus we can now answer the research questions proposed in Sect. 2:

1. By creating a software measurement system with a score that can be traced to concrete architectural flaws, supported by key activities and tools such as the quantification of architecture debt, we helped development teams realize the need to conduct large scale architecture refactoring. The value of architecture measurement has been validated by widespread adoption in our development teams. Thus we now believe that architecture measurement should be integrated into the core daily activities of the software development process.
2. It is possible to measure software architecture quantitatively. We learned that we could obtain measures that reveal the level of severity of architecture smells, and that are consistent with the intuition of architecture experts, development teams, and management. In this way we can provide support for them to do the necessary refactoring.
3. By working with developers and being flexible, not expecting 100% compliance immediately, we found that our teams accepted these measures as meaningful.
4. Finally, our developers determined that the measures that we produced were indeed actionable. They used these measures to plan refactoring activities and those refactorings resulted in substantial improvements to our systems in terms of bug rates, change rates, and effort.

Overall we consider the design and deployment of SAI within Huawei to have been a great success. The process required patience and flexibility, it required as much listening as talking, but in the end produced meaningful results.

Lessons Learned. Through the creation and evolution of SAI we have learned a number of lessons that, we believe, strongly affected our success.

First, at the beginning of the process, we were met with suspicion from development teams. On the surface, their doubts were directed towards the standard. But in reality, their doubts stemmed from the implicit pressure of ongoing performance reviews. At this point, we had to compromise. For teams to accept and adopt the standard smoothly, it was necessary to not only convince them in theory, but also to accept some compromises in practice, as we were proving the value of our approach.

Second, we needed to not only provide supporting tools, but also keep improving its usability, which is a key for development teams to accept the standard and apply it widely.

Third, the evolution of the standard is necessary, but it must be incremental. It was also critical to invite architects from a wide range of teams to participate in the construction of instruments from the beginning.

Fourth, we learned that we need to participate in conferences and learn from the research community. We must continuously assess and adopt new theories and methods from the field of architecture measurement. The process, from learning a new theory or method, to its complete integration into the practice of architecture measurement, is long and challenging.

Fifth, once the development teams were inspired to participate in architecture measurement, and once they gained sufficient confidence in the instrument, they brought unexpected innovations to the architecture measurement standard and solution. The product team who used DRH clustering to guide their refactoring process is an example. Another team proposed and employed the concept of *architecture hotspot* in a simple and practical way.

6   Related Work

In this section, we review related work on (architectural) complexity measures and change measures.

Software Metrics. Various metrics have been used to measure software code complexity in past decades. Cyclomatic complexity [15] calculates the number of linearly independent paths through a program's source code to measure complexity. Various object-oriented metrics, such as the well-known CK metrics [6], LK Metrics [13] and MOOD Metrics [8], were proposed to measure object-oriented programs. Based on software metrics, software measurement has been widely studied. For example, Coleman [7] applied two models for measuring software maintainability. Sjøberg et al. [20] conducted a case study to examine the relations among code metrics and the correlations between these metrics and software maintainability. Instead of focusing on a specific class of metrics, our SAI integrates three types of metrics—structure, class/function and global metrics—to measure software maintainability. This helps development teams to monitor their software in different perspectives.

Change Measures. Change measures can be calculated from a project's version control system and its issue tracking system. Various change measures extracted from history, such as change frequency and code churn, have been used for software measurement. For example, Schulte [17] measure software based on the activeness of each file in the project's revision history. Wong et al. [22] calculated co-changes as the number of times two files have been changed (committed) together in the project's revision history. They also showed that co-change measures contain important information which reveals improper relations—modularity violations—among files. Following Wong et al.'s work [22], Schwanke et al. [18] used structure dependency and change measures to predict defects and showed that modularity violations can arise as the result of implicit assumptions between structurally unrelated files.

Architecture Metrics. Several architecture-level metrics have been proposed to measure architecture quality. Mo et al. [16] introduced Decoupling Level to measure how well a software system is decoupled into small and independent modules. MacCormack et al. [14] defined the Propagation Cost metric to measure how tightly coupled a system is. Bouwers et al. presented two architecture-level metrics, Component Balance [3] and Dependency Profiles [4]. They also investigated the usefulness of these metrics [5], and demonstrated that measurement results matched practitioner intuitions. Our SAI has integrated multiple *architectural* measures. To properly assess and understand a software architecture we used a specific architecture measure for each architecture smell.

Architecture Debt Analysis. Various approaches have been proposed to detect and analyze architecture debt. In an industrial case study [11], the authors presented a cost-benefit model, which was used to estimate the effort that could be saved by a refactoring to decouple the architecture. In the case study of Kazman et al. [12], they used an economic model to assess the effort that could be saved after refactoring the identified architecture debts. Our SAI not only integrates architecture debt analyses, but also integrates other state-of-the art techniques to assist a development team in detecting architecture problems and assessing the technical debt caused by these problems.

7   Conclusions and Future Work

In this paper, we have presented our 4-year experience of implementing a software architecture measurement system within Huawei. Our study has revealed the significant and positive impact of architecture measurement, in terms of ensuring software quality and productivity, and supporting continuous evolution and improvement of architecture. Our experience showed that formulas alone are not enough; it is important to back up formulas with concrete architecture smells. The development teams use these identified smells to determine how to improve their scores, and hence to improve their architecture. We also confirmed that it is important to adopt state-of-the-art analysis approaches—such as DSM analysis and architecture debt quantification—as key activities to better understand the consequences of degrading the architecture and to quantitatively support refactoring decisions. The SAI scores have shown positive correlations with productivity measures for most of our pilot studies. And we have shown that, with some coaching, most product teams eventually adopt and even embrace software architecture measurements. The automatic architecture measurement and guarding solutions, as well as the SAI formula itself, are still being refined to address various issues and challenges, including:

- How to further increase the accuracy of our architecture measures, so that they can be fully consistent with the intuitions of architects and product teams, as well as the market performance of their products?
- How to measure service-oriented architectures and other similar architectures that consist of collections of interacting components, each of which has its own architecture and its own code base?
- Currently our architecture measurement tool is an independent web-based application. We are working to integrate it within an IDE, so that software developers can be immediately alerted to potential software decay. This way, our tools can be fully integrated into development activities, and architecture measurements will become part of the daily routine of software development.
- We also intend to explore AI-based architecture refactoring and evolution, employing machine-learning to make refactoring recommendations.

We believe these explorations will drive the progress, evolution and development of automatic architecture measurement and guarding solutions, as well as SAI itself.

References

1. Baldwin, C.Y., Clark, K.B.: Design Rules, Vol. 1: The Power of Modularity. MIT Press, Cambridge (2000)
2. Bass, L., Clements, P., Kazman, R.: Software Architecture in Practice, 3rd edn. Addison-Wesley, Boston (2012)
3. Bouwers, E., Correia, J.P., van Deursen, A., Visser, J.: Quantifying the analyzability of software architectures. In: 2011 Ninth Working IEEE/IFIP Conference on Software Architecture, pp. 83–92, June 2011
4. Bouwers, E., van Deursen, A., Visser, J.: Dependency profiles for software architecture evaluations, September 2011
5. Bouwers, E., van Deursen, A., Visser, J.: Evaluating usefulness of software metrics: an industrial experience report. In: 2013 35th International Conference on Software Engineering (ICSE), pp. 921–930, May 2013
6. Chidamber, S.R., Kemerer, C.F.: A metrics suite for object oriented design. IEEE Trans. Softw. Eng. 20(6), 476–493 (1994)
7. Coleman, D., Oman, P., Ash, D., Lowther, B.: Using metrics to evaluate software system maintainability. Computer 27, 44–49 (1994)
8. e Abreu, F.B.: The mood metrics set. In: Proceedings of ECOOP 1995 Workshop on Metrics (1995)

9. Fowler, M.: AntiPatterns: Refactoring Software, Architectures, and Projects in Crisis. Addison-Wesley, Boston (1989)

10. Fowler, M.: Refactoring: Improving the Design of Existing Code. Addison-Wesley, Boston (1999)

11. Carriere, J., Kazman, R., Ozkaya, I.: A cost-benefit framework for making architectural decisions in a business context. In: Proceedings of the 32nd International Conference on Software Engineering (ICSE 32), (Capetown, South Africa), May 2010

12. Kazman, R., et al.: A case study in locating the architectural roots of technical debt. In: Proceedings of 37th International Conference on Software Engineering (2015)

13. Lorenz, M., Kidd, J.: Object-Oriented Software Metrics. Prentice Hall, Upper Saddle River (1994)

14. MacCormack, A., Rusnak, J., Baldwin, C.Y.: Exploring the structure of complex software designs: an empirical study of open source and proprietary code. Manag. Sci. **52**(7), 1015–1030 (2006)

15. McCabe, T.J.: A complexity measure. IEEE Trans. Softw. Eng. **2**(4), 308–320 (1976)

16. Mo, R., Cai, Y., Kazman, R., Xiao, L., Feng, Q.: Decoupling level: a new metric for architectural maintenance complexity. In: Proceedings of the 38th International Conference on Software Engineering, pp. 499–510. ACM (2016)

17. Schulte, L., Sajnani, H., Czerwonka, J.: Active files as a measure of software maintainability. In: Companion Proceedings of the 36th International Conference on Software Engineering, ICSE Companion 2014, pp. 34–43. ACM, New York (2014)

18. Schwanke, R., Xiao, L., Cai, Y.: Measuring architecture quality by structure plus history analysis. In: Proceedings of 35th International Conference on Software Engineering, pp. 891–900, May 2013

19. Sethi, K., Cai, Y., Wong, S., Garcia, A., Sant'Anna, C.: From retrospect to prospect: assessing modularity and stability from software architecture. In: Proceedings of the Joint 8th Working IEEE/IFIP International Conference on Software Architecture and 3rd European Conference on Software Architecture, pp. 269–272, September 2009

20. Sjøberg, D.I., Anda, B., Mockus, A.: Questioning software maintenance metrics: a comparative case study. In: Proceedings of the ACM-IEEE International Symposium on Empirical Software Engineering and Measurement, ESEM 2012, pp. 107–110. ACM, New York (2012)

21. Wong, S., Cai, Y.: Improving the efficiency of dependency analysis in logical models. In: Proceedings of the 24th IEEE/ACM International Conference on Automated Software Engineering, pp. 173–184, November 2009

22. Wong, S., Cai, Y., Kim, M., Dalton, M.: Detecting software modularity violations. In: Proceedings of the 33rd International Conference on Software Engineering, pp. 411–420, May 2011

23. Wong, S., Cai, Y., Valetto, G., Simeonov, G., Sethi, K.: Design rule hierarchies and parallelism in software development tasks. In: Proceedings of 24th IEEE/ACM International Conference on Automated Software Engineering, pp. 197–208, November 2009

24. Xiao, L., Cai, Y., Kazman, R.: Design rule spaces: a new form of architecture insight. In: Proceedings of 36th International Conference on Software Engineering (2014)

25. Xiao, L., Cai, Y., Kazman, R., Mo, R., Feng, Q.: Identifying and quantifying architectural debt. In: Proceedings of 38th International Conference on Software Engineering (2016)

Identifying and Prioritizing Architectural Debt Through Architectural Smells: A Case Study in a Large Software Company

Antonio Martini[2,3], Francesca Arcelli Fontana[1(✉)], Andrea Biaggi[1], and Riccardo Roveda[4]

[1] Università degli Studi di Milano-Bicocca, Milan, Italy
arcelli@disco.unimib.it, a.biaggi1@campus.unimib.it
[2] CA Technologies, Barcelona, Spain
[3] University of Oslo, Oslo, Norway
antonio.martini@ifi.uio.no
[4] Alten Italia, Milano, Italy
riccardo.roveda@alten.it

Abstract. Architectural technical debt can have a huge impact on software maintainability and evolution. Hence, different architectural violations, detected as architectural smells, need to be identified and refactored. In this paper, we conducted a multiple case-study on several architectural smells detected in four industrial projects. We conducted an in-depth investigation with a questionnaire, interviews and thorough inspection of the code with the practitioners. We evaluated the negative impact of the technical debt detected by the architectural smells, their difficulty to be refactored and the usefulness of the detection tool. The results show that practitioners appreciated the help of automatic detection, and that they prioritize refactoring architectural debt that causes more negative impact despite the higher refactoring effort.

1 Introduction

Architectural Technical Debt (ATD) can have a huge negative impact on software maintainability and evolution. In a recent survey [1], more than 250 practitioners report that the average time wasted because of the presence of Technical Debt accounts for 37% of the whole development time. From the same study, it is also clear that ATD generates the most negative impact.

ATD is regarded as suboptimal solutions in the architecture of a product. A large number of software components that are too interdependent can be considered as an example of ATD. Suboptimal solutions can cause a negative impact, in the form of extra effort, when maintaining or evolving the project. For example, a component that has a lot of dependencies to many other components, would have ripple effects when changed: every time a bug is fixed or a new functionality is added, the practitioners need extra effort. When this, or other sorts of negative impact, occur, they represent the *interest* of the ATD.

© Springer Nature Switzerland AG 2018
C. E. Cuesta et al. (Eds.): ECSA 2018, LNCS 11048, pp. 320–335, 2018.
https://doi.org/10.1007/978-3-030-00761-4_21

Some ATD can be automatically detected, thanks to identification tools analyzing source code [2–4]. More in particular, existing tools recognize Architectural Smells (AS) [5,6], or else anti-patterns present in the architecture of the project. These patterns can be identified, for instance, by analyzing the dependency graph of the project. An AS is usually a *symptom* of the presence of ATD, and detecting AS can help developers and architects identifying ATD.

Finally, there is a cost associated with the removal of ATD, which is regarded as the *principal* of Technical Debt. ATD is removed by paying the principal in term of time for refactoring the code. The main reason to repay the principal, and to refactor ATD, is to avoid paying its interest [7].

In summary, it is critical to detect ATD, but also to prioritize it by understanding its interest and principal. Although some tools are able to detect AS (and therefore pointing at the possible presence of ATD), there are no studies on what negative impact and cost of refactoring are associated to such ATD and how practitioners prioritize ATD revealed through AS.

Given the previous motivations, in this study we aim at answering the following RQs:

- RQ 1: How do AS help practitioners in identifying ATD?
- RQ 2: How do practitioners prioritize ATD revealed through AS?
- RQ 2.1: How is the AS's negative impact (interest) perceived by the practitioners?
- RQ 2.2: What is the refactoring cost (principal) of AS perceived by the practitioners?

By answering RQ1, we aim at understanding if AS are useful to automatically identify ATD in industrial projects. Answering RQ2 means answering the combination of RQ2.1 and RQ2.2: understanding what negative impact is generated by the ATD and what cost of refactoring is required. This would help identifying which AS are more critical for the practitioners to prioritize.

In summary, with this case-study, we make a first step towards understanding how practitioners can semi-automatically detect and prioritize ATD.

The paper is organized through the following sections: in Sect. 2, we present related works; in Sect. 3, we describe the design of the case study, while in Sect. 4, we present the results; in Sect. 5, we discuss the results with respect to the RQs; in Sect. 6, we outline the threats to validity and finally in Sect. 7 we draw our conclusions.

2   Related Work

To the best of our knowledge, no studies have been conducted on identifying and prioritizing ATD using architectural smells. A recent paper [8] reports a comparative case-study on a component modularization, analyzing the negative impact saved by reworking a single instance of Architectural Debt. The study also reports an ad-hoc measurement project to detect the ATD, but it does not assess AS and does not compare several projects.

Several studies on *code smells* have been conducted in collaboration with practitioners, but not on *architectural smells*. An exploratory survey on code smells has been performed by Yamashita et al. [9]: their results showed that a large proportion of developers did not know about code smells. Soh et al. [10] conducted a study where professionals were hired to perform maintenance tasks on functionally equivalent Java projects in order to assess whether code smells affect maintenance activities. Another empirical study on understanding maintenance problems related to code smells, has been done by Yamashita [11]. Palomba et al. [12] conducted a study on developer's perception of the nature and severity of code smells.

3   Research Design

We conducted a multiple case-study in a large, international company located in Sweden. In particular, we automatically analyzed four projects and we assessed the output with the practitioners responsible for the development and maintenance of such projects.

3.1   Case-Study Design

We designed an embedded, multiple case-study, according to the guidelines in [13]. Our unit of analysis was a project developed by the organization. We conducted an in-depth analysis of four software projects of the same company, described in Sect. 3.2. The investigation included a mix of quantitative and qualitative methods, which is highly recommended in case-studies [13], where it is crucial to reach a detailed understanding of complex systems, such as large software projects.

The objectives of the case-study were:

1. automatically identify the AS in the industrial projects (RQ1)
2. evaluate the output in terms of negative impact (RQ2.1) and cost of refactoring (RQ2.2), to prioritize the ATD.

To identify the AS, we used Arcan [5], a tool for architectural smell detection described in Sect. 3.3. We decided to use Arcan for: reproducibility purposes since the tool is fully available online, it has been previously validated and the formulas used to identify the smells are well known. This allows other researchers to reproduce this study in other organizations and compare the results with ours.

To answer RQ1 and RQ2, for each project, we performed the following steps:

- We conducted a meeting with the team to understand the project.
- The code was analyzed using Arcan. A sample of the detected AS was then selected to be further assessed. We selected 22 AS since understanding in-depth architectural issues, their negative impact and their cost of refactoring was quite time consuming for the practitioners. This did not allow us to evaluate a larger number of AS. However, 22 cases is a reasonable number considering the kind of in-depth analysis that was performed. In particular,

we extracted the AS of three different kinds in a balanced number for each project. We chose the ones that were considered the most critical, according to Arcan's severity measure (see Sect. 3.3). This was done to focus on AS that would be more probably regarded as problematic by the practitioners.

– We conducted a group interview with the team responsible for the analyzed project. We selected participants who had high experience and a higher knowledge of the project. The interview lasted, on average, two to three hours, and included the following activities:

1. First, we introduced Arcan and the AS to the practitioners. We carefully presented the AS types and we explained how they were calculated (including formulas) and what they were expected to reveal.
2. Then, we showed a graphical representation of the smell in the form of a graph, rendered with Neo4J[1], which visualized the involved classes, packages and dependencies.
3. We asked the developers to identify the architectural issue related to the selected AS. In order to avoid speculations, we asked the practitioners to navigate the source code and to share the screen with the researchers and with the other interviewees.
4. Once the architectural issue related to the AS was identified, we conducted an assessment according to the objectives defined in our RQs. In particular, we used the questionnaire described in Sect. 3.4. Such questionnaire was divided in four parts: (1) understanding if the considered smell was pointing at a critical underlying ATD and if it was known (2) assessing the negative impact experienced and estimated by the practitioners. In order to do so, we used a method [14], empirically evaluated, to quantify the negative impact of Technical Debt; (3) assessing the costs and steps necessary for refactoring the AS; (4) understanding what was the current process to evaluate quality and what additional value would the automatic tool give the practitioners.

3.2 Analyzed Projects

The analyzed projects were developed by the same company and they were written in Java: they had different size but they operated in the same field of Product Data Management. A brief description of the projects is outlined in Table 1. The interviewees were nine, two for projects B, C and D and three for project A.

3.3 Data Collection - Automatic Detection of as with Arcan

Arcan [5] is a tool for architectural smell detection in Java projects. An architectural smell can derive from commonly used architectural decisions, intentional or not, that negatively impact internal software quality [15] with large effects on software maintainability [16].

---

[1] https://neo4j.com/.

Table 1. Analyzed industrial projects and architectural smells

Name	Description	Metrics		Architectural Smells				
		NoP	NoC	UD	HL	Class CD	Package CD	AS
A	Product Data Management (PDM)	269	10171	476	1	199	31	707
B	After market	240	7261	98	0	7	6	111
C	Audit project	220	3250	34	1	31	8	74
D	Warehouse management project	166	3067	53	0	49	7	109

Legenda: NoP: Number of Packages, NoC: Number of Classes, Unstable Dependency (UD), Hub-Like Dependency (HL), Cyclic Dependency (CD), Total Architectural smells (AS).

In this study, we considered the following three architectural smells adequately validated in [5,17]:

- **Unstable Dependency (UD):** describes a subsystem (component) that depends on other subsystem that are less stable than itself, with a possible ripple effect of changes in the project.
- **Hub-Like Dependency (HL):** occurs when an abstraction has (outgoing and ingoing) dependencies with a large number of other abstractions.
- **Cyclic Dependency (CD):** refers to a subsystem (component) that is involved in a chain of relations that break the desirable acyclic nature of a subsystems dependency structure. The subsystems involved in a dependency cycle can be hardly released, maintained or reused in isolation. Arcan detects this smell according to different shapes [18].

Moreover, Arcan estimates the *Severity* of each architectural smell [19] according to the values of the metrics used for the AS detection. A *Severity-Score*(AS_k) is evaluated for each instance of AS and according to each type of AS in order to evaluate the criticality of the smell. In our study with the practitioners, we selected the AS instances with the highest Severity, according to each type of AS.

In this work we have considered the above three AS since these AS are detected by an available tool such as Arcan and they are based on dependency issues which certainly represent relevant sources of possible architectural debt. Since this kind of smells do not represent the only source of architectural debt, we will consider in the future other categories of architectural smells. We focused our attention on architectural smells and not on code smells [20], also if some code smells such as for example the God Class smell [21] can have an impact at architectural level and hence it can be considered an architectural smell.

3.4   Data Collection - Survey with Practitioners

The questionnaire carried out during the interviews is reported in Table[2] in [22]. We used the survey tool Google Forms. We asked the practitioners to fill in a form (the same) for each AS.

---

[2] For space reason, it is available at https://drive.google.com/file/d/160TA9Q9jUI UpTBp-Wg7zu87elVa3y1qr/view?usp=sharing.

Identifying Architectural Debt via Architectural Smells (RQ1). We started asking if the analyzed AS was related to a critical architectural issue (ATD) (Q1.1). Only the ones considered as high priority issues were then further analyzed. This was done because we wanted to obtain more in-depth analysis rather than more sub-cases of smells, to better understand the details of the ATD. Then, we asked if the practitioners were already aware of the AS before it was revealed during the interview: this was done to understand if the output of the tool increased the awareness of the practitioners.

Architectural Smells Impact (RQ2.1). This part of the survey aimed at assessing the negative impact of the AS (Table in [22]). The question from 2.1 to 2.6 were adapted from the seven factors reported in [14]. In their paper, Martini et al. carry out an evaluation of these factors and report them as necessary and important for assessing the negative impact of Technical Debt. The assessment of the factors was adjusted, transforming the specific values used in [14] into a generic agreement Likert scale. Although this meant reducing the precision of the assessment, in this study we were interested in assessing a higher number of AS, and we therefore opted for a simplified set of questions. The factors and related questions in [22] are:

- **Reduced Development Speed.** If the speed is reduced, the interest of the ATD is hindering evolvability and maintainability of the system (Q2.1)
- **Bugs related to the TD item.** If many bugs are generated from the ATD, this greatly affects the maintainability of the system and the time wasted to fix bugs instead of developing new features (Q2.2).
- **Other qualities compromised.** There are several qualities that can be affected by ATD, as shown in [7]. Here we used the ones suggested in the ISO standard [23] but excluding maintainability and evolvability (as they are already covered by the previous factors), (Q2.3).
- **Users affected.** ATD might not involve a large part of the system, but can still affect a large number of developers. In this case, the extra cost of the interest would be multiplied by all the "victims" (Q2.4).
- **Frequency of the issue.** The more frequent the negative impact occurs, the worse the interest (Q2.5).
- **Future growth of interest.** To understand the overall negative impact of TD, it is important to assess the current negative impact (already covered by Q2.1–2.5), but we need to understand its future growth [7] as well (Q2.6).
- **Other extra costs.** There might be other context-dependent extra costs to be considered when assessing the interest (Q2.7).
- **Spread in the system.** The larger the portion of the system affected by the TD, the more ripple effects the interest might have on the organization and on the newly added code. This factor was already covered by the Arcan analysis and was included in the selection criteria according to the severity of the smell.

Finally, we asked an overall assessment of the negative impact associated with the AS (Q2.8). The correlation analysis supports the reliability of the chosen method. Such sanity check is explained with more details in Sect. 4.2.

Architectural Smells Refactoring (RQ2.2). The second part focused on refactoring the architectural smell under analysis (Q3.1–3.4). First, we asked what strategy the practitioners would use to remove the smell (Q3.1). Then, we asked an estimation of how much time would be required to remove the smell (Q3.2). We agreed about the possible thresholds with the Chief Architect before the investigation. The thresholds were based on what the companies would consider *Low effort* and *High effort*. The next question aimed at understanding if the refactoring would create negative side effects (Q3.3). In fact, refactoring ATD might optimize one aspect of the system, but it could negatively affect other qualities [24].

Architectural Smells Prioritization (RQ2). We asked the overall priority that the practitioners would give to refactoring the ATD detected by the AS (Q3.4). In particular, we asked the practitioners to consider all the factors assessed so far, including questions 2.1–2.8 and 3.1–3.3. The aim was to understand how the negative impact and cost of refactoring affected the priority given by the practitioners.

Arcan Evaluation to Identify ATD (RQ1). This part included general questions on Arcan, the detected smells and the use of software quality assessment tools during the development process, questions 4.1–4.7 (see Table [22]). The aim of these questions was to collect feedback from practitioners when detecting ATD by identifying architectural smells. In particular, we wanted to understand if the current state of the art on detecting AS would help the practitioners in managing their ATD. We asked for *a)* the difficulties emerged by using Arcan, *b)* the participants' past experiences using software analysis tools, *c)* quality index computation, *d)* estimate which are the most or least important type of architectural smells and *e)* evaluate if they are interested in using a new architectural debt index.

4   Results

Architectural Smells Selection. Table 1 shows the AS found by Arcan in the four industrial projects. As we can see, we had a large amount of Unstable Dependencies (UD). We found only two Hub-like Dependencies (HL), one in project A and one in project C. We also found many Cyclic Dependencies; more at class level (CCD) than at package level (PCD). Given the high amount of some smells (CD and UD) found in the projects, we had to select some AS instances from each category and for each project. For HL, we selected the two instances that we detected, while for UD, CCD and PCD we selected the instances with high severity according to Arcan. After this selection, we obtained the smells of Table 2a. Although Arcan shows the graph with the dependencies and the packages involved in a smell, it was difficult for the practitioners to easily navigate the results for the Package Cyclic Dependency smell, which were thus removed from the analysis.

4.1   Architectural Smells Identification (RQ1)

First, the practitioners assessed whether the AS was pointing to critical ATD issues, causing an increase of technical debt, or not. (Q1.1). In Table 2a, we can see the results of this first screening: on the "Discussed" column we report the number of smells that were initially discussed, while, on the "Problematic" column, we report the number of smells that were recognized as real problems.

From this analysis, we can see that **50% of the AS were considered problematic**, or else related to the presence of ATD. From the qualitative analysis, it is possible to better understand the reasons for the AS that were not considered related to ATD. One of the causes for this result was the kind of software that was assessed. For example, in project A, several Cyclic Dependencies were created by callbacks from anonymous classes in GUI components. When discussed with the practitioners, they clearly stated that *"On the Java server, you would never have this kind of stuff, but here it's kind of natural"*. Callbacks for event listeners in the GUI components could not be easily replaced, and therefore the developers did not recognize CDs as problematic in those specific cases, but rather as a necessary solution. This leads to an interesting context-dependent finding: CDs might not need to be reported when analyzing GUI components.

The few HLs were very well understood and were recognized right away as issues, even without navigating the code.

On the other hand, UDs were not easily understood by the practitioners: it was difficult for them to relate to the concept of Unstable Dependency, and they often disagreed on it being a problem. On the contrary, this kind of dependency was sometimes related to design patterns used on purpose. This is the case of an instance of Unstable Dependency in project A, that was caused by classes that applied a Strategy design pattern.

As a result of this first screening, we performed the subsequent assessment only on the AS listed as "Problematic" in Table 2a.

According to Question 1.2, only half of the problematic smells were known by the practitioners (Table 2a). This shows that the automatically reported AS improved the ATD awareness of the practitioners in 50% of the cases.

4.2   Architectural Smells Prioritization (RQ2)

Architectural Smells Impact (RQ2.1). The answers to questions 2.1–2.6, are shown in Fig. 1a. According to Question 2.1, in most of the cases the detected AS was associated with reduced development speed when adding functionalities, except for Unstable Dependencies: for this type of AS, practitioners seem to agree in 25% of the cases only.

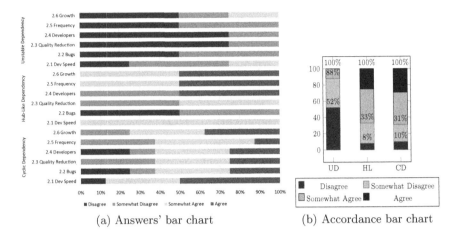

(a) Answers' bar chart   (b) Accordance bar chart

Fig. 1. Answers' for questions 2.1–2.6 (architectural smells impact)

Table 2. Extracted architectural smells results and average answers by architectural smell given to questions Q2.8, Q3.2, Q3.3 and Q3.4

(a) Extracted Smells

Projects	Type of Smell	Discussed	Problematic	Known Yes	No
A	UD	2	0	0	0
	HL	1	1	1	0
	CD	4	1	1	0
B	UD	2	1	0	1
	HL	0	0	0	0
	CD	3	2	0	2
C	UD	1	0	0	0
	HL	1	1	1	0
	CD	3	3	2	1
D	UD	2	1	0	1
	HL	0	0	0	0
	CD	3	1	1	0
	Total	**22**	**11**	**6**	**5**

(b) Answers by smell

Smell ID	Average of Q2.8	Q3.2	Q3.3	Q3.4
CD1	2	2	1	2
CD2	2	2	1	2
CD3	1	2	0	1
CD4	3	3.67	1.67	3
CD5	2.5	2.5	2.5	2
CD6	2.5	2.5	2.5	2
CD7	2.5	2.5	2.5	2
HUB1	1.5	2	0	1
HUB2	2	2	0	3
UD1	0	1	0	1
UD2	1	3	1.67	1
Total	**1.90**	**2.48**	**1.29**	**1.86**

As for Question 2.2, in more than 60% of the cases, the negative impact caused by Cyclic Dependencies is perceived as an increase of the number of bugs, while it does not happen for the other types of architectural smells.

Analyzing Question 2.3, some system qualities are negatively affected by the presence of Cyclic Dependencies in 60% of the cases and of Hub Like in 50%, while Unstable Dependency almost never affects them. Examples of other qualities affected by these ASs were mentioned in the interviews to be especially performance and testability.

According to Question 2.4, Unstable Dependencies seem to have an impact on technical debt that involves only few developers, while the impact seems to be higher for Hub-Like Dependencies (50% of the times) and Cyclic Dependencies (more than 60% of the cases).

As for Question 2.5, the developers perceive often the negative impact of Cyclic Dependencies in 60% of the cases, Hub Like Dependencies in all the cases and Unstable Dependencies in 50%.

According to Question 2.6, it is possible to assert that the impact will grow in the future, at least for every Hub-Like Dependencies and Cyclic Dependencies (75% of the times), but again it seems that we cannot assert the same for Unstable Dependencies.

In addition, Fig. 1b shows an analysis of the answers for each type of architectural smell, where each column represents the degree of accordance for the statements related to the negative impact of each smell.

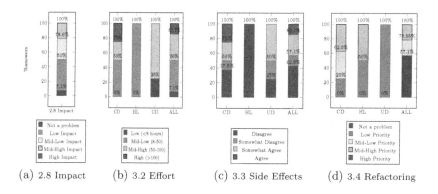

(a) 2.8 Impact   (b) 3.2 Effort   (c) 3.3 Side Effects   (d) 3.4 Refactoring

Fig. 2. Answer's for questions 2.8, 3.2–3.4

According to Question 2.7, architectural smells can also have other impacts and generate problems for writing test cases or fixing conflicts during merging, and, in a few cases, the problems associated to some architectural smells instances, as for example for Cyclic Dependencies, were already identified and added as technical tasks to the backlog to be solved in the next future.

Finally, analyzing the answers to Question 2.8 regarding the overall negative impact, 42.9% Low Impact, 21.4% Medium-Low Impact and 28.6% Medium-High Impact. Moreover, in 7% of the answers (Fig. 2a), the possible negative impact of the AS was not a problem (or negligible).

Architectural Smells Refactoring (RQ2.2). According to Question 3.1, in most of the cases the suggested refactoring requires the split of a class to reduce the responsibility, sometimes to move some logic from a class to another, or to move some logic by creating a new class.

Analyzing Question 3.2, the time for refactoring AS is more than 8 man hours for 93% of the cases and in 14% of the cases, exceeds 100 man hours (Fig. 2b Question 3.2). This was the case for example of a Cyclic Dependency

330   A. Martini et al.

identified in project D. Performing refactoring of this instance of AS, according to the practitioners, would involve reviewing the architecture of a main part of the system and reimplementing the logic revisiting the patterns used in this context.

According to Question 3.3 in 60% of the cases practitioners seem to agree that conducting refactoring would not create side effects.

According to Question 3.4, practitioners assigned *Low priority* to 100% of the UD instances, 50% to the HL and 25% to CD. They assigned higher priorities to the other instances of CD and HL (Fig. 2d Question 3.4). The results on refactoring have been deeply investigated in the following section in order to understand the relationships between the aspects covered by the questions.

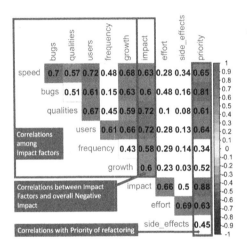

Fig. 3. Correlation analysis among the variables related to impact factors, overall negative impact, side effects, effort and refactoring priority. The white cells represent non-significant correlations (p-value > 0.05)

Correlation Analysis on the Prioritization of ATD. In order to understand the relationships among cost, impact and overall prioritization of ATD, we ran Pearson correlation tests on the agreement scores. In particular, we compared questions 2.1–2.6 (impact factors) 2.8 (overall negative impact), and 3.2–3.4 (effort, refactoring side effects, and overall refactoring priority), shown in Fig. 3. The scores in the white cells represent non-significant results (we set p-value < 0.05 for significance), so we discuss the red cells only.

First, we can see how there is a medium-strong and significant correlation between all the impact factors (2.1–2.6) and the overall negative impact. This confirms that all the chosen factors were contributing to the developers' perceived negative impact, but none of them seems redundant. This finding also confirms that the chosen method, to assess the negative impact of ATD, can be considered sound.

We can observe how the refactoring effort has a strong correlation with the side effects of refactoring the AS. This makes sense, as the most side effects the refactoring would generate, the more costly it would be to remove the ATD.

The strongest correlation is between the priority of refactoring and the overall negative impact (0.88). This shows that the negative impact, perceived by the practitioners, is the main driver for the prioritization of refactoring. This means that, to prioritize ATD, practitioners need to know its impact (or else its interest). It is finally interesting to observe that there is a medium-strong *positive correlation* between the effort and the assigned priority. Although this

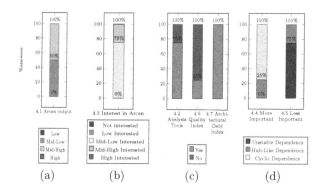

Fig. 4. Answers' stacked charts for questions 4.1–4.7

is counterintuitive (more cost would suggest less priority), this finding implies that practitioners would prefer to refactor ATD that generates negative impact despite its higher cost of refactoring.

Architectural Smell Detection Evaluation (RQ1). According to Question 4.1, half of the practitioners found Arcan's output quite difficult to understand without using the graph generated by Neo4j. According to Question 4.2, 75% of the practitioners make use of software analysis tools during development activity: in particular, they used SonarQube (Fig. 4a Question 4.2); for Question 4.3 all the practitioners expressed at least a *Mid-Low* interest in using Arcan as support during the development of a project (Fig. 4a).

As for Question 4.4, 75 % of the practitioners found that Cyclic Dependency is the most important smell to detect, while (Question 4.5) Unstable Dependency seems to be the less important to detect (Fig. 4d). Lastly (Question 4.6), 75% of the practitioners use an index to measure code quality (Fig. 4a) and, according to Question 4.7, all the practitioners seemed interested in using an architectural debt index based on architectural smells detection (Fig. 4a).

5   Discussion

We discuss the results in relation to each RQs.

RQ 1: How do AS help practitioners in identifying ATD? Given the results outlined in the previous sections, we can assert that AS detection increases awareness on ATD as (1) it highlights issues that should be considered as real problems but were not known according to practitioners and (2) in the few cases where the problem was known, it provided additional unbiased evidence of its presence.

RQ 2.1: How is the architectural smells' negative impact perceived by the practitioners? The results obtained in the analysis suggest that Unstable Dependency is the smell that causes less negative impact compared to the other smells considered in this analysis. In fact, practitioners do not consider this smell as a real problem in most of the cases. Hub-Like Dependency is the one that gives a higher perception of the negative impact and whose effect will grow worse in the future, since all the answers to the corresponding questions (2.6 and 2.8) are "agree" or "somewhat agree".

The smell that seems to be more impactful is Cyclic Dependency, although some of them were not considered real problems, meaning that they don't represent technical debt according to the practitioners.

In conclusion, the detection of these two smells helps practitioners. While the few HL Dependencies were considered a problem, CD need to be better filtered before being a reliable indicator of a serious presence of ATD.

RQ 2.2: What is the refactoring cost of AS? which kind of AS cost more to remove? Cyclic Dependency is the smell that requires more time to be refactored, and the one that creates more side effects during refactoring. For every type of smell, refactoring requires several hours to be performed, in some cases, for Cyclic Dependencies, more 100 man hours. On the contrary, Hub-Like Dependency is the architectural smell that requires a Mid-Low number of hours for refactoring without having any side effect.

RQ 2: How do practitioners prioritize ATD revealed through AS? Combining the results of RQ2.1 and RQ2.2, we can say that Hub-Like Dependencies seem to be the most convenient smell to detect and to refactor (best ratio cost/benefits). Cyclic Dependencies are also important, but need to be better filtered, because some are considered as a necessary coupling, and some have a really high cost of refactoring and therefore it is not clear if they should be prioritized for their removal or not. Finally, Unstable Dependencies are perhaps the less useful smell to detect and refactor.

6   Limitations and Threats to Validity

Validity threats for case studies are proposed in [13].

As for construct validity, there is a possibility that the practitioners misinterpreted what the AS represents or what we asked in the questionnaire. However, we thoroughly mitigated these threats as explained in the research design, with previous workshops explaining the AS.

As for internal validity, it is unlikely that the negative impact reported by the practitioners would be affected by factors that are not the AS, as we were careful to inquire the main causes of negative impact when investigating the code. The correlation analysis do not imply causality per se: however, this threat is mitigated by the construction of the questionnaire and by further qualitative evidence collected, which supports causality.

There is a threat to external validity. The case-study has been conducted in a single organization, although we selected four quite different projects, and a limited amount of AS were in-depth studied.

As for reliability, two researchers were present during the investigation, while the results were checked by multiple researchers. Furthermore, the study is fully reproducible. The practitioners might have been biased when recognizing the negative impact of the code, due to peer pressure. However, they were capable of recognizing several harmful smells.

The results are based on practitioners' experience and perception. This means that the real cost, impact, and the consequent optimal prioritization of ATD might differ from the one reported here. However, practitioners are the ones suffering by ATD and are the final users of AS, so their perception is of utmost importance to understand how to manage ATD using AS.

7   Conclusion and Future Developments

In this paper, we performed a case study within a large software company, to understand how practitioners identify and prioritize Architectural Technical Debt using automatically detected architectural smells. Four industrial projects have been analyzed, and a sample of the detected AS has been thoroughly inspected by the projects' practitioners to find the causes of the issues, and to assess their negative impact and refactoring costs based on their perception and experience. We found which AS pointed at the most harmful Architectural Technical Debt (RQ1), which ones have more impact (RQ2.1), which ones cost more to refactor (RQ2.2) and which ones are, overall, more convenient to detect and prioritize (RQ2).

From the combined results, we can conclude that using AS to identify and prioritize ATD was considered useful: the tool helped identifying half of the problems that were not previously known by the practitioners, and provided evidence for the known ones. However, some AS were not considered high priority, which helps researchers to further improve and filter the automatically revealed AS. Cyclic Dependency was the AS with the worst impact but also the most expensive to refactor, while Hub Like Dependency has also a similar strong negative impact but seems to be the most convenient to detect and to refactor (less costly). On the contrary, Unstable Dependency was not perceived as an issue.

In the future, we plan to perform new case studies in other industrial domains and companies. We aim to better explore the refactoring cost of the smells to improve the prioritization of the smells to be removed first. According to this aspect we would like to ask practitioners to evaluate the usefulness of a new Architectural Debt Index [25], which allows to identify and assess the overall architectural debt of a project by taking into account the severity of each architectural smell. The index can be used to evaluate the most critical parts and to monitor the evolution of the architectural debt during the project history.

Finally, we aim to analyze and detect through Arcan other categories of architectural smells other than those related to dependency issues, such as smells related to the interface (Ambiguous Interface, Redundant Interface and Unstable Interface [26]) or smells related to performance or security issues.

Acknowledgments. The research leading to these results has received funding from the European Union's Horizon 2020 research and innovation programme under the Marie Skłodowska-Curie grant agreement No. 712949 (TECNIOspring PLUS) and from the Agency for Business Competitiveness of the Government of Catalonia. We thank Chalmers University of Technology and University of Gothenburg for the support.

References

1. Besker, T., Martini, A., Bosch, J.: The pricey bill of technical debt: when and by whom will it be paid? In: 2017 IEEE International Conference on Software Maintenance and Evolution (ICSME), pp. 13–23, September 2017
2. Cast Software: Cast (2018). http://www.castsoftware.com/Products
3. Headway Software Technologies: Structure101 (2018). http://structure101.com/products/
4. hello2morrow: Sonargraph (2018). https://www.hello2morrow.com/products/sonargraph
5. Arcelli Fontana, F., Pigazzini, I., Roveda, R., Tamburri, D.A., Zanoni, M., Nitto, E.D.: Arcan: a tool for architectural smells detection. In: International Conference Software Architecture (ICSA 2017) Workshops, Sweden, Gothenburg, pp. 282–285 (2017)
6. Kazman, R., et al.: A case study in locating the architectural roots of technical debt. In: Proceedings of the 37th IEEE International Conference on Software Engineering (ICSE 2015), vol. 2, pp. 179–188 (2015)
7. Martini, A., Bosch, J.: An empirically developed method to aid decisions on architectural technical debt refactoring: AnaConDebt. In: Proceedings of the 38th International Conference on Software Engineering, ICSE 2016, Austin, TX, USA, 14–22 May 2016, Companion Volume, pp. 31–40 (2016)
8. Martini, A., Sikander, E., Madlani, N.: A semi-automated framework for the identification and estimation of Architectural Technical Debt: a comparative case-study on the modularization of a software component. Inf. Softw. Technol. **93**(Suppl. C), 264–279 (2018)
9. Yamashita, A.F., Moonen, L.: Do developers care about code smells? An exploratory survey. In: 20th Working Conference on Reverse Engineering, WCRE 2013, Germany, pp. 242–251 (2013)
10. Soh, Z., Yamashita, A., Khomh, F., Guéhéneuc, Y.: Do code smells impact the effort of different maintenance programming activities? In: IEEE 23rd International Conference on Software Analysis, Evolution, and Reengineering, SANER 2016, Suita, Osaka, Japan, 14–18 March 2016, vol. 1, pp. 393–402 (2016)
11. Yamashita, A.: Assessing the capability of code smells to explain maintenance problems: an empirical study combining quantitative and qualitative data. Empir. Softw. Eng. **19**(4), 1111–1143 (2014)
12. Palomba, F., Bavota, G., Penta, M.D., Oliveto, R., Lucia, A.D.: Do they really smell bad? A study on developers' perception of bad code smells. In: 30th IEEE International Conference on Software Maintenance and Evolution, Victoria, BC, Canada, 29 September–3 October 2014, pp. 101–110 (2014)
13. Runeson, P., Höst, M.: Guidelines for conducting and reporting case study research in software engineering. Empir. Softw. Eng. **14**(2), 131–164 (2009)
14. Martini, A., Bosch, J.: The magnificent seven: towards a systematic estimation of technical debt interest. In: Proceedings of the XP 2017 Scientific Workshops, XP 2017, pp. 7:1–7:5. ACM, New York (2017)

15. Lippert, M., Roock, S.: Refactoring in Large Software Projects: Performing Complex Restructurings Successfully. Wiley, Hoboken (2006)
16. Macia, I., Arcoverde, R., Cirilo, E., Garcia, A., von Staa, A.: Supporting the identification of architecturally-relevant code anomalies. In: Proceedings of the 28th IEEE International Conference on Software Maintenance (ICSM 2012), Italy, pp. 662–665. IEEE (2012)
17. Arcelli Fontana, F., Pigazzini, I., Roveda, R., Zanoni, M.: Automatic detection of instability architectural smells. In: Proceedings of the 32nd International Conference on Software Maintenance and Evolution (ICSME 2016), Raleigh, North Carolina, USA, ERA Track. IEEE, October 2016
18. Al-Mutawa, H.A., Dietrich, J., Marsland, S., McCartin, C.: On the shape of circular dependencies in java programs. In: Proceedings of 23rd Australian Software Engineering Conference (ASWEC 2014), Sydney, Australia, pp. 48–57. IEEE, April 2014
19. Roveda, R.: Identifying and evaluating software architecture erosion. Ph.D. thesis, Università degli studi di Milano - Bicocca, May 2012
20. Fowler, M.: Refactoring: Improving the Design of Existing Code. Addison-Wesley, Boston (1999)
21. Lanza, M., Marinescu, R.: Object-Oriented Metrics in Practice. Springer, Heidelberg (2006). https://doi.org/10.1007/3-540-39538-5
22. ESSeRE Lab: Questionnarie table (2018). https://drive.google.com/file/d/160TA9Q9jUIUpTBp-Wg7zu87elVa3y1qr/view?usp=sharing
23. ISO - International Organization for Standardization: System and software quality models (2015)
24. Arcelli Fontana, F., Roveda, R., Vittori, S., Metelli, A., Saldarini, S., Mazzei, F.: On evaluating the impact of the refactoring of architectural problems on software quality. In: Proceedings of the Scientific Workshop Proceedings of XP 2016, Edinburgh, Scotland, UK, 24 May 2016, p. 21 (2016)
25. Roveda, R., Arcelli Fontana, F., Pigazzini, I., Zanoni, M.: Towards an architectural debt index. In: Proceedings of the Euromicro Conference on Software Engineering and Advanced Applications (SEAA), Technical Debt track, Prague, Czech Republic. IEEE, August 2018
26. Garcia, J., Popescu, D., Edwards, G., Medvidovic, N.: Identifying architectural bad smells. In: CSMR 2009, Germany, pp. 255–258. IEEE (2009)

Software Migration and Architecture Evolution with Industrial Platforms: A Multi-case Study

Konstantinos Plakidas[1]([⊠]), Daniel Schall[2], and Uwe Zdun[1]

[1] Software Architecture Research Group, University of Vienna, Vienna, Austria
{konstantinos.plakidas,uwe.zdun}@univie.ac.at
[2] Siemens Corporate Technology, Vienna, Austria
daniel.schall@siemens.com

Abstract. The software industry increasingly needs to consider architecture evolution in the context of industrial ecosystem platforms. These environments feature a large number third-party offerings with a high variety and complexity of design and technology options. The software architects working on platform migration and in-platform evolution scenarios in such environments require support to find and utilize optimal offerings, ensure design compatibility with various technical and non-technical constraints, and optimize architectures. Based on a multi-case study of three industrial cases, we have derived an architecture knowledge model that provides a basis for supporting software architects in platform migration and in-platform evolution scenarios.

1 Introduction

A common scenario in modern software industry practice is the migration and architectural evolution of legacy systems, usually developed inside a single organization, to cloud platforms. This evolution process typically aims to utilize the various offerings of these platforms, as well as incorporating third-party products from related software ecosystems or integrating devices as part of the Internet of Things (IoT). Unlike the familiar contours of in-house development, architects find themselves confronted with a new production environment that offers a large number and variety of offerings and deployment options, and that is highly dynamic. As a result, industrial platform migration and in-platform evolution is an increasingly challenging undertaking [9].

For the software architects involved in this process, this presents three major challenges: the discovery of a new target environment's parameters (e.g., available technologies, offerings, and constraints); the restructuring and optimization of an application for the target environment; and the subsequent management of its structure across a lifecycle that can span several platforms and deployment configurations. In each case, the architect's decisions are heavily dependent on context—best practices for a specific application domain, available products

© Springer Nature Switzerland AG 2018
C. E. Cuesta et al. (Eds.): ECSA 2018, LNCS 11048, pp. 336–343, 2018.
https://doi.org/10.1007/978-3-030-00761-4_22

and technologies, relevant regulations, desired qualities, and so on. All these constantly change over time and across different use cases and platforms.

Ideally, this context should be captured as knowledge, kept up-to-date, and made available for use by the architects during the decision process. While there are several approaches in the literature on capturing knowledge about architecture evolution decisions [2], they have not yet found widespread adoption in practice, and the community is actively researching on how to make them more lightweight and easier to use [8]. In practice, the evolution process is labor-intensive, error-prone and time-consuming, especially in an enterprise-level application that involves multiple teams, constraints, and features developed over longer periods of time.

This study aims to contribute towards filling this gap by providing a lightweight and reusable approach that enables architects to perform an exploratory analysis of their options in a structured manner. The focus lies not on detailed implementation, but on providing "just enough architecture" [3] for the broad outlines and main design decisions of a project—e.g., programming languages, technologies, architectures—that once taken are "costly to change" [8]. Based on three industrial system cases demanding significant architectural evolution, we performed a multi-case study to derive elements and relationships of an architecture knowledge model, which was then used to support software architects in platform migration and in-platform evolution scenarios.

The paper is structured as follows: Sect. 2 discusses related work. Next, Sect. 3 introduces our research method and the three industrial cases. Sect. 4 describes our approach, and Sect. 5 discusses the results and concludes the paper.

2   Related Work

Software architecture is expected to support the evolution of software systems to keep pace with the shifts in their technical and business environment [2,13]. Accordingly, correct understanding and representation of the architecture are fundamental for a systematic evolution process [13]. Research has produced a large number of patterns and architectural styles, which serve to address recurring design problems [7]; this has been extended to cover new paradigms such as cloud-based architectures [4,10] or microservices [6,16]. Nevertheless, research in the field is still far off from the ideal of "capturing architectural knowledge in a single [...] handbook, which codifies knowledge to make it widely available" [8], as the various approaches are isolated and fragmented. While valuable on their own, in practice many of the approaches require much input from the stakeholders and result in a "collection of documents." This is an overhead that people usually prove unwilling to invest in, especially if the value of the outcome is unclear. Our approach is intended to be a more light-weight alternative with regard to discovery and management of offerings which limits the decisions taken during the architecting process to only the relevant set of constraints. The decision space is limited to manageable proportions by providing only compatible options and their driving forces and consequences.

3   Study Design

The work reported in this paper follows a multi-case study research method. We followed the available guidelines for such case studies in industry [17] for the design of our study. The *research questions* we defined for this study are:

- **RQ1:** to investigate the minimal set of elements and relationships required by software architects to sufficiently represent and specify a software system at a relatively high abstraction level suitable for brownfield development
- **RQ2:** to investigate the minimal set of elements and relationships required to represent the contexts of in-platform evolution and platform migration
- **RQ3:** to investigate how the models resulting from RQ1 and RQ2 can be used to support architectural decisions.

The overall objective was to limit the effort in modelling (compared to existing methods such as [2]). The model must be detailed enough to represent the case study context, while generic enough to avoid overfitting. The main facilities offered by the model would be the management of knowledge, by creating a central knowledge model that can be used to represent any software product, and more importantly the exploitation of that knowledge, by exploiting the links between elements in a knowledge repository to select subsets based on specific criteria. This would allow the architect to browse for "suitable" offerings (i.e., having a desired set of functional and non-functional attributes) for each step of the evolution process; if such were not found, or were not available, the model should be able to provide suggestions for adaptation of existing offerings, or the development of new ones, by exploiting the knowledge base.

In our prior work, we performed a set of *comprehensive studies of the literature* on software architecture decision making [12], quality attributes in such decisions [12], and in software ecosystems [14]. In addition, for this work we exploratively studied the practitioner literature on migration practices and patterns in cloud and IoT platforms (e.g., [1,4,11,15]). As a result we (1) *hypothesised a minimum necessary set of model elements and relations*. Next we defined (2) a *case study protocol template* used for all cases (see [17]) and (3) *sought cases among industrial software systems* with sufficiently complex migration and evolution scenarios. We then (4) *selected three systems for which we could gain access to detailed documentation and key stakeholders*: a Geospatial Analytics System, a Water Management System, and an Edge-Cloud Analytics System. For space reasons, we can not report on them in detail. A case study protocol and detailed model description can be found in a technical report[1]. For each case we first *consulted the available documentation and plans for migration*, and then *consulted architects of the system to close any gaps in our understanding*. We used coding techniques and the constant comparison method borrowed from Grounded Theory [5] to *code the qualitative data* for context elements and relations. After the data had been coded in the first case, we formally modelled the whole case using the resulting model, then applied the same method to the second system (and

---

[1] http://doi.org/10.5281/zenodo.1288459.

after that in the same manner the third system) and thereby iteratively refined the codes, model elements, and relations. Next, we re-modelled the first system (and after that the second and the third system) with the resulting model and resolved any arising inconsistencies. The result is (5) a *semiformal model for platform migration and in-platform evolution*, and three derived case models.

4 Migration and Architecture Evolution

4.1 Evolution Attributes and Process

An application can be considered as comprising its concrete realization (architecture, software components, etc.), and an associated set of attributes (functional and non-functional requirements, etc.) and constraints (dependencies, licenses, legal limitations, etc.) that provide a context that describes and governs its function and usage. The two facets are interdependent: the introduction of a new software component affects the attributes, and predetermined attributes and constraints can affect which components are compatible in a design situation.

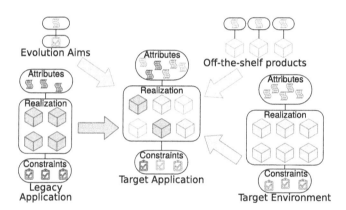

Fig. 1. Element sets involved in a software migration process (simplified). The target application results from a set of decisions trying to fulfil the attributes and constraints of the evolution aims while remaining compatible with the target environment. Legacy components, target environment offerings and off-the-shelf products are available for use as long as they satisfy these constraints.

Software evolution can then be described as the transformation of the specific realization with specific attributes of a *Legacy Application* $\mathcal{L}$ into a new realization with its own attributes, the *Target Application* $\mathcal{T}$. The latter is often deployed in a new *Target Environment* $\mathcal{E}$, as in the specific case of software migration. As shown in Fig. 1, $\mathcal{T}$ results from a mix of different element sets. The coonstraints will result from those carried over from $\mathcal{L}$, the constraints of $\mathcal{E}$, and whatever additional constraints our *Evolution Aims* $\mathcal{A}$ dictate. In addition, $\mathcal{A}$ and $\mathcal{L}$ provide a minimum set of attributes, that the application must realize.

The evolution process is then a search for components and configurations (realization) that are compatible with both the attributes and constraints sets of T. Depending on the context, this idealized view has to be modified: some of the sets may be empty, $\mathcal{A}$ may be minimally described, $\mathcal{L}$ may be insufficiently documented, etc. The relative experience and preferences of architects are also an unknown factor. As a result, the problems and choices that may emerge during the transformation process can not be anticipated beforehand.

Consequently, our focus has been reduced to a minimal core: a single evolution step, either moving (importing) the component from one environment to another, or adapting it (refactoring) to satisfy specific requirement(s). In a migration context, moving effectively copies a component from $\mathcal{L}$, or from some list of $\mathcal{O}$, and imports it into a new environment (T as deployed in $\mathcal{E}$). The presence of the import results in a set of mismatches with the constraints, attributes, and existing state of T, setting off a sequence of adaptation steps in what is in essence an experimentation cycle. If a satisfactory solution to each mismatch is found (or it is considered an affordable trade-off), the next component import from $\mathcal{L}$ takes place, gradually building up T. If the mismatches of a specific import cannot be resolved, then alternative equivalent elements can be imported and tested from the offerings of $\mathcal{E}$ or $\mathcal{O}$. The context of each adaptation decision is thus limited to the imported component and its immediate *operational environment*, and a concurrent adaptation of both the implementation and the attributes takes place, resulting in the final T.

4.2 Migration Scenarios and Model Attributes

Based on the finding from the previous sections, we examined three systems, each representing scenarios typically encountered in industry:

- Migrating a legacy monolithic system into a cloud platform, given a set of business, technical, and legal constraints
- Re-architecting a legacy monolithic system into a cloud-deployed microservice-based architecture
- Requirement-based dynamic selection and allocation of system components on a cloud-edge platform.

The three systems, as well as the resulting detailed model itself, are presented in more detail in the technical report (see footnote 1); here we only present an overview. The model comprises a generic *domain knowledge* representation model which includes five sets (*Capabilities, Applications, Architecture, Technology, Constraints*), and a *software description* model using the elements defined in the former to provide a concrete definition of software products. The main goal of our model is to limit the possible options presented to the architect to manageable levels. The *selection of suitable solutions*, which lies at the root of the trial-and-error approach described above, is carried out by matching individual attributes, either for compatibility (e.g., compatible interfaces or licenses, written in a programming language supported by $\mathcal{E}$) or to discover alternatives (e.g., products with the same functionality). The latter process can require traversing of the domain knowledge *type hierarchy* (e.g., the various categories of data bases or file systems for persistent storage functionality), or of the *versions of a specific product* (e.g., the versions of an ecosystem platform and packages supported).

The more attributes are matched, the narrower the resulting option set. In practice there are usually mismatches which have to be resolved either by resorting to close analogues, or to integrating solutions (e.g., Enterprise Integration Patterns or specific plugins and extensions) which can be used to "bridge" the operational environment of the component with the requirements being pursued. Using this matching approach, a component can be adapted to its new environment. Its external attributes (e.g., its functionality, external interfaces, implementation languages) then become attributes of the composite system. Conversely, since the only thing required to use a component are its external attributes (interfaces, functionality, constraints), *placeholder components* can be defined, whose exact implementation is left undefined. This means that a placeholder can either be dynamically instantiated by using one of multiple compatible solutions (e.g., a placeholder "SQL database"), be implemented by some third party to specification ("compatibility by design"), or can represent a wrapper for an otherwise non-compatible component.

Finally, the model provides concrete architectural guidance by associating attributes and constraints, as well as technologies or applications, with specific architecture patterns and strategies, as well as by indicating the (in)compatibility between patterns. From practical experience with using the model during the microservice-based re-architecting, we realized that the more inexperienced users are overwhelmed by the breadth of architectural options, showing that thearchitecture perspective on its own is unsuitable as an entry point to the design process, and that it had to be refined through combination with other constraints and attributes. This led to the creation of architecture templates, representing common configurations of patterns in combination with components types, functionalities, and constraints.

5 Discussion and Conclusions

Based on the data from a comprehensive literature study and practitioner reports, software evolution of three industrial case scenarios, and interaction with key stakeholders of these projects, we have derived a model for easing software architecture evolution decisions. The scenarios were used to evolve the model, as well as test and validate its functionality. Perforce, such a model operates on a number of assumptions that may not always exist in practice. We assume that a common language between stakeholders exists, so that the same term (e.g., a *Capability* or *Pattern*) will be commonly understood and used in the same way. Likewise, we assume that the descriptions provided to populate the knowledge repository and instanciate our models are accurate and up-to-date. A further problem, which is common to such approaches, is the analysis of the impact of, and tradeoffs between, multiple quality attributes. These are hard to quantify, and vary with context. Thus we can only present a rough ranking of attribute importance and impact, but it is left to the architect to evaluate them. Likewise, the cumulative impact of the individual decisions can only be assessed at the end of the evolution process. The model can support, but not replace the architect. Factors such as personal preferences, past experience, and existing commitments to some technology, can not be anticipated. Nevertheless, our experience working with the model shows that it provides a number of benefits. It creates a common, centrally managed, knowledge repository, which provides a consistent reference model and a framework that links software products, software architecture aspects, business requirements and constraints, and technologies, and allows the easy discovery of interrelations.

The model is also extensible, as new elements, domains, and views can be added easily, while maintaining the same structure. The recursive structure which the *software description* supports means that a variety of offerings can be represented and recomposed at will, with varying levels of detail depending on the context: from a basic template to a complete description. The ability to define templates enforcing consistency in certain key areas is fundamental for industrial ecosystems, and can be used to provide architectural guidance. Furthermore, although developed in the context of software migration, we believe that the model is in practice generalizable for all cases of architecture evolution from greenfield to brownfield, which has much the same requirements and involves the same elements.

Using the model first requires populating the knowledge repository. Though this process can be assisted by tools, it still represents a considerable investment of time and effort. This is an inherent disadvantage of all such approaches, but we believe that the resulting benefits, once this repository is established, outweigh the investment, especially from the view of a keystone organization that has to manage large collections of offerings, and ensure a minimum level of consistency and compliance among the various participants within an ecosystem. The model has the advantage of needing only a high-level description of its elements and features to work; it does not require a full-fledged architecture reconstruction. The full and accurate description of individual components can be deferred to a later time, if and when necessary for their further decomposition. We also expect that, in the context of large ecosystems, software products will share many common elements, encouraging frequent reuse of the generated models, or, analogous to our architecture templates, the creation of prototype applications or application modules. Working directly with the model is often not practical, as the number of attributes involved grows geometrically; this was most clearly seen in the WMS scenario, where the large pattern set had to be structured in pre-defined combinations to become usable. It is therefore our future research plan to realize a web-based decision support tool for the model.

Acknowledgments. This work was partially supported by FFG project DECO (no. 864707) and Austrian Science Fund (FWF) project ADDCompliance.

References

1. New whitepapers on cloud migration: Migrating your existing applications to the AWS cloud, November 2010. https://aws.amazon.com/blogs/aws/new-whitepaper-migrating-your-existing-applications-to-the-aws-cloud/

2. Capilla, R., Jansen, A., Tang, A., Avgeriou, P., Babar, M.A.: 10 years of software architecture knowledge management: practice and future. J. Syst. Softw. **116**, 191–205 (2016)

3. Fairbanks, G.H.: Just Enough Software Architecture. Marshall & Brainerd, Singapore (2010)

4. Fehling, C., Leymann, F., Retter, R., Schupeck, W., Arbitter, P.: Cloud Computing Patterns. Springer, Berlin (2014). https://doi.org/10.1007/978-3-7091-1568-8

5. Glaser, B., Strauss, A.: The Discovery of Grounded Theory. Aldine, Piscataway (1967)

6. Gupta, A.: Microservice design patterns, April 2015. http://blog.arungupta.me/microservice-design-patterns/

7. Harrison, N.B., Avgeriou, P., Zdun, U.: Using patterns to capture architectural decisions. IEEE Softw. **24**(4), 38–45 (2007)

8. Hohpe, G., Ozkaya, I., Zdun, U., Zimmermann, O.: The software architect's role in the digital age. IEEE Softw. **33**(6), 30–39 (2016)

9. Hwang, J., Huang, Y.W., Vukovic, M., Anerousis, N.: Enterprise-scale cloud migration orchestrator. In: 2015 IFIP/IEEE International Symposium on Integrated Network Management (IM), pp. 1002–1007, May 2015

10. Jamshidi, P., Pahl, C., Chinenyeze, S., Liu, X.: Cloud migration patterns: a multi-cloud service architecture perspective. In: Toumani, F., et al. (eds.) ICSOC 2014. LNCS, vol. 8954, pp. 6–19. Springer, Cham (2015). https://doi.org/10.1007/978-3-319-22885-3_2

11. Jamshidi, P., Pahl, C., Mendonça, N.C.: Pattern-based multi-cloud architecture migration. Softw.: Pract. Exp. **47**(9), 1159–1184 (2017)

12. Lytra, I.: Supporting reusable architectural design decisions. Ph.D. thesis, University of Vienna (2015)

13. Medvidovic, N., Taylor, R.N., Rosenblum, D.S.: An architecture-based approach to software evolution. In: Proceedings of the International Workshop on the Principles of Software Evolution, pp. 11–15 (1998)

14. Plakidas, K., Schall, D., Zdun, U.: Evolution of the R software ecosystem: metrics, relationships, and their impact on qualities. J. Syst. Softw. **132**, 119–146 (2017)

15. Reinfurt, L., Breitenbücher, U., Falkenthal, M., Leymann, F., Riegg, A.: Internet of Things patterns. In: Proceedings of the 21st European Conference on Pattern Languages of Programs, pp. 5:1–5:21. ACM, New York (2016)

16. Richardson, C.: Microservices.io. http://microservices.io/

17. Runeson, P., Host, M., Rainer, A., Regnell, B.: Case Study Research in Software Engineering: Guidelines and Examples. Wiley, Hoboken (2012)

Security and Data Architectures

Two Architectural Threat Analysis
Techniques Compared

Katja Tuma[1,2(✉)] and Riccardo Scandariato[1,2]

[1] Chalmers University of Technology, Gothenburg, Sweden
[2] University of Gothenburg, Gothenburg, Sweden
{katja.tuma,riccardo.scandariato}@cse.gu.se

Abstract. In an initial attempt to systematize the research field of architectural threat analysis, this paper presents a comparative study of two threat analysis techniques. In particular, the controlled experiment presented here compares two variants of Microsoft's STRIDE. The two variants differ in the way the analysis is performed. In one case, each component of the software system is considered in isolation and scrutinized for potential security threats. In the other case, the analysis has a wider scope and considers the security threats that might occur in a pair of interacting software components. The study compares the techniques with respect to their effectiveness in finding security threats (benefits) as well as the time that it takes to perform the analysis (cost). We also look into other human aspects which are important for industrial adoption, like, for instance, the perceived difficulty in learning and applying the techniques as well as the overall preference of our experimental participants.

Keywords: Empirical study · Secure software · Threat analysis
STRIDE

1 Introduction

After decades of research and knowledge transfer in the field of "security by design", the software-intensive industries have absorbed the idea that security needs to be addressed throughout the software development lifecycle. Building Security In Maturity Model (BSIMM) [12] collects statistics from 95 companies and gauges their level of adoption with respect to several secure software development techniques. According to the report, security-specific code analysis techniques have successfully found their way into the industrial practice, as two thirds of the surveyed companies adopt them routinely. In this respect, the availability of well-known automated tools has helped significantly. *Architectural threat analysis* is another important pillar of building more secure software and the above-mentioned BSIMM report mentions that about one third of the surveyed companies use architectural threat analysis techniques, like Microsoft's STRIDE [20], attack trees [19], Trike [16], CORAS [11], PASTA [24], threat patterns [2], to cite a few.

© Springer Nature Switzerland AG 2018
C. E. Cuesta et al. (Eds.): ECSA 2018, LNCS 11048, pp. 347–363, 2018.
https://doi.org/10.1007/978-3-030-00761-4_23

Working in collaboration with our industrial partners from the automotive industry, we noticed that Microsoft's STRIDE is well-known and often used. In particular, our partners use the so-called STRIDE-per-element version. In this version, each component of the software system is considered in isolation and scrutinized for potential security threats. However, practitioners advocate for a threat analysis technique that allows them to analyze end-to-end scenarios where several components interact (e.g., to provide a given functionality). In this respect, the STRIDE-per-interaction variant could be more appropriate, as in this variant the analysis has a slightly wider scope and considers the security threats that might occur in a pair of interacting software components. On the other hand, there are also truly end-to-end analysis techniques, like for instance the one proposed by Tuma et al. [23]. From our perspective, it is interesting to study how these alternative techniques differ across the spectrum (analysis of isolated components vs analysis of pair-wise interactions vs analysis of end-to-end scenarios) in terms of performance. In essence, which approach to threat analysis produces more results in a faster way? Consequently, this study focuses on the differences between the analysis of isolated components and the analysis of pair-wise interactions. In current work, we are also comparing the analysis of isolated components with the analysis of end-to-end scenarios.

In the latest publication by Shostack [20] describing Microsoft's STRIDE, the author describes two variants that are dubbed 'STRIDE per element' (analysis of isolated components) and 'STRIDE per interaction' (analysis of pairwise interactions). A more detailed description of the two is provided in Sect. 2. In our study, we divide our participants (110 master students) into two treatment groups (ELEMENT vs INTERACTION), each using one of the two variants of STRIDE to analyze the architectural design of an Internet-of-Things system. For replication purposes of this study, we have created a *companion web-site* [1], where all the material used during the experiment is available. The study analyzes and compares the effectiveness of the two variants in unearthing security treats (benefits) as well as the time that it takes to perform the analysis (cost). We also look into other human aspects which are important to adoption, like the perceived difficulty in learning and applying the techniques as well as the overall preference of our participants.

The rest of the paper is organized as follows. Section 2 provides a primer on the STRIDE variants. Section 3 describes the experiment and states the research hypotheses. Section 4 presents the results, while Sect. 5 discusses them. The threats to validity are listed in Sect. 6. Section 7 discusses the related work and Sect. 8 presents the concluding remarks.

2   Treatments

STRIDE is a threat analysis approach developed to help people identify the types of attacks their software systems are exposed to, especially because of design-level flaws. The name itself is an acronym that stands for the threat categories of Spoofing, Tampering, Repudiation, Information Disclosure, Denial of Service and Elevation of Privilege. For the definition of threat categories, we refer the reader to the documentation of STRIDE [20].

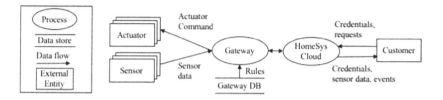

Fig. 1. A high-level DFD of the experimental object.

The analysis is based on a graphical representation of the system architecture as a Data Flow Diagram (DFD). As shown in Fig. 1, a DFD represents how information moves around in a software-based system. The diagram consists of processes (active entities), data flows (exchanged info), external entities (e.g., users or 3rd parties), data stores (e.g., file system) and trust boundaries.

The first step in applying the STRIDE methodology is to create a DFD using the available system documentation. The second step is a systematic exploration of the DFD graph in order to identify the threats. The two STRIDE variants differ in how this exploration is carried out.

STRIDE per Element. Using this approach, the analyst visits every element in the diagram (e.g., starting in the top-left corner). For each element type, STRIDE advises looking into a subset of threat categories. To this aim, STRIDE provides a table mapping element types to threat categories. For instance, the Sensor in Fig. 1 is an external entity, therefore according to STRIDE, the analyst should look into Spoofing and Repudiation threats. For each pair of element type and threat category STRIDE also provides a catalog of example threats that can be used for inspiration by the analyst. With reference to the Sensor, one provided example threat for spoofing a hardware device is IP spoofing.

STRIDE per Interaction. This technique adopts an approach of systematically visiting the interactions in a DFD. Interactions are patterns of DFD elements connected via data flows. The analyst has to first identify the interactions. For instance, "Sensor sends sensor data to Gateway" is a match for the above-mentioned interaction. For each type of interaction STRIDE again advises looking into a subset of threat categories and provides a catalog of example threats. For example, when an external entity is passing input to a process, the analyst is advised to look into Spoofing and Repudiation threats. If there is no logging in place, the Gateway is able to deny having received sensitive information from the Sensor.

3   The Experiment

This section presents the design of a controlled experiment, conducted with participants in an academic setting.

3.1   Experimental Object

As depicted in Fig. 1, the Home Monitoring System (HomeSys) is a system for remote monitoring of residential homes. The purpose of this system is to provide necessary tools for customers to automatically receive and manage notifications about critical events in their homes. The system consists of a smart home gateway which communicates with sensors and actuators and a cloud system which collects data from the gateways and offers a dashboard to the customers. Sensors are analog or digital hardware devices that produce measurements and send them to the gateway. This system includes sensors that detect temperature, humidity, smoke, etc. Actuators are hardware devices that can receive commands from the gateway, like for instance, taking a picture, activating a buzzer or flicking a switch. The gateway is a hardware device which relays measurements to the cloud (via a 3G or WiFi network) and manages the actuators in the residency. The HomeSys cloud is a software system that communicates with the gateways and provides services for the customers, as well the operators of the system.

The system documentation (about 30 pages) includes (1) the description of the problem domain with scenarios, (2) the requirements of the system and (3) a hierarchical architectural description documented in UML. For instance, the documentation includes a UML deployment diagram. The complete description of the system is available with the experimental material [1]. The participants worked on the HomeSys system throughout the entire course before entering the experiment. Therefore, they were very familiar with the object of the experiment and had enough knowledge about the system to understand the problem and complete their task.

3.2   Participants

The participants of this study are 110 first-year master students of Software Engineering, attending a course on "Advanced Software Architecture", taught by the experimenters. In order to gather sufficient data, we have repeated the experiment for two consecutive academic years (2016 and 2017). The participants performed the assigned tasks in teams. Each year, the participants were randomly grouped into teams of about 4 students and assigned one analysis techniques (i.e., treatment groups). In total, we have assigned 14 teams to the ELEMENT and 13 teams to the INTERACTION treatment.

We have collected information with a short questionnaire before the study took place to investigate the background of the participants. As shown in Table 1, it included questions about participants' work experience and perceived familiarity with task-related concepts. Most participants have had previous experience in software development outside the university and consider to have adequate

Table 1. Answers to the entry questionnaire.

Questions and answers [%]			
1. Do you have any working experience in software development outside the university?			
Yes (63)	No (37)		
2. How would you describe your working experience outside the university?			
Profit (39)	Non-profit (8)	Both (27)	NA (26)
3. How would you rate your level of expertise as a programmer?			
Very insufficient (1)	Limited (17)	**Adequate (58)**	Advanced (24)
4. How would you rate your level of familiarity with software design, including the use of UML?			
Very insufficient (2)	Limited (33)	**Adequate (63)**	Advanced (2)
5. How would you rate your level of expertise in security?			
Very insufficient (16)	**Limited (65)**	Adequate (16)	Advanced (3)

knowledge about software design and programming. A large majority of the participants are able to use UML, which is relevant as the study object is documented in such language. The course does not require background knowledge of information security, hence the participants consider to have limited expertise in this area, as expected.

3.3 Task

The teams were presented with the same task on the same experimental object. The task was divided into two sub-tasks: participants were asked to (1) build a DFD based on the provided architectural documentation and (2) analyze the DFD according to the assigned technique.

During the training, participants were provided with guidelines for creating the DFD. First, they had to create a DFD by mapping the nodes from a given deployment diagram into DFD elements. Second, the participants had to use the rest of the documentation (e.g., component and sequence diagrams) to refine the DFD and identify the data flows. The details of training are available online [1].

The second sub-task required a systematic analysis of the DFD according to the techniques described in Sect. 2. The analysis results had to be documented in a report and submitted electronically. The report had to contain a list of identified threats and corresponding descriptions. Threat descriptions were made according to a provided template (available online [1]). The purpose of the template is to simplify and standardize the analysis of the reports. Note that the task has been performed during a supervised lab session. In the lab, the teams were instructed to keep an informal log of the identified threats (lab notes). The preparation of the official report had to be done after the supervised lab. However, we have monitored that the reports did not contain more threats with respect to the work done in the lab (e.g., by taking snapshots in the lab). The snapshots taken during the lab were compared with the final report to capture any threats identified outside the supervised lab. We have not recorded any discrepancies between the snapshots and the reported threats.

Finally, we asked the teams to keep track of the time they spent. To this aim, the teams were instructed to use an online time-tracking tool (www.toggl.com) and submitted their time-sheets electronically at the end of the supervised lab.

3.4   Execution of the Study

The experiment is positioned at the end of a course on software architecture. The topic covered in the experiment aligns with the course content. Participation in the study contributes to the teaching objectives of the course, hence participants were highly motivated. For more details about the experimental material please refer to the companion web site [1].

Entry Questionnaire. A few weeks before the beginning of the study, the participants have been asked to fill in a brief questionnaire about their knowledge and background (see Sect. 3.2).

Training. As part of training for the experiment, the participants attended 2 lectures (mandatory 4 h of training). In the first lecture (2 h) the participants got an introduction to secure design and the use of the DFD notation. The lecture also included a practical exercise on how to build a DFD for a system of similar size as HomeSys. For the second lecture (2 h) participants were split according to their assigned treatment group. Each group received a dedicated lecture explaining the philosophy of STRIDE specific to their treatment group. In addition, participants received only documentation specific to their treatment group. This was done in order to limit the problem of treatment diffusion. An overview of the HomeSys documentation was also given in the second lecture. The students were more than familiar with the system, but the experimenters wanted to be sure that they would be able to navigate the documentation without hiccups. Finally, in a lab session preceding the experiment, the participants were familiarized with the time-keeping tool.

Supervised Lab. The experiment took place in one lab session of 4 h. The session was supervised by the authors and two teaching assistants. At the beginning of the lab, the authors explained the experimental protocol to the participants, e.g., by summarizing the task, mentioning all the provided material, and reminding the participants about the time-tracking tool. Each team was provided with a printed copy of task description, the relevant book chapters, and the documentation of HomeSys. The teams performed the assigned task and kept track of their work by writing lab notes.

Report. The participants were given about a week to write a report documenting the threats they had found during the lab. To this aim, they used their lab notes. Each report contained a figure of the DFD and a list of identified threats, where each threat was documented according to a provided template [1]. In particular, each threat is described with a title, a position in the DFD where the threat is located, a threat category (STRIDE), required attacker capabilities, and a detailed description of the threat itself. The participants were also asked to document their assumptions about the system.

Exit Questionnaire. At the end of the lab session, the participants were asked to fill in an exit questionnaire. Access to the questionnaire was open for a week after the lab session had finished, during which time a few reminders were sent by email. As discussed later, this questionnaire is meant to validate some experimental assumptions (e.g., the participants understood the task and were adequately prepared to carry it out) and to collect additional information about the treatments (e.g., the perceived difficulty of the tasks).

3.5   Measures

We have collected the measure of effort (in minutes) spent by each team on both sub-tasks (DFD creation and threat analysis).

We have also collected the measure of true positives (TP), false positives (FP) and false negatives (FN). True positives are reported threats that are assessed as correct by the experimenters in light of the analyzed DFD and the security assumptions made by the team. False positives are wrong or unrealistic threats reported by the team. Finally, false negatives are threats that are present in the analyzed system but had gone unnoticed by the team.

In order to record the correct threats a "ground truth" has been created by the first author. Incidentally, we decided to let the teams produce their DFD as this activity is an integral part of threat analysis in practice. Ergo, the teams have analyzed slightly different DFDs. A ground truth was built *for each team* to ensure a correct evaluation. For each report, the ground truth was used to identify the correct, incorrect and overlooked threats. In particular, a threat is considered correct if (1) it is identified at the correct location, (2) it is correctly categorized, (3) it has some impact on system assets, (4) the description of the threat agent is correct and (5) the description provided by the team is realistic from a security perspective and does not contradict their assumptions. Oftentimes the teams reported the same threat more than once, using a different title. A threat (either correct or incorrect) that is identified more than once is marked as a duplicate. Note that duplicated threats are intentionally not considered as TP or FP.

3.6   Hypothesis

We have adopted a standard design for a comparative study of one independent variable with two values, i.e., the two treatments of ELEMENT and INTERACTION. Our study investigates three dependent variables: productivity, precision, and recall. In this study we define the *productivity* ($Prod$) of a team as the number of correct threats (TP) per time unit. For each team, *precision* (P) is the percentage of correctly identified threats out of the total number of reported threats ($TP/(TP+FP)$). *Recall* (R) is the percentage of correctly identified threats out of the total number of existing threats ($TP/(TP + FN)$).

We use the Wilcoxon statistical test to determine whether there is a statistical difference in the three dependent variables across the two treatment groups. Accordingly, the null hypotheses are as follows:

H_0^{Prod}: *There is no statistically significant location shift between the average productivity of the two treatment groups.*
H_0^{P}: *There is no statistically significant location shift between the average precision of the two treatment groups.*
H_0^{R}: *There is no statistically significant location shift between the average recall of the two treatment groups.*

4   Results

In this section, we present the results of the study and answer to research questions. All statistical tests have been performed using the two-sample Wilcoxon test of independence with a level of significance equal to 0.05.

4.1   True Positives, False Positives, and False Negatives

Figure 2 reports the number of TP, FP and FN per treatment group. We have observed slightly better averages for the ELEMENT group, compared to the INTERACTION. Namely, the TP is higher (ELEMENT: 14.3, INTERACTION: 11.6), the average number of FP is lower (ELEMENT: 14.2, INTERACTION: 15) and the average number of FN is also lower (ELEMENT: 8.8, INTERACTION: 11.8). However, the analysis shows that there are no significant differences between the amount of TP, FP and FN across treatments groups.

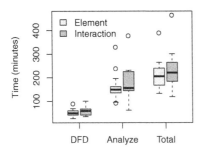 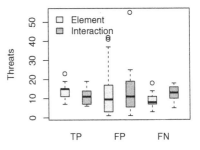

Fig. 2. Average time per sub-task and total time of treatment groups (left) and true positives, false positives, and false negatives (right).

The average number of TP, FP and FN per threat category is depicted in Fig. 3. Overall, both treatment groups visibly focused less on Repudiation and Elevation of Privilege threats compared to other threat categories. A statistical analysis shows that there are significant differences between the TP of the

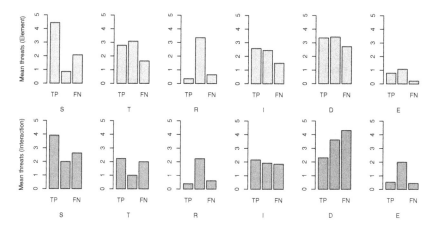

Fig. 3. The mean number of identified threats for per element (top) and per interaction treatment (bottom).

Denial of Service (p-value = 00.02) and Tampering (p-value = 00.007) threat categories across treatments. For the Denial of Service threat category, the ELEMENT treatment group identified on average more TP (statistically significant, p-value = 00.02) and less FN (not significant). For the Tampering threat category, the ELEMENT treatment group identified on average less FN, more TP (statistically significant, p-value = 00.007), and less FP. This might be due to the two methods providing different mapping tables (from DFD to threat categories [20]). The INTERACTION has a lower rate of mappings to the Denial of Service threat category (8/72 = 11% vs 3/20 = 15%). We have also computed the recall when the Denial of Service threats are removed. The results stay similar to what is reported in Fig. 4, i.e., the median recall is not "driven" by the Denial of Service category. Incidentally, there is a similar situation in the mappings for the Tampering category (3/72 = 4% vs 3/20 = 15%). Identified threats from other categories do not differ across treatment groups.

4.2   RQ1: Productivity

As shown in Fig. 2, the average time spent by the teams performing STRIDE per element is 3.5 h, whereas the average time spent per teams performing STRIDE per interaction is 3.95 h (not statistically significant). There is a noticeable difference between time spent on the sub-tasks, with the analysis time being dominant. When looking at differences across the treatments, the ELEMENT group was on average faster in performing both sub-tasks (not statistically significant). It is interesting to notice, that even though both treatments followed the same guidelines for DFD creation, the INTERACTION group created on average DFDs with more elements (discussed in Sect. 5).

The overall productivity of a technique depends on the amount of correctly identified threats (TP). The average productivity of the ELEMENT group is

4.35 TP/h^1. The INTERACTION group turned out to be less productive (**3.27** TP/h). However, the difference is not statistically significant and, hence, the null hypothesis H_0^{Prod} cannot be discarded.

As a possible explanation for lower productivity of the INTERACTION treatment, we highlight that the documentation of the STRIDE per interaction variant is more complex with regard to mapping threats to interactions. As mentioned by Shostack, "STRIDE-per-interaction is too complex to use without a reference chart handy" [20]. Such a reference chart was available to the participants, yet the complexity might still have been too high.

4.3 RQ2: Precision

Figure 4 presents the precision (i.e., the correctness of analysis) of the two treatment groups as an aggregate (left-hand side) and across each individual threat category (right). Overall, the mean precision is **0.60** for both treatment groups. Therefore, null hypothesis H_0^P cannot be rejected. We have also analyzed the differences in precision within threat categories. There is a statistically significant difference in the precision of Tampering threats (ELEMENT: 0.58, INTERACTION: 0.81, p-value = 00.027). A difference can also be observed for the Denial of Service category (not statistically significant).

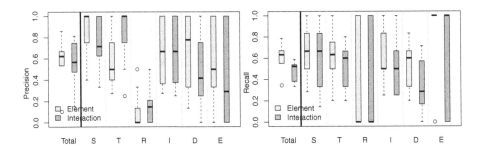

Fig. 4. Precision (left) and recall (right) aggregated across threat categories.

4.4 RQ3: Recall

Shostack states that the "STRIDE-per-interaction leads to the same number of threats as STRIDE-per-element" [20]. Yet in our study, the number of reported threats was higher for the ELEMENT treatment, especially the number of FP (see Fig. 2). Figure 4 presents the recall (i.e., completeness of analysis) of the two treatment groups as aggregate (left-hand side) and across each individual threat category (right). The average recall for the ELEMENT treatment is **0.62**, whereas the average recall of the INTERACTION is **0.49**. The difference is statistically significant (p-value = 0.028). Therefore, null hypothesis H_0^R can be

---

[1] Scandariato et al. [18] reported an average productivity of 1.8 TP/h.

rejected. We have also analyzed the differences within each threat category and found a statistically significant difference in the recall of the Denial of Service category (ELEMENT: 0.55, INTERACTION: 0.34, p-value = 00.014). One possible explanation relates to the fact that the ELEMENT group tends to create smaller DFDs, as discussed in Sect. 5. Alternatively, the difference could be linked to the fact that the threat examples in the documentation are more extensive in case of the ELEMENT treatment and the documentation of the INTERACTION treatment is more complex to navigate (as mentioned in Sect. 4.2). These are interesting hypotheses for future studies.

4.5 Exit Questionnaire

In summary, the two treatments displayed a statistically significant difference only with respect to recall, with the ELEMENT group reporting more complete results (13% better). It is also important to appreciate how the two variants are perceived by the participants. This could have an impact on the successful adoption of the technique and, hence, become a deciding factor beyond the performance indicators investigated in the three research hypotheses.

To this aim, we asked the participants to fill in a questionnaire at the end of the experiment. Due to space limitations, the questions and the answers are not shown here. They are available on the companion web-site [1] under the "Questionnaires" tab. To investigate differences across the treatment groups, we have performed a Cochran-Mantel-Haenszel test (similar to the Chi-square test) with a level of significance equal to 0.05.

In general, participants from both treatment groups agreed about having a clear understanding of the task, though they were sufficiently prepared and were familiar with the experimental object. Overall the task was not too difficult, while the first sub-task of creating the DFD was perceived easier than the second sub-task of analyzing the DFD (for both treatments). According to the documentation, "STRIDE per element is a simplified approach designed to be easily understood by the beginner" [20]. This implies that STRIDE per interaction is perceived by Microsoft as the technique to be used in production. However, according to our results, the techniques are the same (i.e. per element is not simpler than per interaction) in terms of productivity and precision. Concerning the learnability, the teams from both treatment groups agreed that the techniques they used were easy to understand and learn (no significant differences). Although the teams were given sufficient time to carry out the task, both treatment groups perceived the techniques as lengthy and tedious.

The participants from both treatment groups mostly believed that 50–75% of their identified threats were correct. This is a fairly accurate estimation according to the observed precision in this study (0.6). Interestingly, participants were slightly less confident about the completeness of their analysis. The aggregate recall over all teams (regardless of the treatment group) is 0.5 and only less than half of the participants (47.7%) have this perception. Finally, participants generally liked the technique they used but were not especially fond of it either. No significant differences were observed across treatments.

5   Discussion

DFD. The participants followed precise guidelines for DFD creation [1]. As such, the created DFDs have limited variability as well as consistent quality, e.g., we did not find many mistakes in the DFDs. In this study, we have made a deliberate choice to minimize the influence of the DFD creation (common to both treatments) and focus on the alternative techniques of analyzing the DFD (the key difference between the treatments). Figure 5 depicts the number of DFD elements in the models created by the teams. On average, the teams created DFDs with about 26 data flows, 6 processes, 4 data stores, 3 external entities, and 3 trust boundaries. A few differences can be noted. On average, we observed a smaller number of DFD elements in the ELEMENT group (37.4) compared to the INTERACTION group (41.9). This difference is consistent across the different element types, yet not statistically significant.

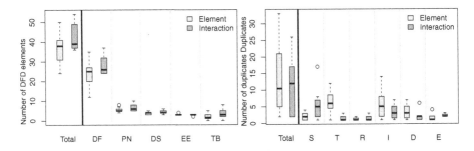

Fig. 5. The average number of DFD elements (DF=data flows, PN=process nodes, DS=data stores, EE=external entity, TB=trust boundaries) (left) and the average number of duplicated threats (right).

Mistakes. As reported in Fig. 5, the teams sometimes reported several threats more than once. Duplicated threats are considered to slow down the analysis process, especially during threat prioritization. Note that the results about productivity (see Sect. 4.2) are not affected by duplicates, as they were discarded.

Most commonly, threats are duplicated due to (i) threat 'fabrication' or (ii) a misuse of the reduction technique. We consider threat fabrication as mistakenly identifying threats in order to achieve complete coverage of the STRIDE category mapping table. Proposed by STRIDE, threat reduction is a technique that aims towards minimizing the number of DFD elements that have to be analyzed. In particular, the reduction enables coupling the elements of the same type in order to analyze them at once. In other words, the threats identified for one DFD element may apply to other elements of the same type.

About 30% of all reported threats were duplicated. Of those, the majority belonged to the ELEMENT group (65%). The mean number of duplicated threats identified by the ELEMENT teams is bigger (6) than the INTERACTION teams (5) (not statistically significant). However, there is a significant difference in the amount of Tampering duplicates across treatments (ELEMENT: 6.27,

INTERACTION: 1.67, p-value = 0.042). Incidentally, we also observed more Spoofing duplicates in the INTERACTION treatment. A possible explanation for fewer duplicates in the INTERACTION group is that the notion of interaction patterns might lend itself useful to a correct use of the reduction technique.

Interestingly, we observed that most teams correctly identified more outsider threats than insider threats. Very often, the reported insider threats were just unrealistic and assessed as false positives.

Analysis Focus. Overall (including duplicated threats and FP), both treatment groups have focused their analysis on 'border' elements of the system, as well as the data flows that pierce through trust boundaries. The reports of the ELEMENT treatment group contain more threats to processes, external entities, and data stores compared to threats to data flows. In contrast, the reports of the INTERACTION treatment group contain more threats to data flows compared to threats to other types of DFD elements. In general, all teams were more likely to identify correct threats to the data flows crossing a trust boundary. This confirms the usefulness of using trust boundaries to focus the attention of the analyst. However, there is a lack of precise guidelines for how and where trust boundaries should be placed, as our teams showed uncertainties in this regard. The teams were more likely to falsely identify threats (FP) to processes and data stores. The participants found the most commonly known threats (e.g., phishing, SQL injection, stealing for credentials or account). Coincidentally, these are more commonly identified on data flows. Correctly identifying a Tampering threat to a data store within system boundaries would mean finding a way to by-pass the system access control or even overcome obstacles like file-locking or other system defenses. This kind of threat requires correct assumptions and more security background. Unfortunately, most teams did not document many (if any) assumptions.

6 Threats to Validity

The time spent for performing the task was measured by the participants themselves. To mitigate this threat, we have continuously reminded the participants to pause and continue measuring time during breaks. The amount of work that was reported was consistent with the reported time, which indicates that this is a minor concern. The use of student participants instead of professionals is a potential issue threatening the generalization of results. This kind of population sampling is sometimes referred to as *convenience sampling* [25]. It is considered controversial due to certain drawbacks [3]. However, studies have shown [6,15,17] that the differences between the performance of professionals and graduate students are often limited. The experiments were conducted by using teams of 3–5 students, which threatens the generalization of results to a single analyst. Nonetheless, the state-of-the-art [7,20,22] advises sound-boarding the analysis with a team of experts in the industrial setting as well. This is what happens in the medium-to-large companies we collaborate with. Finally, the results of this study may be influenced by the experimental object and in turn, may not be applicable to a system of different complexity or from a different domain.

Possible mistakes might have been made during the assessment of the reports and during the creation of the ground truth. In order to avoid over-loading the participants and make them tired, the supervised experiment was performed in a span of 4 h. Additional time was given for documenting the identified threats outside the supervised lab. The teams were not monitored after the experiment has ended, however, we have made sure that the final report included only the threats in the lab notes (e.g., by taking snapshots in the lab).

7   Related Work

McGraw conducted a study including 95 well-known companies [12]. The study analyzes the security practices that are in place in the companies. The BSIMM model does not mention STRIDE per se, rather it highlights the importance of threat analysis. Microsoft has not published evidence of the effectiveness of the STRIDE variants analyzed in this paper. Guidelines, best practices, and shortcomings are discussed, yet there is no evidence about how the two approaches differ in terms of performance [20].

Scandariato et al. [18] have analyzed a previous version of STRIDE-per-element and evaluated the productivity, precision, and recall of the technique in an academic setting. The purpose of their descriptive study was to provide an evidence-based evaluation of the effectiveness of STRIDE. Our study, on the other hand, provides a comparative evaluation (by means of a controlled experiment) of the two latest approaches for STRIDE. Also, our study has a larger number of participants and uses a larger object. We remark that our study has some discrepancies with respect to the observed productivity (4.35 in our study vs. 1.8 threats per hour), precision (0.6 vs. 0.81), and recall (0.62 vs. 0.36). However, a direct comparison is not entirely possible, as the two studies use different versions of STRIDE-per-element (our being the most up-to-date).

A privacy oriented analysis methodology (LINDDUN [4]) has been evaluated with 3 descriptive studies [26]. LINDDUN is inspired by STRIDE and is complementary to it. Both techniques start from a representation of a system, which is described as a DFD. Similarly, the authors assess the productivity, precision (correctness) and recall (completeness) of the technique, as well as its usability.

Labunets et al [10] have performed an empirical comparison of two risk-oriented threat analysis techniques by means of a controlled experiment with students. The aim of the study was to compare the effectiveness and perception of a visual technique with a textual technique. The main findings were that the visual method is more effective for identifying threats than the textual one, while the textual method is slightly more effective for eliciting security requirements.

The work of Karpati, Sindre, Opdahl, and others provide experimental comparisons of several techniques. Opdahl et al. [14] measure the effectiveness, coverage and the perception of the techniques. Karpati et al. [8] present an experimental evaluation of MUC Map diagrams focusing on identification of not only vulnerabilities but also mitigations. Finally, Karpati et al. [9] have experimentally compared MUCs with mal-activity diagrams in terms of efficiency.

Diallo et al. [5] conducted a descriptive comparison of MUCs, attack trees, and Common Criteria [21]. The authors have applied these approaches to the same problem and discuss their observations about the individual technique's strengths and weaknesses. An interesting evaluation of the reusability of threat models (MUC stubs and MUC Maps diagrams, both coupled with attack trees) is presented by Meland et al. [13]. The authors conducted an experiment including seven professional software developers. The study suggests that overall, the productivity is improved by reusing threat models for both techniques.

8   Conclusion

This study has presented an empirical comparison of two variants of a popular threat analysis technique. The comparison has been performed in-vitro by means of a controlled experiment with master students. As presented in Sect. 4, this work provides reproducible analysis and observations about the effectiveness of applying both techniques, in terms of productivity, precision and recall. In summary, with the type of population used in this study (non-experts), our study observed better results with the STRIDE-per-element variant. For instance, STRIDE-per-element yielded 1 additional threat per hour in terms of productivity, with no consequences on the average correctness of the results (i.e., same precision). The proponents of STRIDE have claimed that "STRIDE-per-interaction leads to the same number of threats as STRIDE-per-element" [20]. However, in this study, we have observed a statistically significant higher level of completeness in the results returned by the teams using STRIDE-per-element. This is possibly influenced by the tendency of the STRIDE-per-interaction group to create larger DFD models, which might not be necessarily needed. Another explanation is related to the more complex documentation in the case of the INTERACTION treatment. As security budgets are quite tight in companies, knowing that one variant might be more productive is a useful piece of information.

This work calls for future studies about the effectiveness of the threat analysis variants, especially with more expert analysts. In particular, we are planning a case study in two companies where the local, per-element analysis is compared to a global, end-to-end analysis. Furthermore, it would be beneficial to study the effect on the importance (in terms of risk) of the discovered threats, as well as the quality of the of security requirements that are derived from them.

References

1. Empirical study: Threat modeling. https://sites.google.com/site/empiricalstudythreatanalysis/. Accessed 25 Aug 2017
2. Abe, T., Hayashi, S., Saeki, M.: Modeling security threat patterns to derive negative scenarios. In: 2013 20th Asia-Pacific Software Engineering Conference (APSEC), vol. 1, pp. 58–66. IEEE (2013)

3. Carver, J., Jaccheri, L., Morasca, S., Shull, F.: Issues in using students in empirical studies in software engineering education. In: Proceedings of Ninth International Software Metrics Symposium, pp. 239–249. IEEE (2003)
4. Deng, M., Wuyts, K., Scandariato, R., Preneel, B., Joosen, W.: A privacy threat analysis framework: supporting the elicitation and fulfillment of privacy requirements. Requir. Eng. **16**(1), 3–32 (2011)
5. Diallo, M.H., Romero-Mariona, J., Sim, S.E., Alspaugh, T.A., Richardson, D.J.: A comparative evaluation of three approaches to specifying security requirements. In: 12th Working Conference on Requirements Engineering: Foundation for Software Quality, Luxembourg (2006)
6. Höst, M., Regnell, B., Wohlin, C.: Using students as subjectsa comparative study of students and professionals in lead-time impact assessment. Empir. Softw. Eng. **5**(3), 201–214 (2000)
7. Howard, M., Lipner, S.: The Security Development Lifecycle, vol. 8. Microsoft Press, Redmond (2006)
8. Karpati, P., Opdahl, A.L., Sindre, G.: Experimental comparison of misuse case maps with misuse cases and system architecture diagrams for eliciting security vulnerabilities and mitigations. In: 2011 Sixth International Conference on Availability, Reliability and Security (ARES), pp. 507–514. IEEE (2011)
9. Karpati, P., Sindre, G., Matulevicius, R.: Comparing misuse case and mal-activity diagrams for modelling social engineering attacks. Int. J. Secure Softw. Eng. (IJSSE) **3**(2), 54–73 (2012)
10. Labunets, K., Massacci, F., Paci, F., et al.: An experimental comparison of two risk-based security methods. In: 2013 ACM/IEEE International Symposium on Empirical Software Engineering and Measurement, pp. 163–172. IEEE (2013)
11. Lund, M.S., Solhaug, B., Stølen, K.: A guided tour of the CORAS method. In: Lund, M.S., Solhaug, B., Stølen, K. (eds.) Model-Driven Risk Analysis, pp. 23–43. Springer, Heidelberg (2011). https://doi.org/10.1007/978-3-642-12323-8_3
12. McGraw, G., Migues, S., West, J.: Building security in maturity model (BSIMM). https://www.bsimm.com. Accessed 25 Aug 2017
13. Meland, P.H., Tøndel, I.A., Jensen, J.: Idea: reusability of threat models – two approaches with an experimental evaluation. In: Massacci, F., Wallach, D., Zannone, N. (eds.) ESSoS 2010. LNCS, vol. 5965, pp. 114–122. Springer, Heidelberg (2010). https://doi.org/10.1007/978-3-642-11747-3_9
14. Opdahl, A.L., Sindre, G.: Experimental comparison of attack trees and misuse cases for security threat identification. Inf. Softw. Technol. **51**(5), 916–932 (2009)
15. Runeson, P.: Using students as experiment subjects-an analysis on graduate and freshmen student data. In: Proceedings of the 7th International Conference on Empirical Assessment in Software Engineering, pp. 95–102 (2003)
16. Saitta, P., Larcom, B., Eddington, M.: Trike v. 1 methodology document [draft]. http://dymaxion.org/trike/Trike_v1_Methodology_Documentdraft.pdf
17. Salman, I., Misirli, A.T., Juristo, N.: Are students representatives of professionals in software engineering experiments? In: Proceedings of the 37th International Conference on Software Engineering, vol. 1, pp. 666–676. IEEE Press (2015)
18. Scandariato, R., Wuyts, K., Joosen, W.: A descriptive study of microsofts threat modeling technique. Requir. Eng. **20**(2), 163–180 (2015)
19. Schneier, B.: Attack trees. Dr Dobb's J. **24**(12), 21–29 (1999)
20. Shostack, A.: Threat Modeling: Designing for Security. Wiley, Hoboken (2014)
21. Stoneburner, G., Hayden, C., Feringa, A.: Engineering principles for information technology security (a baseline for achieving security). Technical report, Booz-Allen and Hamilton Inc., Mclean, VA (2001)

22. Torr, P.: Demystifying the threat modeling process. IEEE Secur. Priv. **3**(5), 66–70 (2005)
23. Tuma, K., Scandariato, R., Widman, M., Sandberg, C.: Towards security threats that matter. In: Katsikas, S.K., et al. (eds.) CyberICPS/SECPRE -2017. LNCS, vol. 10683, pp. 47–62. Springer, Cham (2018). https://doi.org/10.1007/978-3-319-72817-9_4
24. UcedaVelez, T., Morana, M.M.: Risk Centric Threat Modeling: Process for Attack Simulation and Threat Analysis. Wiley, Hoboken (2015)
25. Wohlin, C., Höst, M., Henningsson, K.: Empirical research methods in software engineering. In: Conradi, R., Wang, A.I. (eds.) Empirical Methods and Studies in Software Engineering. LNCS, vol. 2765, pp. 7–23. Springer, Heidelberg (2003). https://doi.org/10.1007/978-3-540-45143-3_2
26. Wuyts, K., Scandariato, R., Joosen, W.: Empirical evaluation of a privacy-focused threat modeling methodology. J. Syst. Softw. **96**, 122–138 (2014)

Executing Architectural Models for Big Data Analytics

Camilo Castellanos[✉], Dario Correal, and Juliana-Davila Rodriguez

System Engineering and Computing Department, Universidad de los Andes,
Bogotá, Colombia
{cc.castellanos87,dcorreal,dr.juliana10}@uniandes.edu.co

Abstract. With recent big data analytics (BDA) proliferation, enterprises collect and transform data to perform predictive analyses in a scale
that few years ago were not possible. BDA methodologies involve business, analytics and technology domains. Each domain deals with different
concerns at different abstraction levels, but current BDA development
does not consider the formal integration among these domains. Hence,
deployment procedure usually implies rewriting code to be deployed on
specific IT infrastructures to obtain software aligned to functional and
non-functional requirements. Moreover, previous surveys have reported a
high cost and error-prone transition between analytics development (data
lab) and productive environments. This paper presents ACCORDANT,
a domain specific model (DSM) approach to design and generate data
analytics solutions bridging the gap between analytics and IT architecture domains. To validate the proposal's feasibility and usability, a proof
of concept is developed and evaluated.

1 Introduction

With recent big data and data science proliferation, enterprises collect and transform data to carry out predictive analyses in a scale that few years ago were not
possible. The convergence of Internet of things (IoT), No-SQL databases, distributed computing, data streaming and machine learning (ML) enables us to
extract insights from raw data to add value to the business.

The development of big data analytics (BDA) solutions involves three knowledge domains: business, analytics and technology. In the business domain, business experts have to define business goals and quality scenarios to drive analytics projects. In the analytics domain, these business goals are translated into
specific analytics tasks by data scientists. Finally, in the technology domain,
software architects make decisions in terms of tactics, patterns and deployment
considerations keeping in mind quality attributes.

Research supported by the Center of Excellence and Appropriation in Big Data
and Data Analytics (CAOBA), supported by the Ministry of Information Technologies and Telecommunications of the Republic of Colombia (MinTIC) through
the Colombian Administrative Department of Science, Technology and Innovation
(COLCIENCIAS) within contract No. FP44842-anexo46-2015.

C. E. Cuesta et al. (Eds.): ECSA 2018, LNCS 11048, pp. 364–371, 2018.
https://doi.org/10.1007/978-3-030-00761-4_24

In each domain, stakeholders (i.e. business experts, data scientists and software architects) deal with cross-cutting concerns at different abstraction levels. Due to the lack of techniques and tools to enable articulation and integration of such domains, BDA solutions development presents a high cost and error-prone transition between development and productive environments [1,2]. Though there is a growing interest of companies in big data adoption, real deployments are still scarce ("Deployment Gap" phenomenon).

In the same vein, recent surveys [3,4] have reported that only 13% analytics solutions are "always" deployed, 50% "most of the time", and about 33% "sometimes" or less often. Forty percent of respondents report noticeable delays (weeks or months) in time-to-market. In short, BDA deployment presents problems in model translation, interoperability and stakeholders' communication. These pitfalls are the result of the traditional approach of BDA development where data scientist produce models as source code implemented using ML-driven tools which are focused on analytics perspectives within a controlled environment (data lab). On the other hand, IT architects have to translate these models into software products what it usually implies rewriting code to obtain productive software components deployed on specific IT infrastructures.

Domain Specific Modeling (DSM) is an approach to tackle these concerns. Therefore, we propose ACCORDANT (An exeCutable arChitecture mOdel foR big Data ANalyTics) a DSM approach to design BDA solutions bridging the gap between analytics and IT domains. The specific objectives of this research are: (i) to design a DSM to describe analytics and deployment components for BDA solutions. (ii) To implement a prototype to diagram ACCORDANT models. (iii) To validate our proposal using a proof of concept from real life analytics project. We follow the Design Science Research methodology (DSR) due to its recognized application in information systems and computer science research [5].

The remainder of the document is organized as follows. Section 2 introduces the background. Section 3 synthesizes the related work. Section 4 offers the proposal overview. Section 5 describes the evaluation and Sect. 6 offers the preliminary results. Finally, Sect. 7 draws the conclusions and future work.

2   Background

2.1   Domain Specific Modeling (DSM) in Software Architecture

Domain Specific Modeling enables software to be modular and resilient to changes through the separation of concerns principle by specifying technology–agnostic concepts, relationships and constraints within the domain. An important advantage of DSM is the close mapping problem and solution domains to provide code generation. Moreover, DSM can speed up and optimize the code generated for the specific platform improving the productivity.

Regarding representations, DSM can be expressed in graphical, textual or mixed notation according the domain context. It is possible to embed multiple views or aspects (for example analytics, architecture and deployment) within the domain using different representations which share some elements or links.

2.2 Big Data Analytics Deployment

BDA deployment implies putting the analytics model in productive environments ready to be in continuous operation. Specifically, this phase involves system's architecture definition and how software components will be deployed on technological infrastructure to fulfill the quality scenarios.

The inputs for the deployment phase are the analytics transformations and models built and validated during data preparation, model building and model evaluation. The activities involved in deploy phase range across quality scenarios definition, architecture design, software development, testing, software deployment in computational nodes, and monitoring. Due to the multidisciplinary nature of DBA deployment, different concerns require views and languages.

To offer a smooth transition and interoperability among analytics tools, open standards such as PMML (Predictive Model Markup Language) [6] have been proposed to enable transformations and models interchange. Due to the wide use of these specifications, they are considered de-facto standards of interoperability.

2.3 DevOps and Infrastructure as Code (IaC)

DevOps (Development and Operation) seeks to reduce the separation between development and operation aiming to an automated deployment process. This automatic deployment includes provision of computing resources ready to use. Consequently, the approach of Infrastructure as Code (IaC) supports the DevOps goal dealing with automatic provisioning of computing resources.

3 Related Work

Previous works have proposed methodologies, techniques and tools to integrate analytics and architecture in BDA projects. Indeed, some works have tackled DSM to describe BDA solution.

Gribaudo et al. [7] propose a modeling framework for performance evaluation of systems running applications based on lambda architecture. This modeling framework allows to define stream, batch, storage, computation nodes, computation stages along with performance indices to be simulated and evaluated. Huang et al. [8] introduce a model to design, deploy and configure Hadoop clusters through architecture metamodel and rules which describe BDA infrastructure and deploy automation. Guerriero et al. [9] introduce a DSM offering Big Data design which comprises data, computation, technology-frameworks and deployment concepts. All these works are focused on design, deploy and evaluation of BDA technology infrastructures. However, they leave out functional analytics models to get a integrated BDA solution.

On the other hand, some works have presented DSM to model analytics functions, however they do not tackle architecture and deploy considerations. Breuker in [10] offers initial conceptualization of a DSM and code generation for visual representations of probabilistic models. Lechevalier et al. [11] introduce a

DSM framework for predictive analytics of manufacturing data using Artificial Neural Networks (ANN) to generate analytics models. Sujeeth et al. present in [12] OptiML, a DSL for machine learning which describes analytics functions using a statistical model which cover a subset of ML algorithms, this analytics functions are analyzed and optimized before the code generation. Qualimaster Project [13] is an approach for systemic risks analysis in financial markets using self-adaptation in big data stream processing.

4 Proposal

ACCORDANT bridges the gap of data lab and production environment transition using a domain specific modeling (DSM) for both data scientists and IT architects to describe and integrate their concerns.

This approach looks for offering an extension for DevOps practice, starting from architectural artifacts, instead of source code, for operation deployment. We call this approach: "ArchOps", because we believe that architectural models are first-class entities in software development, deployment and operation.

This proposal is composed by seven steps depicted in Fig. 1: (1) quality scenarios definition, (2) ML models and transformations development (PMML specifications), (3) *Functional Viewpoint* design, (4) *Deployment Viewpoint* design, (5) code generation, (6) deployment and (7) software solution monitoring. In the proposed DSM, we include the *Functional Viewpoint* (*FV*) and *Deployment Viewpoint* (*DV*) proposed by Rozanski and Woods in [14]. Figure 2 offers a high-level view of ACCORDANT metamodel along with its internal viewpoints.

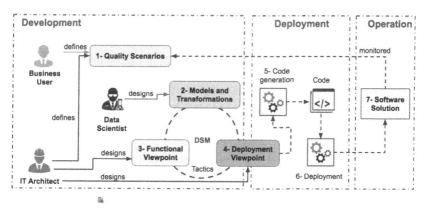

Fig. 1. Proposal overview

Quality scenarios (*QS*) include specific and measurable quality requirements described by source, stimulus, environment, artifact, response and measure. *QS* are defined by business and IT experts to achieve business goals.

Models and transformations contain the artifacts already developed by data scientists using diverse tools within the scope of data lab. Data transformations and models are exported to technology-neutral XML format (conforms to PMML) to be used in the *FV* as analytics building blocks. Both PMML transformations and models have associated a mining schema which describe the data features (inputs and outputs).

Functional Viewpoint (FV) constitutes analytics workflow in terms of ingestion, preparation, analysis and exporting building blocks. *FV* deals with functional requirements to achieve the expected result in analytics projects, and the constructs are described in technology-neutral way, as detailed in Fig. 2. These workflows are described in a component-connector structure which includes *Ingestor* of raw data from source, *Transformer, Estimator, Sink* components, and *Connectors. Estimator* and *Transformer* are the software component realizations of PMML model and data transformer respectively, and the PMML defines their behavior. A *Component* has provided and required *Interfaces* which enable communication with *Connectors*. The data structure of *Interfaces* is inferred from PMML mining schema. Furthermore, *Connectors* transfer data or control flow among components, hence we include a set of connector types: *Event, DataAccess, Stream, Arbitrator* and *Adaptor* following the classification proposed by Taylor et al. in [15] and BDA requirements.

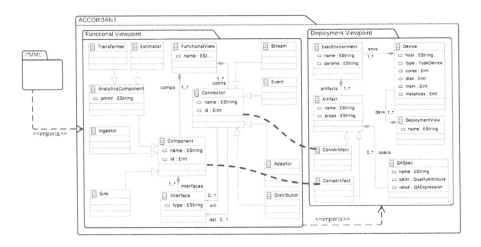

Fig. 2. ACCORDANT metamodel overview

Deployment Viewpoint (DV), depicted in Fig. 2, specifies *Devices* and execution environments (*ExecEnvironment*) where the *Artifacts* are deployed. An *Artifact* is assigned to functional elements (components and connectors) through interviewpoint mappings (in purple). Additionally, to fullfill the *QS*, an *QASpec* determines the quality attribute's requirements for an *Artifact*. In this way, the same *FV* model can be deployed in different *DV* models.

The *Code generation* takes PMMLs, *FV* and *DV* models designed in previous steps and uses model-to-text transformations to generate executable code. To do this, it is necessary to select the target technology manually for each component/connector *Artifact* regarding its *QASpec*. *DV* model also contains the required details for infrastructure provisioning and the *ExecEnvironment-Artifact* assignments. The transformations produce two kind of code: (i) source code (data transformations, estimators, ingestor/sink components and connectors) and (ii) deployment code (IaC).

In the *Deployment* step, IaC previously generated is executed to provisioning technology infrastructure. Generated software code is installed on such infrastructure according *ExecEnvironment-Artifact* assignment. As a result, a BDA solution is running on productive environment aligned to *QS*.

Finally, *analytics software solution* running in a specific infrastructure can be monitored against *QS* to measure how quality attributes are achieved.

5 Evaluation

We built a proof of concept to evaluate the technical feasibility and usability implementing an experiment. The prototype is a web interactive diagramming editor to describe *FV* and *DV*.

The use case implemented is related to delay prediction of a public transport service at Vancouver. Bus trips data are collected from realtime API of Vancouver Transport Operator[1]. We evaluate the interaction of data scientist and IT architect by means of a proof of concept. Data scientist trains and evaluates a regression tree model using a data science-driven tool (Scikit-learn). The model predicts the delay depending of a set of features such as bus trips, routes, stops and time). As a result, this model is exported to PMML.

The QSs are defined by IT architect in terms of performance and modifiability attributes. The first QS specifies that users make 1000 requests to delay prediction service under operations without load, and the responses must have an average latency lower than 2 s. Second QS states that when data scientist produces a new version of the predictive model (new PMML file), it must be updated at runtime in 10 s.

The architect designs *FV* and *DV* models defining two tactics oriented to tackle modifiability and performance scenarios: *Tactic 1*) trip data are collected from Translink API, using an *Ingestor* component, and delivered to *Estimator* component through an *Event* connector. The *Estimator* component contains the PMML regression tree model. *Estimator* component receives incoming data and produces the delay prediction. Then, this delay prediction is sent via second *Event* connector to be stored in a MongoDB collection (*Sink*). *Tactic 2*) is similar to *Tactic 1*, but *DV* model includes horizontal scaling (2 instances) of *Estimator* artifact for load balancing of prediction requests.

---

[1] https://developer.translink.ca/.

The scope of this proof of concept is limited to use the following target technologies: Kubernetes[2] (IaC) OpenScoring[3] (web server for PMML models), Kafka (pub/sub message queue) and MongoDB (NoSQL database) drivers. OpenScoring allows to publish PMML files as REST web services. Kubernetes is used to manage infrastructure's provisioning through IaC. Therefore, code generation (model to text transformations) are implemented only for OpenScoring (*Estimator*), Kafka (*Event* connector) and MongoDB (*Ingestor/Sink*).

We compare the development and deployment time of the use case using traditional approach versus ACCORDANT. In the traditional approach, the model trained by data scientist is recoded as Java component and deployed as a REST service. Kafka Connectors and MongoDB driver are developed and configured manually. Once software components are developed, the deployment process uses Kubernetes.

6   Preliminary Results

After the experimentation, we obtained results in terms of feasibility, ease of use and effectiveness. ACCORDANT allows to design BDA solution integrating analytics models and architectural decisions. Also, ACCORDANT enables to express different concerns and integrate them by means of ACCORDANT viewpoints. The software implementation and deployment are accelerated avoiding recoding and bugs thanks to automatic code generation. Design the whole BDA solution (*FV* and *DV* models) on ACCORDANT, and the real deployment using Kubernetes takes 25 min reducing the time-to-market compared to traditional approach which takes 150 min.

Regarding the quality scenarios, both Tactic 1 and Tactic 2 fulfill the modifiability scenario enabling to update analytic model at runtime in 10 s by means of OpenScoring REST services. Although both tactics achieve time responses average lower than 2 s, tactic 1 presents a better performance (1,328 ms) than tactic 2 (1,785 ms). The monitoring shows a higher latency when prediction results are stored in MongoDB through driver. It could imply that more *Estimator* instances could overload the MongoDB access generating a slight additional latency; therefore, scaling of *Estimator* component should require to scale the other associated components.

7   Conclusions

We present a DSM approach in BDA deployment which enables to deliver BDA solution in production avoiding software recoding. Furthermore, we could reduce time-to-market and programming errors along with speeding up the tactics design and infrastructure provisioning. We validate the feasibility and use of the DSM proposed through experimentation with a case study and proof of concept.

---

[2] https://kubernetes.io/.
[3] https://openscoring.io/.

The building of DSM editor is time consuming, and the customization is not easy. Hence, we are going to explore models@run.time frameworks to improve and accelerate the prototypes building. In some cases, PMML transformation are not enough (e.g. join functions) to implement an whole solution, so PMML could be extended including new functions to broaden the spectrum of usability. Improvement in terms of technologies catalog and automatic monitoring of QS can be developed in future iterations. The selection of target technology for connectors and components could be supported using recommender system or heuristics rules based on the quality attribute specification of each artifact.

Finally, a deeper and more rigorous evaluation is necessary to evidence that an artifact is both applicable and useful in practice from three realities: real tasks, real systems, and real users.

References

1. Chen, H.M., Kazman, R., Haziyev, S.: Agile big data analytics for web-based systems: an architecture-centric approach. IEEE Trans. Big Data **2**(3), 234–248 (2016)
2. Wegener, D., Rüping, S.: On Reusing Data Mining in Business Processes - A Pattern-Based Approach (2011)
3. Rexer, K.: 2013 Data Miner Survey. Technical report, Rexer Analytics (2013)
4. Rexer, K., Gearan, P., Allen, H.: 2015 Data Science Survey. Technical report, Rexer Analytics (2016)
5. Gregor, S., Hevner, A.R.: Positioning and presenting design science research for maximum impact. MIS Q. **37**(2), 337–355 (2013)
6. Guazzelli, A., Zeller, M., Wen-Ching, L., Williams, G.: PMML: an open standard for sharing models. R J. **1**(1), 60–65 (2009)
7. Gribaudo, M., Iacono, M., Kiran, M.: A performance modeling framework for lambda architecture based applications. Future Gener. Comput. Syst. **86**, 1032–1041 (2017)
8. Huang, Y., Lan, X., Chen, X., Guo, W.: Towards Model Based Approach to Hadoop Deployment and Configuration. In: 12th WISA, IEEE, pp. 79–84 (2015)
9. Guerriero, M., Tajfar, S., Tamburri, D., Di Nitto, E.: Towards a model-driven design tool for big data architectures. In: 2nd IWBDSE (2016)
10. Breuker, D.: Towards model-driven engineering for big data analytics - an exploratory analysis of domain-specific languages for machine learning. In: 47th International Conference on System Sciences, pp. 758–767. IEEE (2014)
11. Lechevalier, D., Ak, R., Lee, Y.T., Hudak, S., Foufou, S.: A neural network meta-model and its application for manufacturing. In: 2015 IEEE International Conference on Big Data (2015)
12. Sujeeth, A.K., et al.: OptiML: an implicitly parallel domain-specific language for machine learning. In: 28th ICML, pp. 609–616 (2011)
13. Alrifai, M., Eichelberger, H., Qui, C., Sizonenko, R., Burkhard, S., Chrysos, G.: QualiMaster quality-aware processing pipeline modeling. Technical report, Quali-Master Project (2014)
14. Rozanski, N., Woods, E.: Software Systems Architecture: Working with Stakeholders Using Viewpoints and Perspectives. Addison-Wesley, Boston (2005)
15. Taylor, R.N., Medvidovic, N., Dashofy, E.: Software Architecture: Foundations, Theory and Practice (2010)

Author Index